FROMMER'S

COMPREHENSIVE TRAVEL GUIDE

BANGKOK

2ND EDITION

by Ron Bozman and Kyle McCarthy
Assisted by John Levy

MACMILLAN • USA

About the Authors: **Kyle McCarthy** has coauthored Frommer Guides to Greece, Southeast Asia, and Thailand and written for numerous periodicals. **Ron Bozman,** a former *Time* correspondent, has researched the Mediterranean and Southeast Asia for Frommer's between assignments as a producer of feature films.

MACMILLAN TRAVEL

A Prentice Hall Macmillan Company
15 Columbus Circle
New York, NY 10023

ISBN 0-671-84918-2
ISSN 1055-5374

Design by Robert Bull Design
Maps by Ortelius Design

SPECIAL SALES

Bulk purchases (10+ copies) of Frommer's Travel Guides are available to corporations at special discounts. The special sales department can produce custom editions to be used as premiums and/or for sales promotion to suit individual needs. Existing editions can be produced with custom cover imprints such as a corporate logo. For more information, write to special sales, Prentice Hall, Paramount Communications Building, 15 Columbus Circle, New York, NY 10023.

Manufactured in the United States of America

CONTENTS

1 INTRODUCING BANGKOK 1

1. Geography, History & Politics 2
2. The People 6
3. Art, Architecture & Literature 7
4. Religion, Myth & Folklore 11
5. Performing Arts & Evening
   Entertainment 15
6. Food & Drink 16
7. Recommended Books & Films 18

SPECIAL FEATURES
- *What's Special About
  Bangkok 2*
- *Dateline 3*

2 PLANNING A TRIP TO BANGKOK 21

1. Information, Entry Requirements &
   Money 21
2. When to Go—Climate, Holidays &
   Events 24
3. Preparing for Your Trip 26
4. What to Pack 29
5. Tips for the Disabled, Seniors, Singles,
   Families & Students 30
6. Getting There 32

SPECIAL FEATURES
- *What Things Cost in
  Bangkok 23*
- *Bangkok Calendar of
  Events 25*
- *Frommer's Smart
  Traveler: Airfares 34*

3 GETTING TO KNOW BANGKOK 36

1. Orientation 37
2. Getting Around 43
3. Networks & Resources 57
4. Moving On—Travel Services &
   Systems 57

SPECIAL FEATURE
- *Fast Facts:
  Bangkok 47*

4 BANGKOK ACCOMMODATIONS 61

1. On the River 62
2. Historic Bangkok—Near the
   Grand Palace 71
3. The Business District 75
4. The Shopping/Embassy Area 82
5. Around the Railroad Station 91
6. Near the Airport 92

SPECIAL FEATURES
- *Frommer's Smart
  Traveler: Hotels 64*
- *Frommer's Cool For
  Kids: Hotels 67*

5 BANGKOK DINING 94

1. On the River   95
2. Historic Bangkok—Near the Grand Palace   97
3. The Business District   100
4. The Shopping/Embassy Area   106
5. Chinatown   115
6. Specialty Dining   116

SPECIAL FEATURES
- *Frommer's Smart Traveler: Restaurants 96*
- *Frommer's Cool for Kids: Restaurants 105*

6 WHAT TO SEE & DO IN BANGKOK 121

1. The Top Attractions   121
2. More Attractions   131
3. Cool for Kids   136
4. Organized Tours   137
5. Sports & Recreation   138

SPECIAL FEATURES
- *Suggested Itineraries 121*
- *Did You Know 123*
- *Frommer's Favorite Bangkok Experiences 129*

7 STROLLING AROUND BANGKOK 140

1. Wat's What   140
2. Chinatown   144
3. Thonburi   147

8 BANGKOK SHOPPING 151

1. The Shopping Scene   151
2. Shopping A to Z   152

9 BANGKOK NIGHTS 173

1. The Performing Arts   173
2. The Club & Music Scene   174
3. The Bar Scene   177
4. More Entertainment   179

SPECIAL FEATURE
- *Major Concert Halls & Theaters 174*

10 DAY TRIPS FROM BANGKOK 180

1. River Trips to Ayutthaya & Nonthaburi   180
2. Bang Pa-In   181
3. Floating Market at Damnoen Saduak   182
4. The Ancient City   182
5. Samutprakarn Crocodile Farm   183
6. Rose Garden Country Resort   183
7. Samphran Elephant Ground & Zoo   184
8. Nakhon Pathom   184
9. Water Parks   185

11 EASY WEEKEND EXCURSIONS FROM BANGKOK 187

1. Ayutthaya 187
2. Pattaya 193
3. Kanchanaburi 209
4. Hua Hin/Cha-Am 213
5. Lopburi 226

APPENDIX 229

A. Vocabulary 229
B. Menu Savvy 230
C. Glossary 235
D. Conversion Tables 236

INDEX 237

LIST OF MAPS

THAILAND 33

BANGKOK

Bangkok Orientation 38–39
Bangkok
  Accommodations 68–69
Bangkok Dining 102–103
Bangkok Attractions 126–127

Shopping in the Markets of
  Central Bangkok 154–155
Shopping Along Sukhumvit
  Road 157
Shopping in the Chinatown
  Area 159

WALKING TOUR MAPS

Walking Tour—Wat's
  What 143

Walking Tour—
  Chinatown 145
Walking Tour—Thonburi 149

REGIONAL MAPS

Bangkok Excursions 185
Ayutthaya 191

Pattaya 195
Hua Hin & Cha-Am 219

ACKNOWLEDGMENTS

This first update of the Bangkok City Guide owes its spirit and enthusiasm to our 20-month old son, Regan, who delighted in the many "Budda houses" and "tuk-tuks" he saw throughout our research. His fresh outlook, combined with the Thais' boundless affection for children, renewed our love for this rapidly changing country and its gracious people.

In addition, we owe tremendous gratitude to Khun Sumontha Nakornthab and her excellent staff at TAT: our old friend Peck Chalermlap, Chattan Kunjara, and Suraphon Svetasreni and Mr. Nat in the TAT's New York office.

We'd also like to thank some of our many friends in Bangkok for revealing their favorite haunts and sharing their hard-won insights into a sometimes frustrating and mysterious place. Kanchari Buranasomphob, Frederic Lucron, Jonathan Hayssen, and Jane Puranananda came up with the hot and new; Imtiaz Muqbil and Israporn Posayanond provided an overview on the city's politico-social scene; Lem Morgan passed on his travel tips.

Khop Khun Krap—for the many kindnesses extended by Michael Bamberg, Alan Guignon, Marion Darby, Sakchai Srongprapa, Kathy Barbour, Marion Harris, Caroline Ward, Matthias Wiesmann, and Supachawee Bunyaketu—for their diligence, Junpen Tangjitvisuth and Chalida Thanakitcharoensuk—and for their continuous support, everyone at Macmillan Travel.

ABOUT THIS FROMMER GUIDE

What Is a Frommer City Guide? It's a comprehensive, easy-to-use guide to the best travel values in all price ranges—from very expensive to budget. The one guidebook to take along on any trip.

WHAT THE SYMBOLS MEAN

 FROMMER'S FAVORITES—hotels, restaurants, attractions, and entertainments you should not miss

 SUPER-SPECIAL VALUES—really exceptional values

 FROMMER'S SMART TRAVELER TIPS—hints on how to secure the best value for your money

IN HOTEL AND OTHER LISTINGS

The following symbols refer to the standard amenities available in all rooms:

A/C air conditioning   TEL telephone   TV television
MINIBAR refrigerator stocked with beverages and snacks

The following abbreviations are used for credit cards:

AE American Express   DISC Discover   JCB Card (Japan)
CB Carte Blanche   ER enRoute   MC MasterCard
DC Diners Club   EURO Eurocard   V Visa

TRIP PLANNING WITH THIS GUIDE

Use the following features:

What Things Cost In . . . to help you plan your daily budget
Calendar of Events . . . to plan for or avoid
Suggested Itineraries . . . for seeing the city
What's Special About Checklist . . . a summary of the city's highlights—which lets you check off those that appeal most to you
Easy-to-Read Maps . . . walking tours, city sights, hotel and restaurant locations—all referring to or keyed to the text
Fast Facts . . . all the essentials at a glance: currency, embassies, emergencies, safety, taxes, tipping, and more

OTHER SPECIAL FROMMER FEATURES

Cool for Kids—hotels, restaurants, and attractions
Did You Know . . . ?—offbeat, fun facts
Impressions—what others have said

INVITATION TO THE READERS

In researching this book, we have come across many wonderful establishments, the best of which I have included here. We are sure that many of you will also come across appealing hotels, inns, restaurants, guesthouses, shops, and attractions. Please don't keep them to yourself. Share your experiences, especially if you want to comment on places that have been included in this edition that have changed for the worse. Address your letters to Kyle McCarthy or Ron Bozman, Macmillan Travel, 15 Columbus Circle, New York, NY 10023.

A DISCLAIMER

Prices fluctuate in the course of time, and travel information changes under the impact of the varied and volatile factors that affect the travel industry. Neither the author nor the publisher can be held responsible for the experiences of readers while traveling. Reader are invited to write to the publisher with ideas, comments, and suggestions for future editions.

SAFETY ADVISORY

Whenever you're traveling in an unfamiliar city or country, stay alert. Be aware of your immediate surroundings. Wear a money belt and keep a close eye on your possessions. Be particularly careful with cameras, purses, and wallets, all favorite targets of thieves and pickpockets.

CHAPTER 1

INTRODUCING BANGKOK

- **WHAT'S SPECIAL ABOUT BANGKOK**
1. **GEOGRAPHY, HISTORY & POLITICS**
- **DATELINE**
2. **THE PEOPLE**
3. **ART, ARCHITECTURE & LITERATURE**
4. **RELIGION, MYTH & FOLKLORE**
5. **PERFORMING ARTS & EVENING ENTERTAINMENT**
6. **FOOD & DRINK**
7. **RECOMMENDED BOOKS & FILMS**

Many first-time visitors to Southeast Asia include Bangkok on their grand tour with little idea of what they will actually experience. Although some arrive expecting to find an exotic microcosm of the "mysterious East," we have come to know the city as a richly complex, sophisticated, fast-growing, badly polluted, and traffic-plagued place that is as much an assault as a revelation on one's sensibilities. Once known as the Venice of the East, Bangkok has lost some charm, but remains the region's most compelling capital.

Bangkok is an ancient riverine city, with the mighty Chao Phraya River, a network of klongs (canals), and the Floating Market supporting thousands of residents. Home of Wat Phra Kaeo (Temple of the Emerald Buddha) and the Grand Palace, it contains a remarkable concentration of other wats (temples), museums, and regal monuments. Within its urban sprawl are legendary Thai, Chinese, and Indian markets that rival anything on the Asian continent. In the outer sections of Bangkok are the hastily built, less alluring neighborhoods where many of the city's six million residents live, working six days a week to power one of the fastest-growing economies in the world.

Centuries after the first traveling European dignitaries and writers returned home talking of the Land of Smiles and the personal inner serenity engendered by its ancient Buddhist culture, as well as the Thais' fierce independence ("Thailand" means "Land of the Free"), travelers still find the country's sights and sounds, people and customs enduringly impressive. In fact, modern-day Bangkok is a tourist mecca, a city with probably the greatest concentration of luxury hotels in the world, made even more special by the Thais' deeply gracious hospitality. Bangkok also boasts a bounty of inexpensive restaurants featuring sumptuous Thai and international cuisines.

There is unrivaled shopping for Southeast Asian handcrafts; Thai, Chinese, and Burmese antiques; bargain sportswear and high-fashion accessories; homespun raw and top-grade silks; and the highest-quality jewelry. One night in Bangkok is plenty of time to

WHAT'S SPECIAL ABOUT BANGKOK

Architectural Highlights

- ☐ The Grand Palace, a fascinating complex of royal buildings and temples, surrounded by Garuda figures and *naga* snake-guardians.
- ☐ Wat Arun, a Khmer-style *prang* (tower) decorated in cracked tiles and porcelain that casts its slender, towering shadow over the Chao Phraya River.
- ☐ The turn-of-the-century Authors' Wing in the deluxe Oriental hotel, with its colonial charm and legacy of literary guests.
- ☐ The 81-room gingerbread Victorian, golden teak Vimanmek Mansion Museum, built for King Chulalongkorn the Great (Rama V).
- ☐ The stunning blend of contemporary comfort, superb Asian art, and classic Thai architecture on view at Jim Thompson's House.
- ☐ Wang Suan Pakkard, the late Princess Chumbhot's five traditional Thai houses, lovely gardens, private klong, and collection of Thai art and antiquities.

Religious Shrines

- ☐ Wat Po's reclining Buddha and its famous School of Thai Healing Massage.
- ☐ The beloved jade Emerald Buddha housed in the royal Wat Phra Kaeo.

The River and the Canals

- ☐ Adventurous, self-guided klong (canal) tours by river taxi through Bangkok's floating suburbs.
- ☐ Romantic moonlit cruises on the Chao Phraya River, the perfect venue for Thai cuisine and dancing.

experience the intense nightlife scene, varied and affordable enough to satisfy both the cultural and physical hedonist.

Bangkok also makes a perfect base for day trips by bus or railroad, as well as more extended tours south to Thailand's palm-fringed beaches or north to its verdant hills.

The pastoral life and easy grace of old Siam may be gone, but its natural and cultural wonders survive. And despite the growing number of touts, the Thai people's warmth gives many a modern traveler cause to fall in love with both raucous Bangkok and its cordial hosts.

1. GEOGRAPHY, HISTORY & POLITICS

GEOGRAPHY With a land area of 513,115 square kilometers (198,114 square miles), about the size of France or Texas, Thailand contains four distinct regions and shares borders with Myanmar (formerly Burma) to the west, Laos to the north, Kampuchea (formerly Cambodia) to the east, and Malaysia to the south. The mountainous north is filled with teak forests where elephants still do the work of machines, with Chiang Mai and Chiang Rai the most significant towns. The Khorat Plateau of the semiarid northeastern region, home to some of the world's first civilizations, is a fascinating area long ignored by tourists. Bangkok lies in the central plain on the mighty Chao Phraya River, whose waters come from the Ping, Wang, Yom, and Nan rivers in the northern plains. Because it was built on an alluvial plain, the city is flat. South of Bangkok, the Southern Peninsula is a thin thread of land that stretches all the way to Malaysia, flanked by Thailand's favorite beach resorts and islands.

HISTORY Bangkok was not always the capital and is, in fact, fairly young as great cities go. Thailand's history begins with a Bronze Age culture between 2,000 and 250 B.C. In the 8th century, the ancestors of the Thais began to move south from China to settle Thailand's hills and valleys. In the 10th and 11th centuries, Thailand was dominated by the great Khmer civilization, whose power began to wane in the 12th century. By the 13th century, the kingdom of Sukhothai had achieved regional supremacy over the Khmer in central Thailand, only to decline in the latter half of the 14th century. In the mid-14th century, Ayutthaya (about 76km [47 miles] north of Bangkok) rose to dominate the entire region. This second kingdom of Siam grew and flourished (reaching a population of more than a million inhabitants) until it was completely destroyed by the Burmese in 1767.

After Ayutthaya's king died (from exhaustion), his leading general, Phya Tak, led the remaining troops south to a small village on the Chao Phraya River called Thonburi. Phya Tak was soon crowned king and given the royal title Boromaraja IV. History has always referred to him as King Taksin.

Thonburi and Bangkok had grown up on opposite sides of the Chao Phraya River. Thonburi was chosen as the new Siamese capital for several reasons: It was farther from the Burmese territories, small enough to defend, near to the Indian Ocean (so that arms and goods could easily be imported), and situated so that river access to the north could easily be controlled. Taksin reunified the Thai people and ruled for the next 15 years, but he seems to have slowly become monomaniacal, even proclaiming

DATELINE

• **6th to 9th centuries** The Dvaravati Kingdom spreads Buddhism throughout the region between the Khmer and Burmese empires.

• **9th to 12th centuries** Khmers from Angkor region take over and introduce Hinduism and Indian culture.

• **1351** Kingdom of Ayutthaya founded in Chao Phraya River basin; dominates entire region for four centuries. Bangkok and Thonburi grow up on opposite sides of the river in the south.

• **1767** Ayutthaya is destroyed by the Burmese; Phya Tak becomes King Taksin and chooses Thonburi as his capital city.

• **1782** Rama I ascends the throne; he moves his capital to Bangkok, across the river. The Buddhist Scriptures *(continues)*

DATELINE

are revised, and
Wat Po and Wat
Suthat constructed.

- **1809–24** King
Rama II, a great
patron of the arts,
rewrites the Hindu
Ramayana as the
Ramakien, and
constructs Wat
Arun. He reopens
contact with the
West.

- **1851–68** King
Mongkut (Rama IV),
with his knowledge
of Western
languages and
customs, keeps
Siam independent
of European
colonization and
expands trade and
diplomacy.

- **1862–1910** King
Chulalongkorn the
Great (Rama V)
reforms Thai
society, abolishing
slavery and the
custom of
prostration before
the king. Industrial
development begins
with the first railroad
trains and motor
cars.

- **1910–25** Rama
VI opens Siam's
first university and
makes primary
education
compulsory. Siam
joins World War I
on the Allied side.

- **1932** People's
Party seizes power
from the ineffectual
Rama VII, abolishes
absolute monarchy,
and tries to install a

(continues)

that he was a Buddha incarnate requiring proper reverence from the monks. He was deposed and executed in 1782. Taksin's top general, who held the title Chao Phrya Chakri, took the throne as Rama I, thus founding the Chakri dynasty, which continues to this day.

One of Rama I's first acts was to move the capital across the river near the quiet trading village of Bangkok (Village of the Wild Plums) in 1782. The new city was always known to the Thais as Krung Thep (City of Angels). The king built his palace in an area called Rattanakosin (The Jewel of India), where he ordered a network of klongs dug around a bend in the river to create an island, which would be more defensible. Those klongs still exist today. To establish cultural continuity, Rama I built the city on the model of Ayutthaya—but surpassing it. He also enacted a series of laws, the Tra Sam Duang (Law of the Three Seals), which incorporated administrative and economic principles from both the Sukhothai and the Ayutthaya kingdoms.

The reign of the first three Ramas in the early Bangkok period was a time in which law and the social order developed and matured, and the power of the monarchy was consolidated. In the late 18th and early 19th centuries, foreign trade flourished as well, primarily with China. With it came a flood of Chinese immigrants, so that by the mid-19th century, more than half of Bangkok's 400,000 residents were Chinese; from here, they dominated the internal commerce of the country. Western traders returned and treaties were consummated with European powers, and even with the United States (1833).

King Mongkut, Rama IV, refined foreign policy even further, greatly expanding trade and treaties, and brought the kingdom into the modern age. Due to his shrewd brokerage of competing foreign powers, Thailand maintained a studied and finely balanced neutrality that made it the only country in the region to escape colonial rule. One of Mongkut's key moves was to cede all rights in Cambodia to the French (1867), an act that would have great import in 20th-century history. Western influence on medicine and culture was welcomed, though the Thais remained generally immune to repeated Western missionary attempts at conversion. During this era the English tutor Anna Leonowens, later made famous in

Margaret Landon's *Anna and the King of Siam*, was in residence. Her legendary influence on Rama IV is thought to be greatly exaggerated and the stories of her importance to the "uneducated" king are offensive to most Thais.

In 1868, Mongkut was succeeded by his son King Chulalongkorn, Rama V, who continued the policy of foreign conciliation, granting further rights to the French in Laos and Cambodia and to the British in British Malaya. He also brought about massive internal changes with the abolition of slavery, the establishment of state-provided education, and the introduction of railway lines and telegraph systems. Western models of government were borrowed and adapted.

The monarchy's absolute status was forever changed by the coup in 1932 when members of the educated ruling class seized power, imprisoned the royal family, and attained acceptance of constitutional rule, complete with a parliamentary-style National Assembly and the king as a constitutional monarch. However, the new government soon fell apart, and the military seized control in the aftermath. In 1939, the name of the country was changed from Siam to Thailand.

Although Thailand was officially a supporter of the Allies during World War I, in World War II the policy, by necessity, was pro-Japanese. Though the Thais had attempted to maintain neutrality, they were helpless before the superior Japanese forces, and on December 21, 1941, 13 days after Pearl Harbor, they signed a treaty with Japan. The Japanese agreed to help the Thais regain territories lost to the British, and the Thais agreed to assist Japan in the war. A month later, British and American planes bombed Bangkok and other towns, and Thailand declared war on the United States and Great Britain. After the conflict, however, the Thai National Assembly repudiated the declaration of war and agreed to return Burma and Malaysia to Great Britain. Always the diplomats, the Thais survived World War II intact and independent.

From then until the early 1970's, the military maintained control of the government. In late 1973, student discontent with military rule exploded and led to clashes with the police and army; more than 100 students were killed. The government was dismissed by the current king, Bhumibol (Rama IX), and eventually a democratic

DATELINE

constitutional government.

• **1939** Field Marshal Pibul Songgram becomes premier. The Kingdom of Siam is renamed Thailand, "Land of the Free."

• **1941** Thailand becomes Japan's ally in World War II.

• **1946** Thailand admitted to the United Nations.

• **1951** The Western-educated King Bhumibol Adulyadej ascends the throne as Rama IX.

• **1968** After several coups and years of military rule, a new constitution is drafted to establish a parliamentary government.

• **1971** Martial law is imposed, the constitution abolished, and the parliament disbanded.

• **1973** After huge student protests, a short-lived democratic government is installed.

• **1991** The prime minister, Chatichai Choonhaven, is ousted in a military coup aimed at "restoring order," after years of repeated military coups, growing restlessness, and calls for democracy.

regime was instituted. But it lasted only three years, and in 1976, after renewed clashes with rebelling students, the military dismissed the civilian government and resumed power. Since then, there have been numerous coups, the most recent of which occurred in early 1991, when the military forced the prime minister to resign, replacing him with their own choice, General Suchinda Kraprayoon. In May of 1992, after mounting protests and calls for democratic reforms, the military cracked down on public demonstrations and several students were killed. The king managed to quell the ensuing violence by publicly scolding both the prime minister, as head of the military, and the opposition leaders. A compromise was reached; General Suchinda stepped down, and businessman Anand Panyarachun, who had run the interim government after the coup, reascended to the prime minister's position.

General elections were held in September 1992, and Chuan Leekpai was elected the new prime minister, heading a very fragile five-party coalition. At our recent visit, the most pressing issues on his agenda were decentralization of the economy (which is currently strong—the GDP is growing at 7.5% per annum; whereas inflation stands at a mere 3.6%), redistributing the wealth in the rural areas, solving Bangkok's traffic and environmental problems, and ridding the government of corruption.

POLITICS   The current form of government, defined in 1932 and in the newer constitution of 1978, is a constitutional monarchy, with the king as chief of state and the prime minister as head of government. There is a bicameral National Assembly and three levels of courts.

King Bhumibol Adulyadej, Rama IX, is a greatly revered, progressive man. Born in the United States (where his father was a student), he was educated in Europe. He and his wife, Queen Sirikit, are very devoted to their subjects and their royal duties. The king has a special interest in agricultural projects, and the queen concentrates on home industries.

2. THE PEOPLE

Thailand's population was estimated at almost 60 million in 1992, making it then the world's 20th most populous country. Approximately 6.3 million people live in Bangkok, whose population has grown more than 5% annually since 1961. Almost half the population is under age 30, with an impressive literacy rate of 89%.

After 1975, over a million refugees fled to Thailand from surrounding Indo-Chinese countries. Since the Vietnam War, Laotians, Vietnamese, and the Cambodians have been housed in camps along the eastern border. The Thai government and various international aid organizations are attempting to repatriate them in the wake of the Cambodian Peace Accord.

ETHNIC GROUPS   Approximately 84% of Thailand's population are ethnically Thai, 12% are Chinese, and 4% come from other ethnic groups or the various hill tribes. The lineage of the Thai people is still a matter of dispute. The prevailing theory is that the Thais (or Tais), who had a unified culture by the 7th century, migrated south from southwestern China's Yunnan Province. They settled in independent states throughout the north of what is now Thailand during the 11th and 12th centuries and were united during the Sukhothai period, beginning in the 13th century.

Thai culture was shaped primarily by settlers from the great Mon civilization of southern Burma and central Thailand and by the Khmer peoples of the Mekong Valley to the north and east, both of whom were heavily influenced by Indian culture. Individual Tibeto-Burman tribes also played a role in shaping Thai culture. The Thai language, in various forms, is spoken today by a wide variety of groups in Burma, Thailand, Laos, Vietnam, and southern China. It has even been found in Assam, in eastern India.

Others believe the Thai people were Thailand's indigenous inhabitants, forced out of the country by more powerful Mon and Khmer invaders. According to this theory, the Thais fled north to China's Yunnan Province and returned to their homeland, under pressure from the Mongolians, during the 11th and 12th centuries.

In Bangkok you'll find the true melting pot of all these cultures, commingled with the Indian and Chinese strains that have long existed in the country.

Although they number a scant 575,000 households, the six main hill tribes of the north contribute a great deal to Thailand's ethnic diversity. The principal groups are the Karen, Hmong, Lahu, Mien, Akha, and Lisu, and all of them live in the hills around Chiang Mai. Their colorful textiles, jewelry, and other handcrafts can be found in Bangkok shops.

Western influence first appeared in the 16th century, when Portuguese missionaries arrived in the Siamese capital of Ayutthaya. The Dutch, French, English, and Danes all established trade missions here in the early 17th century, and the Thais sent embassies to European courts. The Chinese were early traders and have continued their major position in Thai commerce to this day.

3. ART, ARCHITECTURE & LITERATURE

ARCHITECTURE & SCULPTURE Most accounts of Thai art history begin with the so-called Nanchao Period (A.D. 650–1250) during which Chinese and associated ethnic minorities migrated south into the land that would become a unified country during the early years of the 13th century. Yet the real story begins during the Neolithic era in which such places as the Spirit Cave in Mae Hong Son and the settlements in and around Ban Chiang in the Northeast developed into sophisticated agrarian cultures. Their religion was animistic and its art is similar to the Geometric Period in early Greek art; large primitively fired ceramic red vessels are painted with bold black spirals and other abstract designs. Opened graves indicate some aesthetically crude but metallurgically sophisticated sculpture, mostly of animals, as well as finely crafted jewelry.

A gulf of over 2,000 years separates the Neolithic period from the Nanchao era; there are few extant art forms from this early time though it's thought that Buddhist missionaries from India and Sri Lanka imported aesthetic ideas from the subcontinent. Only with the direct connection between Thailand and China, Burma, Indonesia, Cambodia, and, most important, Sri Lanka and India, is there solid evidence of a true Thai art in the making. The dominant influence of Indian styles can be seen in the art of several Southeast Asian peoples: Dvaravati (Mon), Khmer (Cambodia), Burmese, and Srivijaya (Javanese), all of whom either settled in Thailand or traded with the Thai people. Of these, the Dvaravati were initially the most influential. Their artisans' style, from the 6th to the 10th century, is most similar to the so-called Gupta style of traditional Indian art and architecture and is most evident in the central and northeast section of the country. Unfortunately, the vast majority of sculpture and painting was destroyed when most Dvaravati-influenced buildings were either left to ruin or converted to Mahayana Buddhist structures, but what survives are the precursors to the Khmer *prang* or cactus-shaped towers with carved images of Hindu deities set in niches. The style of construction is a direct imitation of both early Hindu and Sri Lankan forms, with most buildings made from carved sandstone.

The Khmer (Cambodian/Hindu) empire was well established within Thailand from the 11th to the 13th century and with it came the country's second significant influence. The two most important aspects of Khmer art and architecture (as they relate to later Thai styles) are the fluid, sinewy shapes evident in Khmer stone religious sculpture, and the layout of both civil and religious buildings. Khmer stone carvers paired the elaborate ornamentation of Indian art with the abstract style of Chinese sculpture; friezes above lintels in such temples as Phimai are examples of the former, while the serene Khmer figural representation on display in Jim Thompson's House are excellent examples of the latter. Khmer architects built travel halts (government-built inns) and religious complexes that would later serve as models for the much larger Thai "wat" (a cluster of religious buildings surrounded by a wall and gateways).

The kingdoms in Chiang Mai and Sukhothai brought forward the next major advances in Thai sculpture and architecture. A lasting legacy of the Sukhothai Period is its sculpture, characterized by the parrot-nose Buddha, either sitting or, more typically, walking. These Buddhas are considered the best ever produced, and the period is regarded as the zenith of Thai culture. Hindu cultural hegemony was swept away as the layout and decorative style of the Khmer capitals was expanded and furthered. With the inclusion of Chinese wooden building techniques and polychromatic schemes and Javanese-influenced carved, flowing lines, the wat, with its murals, Buddhist sculpture, and spacious religious and administrative buildings, defined the first "pure" Thai Buddhist style. During this period came the mainstays of Thai wat architecture (in order of ar-

---

IMPRESSIONS

From the very beginning I was charmed by Bangkok . . . I liked its polite, gentle, handsome people, its temples, flowers, and canals, the relaxed and peaceful rhythm of life here.
—S. J. PERELMAN, *WESTWARD HA!*

tistic importance): the *phra chedi (stupa), bot, vihara, phra prang, mondop,* and *pra sat.*

The phra chedi or stupa is the most venerated structure. Originally it enshrined relics of the Buddha, later of holy men and kings, and is the equivalent symbolically of the Christian cross. The structure consists of a drum (basement) and dome (tumulus) surmounted by a cubical chair representative of the seated Buddha and over it the *chatra* or umbrella in one or many tiers. There are many different forms extant in Thailand.

The bot is where the *bhikku* (monks) meditate and all ceremonies are performed. It consists of either one large nave or one nave with lateral aisles. The Buddha image is enshrined here. It is built on a rectangular plan. At the end of each ridge of the roof are graceful finials, called *chofa* (sky tassles), which are reminiscent of animal horns but are thought to represent celestial geese or the Garuda. The triangular gables are enriched with gilded wooden ornamentation and glass mosaic.

The vihara or *viharn* is a replica of the bot that is used to house Buddha images.

The phra prang, which originated with the corner tower of the Khmer temple, is a new form of Thai stupa, elliptical in shape. The interior contains images of the Buddha.

The mondop may be of wood or brick. On a square pillared base the pyramidal roof is formed by a series of receding stories, enriched with the same decoration and tapering off in a pinnacle. It may serve to enshrine some holy object, or it may serve as a kind of library and storeroom for religious ceremonial objects, as it does at Wat Phra Kaeo.

The pra sat is a direct descendant of the Greek cross-shaped Khmer temple. At the center is a square sanctuary with a domed *sikhara* and four porchlike antechambers which project from the main body of the building. The rooflines of these porches are lower than that of the main building, giving the whole a steplike contour. The pra sat serves either as the royal throne hall or as a shrine for some venerated objects such as the pra sat of Wat Phra Kaeo, which enshrines the statues of the kings of the present dynasty.

Less important architectural structures include the *ho trai* or library housing palm-leaf books; the *sala,* an open pavilion used for resting; and the *ho rakhang,* the Thai belfry.

The Ayutthaya and Bangkok periods furthered the Sukhothai style, bringing refinements in materials and design. During the Ayutthaya period there was a Khmer revival; the Ayutthaya kings briefly flirted with Hinduism, with the result that they built a number of Neo-Khmer style temples and edifices. The art and architecture evident in early Bangkok was directly inspired by the dominant styles in Ayutthaya, the country's earlier capital. After the destruction of Ayutthaya in the 18th century, the new leaders, having established their foothold in Thonburi (and soon to move across the Chao Phraya to Bangkok), tried to rebuild many of the most distinctive buildings in the so-called Ayutthaya mold. This meant incorporating older Khmer (such as Wat Arun), Chinese, northern

○ **The wat, with its murals, sculpture, and spacious buildings defined the first "pure" Thai Buddhist style**

Thai, and (to a lesser degree) Western modes into contemporary wats, palaces, sculpture, and murals.

The last major influence in Thailand's architectural and artistic development was of Western origin—many would say that it is the single most important style today. Beginning with the opening up to Europe during the latter days of the Ayutthaya period, Jesuit missionaries and French merchants brought with them decidedly baroque fashions. Although the country was circumspect about its continuing relations with the West, it did follow and incorporate many of the prevailing styles of the day. The Marble Wat is an obvious example of this melding of Thai/European style.

Modern architectural development is almost indistinguishable from that of other fast-growing Asian capitals, particularly Hong Kong and Singapore. Typical Thai wooden house blocks are cleared, klongs are filled in, and wide boulevards are created. In place of traditional Thai architecture are high-rise office and apartment complexes that bear little connection to past traditions.

PAINTING   Murals, paintings on cloth, and manuscripts are the largest and most important examples of Thai painting, along with designs in gold leaf and black lacquer found on doors, bookcases, chests, and screens.

The subjects of traditional Thai painting are mainly religious, depicting the life of the Buddha. The Jataka scenes narrate the many lives of the Buddha prior to his Enlightenment, or scenes from the *Ramakien* (see below).

Usually, though not always, the murals are placed as follows: On the top part of the wall facing the main image of the Buddha there is a scene representing the unsuccessful temptation of the Buddha by Mara. Behind the Buddha image will probably be scenes of the Buddhist cosmos or of Hell. Scenes from the life of the Buddha or from the Jataka stories—the most famous being the Mahachat (the final life of the Buddha before his Enlightenment) or the Thotsachat (the last 10 lives of the Buddha)—are usually pictured on the other two walls. These murals are often surmounted by rows of seated Buddhas.

In Thai painting there is no Western perspective or shadow. Landscape in itself is not considered important, being only the background setting for the action of the story. In mural painting the paint (traditionally made of mineral and earth pigments) is applied to dry plaster. The brushes, made of tree roots, give Thai painting its distinctive solid wirelike line as compared to Chinese and other Oriental brush painting. The wooden brushes are used for broad lines and stippling; cow's hair brushes are used for detail and finer work.

Only a few examples of pre-17th-century work have survived the humid climate. The first fairly well preserved paintings were found at Ayutthaya at Wat Ratachaburana and in a chedi at Wat Mahathat. From the fall of Ayutthaya to the mid-19th-century, murals grew in complexity and richness of color, heightened by lavish use of gold leaf. Good examples can be seen in Thonburi at Wat Suwannaram, in Bangkok at Wat Suthat, and in the Buddhaisawan chapel in the National Museum.

In Northern Thailand painting is more Burmese in style, less luxurious and cooler in tone than the Bangkok school. In Wat Pra Sing in Chiang Mai, one of the walls narrates the story of Sang Thong about a prince born in a golden conch shell. Look at the work closely and you will find humorous touches even in the most reverent scenes, like the man flirting with a group of girls while a cat stalks a female on the roof above his head.

Traditional Thai painting began to die in the mid-19th century when Western oil paints and techniques were introduced. An interesting early example of this development incorporating some elements of shading and perspective can be seen on the upper portion of walls at Wat Bovornivet, where King Mongkut ordered the painting of Western scenes including a windmill, Mount Vernon, and Versailles, as an educational mural.

LITERATURE Although there are several great works of literature representative of the Thai cultural tradition, there are two best known in the West that visitors will most likely come across, either portrayed artistically in murals or dramatically in the *khon* and in shadow plays. The first is the *Ramakien*, based on the Hindu epic, the *Ramayana*, that tells the story of the triumph of Rama, rightful king of Ayutthaya, over Tosakanth, the evil king of the island of Longka—the triumph of good over evil. Derived from the sacred book of the Hindus, the *Ramakien* as such has no sanctity to a Thai; rather it's profane entertainment.

○ **The Thai language was first set in print in 1828**

The second is the *Mahachat,* a story beloved of the Thai people. It is the story of the Lord Buddha in his last-incarnation-but-one-on-earth as Prince Wetsandon. The story of Prince Wetsandon's selfless life, which prepared the Lord Buddha for his final enlightenment, represents to the Thais an ideal for faith, and the story is recited at the mid-year Autumnal Festival by specially trained monks. Originally composed in Pali, it has been a source of great inspiration for Thai art and poetry, and exists in many versions.

It was only in 1828 that the Thai language was first set in print. Before that time, works of literature were written on folded scrolls that were both difficult and expensive to produce. And while much poetry and many plays have been written, not a great deal of Thai literature has been translated.

Among the current generation of Thai writers whose works are available in English or French, none is better known that Pira Sudham, whose most recent work is *Monsoon Country*. Pira hails from Isan, and his books reflect the struggles inherent in living between the Western and Thai worlds. In 1990 he was nominated for the Nobel Prize in literature; his other titles are *People of Esarn* and *Siamese Drama*. Among other well-regarded contemporary writers available in translation are Kukrit Pramoj and Suwanee Sukonta.

4. RELIGION, MYTH & FOLKLORE

RELIGION Anyone visiting Thailand cannot fully appreciate the culture without some understanding of Buddhism, which is followed by 90% of the population. Buddha was a great Indian sage born in the 6th century B.C. Born Siddhartha Gautama, a noble prince sheltered from the outside world, he left the palace one day and encountered first an old man, then a sick man, and then a corpse. He concluded that all is suffering and resolved to search for relief from that suffering. He went into the forest and lived there for many years as a solitary ascetic and ultimately achieved enlightenment while sitting under a sacred fig tree. The highlights of his life were his temptation by Mara (evil) who sent his daughters to seduce him; his protection by Serpent King Mucalinda from raging floods that followed a seven-day storm; the First Sermon on the Wheel of Law given in the Deer Park at Sarnath, India; and his death and cremation. After his death, two schools arose among his followers. The oldest and probably closest to the original is Theravada (Doctrine of the Elders), sometimes referred to less correctly as Hinayana (the Small Vehicle), which prevails in Sri Lanka, Myanmar, Thailand, and Cambodia. Mahayana (the Large Vehicle) is practiced in China, Korea, and Japan. In addition, Tibetan Buddhism and Zen Buddhism could be considered schools of their own.

> ○ **Ninety percent of Thailand's population follow Buddhism**

The basic Buddhist document is the Pali canon, which was recorded in writing in the 1st century A.D. The doctrine is essentially an ethical and psychological system in which no deity plays a role. A religion without a God, it is mystical in the sense that it strives for the intuitive realization of the oneness of the universe. It has no pope or priests and no secular authority. It requires that individuals work out their own salvation as commanded by the Buddha himself to "look within, thou art the Buddha," and in his final words, "work out your own salvation with diligence." The open pagoda design of the temples reflects the openness and accessibility to all of the teaching, which admits no caste, sex, or race superiority. It is tolerant and seeks no converts.

So what, you may ask, are the people doing who enter the temple and prostrate themselves before the Buddha, place their hands together in a gesture of worship, light incense, and make offerings of fruit and flowers? What role exactly does the Buddha image play and how did the image become so prevalent? Here's how it happened. At his death the Buddha's disciples were distraught at the prospect of losing their great and beloved teacher, and they asked how they might remember him. Buddha granted them permission to make pilgrimages to the Great Events of his career and to gather his bodily relics and place them in stupas or mounds to remind them of his life and his teachings and to make their hearts glad and happy. And so stupas were built and the events of his life remembered by making symbolic representations of the elements of those events. It was a short step from there to making representations of the Buddha himself. Buddha images were first invented about the beginning of the Christian era and have been created by artists ever since. The images are honored in the same way that any great teacher is honored and revered in the Eastern tradition; they are not objects of worship but images that in their physical form radiate spirituality and convey the essence of Buddhist teachings—serenity, enlightenment, purity of mind, purity of tongue, and purity of action. They are in many ways considered living things that have "teja" or energy of their own. They are therefore often presented with robes. For example, the Emerald Buddha has three changes of costume: princely attire for the hot season, a monastic robe for the rainy season, and a mantle of gold mesh for the cool season. Similar energy is felt to inhere in the miniature buddhas that are worn as talismans to protect against evil spirits.

Buddhism has one aim and one aim only: to abolish suffering. It proposes to do so by purely human means, by ridding oneself of the causes of suffering—craving, malice, and delusion. All Buddhist individuals are expected to eliminate craving and malice by exercising self-restraint and showing kindness to all creatures or "sentient beings." Only the monks, though, are able to participate directly in the struggle against delusion.

Other aspects of the philosophy include the law of karma whereby every action has effects, and the energy of past action, good or evil, continues forever and is "reborn." (Some argue, though, that the Buddha took transmigration quite literally.) As a consequence, "tam bun" or "making merit" is taken very seriously. This can be done by entering the monkhood for a few days or months, helping in the construction of a monastery or a stupa, contributing to education, giving alms, or performing any act of kindness no matter how small. When the monks go daily with their begging bowls from house to house they are giving the people an opportunity to make merit; similarly, the boys whom you will see carrying caged birds that can be freed for a fee are allowing people to make merit by freeing the bird from the cage. When making merit, it is the motive that is all important—the intention of the mind at the time of the action determines the karmic outcome, not the action itself. Buddhism calls for self-reliance; the individual embarks alone of the Noble Eightfold Path to Nirvana following the teachings that include the exhortations "to cease to do evil, learn to do good, cleanse your own heart."

Although Buddhism first came to Thailand in the 3rd century B.C., when missionaries sent by King Aśoka of India arrived at Suvannabhumi, near present-day Nakhon Pathom, it was not until the 14th century, when the reigning king sent to Ceylon for a Theravadan bhikku (ascetic—a spiritual leader), that the *sangha* (monastic order) was established. The king entered the order, thus beginning the close connection between the royal house and the sangha that continues to this day.

Most Chinese and Vietnamese living in Thailand follow Mahayana Buddhism (there are 34 such monasteries in the country).

Some of the rituals that you will observe in Thailand is derived from Chinese and Indian traditions (including Confucianism and Brahmanism). For a living example of the Brahmanical tradition, stop by the Erawan shrine in Bangkok and watch the supplicants lighting joss sticks and asking for the god's help. (One of the reasons why the crowds are so thick here is that one man won the lottery after worshiping at the shrine.)

Other religions and philosophies are also followed in Thailand including Islam, Christianity, Hinduism, and Sikhism. Sunni Islam is followed by more than two million Thais, mostly of Malay origin, descendants of the Muslim traders and missionaries who spread their teachings in the southern peninsula in the early 13th century. There are approximately 2,000 mosques in Thailand.

Christianity has spread throughout Thailand since the 16th century by generations of Jesuit, Dominican, and Franciscan missionaries from Europe and America. Even with centuries of evangelism, however, there are only a quarter of a million Christians living in the country. Yet Thais have accepted much that has come from the Christian missionaries, particularly ideas on education, health, and science. Part of the reason that Christianity has failed to establish itself in the country is that the Thai inner spirit is unwilling to accept a limited or exclusive faith. One of our favorite stories is about a remark by King Mongkut (the king in *Anna and the King of Siam*) to a group of visiting missionaries: "What you teach us to do is admirable, but what you teach us to believe is foolish."

The king is dubbed Upholder of All Religions and, though a Buddhist, he is a testament to the Thai sense of tolerance and diversity that charges him to protect all beliefs. Still, it is the network of more than 27,000 Buddhist monasteries that most occupies the attention of the king and government.

MYTH & FOLKLORE Thai myth is principally derived from the Indian epic, the *Ramayana*. The Thai version, called the *Ramakien*, is a restatement of the epic text that is best known in Indonesian culture, especially as it is dramatized in the *wayang kulit* or shadow-puppet plays. These stories involve brave kings and queens, heroic deeds, historical battles, animals that are transformed into people (and vice versa), clowns, and touching love stories. Many of the country's writers have taken classic stories from the *Ramakien* and updated them.

There is much that could be classified as folklore in Thai village life, particularly in rural areas. It's too vast a topic to go into here, but there are some elements that you will certainly notice on your travels. For example, ancestor and spirit worship exists everywhere, even in Bangkok where you will see "spirit houses," small replicas of houses standing on a pedestal that are filled with flowers, fruit, ribbons, and burning incense. These are shelters for gods who watch over the household; if a householder adds to his house, then he will also expand the spirit house. There are family spirits, rice spirits, tree spirits, village spirits—all kinds of spirits that inform many village customs. They are vestiges of the animism that was practiced before the advent of Buddhism. In some ways these spirits help to encourage social harmony and the resolution of village conflicts, insofar as an individual who alienates the local spirits is a threat to the safety and well-being of the community.

Many of the festivals that are celebrated in Thailand derive from the same animistic roots, like the rain-generating skyrocket festival *bun bang fai* in Northeast Thailand or Loy Krathong when offerings are made to the water goddess. For further discussion of this fascinating topic, see "Recommended Books and Films" later in this chapter.

A rich folklore tradition also exists among the ethnic hill tribes in the north of Thailand. Each culture has its own story about the

---

IMPRESSIONS

Fundamentally the culture of Thailand may be summed up in one word, religion. For everything, arts and literature, social system, habits and customs is developed around their religion . . . to the people as a whole religious culture is still a living force.
—PHYA ANUMAN RAJADHON, *ESSAY ON THAI FOLKLORE*, 1968

IMPRESSIONS

It is a country of perpetual symbol. Mermaids and sirens in the waters, ogres and giants on the land, nymphs in the forests, ghosts and spirits everywhere, dragons and fire-spitting serpents. . . . A country of unceasing pageantry.
—BISHOP PALLEGOIX,
DESCRIPTION DU ROYAUME THAI, 1854

creation of the world and that people's place in the universe. The characters, rituals, and traditions within this much-studied segment is well described in Paul and Elaine Lewis's *Peoples of the Golden Triangle.*

5. PERFORMING ARTS & EVENING ENTERTAINMENT

There is much to see throughout the country in performing arts, particularly during the many festivals and holidays. Thai dance, with its subtle gestures and elegant costumes, is more than 300 years old. It is the best-known Thai art form and is frequently performed.

The khon, the dramatic masked performance of the *Ramakien,* is what most visitors will encounter. Incidents are dramatized from the story that tells of the war between Rama, rightful king of Ayutthaya, and Tosakanth, evil king of the island of Longka, who abducts Rama's wife, Sita. Rama is aided by his brother Lakshman and several monkey chieftains, including Hanuman, with troops of monkeys. Tosakanth's allies are various demons (*Asuras, Rakshas,* and *Yakshas*). At one time all the performers wore masks, but today the players of divine and human roles no longer wear masks; only the simians and demons do. The masks are magnificent. There are 100 masks for the demons alone, and each is distinguished by its shape, color, and facial characteristics. The *Ramakien* stories are also told in the shadow-puppet plays.

Thai musical composition uses the diatonic scale of seven full tones (no semitones) within an octave and uses simple duple time rather than compound time. It is performed by a *piphat* band, consisting of woodwind and percussion. The first is represented by a single instrument, the *pi-nai,* a cylindrical rosewood instrument with a reed that produces a piercing tone similar to a bagpipe. The percussion is divided into gongs, drums, and other metal percussive instruments. The *ranad ek* is shaped like a wooden boat on a stand. Across it are hung 21 gradated resonance bars (like a xylophone). Its cousin is the *ranad thong ek,* which is shaped like a tapered box. There are also deep-toned versions of both of these. The *gong wong yai,* which plays the principal melody, consists of a large oval frame of rattan or cane about 2 feet high and 5 feet from front to back, which is strung with 16 metal discs of different pitches. The player sits in the circle beating them with hard and soft sticks. The

❂ **Thai dance is more than 300 years old**

gong wong lek is similar but smaller, while the *gong hoi* is a set of three very sonorous gongs, often beautifully decorated, suspended from a stand, and played with padded sticks. The drums are represented by the *tapone,* a bulging drum on a stand that has different-size ends, one covered with ox or wild goat skin and the other with calf skin. Its sound effects are regulated by the application of a thick rice and ash paste. The *song na,* a thinner version of the tapone, is played on the lap. The *klong thad* is a very large drum that stands up on end. Both ends are the same size and only one side is beaten with thick bamboo sticks. *Charb Lek* and *charb yai* are small and large cymbals, respectively. The *ching* are small, heavy cup-shaped cymbals that are much more resonant than the triangle. These play the role of the conductor setting the rhythm and the pace of the orchestra.

6. FOOD & DRINK

FOOD Food is one of the true joys of traveling in Thailand—in fact, we think of the country as the culinary Italy of Southeast Asia. If you aren't familiar with Thai cooking, imagine the best of Chinese ingredients and preparation combined with the sophistication of Indian spicing, topped off with red and green chili. The cooking styles available in Bangkok run the gamut from the northern kantoke to southern tiger prawns; in other words, you can find nearly any style of Thai (and Western) cooking in the capital.

THAI CUISINE Basic ingredients include a cornucopia of shellfish, fish, meat, fresh fruits and vegetables (limes, tamarind, asparagus, bean sprouts, carrots, mushrooms, morning glory, spinach, bamboo shoots), and herbs and spices (basil, lemongrass, mint, chili, garlic, coriander). Thai cooking also uses coconut milk, curry paste, peanuts, and a large variety of noodles and rice. In the classic cuisine, the five basic flavors (sweet, salty, sour, bitter, hot) must be in balance, and every menu should include some of each.

We've included a helpful menu and guide to ordering food in the appendix. Among the dishes you'll find throughout Bangkok are: tom yam goong, a Thai hot-and-sour shrimp soup; satay, charcoal-broiled chicken, beef, or pork strips skewered on a bamboo stick, then dipped in a peanut-coconut curry sauce; spring rolls, similar to egg rolls but thinner and usually containing only vegetables; larb, a spicy chicken or ground-beef concoction with mint and lime flavoring; salads with a dressing of onions, chili peppers, lime juice, and fish sauce; pad thai, literally "Thai noodles," a dish consisting of rice noodles, large shrimp, eggs, peanuts, fresh bean sprouts, lime, and a delicious sauce (this is one of our favorites, and you can find it everywhere); khao soi, a northern curried soup served at small food stalls; a wide range of curries, flavored with coriander, chili, garlic, and fish sauce or coconut milk; tod man pla, one of many preparations of fish, this one spicy; sticky rice, served in the north and made from glutinous rice, prepared with vegetables and wrapped in a banana leaf; and Thai

❍ **Food is one of the joys of traveling in Thailand**

fried rice, a simple dish made with whatever the kitchen has on hand.

As a word of caution, the Thai palate relishes incredibly spicy food, normally much hotter than is tolerated in even the most piquant Western cuisine. Protect yourself with *"mai phet, farang,"* meaning "not spicy, foreigner." If you begin to suffer from Thai-food burnout, visit a Chinese restaurant. Most of the Chinese cuisine in Thailand is from Yunnan Province or Canton, meaning delicious food with restrained spices. However, most Thai and Chinese food, particularly in the cheaper restaurants and food stalls, is cooked with lots of MSG (known locally as "Ajinomoto" because of the popular Japanese brand widely used), and it's almost impossible to avoid.

Traditionally, Thai menus don't offer fancy desserts. Most you'll find are coconut-milk-based sweets or a variety of fruit-flavored custards, but the local fruit is luscious enough for a perfect dessert. Familiar fruits are pineapples (eaten with salt to heighten the flavor), mangoes, bananas, guavas, papayas, coconuts, watermelons, and the newest rage, apples grown in the royal orchards. Less familiar are durian (in season during June and July), which tastes wonderful but smells odious; mangosteen (available April to September), a purplish hard-skinned fruit with delicate whitish pink segments that melt in the mouth; jackfruit (available year-round), which is large and yellow-brown, with a thick, thorned skin that envelops tangy-flavored flesh; lychee; longan (available July to October), small and brown-skinned, with very sweet white flesh; tamarind, a spicy little fruit in a pod that you can eat fresh (it's also used to make a delicious spicy sweet-and-sour sauce); rambutan (available May to July), which is small, red, and hairy, with transparent sweet flesh clustered round a woody seed; pomelo (available October to December), similar to a grapefruit, but less juicy. By the way, some of these fruits are served as salads—the raw green papaya, for example, is particularly delicious.

With such an international community, it's not surprising that in Bangkok a large assortment of European-style cuisines can be found. Don't be surprised if your Thai host suggests visiting one of the French or Italian restaurants; they are extremely popular and often quite good. If you do take in a Western-style restaurant, try those unique dishes that combine traditional European recipes with native Thai ingredients.

Thailand also has many Indian restaurants, with a wide variety of vegetarian dishes. We've found that most of these serve the less spicy northern cuisine, not the fiery dishes from the south.

DINING CUSTOMS The Thai family usually has an early breakfast of khao tom, a rice soup (made from leftovers) to which chicken, seafood, or meat may be added. Typically, it's served with a barely cooked egg floating on top and a variety of pickled vegetables, relishes, and spicy condiments to add flavor. It's our favorite breakfast, and widely available at even the poshest hotels.

The Thais take eating very seriously, so businesspeople allow two to three hours for lunch. A formal business luncheon consists of several dishes, but most casual diners have a one-course rice, noodle, or curry dish. For two tourists, two hot dishes and perhaps a cold salad (mostly of the "not spicy" variety) are a satisfying way to sample new foods. Most restaurants offer lunch from noon to 2 pm. Many close until 6 or 7 pm, when they reopen for dinner.

Thais often stop at one of the ubiquitous food stalls for a large bowl of noodle soup (served with meat, fish, or poultry) or dine at a department-store food hall or market, where they can buy snacks from many different vendors and have a seat. Snacking from streetside food stalls—the source of the best Thai food, some would claim—is popular throughout the day.

Dinner, the main meal of the day, consists of a soup (gaeng jued); a curried dish (gaeng ped); a steamed, fried, stir-fried, or grilled dish (nueng, thod, paad, or yaang); a side dish of salad or condiments (krueang kiang); steamed rice (khao); and some fruit (polamai). Two Thais dining out may share four dishes (of different textures and spiciness), always helping themselves to a little portion at a time (so as not to appear gluttonous). Dishes are brought to the table as they're cooked and eaten in any order.

Bangkok's elite often follow the lead of their Singapore and Hong Kong neighbors by entertaining guests at Chinese, French, or continental restaurants, often located in the city's best hotels. For those at the other end of the economic spectrum, American-style fast-food restaurants have become popular dating venues. Many travelers use their evening meals to sample Thai buffets or banquet menus, prepared in conjunction with classical music and dance performances.

DRINK Bangkok has many bars, and liquor and beer are also widely available in stores, restaurants, and hotels. Locally made whisky, such as Mekong, is very popular. Johnnie Walker Black is still one of the most highly prized gifts you can give. Several fine varieties of beer are brewed in the country; the best known are Singha and a locally brewed German beer, Kloster. There isn't much in the way of Thai wine. Most wine is imported and incredibly expensive; mediocre ones are readily available in Bangkok but not in the countryside, except in Western restaurants.

---

7. RECOMMENDED BOOKS & FILMS

BOOKS

HISTORY For an entertaining and well-written history of Bangkok, read Alec Waugh's *Bangkok, Story of a City* (Boston: Little Brown, 1971). William Warren's *Bangkok's Waterways* (Bangkok: Asia Books, 1989) provides an entertaining tour of the river and klongs of contemporary Bangkok.

For a historical overview of the region, try D. G. E. Hall's *A History of Southeast Asia* (London: Macmillan, 1977). For a history of the country, we recommend M. L. Jumsai's *Popular History of Thailand* (Bangkok: Chalermnit, 1970), W. A. R. Wood's *A History of Siam* (London: Unwin, 1979), or David K. Wayatt's fine *Thailand: A Short History* (Bangkok/London: Thai Wattana Panich/ Yale University Press, 1984).

There are three newer works we appreciate as much for their literary value as for their insights into specific periods: Reginald

Campbell's *Teak-Wallah* (Oxford University Press, 1985) chronicles the days of a young English teak inspector in northern Thailand at the turn of the century; Collin Piprell's *Bangkok Knights* (Editions Duang Kamol, D. K. Books, 1991) is a collection of short stories by a Canadian resident, set in contemporary Bangkok; Samitsuda Ekachai's collection of interviews with residents of Isan in *Behind the Smile* (Development Support Committee, 1990) is a fascinating look at life in the Northeast.

RELIGION & CULTURE For a better understanding of Buddhism and the customs and culture of the country the following titles are all filled with fascinating material. The first two are easily available; the rest can be found in English bookstores in Thailand. *Buddhism* by Christmas Humphreys (Penguin, 1987) gives a good, clear explanation of Buddhism including an extensive discussion of Theravada. *Three Ways of Asian Wisdom* by Nancy Wilson Ross (Simon & Schuster, 1966) is a classic, providing brilliant explication of the complex intuitions at the heart of Hinduism, Buddhism, and Zen. *Essays on Thai Folklore* (Bangkok: Editions Duang Kamol, 1968) by Phya Anuman Rajadhon, who was president of the Siam Society, is filled with descriptions and explanations of rites, rituals, ceremonies, and traditional folktales. His *Some Traditions of the Thai* concentrates on birth customs. *Reflections on Thai Culture* by William J. Klausner (Siam Society, 1987) is a collection of essays about traditional village life, popular Buddhism, the law, and customs, covering everything from *krengjai* (deference and consideration), gift-giving, and the meaning of *sanuk* (fun) to bargaining, body language, taboos, and eating habits. *More Thai Ways* (Allied Newspapers, 1982) by Denis Segaller, an Englishman now living in Thailand, takes a loving look at Thai people and customs touching on all kinds of things: the royal barge procession, the relationship of the people to the monarchy, language, fruits, flowers, ceremonies, and much more.

ART & LITERATURE Among the best works on art and sculpture are Piriya Krairiksh's *The Sacred Image and Art in Thailand* (Bangkok: White Lotus, 1980) and Reginald LeMay's *The Culture of Southeast Asia* (London: Unwin, 1954).

Literary works in English include Anna Leonowens's *The English Governess at the Siamese Court*, published in 1870; and Margaret Landon's 1944 *Anna and the King of Siam;* William Warren's *Jim Thompson: The Legendary American* (Boston: Houghton Mifflin; now out of print but available in libraries); and Ernest Young's *The Kingdom of the Yellow Robe* (New York: AMS Press, 1988).

The most important Thai literary suggestion is the epic work, *Ramakien*, based on the *Ramayana*, and available in libraries. Contemporary works of Thai literature are *Monsoon Country* by Pira Sudham (Bangkok: Shire Books, 1988); *Four Reigns and Red Bamboo* by Kukrit Pramoj (Bangkok: D. K. Books, 1981); and *A Man Called Karn* by Suwannee Sukonta (Bangkok: Bannakarn).

For a savvy look at Thai design and home styles, try *Thai Style* (Bangkok: Asia Books, 1988) by William Warren and Luca Tettoni.

TRAVEL For 19th-century descriptions of travel in Thailand, we recommend *Temples and Elephants* (Oxford University Press, 1986), a delightful account written in 1884 during King

Chulalongkorn's reign by Carl Bock. W. Somerset Maugham's *The Gentleman in the Parlor* (London: William Heinemann Ltd., 1930) is an interesting account of travels in Burma and Thailand.

If you're planning an extensive tour of the country, we recommend *Frommer's Thailand '95* (New York: Prentice Hall Travel) as a travel guide, and the APA Insight Guides, *Thailand* and *Bangkok* (distributed by Prentice Hall Travel), for in-depth historical and cultural background.

A good introduction for businesspeople who intend to work in the country is *Conflict or Communication*, reprinted from *Business in Thailand* (Bangkok [Phetchaburi Road]: Business Information and Research Co.). If you plan to live in Thailand—particularly in Bangkok—for an extended amount of time, the *Bangkok Guide* (Bangkok: Australian–New Zealand Women's Group, revised 1990) is an excellent reference handbook that will ease your move.

FILMS Few films have been made about Bangkok (or Thailand for that matter). Most familiar to Westerners are the two versions of *Anna and the King of Siam*, with Rex Harrison and Irene Dunne (1946), and the later musical adaptation with Yul Brynner and Deborah Kerr, *The King and I* (1956). Both films were shot in Hollywood on sound stages, and are banned in Thailand because they're considered disrespectful of the king.

However, many films about other Southeast Asian countries have been shot on location in Thailand. There have been a spate of films about Vietnam and Cambodia filmed in Thailand: *The Deer Hunter* (1978) was partially filmed there; *The Killing Fields* (1984); *Casualties of War* (1984), shot on the island of Phuket; *Air America* (1990); *Good Morning, Vietnam* (1987); *Rambo III* (1988); and Oliver Stone's *Heaven and Earth* (1993).

Earlier films shot in Bangkok were *The Bridge on the River Kwai* (1957); *The Ugly American* (1963), shot in Bangkok; and *The Man with the Golden Gun*, filmed in Bangkok and Phuket.

CHAPTER 2

PLANNING A TRIP TO BANGKOK

1. **INFORMATION, ENTRY REQUIREMENTS & MONEY**
- **WHAT THINGS COST IN BANGKOK**
2. **WHEN TO GO— CLIMATE, HOLIDAYS & EVENTS**
- **BANGKOK CALENDAR OF EVENTS**
3. **PREPARING FOR YOUR TRIP**
4. **WHAT TO PACK**
5. **TIPS FOR THE DISABLED, SENIORS, SINGLES, FAMILIES & STUDENTS**
6. **GETTING THERE**
- **FROMMER'S SMART TRAVELER: AIRFARES**

This chapter is devoted to the where, when, and how of your trip—the advance planning issues required to get it together and take it on the road. It should help you budget your trip and resolve other important questions: when to go; whether or not to join a tour; what pretrip health precautions to take; what insurance coverage is needed; where to obtain more information about the destination; and so on.

1. INFORMATION, ENTRY REQUIRE- MENTS & MONEY

INFORMATION

A major source of free and excellent information is the **Tourism Authority of Thailand (TAT)**, with offices throughout the world. Consult the TAT on travel plans, hotels, transportation options, and current schedules for festivals and holidays. A multilingual Tourist Police force, part of the TAT in all major tourist areas within Thailand, is helpful in emergencies (such as filing police reports for theft) and can provide local information.

In the **United States, United Kingdom,** and **Australia,** you'll find TAT offices at the following addresses: 3440 Wilshire Blvd., Suite 1100, Los Angeles, CA 90010 (tel. 213/382-2353; fax 213/380-6476); 5 World Trade Center, Suite 3443, New York, NY 10048 (tel. 212/432-0433; fax 212/912-0920); 303 E. Wacker Dr., Suite 400, Chicago, IL 60601 (tel. 312/819-3990); 49 Albemarle St., London WIX 3FE, England, U.K. (tel. 071/499-7679; fax 071/629-5519); and Royal Exchange Building, 12th floor, 56 Pitt St., Sydney 2000, Australia (tel. 02/247-7549; fax 02/251-2465).

You can also contact the **Royal Thai Consulate General** at these addresses in the United States: 351 E. 52nd St., New York, NY 10022 (tel. 212/754-1770); 35 E. Wacker Dr., Suite 1834, Chicago, IL 60601 (tel. 312/236-2447; and 801 N. La Brea Ave., Los

Angeles, CA 90038 (tel. 213/937-1894). Or: the **Royal Thai Embassy,** 2300 Kalorama Rd. NW, Washington, DC 20008 (tel. 202/ 483-7200). Or contact the **Royal Thai Embassy** in your home country. For additional information in other Asian cities, contact **Thai Airways International.**

Follow your local newspapers for current information about the state of affairs in Thailand and Southeast Asia. Travelers should contact the **Travel Advisory Service, U.S. Department of State** (tel. 202/647-5225), to see if any recent travel advisories have been issued about the area.

ENTRY REQUIREMENTS

All visitors to Thailand must carry a valid passport along with proof of onward passage (either a return or a through ticket). Entry and departure must be through the airport or one of the major ports of entry; check with the Thai consulate or embassy in your country if you plan to enter Thailand via an exotic port.

Visas are not required if you are staying up to 15 days, are a national of one of 41 designated countries, and have proof of return passage. A 15-day visa can be issued at Don Muang International Airport to nationals of 80 other countries, with proof of return passage. Visa-free entry cannot be extended. To stay longer than 15 days, you must apply for a 60-day tourist visa or a 30-day transit visa at any Thai embassy or consulate. A valid passport, two photographs, and $10 are required for a transit visa, with a charge of $15 for a tourist visa and $20 for a nonimmigrant (business) visa. Businesspeople need a visa for making business contacts, calls, or meetings, as well as for employment. A nonimmigrant visa for up to 90 days can be obtained with a letter from your employer stating the purpose and length of your stay. If you have a question as to which type of visa is required (if any), call or write the nearest Thai embassy or consulate. The entire process takes one business day when you apply in person, and all visas must be used within 90 days of issuance.

Check at the nearest Thai embassy or consulate for up-to-date information about health certificates that may be required for entry. As of this writing, there were no inoculations required, other than for tourists coming from an infected zone.

There are no restrictions on the import of foreign currencies or traveler's checks. But you cannot export foreign currency in excess of $10,000 unless it is declared to Customs upon arrival. Individuals may bring a maximum of 2,000 baht (4,000 baht per family) into the country and may take out a maximum of 500 baht (1,000 baht per family) upon exit.

MONEY

CASH/CURRENCY The Thai unit of currency is the **baht** (you will see it written B), divided into 100 **satang** (though you'll rarely see a satang coin). Copper-colored satang coins come in denominations of 25 and 50 satang; silver-colored baht coins come in denominations of 1B, 2B, and 5B (note that the 1B and old 5B coins are the same size). Baht notes come in denominations of 10B (brown), 20B (green), 100B (red), and 500B (purple). The exchange rate at the time of publication was 25B for $1 U.S., making 1B equal to 4¢ U.S.

THE THAI BAHT

This table provides the approximate exchange values (rounded off) of the baht, the U.S. dollar, and—for British travelers—the pound. The rates given here fluctuate and may not be the same when you travel to Thailand—use this table only as a guide.

Baht	U.S.$	U.K.£	Baht	U.S.$	U.K.£
1	0.04	0.03	500	20.00	15.00
5	0.20	0.15	750	30.00	22.50
10	0.40	0.30	1,000	40.00	30.00
15	0.60	0.45	1,250	50.00	37.50
20	0.80	0.60	1,500	60.00	45.00
25	1.00	0.75	1,750	70.00	52.50
50	2.00	1.50	2,000	80.00	60.00
75	3.00	2.25	2,250	90.00	67.50
100	4.00	3.00	2,500	100.00	75.00
125	5.00	3.75	2,750	110.00	82.50
150	6.00	4.50	3,000	120.00	90.00
175	7.00	5.25	3,250	130.00	97.50
200	8.00	6.00	3,500	140.00	105.00
250	10.00	7.50	4,00	160.00	120.00

WHAT THINGS COST IN BANGKOK	U.S. $
Taxi from the airport to the city center	12.00
Local telephone call (private pay phone)	.20
Double at The Oriental (very expensive)	300.00
Double at Wall Street Inn (moderate)	92.00
Double at Peachy Guesthouse (budget)	6.20
Lunch for one at Ban Chiang (inexpensive)	9.00
Lunch for one at Suda Restaurant (budget)	5.00
Dinner for one, without wine, at Sala Thip (moderate)	20.00
Dinner for one, without wine, at Lemongrass (inexpensive)	17.00
Dinner for one, without wine, at M. K. Restaurant (budget)	6.50
Pint of beer	3.20
Coca-Cola	.95
Cup of coffee	.60
Roll of ASA 100 Kodacolor film, 36 exposures	4.80
Admission to the National Museum	1.00
Movie ticket	2.00

CREDIT CARDS & TRAVELER'S CHECKS Nearly all international hotels and larger businesses accept major credit cards, but almost none accept personal checks. Most establishments add a 3% to 5% surcharge (despite protests by the credit-card companies) for payment by credit card. Traveler's checks are negotiable at most banks, hotels, restaurants, and tourist-oriented shops, but you'll receive a better rate cashing them at commercial banks. In smaller towns and remote provinces, baht will be the only acceptable currency.

---

2. WHEN TO GO—CLIMATE, HOLIDAYS & EVENTS

CLIMATE Thailand has two distinct climatic areas: the humid south, which is tropical; and the humid north, which is a tropical savanna.

There are three distinct seasons (except in the more temperate south). The hot season lasts from March to May, temperatures averaging in the upper 90s Fahrenheit (mid-30s Celsius). The rainy season lasts from June to October, the temperature averaging 84°F (29°C), with 90% humidity. The cool season, from November to February, has temperatures from the high 70s to low 80s Fahrenheit (26°C).

In the north, particularly in the hills around Chiang Mai, temperatures can go down to the low 60s (16°C). The southern half of the country, particularly the southern Malay Peninsula, has intermittent showers year-round and daily ones during the monsoon, with temperatures averaging in the low 80s (30°C). However, Thailand's monsoon isn't as imposing as in other Asian countries—you can actually travel around the country in some comfort.

HOLIDAYS Many holidays are based on the Thai lunar calendar; check with the TAT for the current year's schedule.

Besides New Year's Eve and New Year's Day, there is the Buddhist New Year's water-throwing festival, Songkran (Apr 12–14), and the Chinese New Year (late Jan/early Feb)—the national holidays are as follows: Magha Puja (Feb), celebrating the day the Buddha preached his doctrines; Chakri Day (Apr 6), commemorating the founding of the Chakri dynasty (the reigning dynasty); Coronation Day (May 5), honoring the coronation of His Majesty King Bhumibol in 1950; Visakha Puja (mid-May), marking the birth, enlightenment, and death of the Buddha; Asalha Puja (July), signaling the beginning of the Rains' Retreat and the three-month period of meditation for all Buddhist monks; Her Majesty the Queen's birthday, also Mother's Day (Aug 12); Thot Kathin (Oct), during which monks are presented with new robes; Chulalongkorn Day (Oct 23), honoring the country's favorite king; Loy Krathong (early Nov), one of Thailand's greatest holidays, honoring the water spirit and serving as a day to wash away sins committed during the previous year; His Majesty the King's birthday, also Father's Day (Dec 5); and Constitution Day (Dec 10), recognizing Thailand's first constitution in 1932.

BANGKOK CALENDAR OF EVENTS

JANUARY

☐ **Elephant Roundup and Handcraft Fair** (Ayutthaya). Weeklong festival with elephant-training demonstrations and handcrafts fair. End of month.

FEBRUARY/MARCH

☐ **Corrections Department Handcraft Fair.** Moderately priced handcrafts made by Thai prisoners from all regions are for sale.

MARCH

☐ **Bangkok International Jewelry Fair.** Promotional displays by Thai and international designers and manufacturers. Middle of month.

APRIL

☐ **Pattaya Festival** (Pattaya). Arts, fireworks, beauty pageant. First week.

☉ INTERNATIONAL KITE FESTIVAL Contests and displays.
   Where: Sanam Luang Parade Ground, near the National Museum. **When:** Third week in April. **How:** Open event.

☐ **Bangkok Ready-to-wear Fair.** Promotional displays of garments, fabrics, and accessories made in Thailand for export. Last week.

MAY

☐ **Royal Ploughing Festival** (nationwide). Demonstrations, plus royal blessings to mark the commencement of the rice-planting cycle. First week.
☐ **Foodex and Hotelex Foodpack.** Promotional displays of food products and food-packaging equipment for the trade. Last week.

AUGUST

☐ **Thailand Tourism Festival.** Promotional displays from various regions for visiting international travel-industry people. Middle of month.

SEPTEMBER

☐ **Thailand International Swan Boat Races.** Races and parades to mark the end of the rains. Middle of month.
☐ **Bangkok Gems and Jewelry Fair.** Promotional displays by Thai and international designers and manufacturers. Middle of month.

OCTOBER

☐ **Thai Leather Goods.** Promotional displays by Thai and international manufacturers for retail buyers. End of month.

☐ **Vegetarian Festival.** In honor of the Chinese religions, restaurants serve special vegetarian meals.

NOVEMBER

☐ **River Kwai Bridge Week** (Kanchanaburi). Historical exhibits, *son et lumière* at bridge, train rides, cultural performances. End of month.

☐ **Bangkok Marathon.** Both a full marathon and a half marathon are run through the city, across its bridges, and around Thonburi. End of month.

DECEMBER

✪ *KING'S BIRTHDAY AND TROOPING OF THE COLORS.* Celebrations go on nationwide for about a week, and include a parade of the elite Royal Guards and military troops and fireworks displays.

Where: Near the Grand Palace. *When:* First week in December (the king's birthday is December 3). *How:* Public event.

☐ **Made in Thailand.** Promotional display of locally produced handcrafts, technical equipment, machinery, etc., for export. Beginning of month.

☐ **Gift Show.** Promotional displays of gifts for year-end giving to educate local consumers about new products. End of month.

---

3. PREPARING FOR YOUR TRIP

HEALTH

Although you shouldn't anticipate any health problems, it's best to be aware of potential concerns associated with travel to exotic lands. First, consult your doctor regarding his or her recommendations on immunizations and inoculations (none are legally required for entrance into Thailand) at least one month before departure. Malaria, Japanese encephalitis, typhoid, and hepatitis A are endemic to some rural parts of Thailand, and some prophylaxis may be recommended. You can also call the **Centers for Disease Control and Prevention** (tel. 404/332-4559) or order the current edition of its book *Health Information for International Travel.*

Do *not* drink the tap water, even in Bangkok, where the Municipal Authority purifies it. Make sure water is boiled or bottled, and that boiled water has been used to make ice cubes. Avoid salads and fresh dairy products, including ice cream, and unpeeled fruit or vegetables except at the larger hotels and restaurants; even there, inquire whether fresh products are washed with purified water. We love to eat street food, but exercise caution; check to see if oil and ingredients look fresh, and never eat ice cream or anything raw prepared at a street stand, especially seafood.

Don't swim in freshwater streams or pools (other than chlorinated hotel pools), as they are probably contaminated. If you're making any side trips to the beach resorts, avoid the ocean near sewage-pipe outlets and freshwater streams, because of contaminated water (especially around Pattaya) and the poisonous sea snakes that inhabit these areas. Be especially careful of coral reefs (such as those along Phuket), jellyfish, and sea urchins, and treat all cuts or stings immediately by cleaning and applying an antibiotic cream. Ear infections are a common problem, so dry your ears thoroughly after you swim.

Avoid sunstroke or heat exhaustion by exercising caution about physical activity, especially in the hot season. Above all, drink lots of liquid to avoid dehydration; inexpensive bottled water is widely sold. Refrain from excessive exposure to the sun, use a strong sunscreen, and wear a hat for protection. Restricting alcohol consumption and eating lightly will help acclimatization. Diarrhea is to be expected in the adjustment to a new cuisine and climate. If it persists beyond 48 hours or is accompanied by fever or dehydration, consult a doctor.

The **U.S. Embassy Medical Unit** (tel. 252-5040) is extremely knowledgeable about local maladies and can refer you to local physicians or hospitals for appropriate treatment.

SEX Every day you're in Thailand, in any part of the country, you will see foreigners enjoying the company of Thai women and men. Although prostitution is illegal, it is as much a product of the tourism industry as superb hotels and stunning beaches.

To many, the Thai sense of morality may seem contradictory and confusing. As devout followers of Buddhism, Thais should theoretically eschew lust as a worldly sin. Yet Thai men openly frequent brothels after marriage, while condemning the prostitutes who work there.

Stemming from a legacy of royal patronage and social acceptance, the oldest profession has been part of Thailand's economy for centuries. In poor, uneducated, rural families, where sons are counted on as farm labor, sex has become an unfortunate income-earning occupation for daughters. However, girls sent to the big cities as CSWs (the official term is "commercial sex worker") can quietly retire, return to their villages, and even get married. Thai society tends to ignore men employed as CSWs; although homosexuality is not condoned, most turn a blind eye to it and to the more blatant transvestism seen in the major cities.

Although the majority of CSWs were foreign until the 1930s, today this burgeoning industry has an estimated 800,000 Thai-born CSWs (with an additional 70,000 working in Japan), who outnumber schoolteachers by at least 30%. Despite these numbers, there are not enough CSWs to satisfy demand. The continuing growth in tourist arrivals has meant a tremendous increase in new clientele while increased rural employment opportunities and education have created a shortage of willing workers. Because clients are insisting on younger and younger CSWs in the foolhardy belief that children will be AIDS-free, Thailand currently has the world's largest child sex industry. Many traders promise parents urban employment opportunities (such as domestic service, waitressing, or housekeeping work), then enslave male and female children in sex clubs and massage parlors. *Time* magazine has reported that girls as young as 12 years have been sold to sex dealers for sums up to 200,000B ($8,000), while the daughters of poor hill tribe families may fetch only 1,000B ($40). All sources agree that minors (under 15 years) now make up at least 20% of the CSW labor force and that up to 50% are HIV-positive.

Since sex has become a standard stop on the tourist itinerary, Thailand has had to aggressively develop research and education programs on the subject of AIDS. The largest nongovernmental organization in Thailand, the Population and Community Development Agency (PDA), has enlarged the scope of rural development programs from family planning and cottage-industry schemes to running informational seminars for CSWs and the distribution of condoms. Even the Royal family is involved: HRH Princess Chulaporn Walailuke, founder of the Chulaporn Research Institute and an internationally known activist, sponsored the 1990 International Global AIDS Conference in Bangkok and continues to be active.

As elsewhere, when it comes to AIDS prevention, education and practice are still worlds apart. According to EMPOWER, an activist group founded by Bangkok's CSWs to provide education and health care, CSWs cannot convince most of their clients to wear condoms. The government currently estimates 400,000 AIDS virus carriers nationwide. Mr. Mechai Viravaidya, PDA's secretary-general and an interim cabinet member in Thailand's current government, predicts that more than 2 million people (out of a population of 57 million), or about 40% of the world's AIDS carriers, will be infected by the year 2000. That's a trend that all visitors to the Land of Smiles can help reverse by respecting the CSWs' efforts to prevent AIDS.

INSURANCE

Check your insurance policy before departure to make sure that overseas medical treatment, hospitalization, and medical evacuation are fully covered. Contact your own insurance company (or any membership organization such as AAA) to see if they can provide a rider to cover trip cancellation, baggage insurance, and any uncovered medical expenses. Make arrangements with someone at home who will assume financial responsibility for your medical care or who will be able to wire you funds in case of emergency.

IN THE UNITED STATES Several travel-insurance and -assistance companies offer short-term policies to cover trip cancellation costs, medical bills, medical transportation, and baggage insurance. **International SOS Assistance, Inc.,** Eight Neshaminy Interplex, Suite 207, Trevose, PA 19053 (tel. toll free 800/523-8930), or P.O. Box 466, place Bonaventure, Montréal PQ H5A 1C1, Canada (tel. 514/874-7674), provides emergency evacuation services to members for a small fee (an air-ambulance evacuation with accompanying medical personnel can run as high as $25,000), plus other coverage at reasonable rates.

Two recommended companies that issue temporary policies (fees are based on amount of coverage and duration of trip) are **Healthcare Global,** c/o Wallach & Company, Inc., 107 W. Federal St. (P.O. Box 480) Middleburg, VA 22117 (tel. toll free 800/237-6615), and **Travel Guard Internationale,** c/o Transamerica Premier Insurance Co., 1100 Center Point Dr., Stevens Point, WI 54481-9970 (tel. toll free 800/782-5151). Travmed, issued by the **International Travelers Assistance Association of Baltimore** (tel. toll free 800/732-5309), is another policy with a low deductible and good coverage.

IN THE UNITED KINGDOM You might contact **Columbus Travel Insurance Ltd.** (tel. 071/375-0011), or, for students, **Campus Travel** (tel. 071/730-3402). **Endsleigh** (97–107 Southampton Row, London WC1B, tel. 071/436-4451) is reputable and inexpensive, offering a month's coverage for between £41 and £49.

---

4. WHAT TO PACK

CLOTHING Light, casual clothing is your best defense against the heat. Breathable cottons or linens are far preferable to synthetics, and hotels usually offer prompt, inexpensive laundry service. Bangkok society is relatively formal; wear modest styles (no strapless blouses or shorts, for example), especially if you are touring wats (temples), royal buildings, or other religious monuments. Since you are often required to remove your shoes in religious buildings, we suggest easy-to-remove footwear, such as sandals or slip-on shoes. At the beaches, nudity is illegal and offensive to local residents.

Men should generally wear long pants, though longer shorts are acceptable in beach communities. Pressed cotton pants, a shirt, and a tie (a jacket is optional, depending on the formality of the meeting) are appropriate for business and government meetings; a coat and tie are proper for evening engagements. Women should not wear short or revealing clothing; casual dresses or skirts and blouses are appropriate for evening. Though it's very fashionable, we try not to wear black; it's considered—at least among the more traditional Thais—an unlucky color. During the winter, bring a light sweater; during the monsoon, bring an umbrella.

OTHER ITEMS If you wear eyeglasses or contact lenses, you should carry an extra pair. If you're traveling outside of Bangkok to rural towns, a small flashlight will come in handy during the occasional power blackouts. If you're a low-budget traveler, bring along a towel and soap, as the cheapest hostels will not provide them.

Many common nonprescription medications and toiletries are widely available, but we always carry our favorite sunscreen and mosquito repellent with us. You may also want to carry premoistened towelettes, effective for cleaning your hands before dining and for refreshing yourself in the heat.

5. TIPS FOR THE DISABLED, SENIORS, SINGLES, FAMILIES & STUDENTS

FOR THE DISABLED Thailand is a rapidly developing country with as yet very few conveniences for the physically impaired traveler. In the major cities, vehicular traffic is extreme; sidewalks, where provided, are poorly paved and congested with vendors. In the rural areas, roads are commonly unpaved or damaged by the weather (heat and monsoon rains), making wheelchair access very difficult. Hotels in the major cities have elevators to upper floors, and, often, wheelchair-ramp access to other areas; in the provinces, however, only the most expensive establishments will have these amenities.

However, there are tour operators who design trips specifically for the disabled. **People and Places Inc.,** 483 Elmwood Ave., Buffalo, NY 14222 (tel. 716/886-6240), runs small escorted tours to some international destinations (the itineraries change regularly) for adults with developmental disabilities. The **Evergreen Travel Service,** 4114 198th SW, Suite 13, Lynnwood, WA 98036 (tel. 206/776-1184), has had success with tours for the sight-impaired to Thailand, and also organizes overland trips and cruises for the mobility-impaired and wheelchair-disabled.

FOR SENIORS Several tour operators cater to the burgeoning market for older travelers, offering stops in Bangkok and sometimes the Thai islands on their 21- to 28-day Round-the-Orient holidays. The best-known organization is the **American Association of Retired Persons,** whose **AARP Travel Service,** c/o Amoco Motoring Plan (tel. toll free 800/334-3300), has designed several varied, good-value tours for their members. **Saga Holidays,** 222 Berkeley St., Boston, MA 02116 (tel. toll free 800/343-0273), is another travel company committed to working with seniors. They offer 4 days in Bangkok as part of their 20-day Great Cities of Asia tour, or a 14-day trip (with possible extensions to other Asian cities) visiting sights exclusively in Thailand. Another excellent organization known for its study tours is **Elderhostel,** 75 Federal St., Boston, MA 02110 (tel. 617/426-8056). In 1994, Elderhostel offered 10 different 21-day trips during the winter that included 8 days of study at Thammasat University in Bangkok and 7 days of study at Payap or Chiang Mai University in Chiang Mai, as well as many sightseeing excursions from about $3,000, including airfare from Los Angeles.

FOR SINGLES Unlike many other destinations, Thailand is a very comfortable place for single travelers. The Thais are remarkably warm and hospitable, and single men and women are treated with great respect. However, if you're looking for a travel companion, we can recommend a few resources.

Great Expeditions, P.O. Box 8000-411, Abbotsford, BC V2S 6H1, Canada (tel. 604/852-6170), one of our favorite adventure-travel magazines, has a classified section in each bimonthly issue where travelers looking for companions can advertise.

The **Travel Companion Exchange,** P.O. Box 833, Amityville, NY 11701 (tel. 516/454-0880), is a well-respected organization whose members fill out a questionnaire, pay $36 to $66 for a six-month listing, then receive a listing of their own with brief biographies and/or needs/interests/concerns of potential travel partners. The regular newsletter is filled with travel tips, airfare bargains, and many testimonials to the organization's success, including letters from couples who got engaged after traveling through Thailand!

Also, a few tour operators are beginning to take single travelers into account, pairing those who sign up for the same tour so that they can share room costs and have company.

FOR FAMILIES The natural innocence and curiosity of children make them delightful traveling companions, especially in Thailand, where children play a part in most daily activities. Although you'll probably find your movements somewhat restricted, a child's openness with strangers can win many friends and generate unexpected adventures.

For general tips about traveling with children, you can subscribe to the *Family Travel Times* newsletter ($55 annually), published by **Travel With Your Children (TWYCH)**, 45 W. 18th St., New York, NY 10011 (tel.212/206-0688). Every Wednesday from 10 am to 1 pm, additional phone advice is available to members.

Bangkok has some fun, educational, and inexpensive activities (museums, boat trips, zoos, architectural and cultural displays), but we think they're better suited for children old enough to appreciate them. Unless you're headed for the beach or another resort destination, you may find smaller children less interested in the sights, sounds, and spicy foods of this often hot, sticky country. In Chapters 4 and 5, we've noted the places of most interest to children in the special feature called "Cool for Kids."

Many tourist facilities are geared to families. You can get a transportation discount for small children on trains (as well as some ferries), plus a 50% discount for children up to the age of 12 on most group-tour rates and admission fees. Hotels allow children up to 12 to stay free in the same room as their parents. Babysitting is widely available through the reception desks of most hotels, if you give advance notice.

Some words of caution are in order. Finding your favorite brand of baby products in Bangkok and the major resorts is possible, but in the outer provinces it probably won't be. Be sure to serve your children only bottled or boiled water (and ice cubes made from boiled water), and make sure they use bottled water to brush their teeth. Car seats are a novelty unavailable from most rental companies; if you plan to drive, bring your own, plus some extra straps (it may then double as a high seat) although the top hotels all have high chairs available. A portable stroller will facilitate sightseeing in the larger cities, but it may be a burden in rural destinations where unpaved roads and no sidewalks are the norm. We took our 2-year-old everywhere in a backpack—fun for him but tiring! Although Bangkok has some excellent medical facilities, consult with your physician before departure for advice on health precautions and procedures in case of an emergency.

FOR STUDENTS Students should first contact their educational institutions about any travel programs or discounts being offered.

One of the largest and most efficient educational organizations in America is the **Council on International Educational Exchange (CIEE)**, 205 E. 42nd St., 14th floor, New York, NY 10017 (tel. 212/661-1450). Through their subsidiary, Council

Travel Services, with 43 American offices, you can book discounted student, youth, and teacher fares to many international destinations. They also sell the International Student ID Card, the Youth ID Card, the Teacher ID Card, and memberships to the International Youth Hostel Federation (there are many IYHF affiliate hostels throughout Thailand).

Museums throughout Thailand offer a 50% discount to students.

6. GETTING THERE

Bangkok is centrally located in Southeast Asia and functions as a hub city for many international carriers, making it exceptionally easy to reach. Most international air carriers fly to Bangkok. In addition, there is train service from Singapore and Malaysia, as well as cruise-line or freighter service from various Asian ports. Only privately owned (not rented) cars can be driven into the country along the Malaysian frontier.

BY AIR

FROM NORTH AMERICA

One of the most relaxing, yet exotic, ways to reach Thailand is on **Thai Airways International** (tel. toll free 800/426-5204), the country's gracious and efficient international airline. Thai flies four days a week from several U.S. cities via Los Angeles and Seoul to Bangkok. In 1994 the Los Angeles–originating advance-purchase excursion fare was $1,150 round-trip plus $75 more for one stopover in Seoul, Hong Kong, or Taipei. Business-class tickets run $2,270 with one stopover allowed for $75; first-class seats cost $5,000 with unlimited stopovers. Thai Airways also offers good-value air-and-land packages that combine discounted hotels and guided day trips with your airline ticket. Call Royal Orchid Holidays (tel. toll free 800/426-5204) for information.

Northwest Airlines (tel. toll free 800/447-4747) has daily flights from New York and the West Coast (Los Angeles, Seattle, or San Francisco) via Tokyo to Bangkok. The 1994 weekday advance-purchase fare from the West Coast was $1,020 or $1,320 from New York, round-trip, with one stopover allowed. Northwest's weekend flight ($100 surcharge) also allows one free stopover. Northwest flies daily from Montréal or Toronto to Bangkok via Detroit and Tokyo ($1,350 on a midweek advance-purchase excursion fare).

Canadian Airlines International (tel. toll free 800/426-7000) flies Saturday through Thursday from Vancouver, B.C., or Toronto to Bangkok via Tokyo. In 1994 the advance-purchase excursion fare was $1,132 U.S. round-trip from Vancouver, $1,323 U.S. from Toronto, with $43 U.S. for one stopover. Business-class tickets run $2,187 U.S. or $2,642 U.S. respectively, with one stopover allowed for an extra $43 U.S.; first-class seats cost $5,202 U.S. from either city, with unlimited stopovers. Contact Canadian Airlines or your travel agent about special connecting fares from Montréal and other Canadian cities.

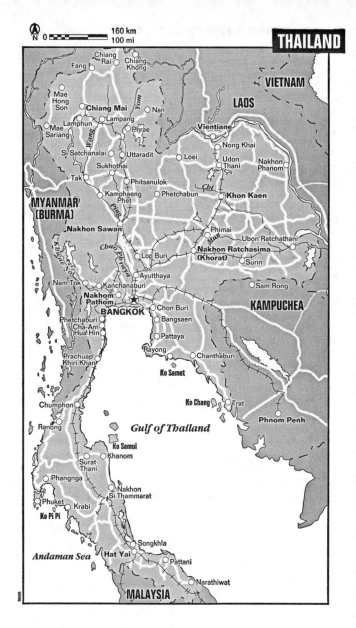

United Airlines (tel. toll free 800/538-2929) is the largest carrier crossing the Pacific. United flies daily to Bangkok from Canada
(Toronto or Vancouver via the U.S.) and from major U.S. cities via
Tokyo (daily) or Taipei (several days a week). The 1994 weekday
advance-purchase excursion fare from New York was $1,300
round-trip, with one stopover allowed. Tickets in business class run
$3,812 from New York; first class is $6,060; both fares include

unlimited stopovers. United also offers Bangkok air-and-land packages; for information, call toll free 800/351-4200.

Delta Airlines (tel. toll free 800/241-4141) now flies four times weekly via Portland, Oregon, Taipei, and Seoul to Bangkok. Their midweek advance-purchase excursion fare in 1994 sold for $1,000 ($100 surcharge for weekend travel), including one free stopover in Taipei or Seoul, and up to two more stopovers at $75 each (including Tokyo for this fee). Business-class passengers would pay $2,952, first class $5,000, with both fares including free stopovers.

Travelers who prefer to make their stopovers in Europe should consider **KLM Royal Dutch Airlines** (tel. toll free 800/374-7747), which flies to Bangkok via Amsterdam, or **Finnair** (tel. toll free 800/950-5000), which flies via Helsinki. The transatlantic routing from North America is currently more expensive than the transpacific ones commonly used, but it's actually a faster and sometimes easier flight.

FROM THE UNITED KINGDOM

Top-flight carriers offering daily service from London's Heathrow Airport direct to Bangkok include **British Airways** (tel. 081/897-4000), **Qantas** (tel. 0345/747-767), and **Thai Airways International** (tel. 071/499-9113). At press time, high-season first-class return tickets on these airlines cost between £4,200 and £6,500; business-class return tickets ran between £2,150 and £3,260. Significant discounts can be had by taking an indirect flight on a carrier such as **Finnair** (via Helsinki, tel. 071/408-1222), or by

---

 FROMMER'S SMART TRAVELER: AIRFARES

1. Shop all the airlines that fly to Thailand, asking about their lowest-priced fares and special excursions. Don't forget the Asian national carriers, such as Philippine Airlines, MAS, Garuda Indonesia, Korean Airlines, etc., which may offer special Bangkok fares combined with routing through their country's capital city.

2. Check the weekend travel section of your local newspaper, plus the Sunday editions of the *New York Times* and *Los Angeles Times* for advertised discount fares and charter operators. London's *Time Out* advertises many discount travel agencies.

3. Consult your travel agent about special round-the-world fares.

4. Call around to consolidators (discount air-ticket sellers who profit by buying unused seats in bulk from various airlines), and be prepared to leave on short notice. Some recommended consolidators: **Council Charter** (tel. toll free 800/223-7402) or **Travac** (tel. toll free 800/872-8800) in the U.S., or **Flight Solutions** (tel. 071/232-1864) and **Trailfinders** (tel. 071/938-3366) in London.

purchasing through a discounted flight agent such as **Campus Travel** (52 Grosvenor Gardens, London SW1W 0AG, tel. 071/730-3402, and many other locations) or **STA Travel** (74 Old Brompton Rd., London SW7, tel. 071/937-9962). If you do work with a discounted flight agent, or "bucket shop," make sure that the company you deal with is a member of the IATA, ABTA, or ATOL. Finally, some good deals can be found by checking **CEEFAX**, a British television information service which is broadcast into many private homes and hotels and runs details of package holidays and flights all round the world.

BY TRAIN

Train service on the **State Railway of Thailand** originates in Singapore, passes through Malaysia (stopping in Kuala Lumpur and Butterworth), and terminates in Bangkok. The 1994 fare ran about $150 for an air-conditioned first-class sleeping berth. The entire 1,860-kilometer (1,153-mile) trip takes 31 hours, plus a 10-hour layover in Kuala Lumpur.

At last, the Orient-Express Group, operators of the deluxe private train service from London to Istanbul, will begin operating private trips on the Eastern & Oriental Express in 1994. Once a week, the luxuriously appointed train will make the 41-hour trip between Bangkok and Singapore (stops in Kuala Lumpur, Penang, Surat Thani, and Hua Hin). Air-conditioned twin cabins with private bathrooms will start at $390 per person, one way, including meals; call them in the U.S. for more information (tel. toll free 800/524-2420).

BY BUS

There is limited private bus transportation between Singapore or Malaysia and Hat Yai in southern Thailand. From there, you can catch a long-distance bus or train directly to Bangkok. Although catching a series of buses may be cheaper than the express train service (see above), it will not be nearly as comfortable.

BY SHIP

A few international cruise companies sail to Thailand, docking near Pattaya. **Ocean Pearl Lines,** with four to six annual departures to Asian ports (including Bangkok), is one of the best known. For current schedules and information, contact your travel agent.

PACKAGE TOURS

Several tour operators within Thailand offer package tours (usually by bus) originating in Bangkok and including the major resort or cultural or historical destination that interests you.

World Travel Service Ltd., 1053 Charoen Krung Rd., 10500 Bangkok (tel. 02/233-5900), is one of the oldest and best of these. An American company that specializes in Thailand is **Absolute Asia,** 155 W. 68th St., Suite 525, New York, NY 10023 (tel. toll free 800/736-8187 or 212/595-5782). Contact both companies directly or inquire through your travel agent for information.

CHAPTER 3

GETTING TO KNOW BANGKOK

1. ORIENTATION

2. GETTING AROUND

• **FAST FACTS: BANGKOK**

3. NETWORKS & RESOURCES

4. MOVING ON— TRAVEL SERVICES & SYSTEMS

Vintage 19th-century photographs of Bangkok show vivid images of life on the Chao Phraya River, bustling with bobbing vessels that ranged from the humble rowboats to elaborate royal barges. Built along the banks of the broad, S-shaped river, the city spread inland through a network of klongs (canals) that rivaled the intricacy—though never the elegance—of Venice. As Bangkok developed and became more densely populated, more and more of the klongs were filled in to create broad thoroughfares.

The capital's central location still makes it both the region's and the country's major cultural and transportation hub. Bangkok has palaces, museums, and wats, three bus stations, a centrally located train station, and a huge, modernized airport (with another to follow in 1997) that is maddeningly close to town but seems to move farther toward Tibet as you creep through the dense traffic. Expect an hour-long ride from the airport into the city, and at least that long from one end of town to the other. Within the city, buses, minivans, taxis and *tuk-tuks* (motorized three-wheelers; aka *samlors*) cruise the broad avenues and provide inexpensive and reliable transportation.

Bangkok offers so much to see and do, but the sooty air, eye-irritating fumes, and din of motorbikes can make an outing into an unpleasant chore. What's being done about it?

The government is trying to reduce air contaminants caused by vehicle emissions, the burning of coal, and industrial waste from the factory zone on the city's outskirts. When the National Environment Board issued price increases and offered incentives to use unleaded gasoline, its market share increased by 24% overnight. The Industrial Estate Authority enforces strict new environmental standards for industry by assigning "Environmental Managers" to businesses. Waste-water treatment plants have been built and an intensive public education campaign is underway. However, widespread corruption and bureaucratic mismanagement have meant that enforcement of many laws and programs is erratic at best.

The traffic is another issue. Some of the statistics and guesstimates that earned Bangkok the title "Gridlock City": There was a 12-mile-long traffic jam down Sukhumvit Road during the 1991 rainy season. Five hundred new vehicles were purchased in Bangkok every hour of 1992. According to a 1993 survey, businesspeople spent 40 working days per year waiting in traffic. After years of expectation, Bangkok's $1.1 billion Second Stage Expressway opened in September 1993, but only after four months of haggling with the contractors who built it.

Solutions? Plans for an underground subway have been scrapped by findings that Bangkok's foundation is too unstable to support one. Plans for an overhead skytrain have been scrapped because engineers determined that at least two lanes of traffic below its route would be eliminated by supports. But dozens of other plans are being studied, including paving over the extant klongs to create roads, and digging out the paved-over klongs to create waterways.

At our most recent visit, after a plea by His Majesty the King, the highly respected former prime minister Anand Panyarachun and the highly respected AIDS activist Meechai Viravaid had teamed up to form a private Bangkok Traffic Task Force. Hopefully they'll have some answers by the time you read this.

In the meanwhile, let's look at ways to make the most of the city as we know and love it.

1. ORIENTATION

ARRIVING

BY PLANE

AIRPORT Bangkok is a major hub for air travel in Southeast Asia, with more than 70 airlines providing service. All international and domestic flights come to and go from **Don Muang International Airport,** located 22 kilometers (14 miles) north of the heart of the city and constantly undergoing expansion. International and domestic flights arrive at different terminals, a 1-kilometer (.6-mile) walk or a free shuttle ride apart.

Travelers arriving at the **International Terminal** will find a wide range of services awaiting them, available for 24 hours a day unless otherwise noted: free luggage carts, found at arrival gates and a welcome aid for the record-length walk between gates and the terminal; luggage storage for 20B (80¢) per day, with a three-month maximum; currency-exchange banks with rates equal to those of city banks; a post office with overseas telephone service; an Airport Information booth and a Tourism Authority of Thailand (TAT) booth, open from 8am to midnight (tel. 523-8972); a Thai Hotel Association desk, which will assist you in finding available accommodations; restaurants, serving both Thai and international food; and the first-class, Amari Airport Hotel (see Chapter 4), a short walk or free shuttle ride away.

The **Domestic Terminal** offers most of these services, 24 hours unless noted: luggage storage, for 20B (80¢) a day, 14-day limit, is open daily from 6am to 11pm; a post office with overseas telephone service; a foreign exchange bank; a Thai Hotel Association desk; and a cafeteria-style coffee shop, open daily from 6:30am to 11:15pm.

THAILAND
★ Bangkok

Business District **9**
Chinatown **3**
Chitralada Palace **7**
Dusit Zoo **6**
General Post Office **5**
Grand Palace/
  Rattanakosin Area **2**
Lumpini Park **11**
Queen Sirikit
  Convention Center **14**
River Area **4**
Royal Bangkok
  Sports Club **10**
Royal Turf Club **8**
Shopping/Embassy Area **13**
Thonburi Railway Station **1**
Tourist Police **12**

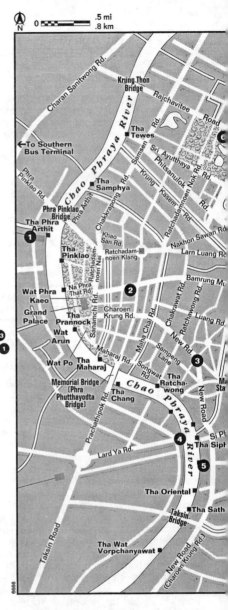

The airport provides a **free shuttle service** between the Domestic and International Terminals, with buses every 10 minutes. If you have light luggage, you might find it more enjoyable (and sometimes faster) to walk.

For general airport information, call 535-1111; for information about arriving or departing domestic flights, call 535-2081, 535-1253, or 523-6121; for information on international flights, call 535-1254.

To Northern
Bus Terminal
& Weekend Market

To Don Muang
Int'l Airport

Phahol Yothin Road

Wipawadi Rangsit

Rama VI Rajchavitee Rd.

Sri Ayutthaya Road

Phetchaburi Road

Klong-Saensaep

New Phetchaburi Road

Rama I Road

Rama VI Road

Siam
Square

Ploenchit Road

13

Lang Suan Ln.

Soi 19

Soi 21 (Asoke)

Chulalong-
korn
University

Phayathai Road

Henri Dunant Road

Rajdamri (Rat Damri) Rd.

10

Sol Sarasin

Soi Ruam
Rudee

Soi Nana

Expressway

Sukhumvit Road

Wireless Rd.

Rama IV Road

12   **11**

Surawong Rd.

Soi Saladang

Convent Rd.

Patpong

Soi Pipat

14

Ratchadaphis Rd.

n Road

rth Sathorn Road

uth Sathorn Road

Soi
Atakan
Prasit

Soi Ngam Dupli

Rama IV Road

River Taxi Pier

Passengers on domestic flights pay a 20B (80¢) departure tax, while those on international flights pay 200B ($8). Children under 2 are exempt.

GETTING TO & FROM THE AIRPORT Most of the expensive and very expensive hotels will arrange to pick up guests if requested in advance, at a typical charge of 450B ($18).

You can easily arrange a very comfortable **sedan** to your hotel at the **Thai Airways Limousine desk,** found at Counter 7, just opposite the Customs exit. These sedans seat four, are usually driven by English-speaking drivers, and cost 400B ($16) for a car, or 650B ($26) for a Mercedes, to most hotels. To arrange a pickup in the city, call 533-6208.

The **Thai Airways Limousine minivan** will take you to your hotel, stopping at other hotels on the way, for 100B ($4) per person.

Public taxis are a better value than the Thai Airways limos, though a compromise in comfort. The fare is determined by a fixed schedule and varies with the distance from the airport, averaging 250B ($10) to most hotels in central Bangkok. There is a Public Taxi Queue inside the International Terminal (turn left out of Customs and walk toward the Meeting Area) where you are told the fare and assigned a taxi. At the Domestic Terminal, you'll find it just outside the front door. The dispatcher will give you a card that specifies the fare and provides a check against possible price gouging. Most legal taxi drivers speak some English. Don't let one take you to the wrong hotel, where the driver may get a kickback.

Public buses no. 4, 29, 10, and 13 run between Bangkok's main streets and the airport for 6B to 20B (28¢ to 80¢), a journey we wouldn't recommend.

There is a **car-service desk** inside the Domestic Terminal (comparable to the Thai Airways Limousine desk), which provides the fancier sedans into the city.

The **Airport Express Train** runs between the central Hua Lampong Railroad Station (tel. 223-7461) and the Don Muang station near the airport six times daily. For 125B ($5) you can save lots of hassle with their 35-minute express train and 15-minute air-conditioned shuttle direct to your terminal. Tickets can be purchased at Hua Lampong, track 12; Thai Airways Limousine Counter, no. 7, in the International Arrivals Hall; or at Thai's counter in the Arrivals Hall of the Domestic Terminal.

BY TRAIN

You can travel by train from Singapore, via Butterworth Station in Penang, Malaysia, to Bangkok. Passengers arrive at **Hua Lampong Railroad Station,** east of Chinatown at the intersection of Rama IV Road and Krung Kasem Road (tel. 223-7461 or 223-3762). We recommend two average hotels nearby, but if you're planning on staying in Bangkok for more than one day, study Chapter 4 for better choices or check with the Thai Hotel Association desk in the station, then take a tuk-tuk or a taxi from the station. More detailed information about traveling by train can be found in Section 4 of this chapter.

BY BUS

Passengers arriving by bus will find themselves at one of Bangkok's three bus stations, depending on the area of the country they've come from. For more information, see Section 4 of this chapter.

TOURIST INFORMATION

The **Tourism Authority of Thailand (TAT)** offers very thorough and accurate information about all aspects of traveling in the country. You'll find their counter in the International Terminal of Don Muang International Airport (tel. 02/523-8972), open daily from 8:30am to 4:30pm. Unfortunately, most flights from the United

States arrive after midnight, so you'll have to venture to their main office, at 372 Bamrung Muang Rd. (tel. 02/226-0060 or 02/226-0085) east of the Grand Palace Area, open daily from 8:30am to 4:30pm. At both offices their very capable staff can answer questions about both Bangkok and the rest of the country and can give you a wide variety of excellent brochures and maps. You can also call the information numbers for assistance from free yellow telephones at Wat Phra Kaeo, the Erawan Shrine at the Ratchaprasong intersection, in Patpong, and at the corner of Silom and New roads. If you have problems, call the Tourist Police (tel. 1699 or 221-6206-10).

Travel Tip: Save yourself a long journey to the TAT by starting at your own hotel front desk. We've found concierges and reception clerks to be extremely knowledgeable and helpful in providing basic information for tourists.

CITY LAYOUT

MAIN ARTERIES & STREETS   Bangkok's most significant axis is still the **Chao Phraya River,** which meanders on a north–south line through the heart of the city and divides Bangkok from Thonburi on its western bank. Along its eastern bank are most of the major tourist sites, including (from north to south) the National Museum and the National Theater, the Grand Palace and Wat Phra Kaeo (repository of the Emerald Buddha), the Reclining Buddha at Wat Po, the Khmer-style complex of Wat Arun on the Thonburi side, the city's historic Chinatown, the golden trio of luxury hotels (The Oriental, the Shangri-La, and the Royal Orchid Sheraton), and the River City Shopping Complex.

The river is spanned by four major bridges. The **Krung Thon Bridge** crosses at the northern end of the city, with its major artery, **Rajchavitee Road,** leading east to the Vimanmek Mansion Museum, the Dusit Zoo, Wat Benchamabophit (the Marble Wat; off Rama V Road), the Chitralada Palace, the Victory Monument, and Wang Suan Pakkard (off Sri [pronounced SHREE] Ayutthaya Road). On the Thonburi side of the **Phra Pinklao Bridge,** along **Klong Bangkok Noi,** is the Royal Barge Museum. **Ratchadamnoen Klang Road** crosses the bridge close to the National Museum and the National Theater on the Bangkok side, continuing east past the Democracy Monument and becoming first Larn Luang Road, then **Phetchaburi Road** (and later **New Phetchaburi Road**).

Running parallel to and south of Phetchaburi Road is **Rama I Road,** one of the city's most important avenues, which runs east and eventually becomes **Ploenchit Road** and, ultimately, **Sukhumvit Road,** home to many excellent restaurants and shopping arcades. Jim Thompson's House is off Rama I Road, along Klong Mahanak. Siam Square and the Mah Boon Krong Center (M.B.K. Shopping Center), two of Bangkok's largest shopping malls, are along Rama I Road, as are the Royal Bangkok Sports Club (and racetrack), several foreign embassies, some of the city's largest office buildings, and several of Bangkok's best hotels, including the Hilton International (on Wireless or Wittayu Road) and The Regent, Bangkok (on Rajdamri Road).

The **Memorial Bridge** leads north from Thonburi directly into Chinatown, Sampeng Lane, and many specialized markets, one of the most richly ethnic of neighborhoods. The southernmost of the major crossings is the **Taksin Bridge,** or **Sathorn Bridge,** crossing from Thonburi east over to the Bangkok side just south of the Shangri-La Hotel. This street is **Sathorn Road** and it intersects with Rama IV Road at Lumpini Park. Running parallel, to the north of Sathorn Road, are **Silom Road** and **Surawong Road,** both important for shopping, restaurants, hotels, and evening entertainment (including notorious Patpong, home to Bangkok's wild sex-club scene). **Rama IV Road,** which begins as Charoen Krung Road in Chinatown, leads east past the Golden Buddha at Wat Traimit, Hua Lampong Railroad Station, the Red Cross Snake Farm, and several hotels, including the deluxe Dusit Thani.

FINDING AN ADDRESS Good luck! Street numbers follow Western conventions, to a point, in that even-numbered addresses are on one side of the street and odd-numbered addresses are on the opposite side. Most addresses are subdivided by a **/** symbol, as in 123/4 Silom Road, which is a variation on sequential numbering that accounts for new construction. Be aware that 123 Silom Road and 124 Silom Road will be on opposite sides of the street, but not necessarily close to each other. You'll find the term *soi* frequently in addresses. A soi is a small lane off a major street. So, 45 Soi 23, Sukhumvit Road (also written 45 Soi Sukhumvit 23) is found at no. 45 on Soi 23, which runs perpendicular to Sukhumvit Road. All even-numbered sois will be on one side of the main road, all odd-numbered sois on the opposite side, though Soi 21 and Soi 20 may be far apart.

It's also a good idea to ask the concierge or desk clerk at your hotel to write the address of your destination in Thai to assist in dealing with taxi drivers. Many do not speak English or, if they do, may not understand your pronunciation of a street address. Many hotels will give you a card with their own address in Thai to assist on your return trip.

NEIGHBORHOODS IN BRIEF We've divided the city into several neighborhoods and organized hotels and dining options within these categories. The distinctions are broad and somewhat imprecise, in that the Shopping/Embassy Area also includes a number of office buildings, and the Business District also includes a number of embassies and shopping complexes. Still, our categories should help you organize the city during your stay.

Historic Bangkok—Near the Grand Palace This area, the site of the original Bangkok capital, lay within the confines of Rattanakosin Island, created as a defense measure by King Rama I. A klong, now called Klong Ong Ang, was dug from a point at a bend in the Chao Phraya River (near what is now the Memorial Bridge), running north, then turning east near Wat Saket, where it became Klong Banglamphu and rejoined the river north of the Phra Pinklao Bridge.

The area includes a majority of the tourist sites, beginning with Wat Po, the Grand Palace, and Wat Phra Kaeo, then continuing north to the Dusit Zoo and the Vimanmek Mansion Museum. There are numerous historic wats, the National Museum, the National Theater, and the National Library. There are only a handful of first-class and moderate hotels in this area, but their proximity to the sites makes it an attractive area to stay in. Low-budget travelers will find an especially rich choice of guest houses and cheap hotels.

On the River Though the Chao Phraya River runs far beyond the city limits of Bangkok, the River Area is roughly that area containing Bangkok's grand riverside hotels. We also include two other hotels in this category, as well as the River City Shopping Complex and some other, smaller shopping malls.

The Business District The Business District is bounded by Rama IV Road on the east, Chinatown on the north, New Road (near the river) on the west, and Sathorn Road on the south. Silom Road and Surawong Road run east–west through the center. As its name implies, many banks and businesses have offices in this area, as do a number of embassies, many shops and malls, and the famous Patpong nightlife area. Good restaurants and high-quality hotels abound.

The Shopping/Embassy Area This includes the neighborhoods on either side of the thoroughfare called Rama I Road on its western end, then Ploenchit Road as it runs east and crosses Rajdamri Road, and finally, Sukhumvit Road as it crosses under the airport freeway. Here are several deluxe hotels, many first-class and moderate hotels, numerous shopping complexes, the newer office buildings, most of the Western embassies, and a large concentration of the expatriate community.

Chinatown Once home to the majority of Bangkok's Chinese citizens, Chinatown is still a unique enclave. It's located north of the river (which bends to run east–west here), west of the Business District, and east of the Grand Palace Area. There are few hotels. It is rich in ethnic character however, and we strongly recommend a walking tour (see Chapter 7).

Thonburi This area on the west bank of the Chao Phraya River was Siam's capital until the reign of Rama I and still remains a quiet and fairly unchanged collection of neighborhoods where few tourists ever venture. You'll find some wonderful wats and one of our favorite walking tours (see Section 3 of Chapter 7).

MAPS There are three excellent Bangkok maps. The first is "Latest Tour Guide to Bangkok & Thailand"—affectionately called "The Bus Map." It costs 60B ($2.40) and is available at most bookstores, though the TAT sells it for less at their main office. The "Bangkok Thailand Guide Map," by Discovery Map, is a slightly more up-to-date version of "The Bus Map" and also costs 60B ($2.40). Both are acceptable as authoritative street guides. The third map we enthusiastically suggest you carry is Nancy Chandler's "Map of Bangkok"—alias "The Market Map and Much More." Nancy, a graphic designer who lived in Bangkok for 19 years, uses her keen eye for quality and value (not to mention the bizarre) to fashion a colorful guide focused on Bangkok's rich markets, shopping opportunities, and sightseeing highlights. The map costs 110B ($4.40) and is available at most bookstores. Most hotels provide Bangkok guides with simple maps free for the asking.

2. GETTING AROUND

Getting around Bangkok is an experience to be forgotten, unless you are clever. The traffic, already legendary, is getting worse.

Driving through the narrow streets of Chinatown during the business day is like waiting to exit a crowded parking lot. Yet certain major thoroughfares are reminiscent of the broad boulevards of European capitals—and, in fact, were patterned after them. Almost all sites and tourist services are located near the river and are easily reached from other river points by the excellent and inexpensive Chao Phraya Express Boat system. Taxis are still a relative bargain and are the best alternative if you are not on the river. The open-air tuk-tuks are recommended only for short trips, as they expose you to heavy doses of automotive fumes.

Most of the main streets are one way, and getting from here to there requires some thought. Plot your route carefully and decide whether river, klong, or land transportation is better. If you're near the river and traveling during daylight hours, it's no contest. Hop on a boat. The most arduous taxi ride will be the one from the Sukhumvit Area to the Grand Palace Area at almost any time of day, a journey that can stretch to well over an hour.

BY PUBLIC TRANSPORTATION

BUS Unfortunately, the very cheap (4B[16¢]), frequent, and fairly fast public bus system must be used with care because of pickpockets, purse slashers, and other petty criminals who take advantage of the densely crowded conditions. If you prefer the public bus, take the air-conditioned ones for a few baht extra; keep your possessions in front of you, carry only what you can afford to lose, and stay away from the back door, where most thieves operate. "The Bus Map" (aka "Latest Tour Guide to Bangkok & Thailand") provides route information.

MINIBUSES Until the government supplies the promised fleet of new air-conditioned public buses, the private sector has taken mass transit into its own hands with several fleets of air-conditioned, express-service minibuses. They ply all the major thoroughfares, stopping at main intersections only during rush hours. The green and red/white ones cost 3.50B (14¢); the blue/white and pale green ones cost 2.50B (10¢); the pink/red ones offer mobile pay phones and cost 15B (60¢).

BOAT We're unabashed fans of travel on the Chao Phraya River. It's an efficient, inexpensive, and fairly tranquil way to get around and provides a remarkable window on local life. Branching off from the river is the ancient network of klongs, most of which are serviced by the basic long-tail boats (*hang yao*).

The **Chao Phraya Express Company** (tel. 222-5330) operates a system of ferries that run up and down the river, stopping at the many piers (*thas*) on both sides of the river. Cross-river ferries carry passengers back and forth from almost every express-boat pier, though often from a separate landing. Most tourists will

IMPRESSIONS

Bangkok has been so loved because it is the expression of Thais themselves of their lightheartedness, their love of beauty, their reverence for tradition, their sense of freedom, their extravagance, their devotion to their creeds—to characteristics that are constant and continuing in themselves.
—ALEC WAUGH, *BANGKOK, STORY OF A CITY*, 1971

board the express boats near The Oriental, at the pier just south of the hotel, or at the Siphya Pier, just south of the Royal Orchid Sheraton. There are numerous other piers (many of which charge a 1B [4¢] entrance fee), though most are hard to find: ask your hotel desk for guidance, ask on the street, or look for small signs pointing the way to express-boat piers.

An express boat is a long white boat with a pointed bow and a large number near the front. It carries the Chao Phraya Express logo on the side, and has bench seats and open sides. Don't confuse the express boat with the smaller, cross-river ferry, distinguished by its squatter shape and rounded bow.

Boats pull up and pause for a fleeting moment, so boarding passengers must step lively. Fares are based on distance. The on-board ticket taker will ask your destination and charge between 4B and 10B (16¢ and 40¢) for the trip, the best deal in town. To exit, move to the back of the boat and be ready to hop off. As on any public conveyance in Bangkok keep a close hand on your purse, wallet, or camera. Cross-river ferries will usually cost 2B to 3B (8¢ to 12¢). Both express boats and ferries operate daily between the hours of 6am and 6pm, with boats arriving every 10 minutes or so.

Navigating the express-boat system can be tricky, since the names of the docks give little hint of the tourist sites near them. However, most ticket takers speak English and will guide you to your destination. The main landmarks and the piers nearest to them are follows:

- Shangri-La Hotel: Sathorn Pier
- Oriental Hotel: Oriental Pier
- Royal Orchid Sheraton: Siphya Pier
- River City: River City Pier
- Chinatown: Ratchawong Pier, south of Memorial Bridge; or Saphan Phut Pier, north of bridge
- Wat Po: Thien Pier
- Grand Palace and Wat Phra Kaeo: Chang Pier
- National Museum and National Theater: Maharaj Pier
- Wat Arun: Thien Pier; transfer to cross-river ferry

Long-tail boats provide ferrylike transportation through the inland klongs on the Thonburi side, leaving when full from the Ratchawong, Thien, Chang, and Maharaj piers. Allow an hour to take a ride on one, just to see the fascinating neighborhoods across the river. The fare should be 5B to 10B (20¢ to 50¢). Get off at any stop and take another boat back.

Those looking for adventure or those staying in the Shopping/Embassy Area should try the system of long-tail boats operating on Klong Mahanak, which runs parallel to and between Phetchaburi Road and Rama I/Ploenchit/Sukhumvit Road. You can board at most major cross-streets (such as Rajdamri, Wireless, or Soi Asoke no. 21) and ride to the western end, near Wat Saket and the Democracy Monument.

The government has joined what began as a private venture with new, larger "River Buses" that ply the length of this major east-west klong, also known as Saensaep, or "deep pain." The name doesn't reflect the service, which is efficient, incredibly easier and faster than taxis, and so friendly (two secretaries happily caught Ron when he fell on them while trying to climb into the shallow bench seats). We *love* this klong ferry. If you're heading all the way west to Wat Saket, you may have to transfer to a smaller, shallow-draught boat at the Krung Kasem Road intersection. Fares run from 7B to 15B (28¢ to 60¢) depending on distance, and include transfers. This is definitely an adventure, as the klong's appearance and odor can get pretty funky, especially in the hot season. But it's cheap, quick, fun, and a terrific way to meet people.

READERS RECOMMEND

Klong Ferry from Banglamphu. *"The 'sewer taxi' I took runs right to the Hua Lampong Railway station from the National Library area, right behind the P.S. Guesthouse. This is the only way to do daytrips out of Bangkok as far as I'm concerned. So long as you get back by 6pm when the sewer taxi stops running, you can have a totally traffic-free Bangkok experience (Joy!) for only 8B, with a fascinating view of the city's underbelly."*— Ariel Zeitlin, New York, NY.

BY TAXI

Since the government revolutionized the taxi industry by requiring drivers to have and use meters, traveling around Bangkok has not been the same! During the lifetime of this guidebook, unmetered taxis will be completely phased out of the scene. No more strong-arming drivers to accept the standard fare to a destination! No more pleading with hotel doormen to resolve fare conflict at the curb! No more zooming through unknown streets to justify inflated fares! Great!—yes, but . . .

We found it impossible to hail a "Taxi Meter" (as they're known by their rooftop signs) with a driver who knew where he was going. It seems all the long-standing professional drivers who speak some tourist English are sticking with their unmetered taxis (they actually will insist on a higher fare than a meter would read) till the bitter end, and only rural immigrants seeking work will drive with meters. Soon enough the situation will improve, and taxis are still comfortable, mostly air-conditioned, and extremely cheap. The flagfall is 35B ($1.40) and goes up, very slowly, by time and distance; it's difficult to reach 100B ($4) in a cross-city trip. Tipping is not expected, though certainly welcome from tourists.

Hotels, of course, offer private luxury cars, like Mercedes-Benz, if you request a "taxi" from the concierge. Rates run approximately double the taxi fare, or about 400B ($16) per hour.

READERS RECOMMEND

Transportation Tip: *"It was great to know ahead of time from your book to negotiate our fare with tuk-tuk drivers. Our daughter loved going places on the tuk-tuks. Some of the drivers sure were set on their prices. One time we asked three different drivers before we found one to take us where we wanted to go—for the right price."*
— Rose Shaffer, Boeing Peace Sentinel

BY CAR

If you can afford it, we recommend hiring a car for some parts of your Bangkok experience, as it will be more efficient and comfortable than finding taxis, particularly for shoppers.

The best, and most expensive, cars for hire are provided at the major hotels. These will be fancier cars, like Volvos or high-end Japanese cars; the drivers will speak English; and the price will start at 250B ($10) for almost any trip. They can be hired with driver by the hour for about 400B ($16) per hour, with a 3-hour minimum. The day rate will range from 2,000B ($80) to 3,000B ($120) for a 9-hour day, with 200 kilometers (120 miles) included. You can arrange this through your hotel's transportation desk or through a travel agent. **Sea Tour Company** (tel. 251-4862) and **World Travel Service** (tel. 233-5900) are two companies that can also arrange English-speaking guides to lead you on a customized tour, at the same rate! Be advised that Avis and Hertz also offer chauffeured cars, but they are the most expensive options, costing about a third more than local car services.

Of course, you can drive yourself around Bangkok, but we're not sure why you'd want to.

BY TUK-TUK

As it used to be with a taxi, to get about by a three-wheeled, motor-driven tuk-tuk (known formally as a samlor), you'll have to negotiate your fare. Expect to pay 40B to 100B ($1.60 to $4) for a given trip, about 25B ($1) less than a taxi fare over a similar distance. The disadvantage of tuk-tuks is that they're noisy, open-air, and thrilling, but you're exposed to the fumes of traffic and can find yourself gasping for breath at the end of a long, hot ride. We recommend them to experience short trips or for longer trips at nonpeak hours, when you're less likely to get stuck in a jam. Tipping is not expected.

ON FOOT

It's easy and safe to walk around Bangkok, though you'll find the traffic congestion generates so much pollution that you'll probably limit your walking to certain neighborhoods and smaller streets. We've suggested walking tours for areas that are easily toured on foot (see Chapter 7).

 BANGKOK

Airlines See Section 1 of this chapter.
Airport See Section 1 of this chapter.
American Express The American Express agent in Thailand is Sea Tours Company, in Suite 413–414 on the fourth floor of the Siam Center, 965 Rama I Rd., between Henri Dunant Road and Phayathai Road (tel. 251-4862). Hours are 8:30am to 4:30pm Monday through Friday, 8:30am to 11:30pm on Saturday; closed Sunday. You can receive mail here, cash emergency checks against your American Express Card, obtain refunds, and report lost credit cards and traveler's checks. (American Express also operates a 24-hour telephone service for lost cards and traveler's checks: 273-0022.) You must bring your passport for all transactions. Sea Tours offers American Express services at their regional offices in Chiang Mai and Phuket.
Note: This office does not cash traveler's checks except in emergency cases. You'll have to go to a bank or change booth.

Area Code The telephone area code for Bangkok and vicinity is 02. The country code is 66.

Babysitters Most hotels can arrange a babysitter, but all require some notice—from a few hours to a full day.

Banking Many American banks maintain offices in Bangkok, including Bank of America, 2/2 Wireless Rd., next door to the Hilton (tel. 251-6333); Chase Manhattan, in the Siam Center, 965 Rama I Rd. (tel. 252-1141); and Citibank, 127 Sathorn Rd. (tel. 213-2442). However, an American customer of one of these banks cannot use them as branches of the domestic bank; to access personal funds from an American account will require making special arrangements before leaving the States.

Americans with bank cash cards that are part of the Cirrus network can withdraw Thai money from their accounts at a number of **cash machines** located around town. Some convenient locations: the Royal Orchid Exchange Office, opposite the Royal Orchid Sheraton on Siphya Road; all Robinson Department Stores; the Patpong Exchange Office, 3 Patpong Rd. Before you leave home, you will need to establish a four-digit identification code on your account.

Bookstores You'll find a number of bookstores offering a wide variety of English-language books. One of our favorites for their extensive selection of books on Thailand and Asia is Asia Books, with stores at 221 Sukhumvit Rd. (between Soi 15 and Soi 17; tel. 252-7277); on the ground and third floor of the Landmark Plaza Building (tel. 252-5839) on Sukhumvit Road at Soi 4; in Thaniya Plaza (tel. 231-2106) on Silom Road in the new Times Square (tel. 250-0162) opposite Robinson's on Sukhumvit; and in the Peninsula Plaza mall near The Regent of Bangkok on Rajdamri Road, south of Rama I Road (tel. 253-9786). All are open from 10am to 8 or 9pm. You'll find a good selection of English-language paperbacks at D.K Bookshops, 244–6 Siam Sq. on Rama I Road (tel. 251-6335). The Bookseller Co. Ltd., 81 Patpong Rd., off Silom Road (tel. 233-1717), also has a fine selection of English-language books, magazines, and cards, and is open daily from 9am to midnight. Almost every international-class hotel has a newsstand; however, the selection of books is usually limited.

Business Hours **Government offices,** including branch post offices, are open Monday through Friday from 8:30am to 4:30pm, with a lunch break from noon to 1pm. They are generally closed on weekends and holidays. The **General Post Office** is open Monday through Friday 8am to 8pm, on Saturday, Sunday, and holidays from 8am to 1pm. **Private businesses** are generally open daily from 8am to 5pm; some open a half day on Saturday. **Department stores** are usually open daily from 10am to 8 or 9pm. **Shops,** particularly those that cater to the tourist trade, are often open daily from 8:30am to 7 or 8pm.

Car Rentals See Section 2 of this chapter.

Climate See Section 2 of Chapter 2.

Courier Services Bangkok is serviced by most major international courier services, including Federal Express (tel. 367-3222), DHL Worldwide Express (tel. 207-8407), and United Parcel Service (tel. 513-1109). A 2-pound package would cost $48 (plus duty, if any) to ship to the U.S. by Federal Express and would take at least 2 days.

Credit Cards Most hotels and larger restaurants take credit cards, though smaller guesthouses and local restaurants will not.

Smaller establishments that do take credit cards sometimes take only MasterCard or VISA. For lost credit cards, call American Express at 253-0990; Diners Club at 235-7305; MasterCard and VISA at 252-2212. Some smaller hotels add a surcharge of 3% to 5% for credit-card charges. The credit-card companies do not recognize this practice and will refund the surcharge if notified.

Currency   See Section 1 of Chapter 2.

Currency Exchange   There are bank branches all over the city, most of which will exchange foreign currency Monday through Friday between 8:30am and 3:30pm. Exchange booths affiliated with the major banks are found in areas with high concentrations of tourist traffic; they charge the same rates as banks. Most are open seven days a week, from as early as 7am to as late as 9pm. All charge a commission (usually 5B [20¢]) and government tax (3B [12¢]). It's essential to bring your passport for changing money, as a photocopy will not always suffice.

Check with the desk or concierge at your hotel for the exchange bank or booth nearest you. Make sure that the booths are affiliated with a bank to insure that you are getting the best exchange rates. Hotel exchange rates will usually be 1B to 3B (4¢ to 12¢) less than those offered at banks. The airport banks charge the same rate and commission as banks in town, though rates vary slightly between banks.

Dentists/Doctors   Thailand has an excellent medical care system with many fine doctors and dentists. Most medical personnel speak English and many were trained in the United States. Most of the better hotels have doctors and/or nurses on staff or on call who can treat minor maladies and supervise treatment of more serious problems. Check first with your concierge for assistance, then contact your country's consulate if you need further help. U.S. citizens can call the U.S. Embassy Medical Unit (tel. 242-5040), open Monday through Friday from 7:30am to 4:30pm, for a list recommended physicians and dentists. See "Emergencies" and "Hospitals," below, for crisis advice.

Driving Rules   See Section 2 of this chapter.

Drugstores   Bangkok has a great many drugstores, though the drugs dispersed may differ widely in quality. Always check the expiration date, if there is one, on the drug label. Among the better outlets are the British Dispensary, 109 Sukhumvit Rd., near Soi 5 (tel. 252-8056), and also on the corner of New Road and Oriental Lane (tel. 234-0174); and the Phuket Dispensary, 383 Sukhumvit Rd., near Soi 21 (tel. 252-9179). For additional recommendations, call the medical unit at your consulate or ask the concierge at your hotel.

Electricity   Electric current in Thailand carries 220 volts at 50 cycles. Most hotels have 110-volt outlets in the bathrooms for electric shavers.

Embassies/Consulates   Most tourists will need only the consular section of their embassy. The U.S. Embassy, 95 Wireless Rd. (tel. 252-5040), is open for consular services Monday through Friday from 7:30 to 10am and noon to 4:30pm. There are regional consular offices in Songhkla, Chiang Mai, and Udorn. The British Embassy, 1031 Ploenchit Rd., off Wireless Road (tel. 253-0191), is open to the public Monday through Thursday from 8 to 11am and 1 to 3:30pm, on Friday from 8am to noon. The Canadian Embassy, on the 11th floor of the Boonmitr Building, 138 Silom Rd., P.O. Box 2090 (tel. 237-4126; fax 236-6463), is open Monday through Thursday from 8am to 12:30pm and 1:30 to 4:30pm, Friday until 1pm only. The Australian Embassy, 37 S. Sathorn Rd. (tel. 287-2680), is open daily from 9:30am to 12:30pm and 2 to 3:30pm. The New Zealand Embassy, 93 Wireless Rd. (tel. 251-8165), is open Monday through Friday from 8am to noon and 1:30 to 4pm.

Most embassies will deal with emergency situations on a 24-hour basis. If you are seriously injured or ill, do not hesitate to call your embassy for assistance.

Emergencies In any emergency, first call the Tourist Police at **1699** or **221-6206-10**. Someone there will speak English. (The local emergency number is **191**, but the operator will probably speak little English.) In case of fire, call **199** or **281-1544**. In a serious emergency situation, first call your hotel front desk, then your country's consulate for advice. For health emergencies, see "Hospitals," below.

Etiquette Though life in Thailand is fairly casual, there is a very defined sense of propriety. Thais have great reverence for the royal family and religious figures. Disrespect for either will cause great offense. Women should never touch a monk. If a woman wants to give something to a monk, she should put the object down and let him pick it up. Great respect is also shown to parents and elders.

Thais consider the soles of the feet unclean; pointing your toes or the soles of your feet at someone is considered impolite. When you enter a temple, remove your shoes and be sure not to point your toes at the Buddha. (Shoes should also be removed when entering an Islamic shrine or, indeed, a private home.) Sit down and fold your legs to the side. Be careful not to cross your legs, especially during an official government visit. Do not climb on or pose in front of a Buddhist figure.

It is an insult to touch someone on the head, the highest spiritual point of the body. Avoid pats on the head or back.

During an official or business call, coffee or tea will probably be served. Wait until your host invites you to drink (usually just before the visit is to end) before touching your cup or glass. When eating with others, do not fill your plate with food. Take a small amount (a few bites at most), or your host may think you a glutton.

Thais rarely offend or disturb other people. Public anger is absolutely taboo. It is very rude and, ultimately, ineffective for Westerners to respond to private problems with anger or raised voices. Above all, find a way for your rival to save face. Be insistent, but smile and remain calm. Public affection, with the possible exception of hand-holding, should be kept to a minimum.

A lovely Thai greeting is the *wai* (pronounced "why"): place your palms together, raise the tips of your index fingers to eye level, and make a subtle bow from the waist while bending your knees. The wai honors a person's presence and is done with all but children and service people. Don't be surprised if you are addressed by your first name—such as Mr. John or Ms. Kyle—which is normal etiquette and is not considered informal.

Even though this is a tropical country and you've probably come in search of the ultimate beach experience, it is somewhat offensive to Thai people for tourists to go shirtless and even to wear shorts, except at the beach. It is forbidden for men or women to wear shorts in temples.

Eyeglasses In all the major shopping areas of the city, you'll find optical shops, most of which can provide replacement glasses within 24 hours at reasonable prices. For eye problems, try the Bangkok Eye Clinic, 430/35 Siam Sq. on Rama I Road, between Phayathai Road and Henri Dunant Road (tel. 253-1917), or the Rutnin Eye Hospital, 80 Soi 21, Sukhumvit Road (tel. 258-0442).

Hairdressers/Barbers The locally recommended hairdressers cut both women's and men's hair. Among them are The Best, in the Nai Lert Park Building, 87 Sukhumvit Rd., near Soi 5 (tel. 251-1358), with another location at Soi 21, Sukhumvit Road (tel. 258-3621). Most of the international hotels also have haircutting services.

Holidays See Section 2 of Chapter 2.

Hospitals There are many fine medical facilities in the Bangkok area. If you are at your hotel and become ill, first contact the front desk for help in getting medical assistance. All hospitals listed here offer 24-hour emergency-room care and ambulance service. Be advised that you may need your passport and a deposit of up to 20,000B ($800) before you are admitted; bills must be settled before you leave. Your domestic medical insurance policy will probably not be accepted for payment, though major credit cards will be. In an emergency, call 1699 or 221-6206 or 281-5051 for assistance or for the location of the nearest infirmary. Among the best hospitals with English-speaking staff are Bumrungrat Medical Center and Hospital, 33 Soi 3, Sukhumvit Road (tel. 253-0259); Bangkok Nursing Home, 9 Convent Rd., between Silom Road and Sathorn Road, south of Rama IV Road (tel. 233-2610). Both the public Chulalongkorn Hospital (tel. 252-8181) and Ramathibodi University Hospital (tel. 246-0024) are leading teaching and research facilities and are located on Rama IV Road. The Bangkok General Hospital, which is the public hospital, and especially good for coronary problems, is found at 2 Soi Soonvijai 7, New Phetchaburi Road (tel. 318-0066). Accident victims are often taken to the **police hospital** (tel. 252-8111, the central emergency number).

Hotlines There is a volunteer Hot Line (tel. 277-7699 or 277-8811) for those in emotional distress. The Samaritans of Bangkok (tel. 236-7465 or 249-9977), a nonreligious group of volunteers, offers English-language counseling. Alcoholics Anonymous has several groups in town, one chapter meeting several times a week at the Holy Redeemer Church, 123/19 Ruam Rudee, off Wireless Road (tel. 256-6570 or 256-6305).

Information See Section 1 of Chapter 2 and Section 1 of this chapter.

Language Thai people welcome those who attempt to speak their language. The *Thai Phrasebook*, published by Lonely Planet Publications, is a useful guide for everyday phrases. It's available in the travel section of most American bookstores.

Laundry/Dry Cleaning Most hotels offer laundry and dry-cleaning services, and the work is usually very good. Locals recommend the dry cleaners at the Dusit Thani, Erawan Dry Cleaners, located in the basement of the Landmark of Bangkok. Another we recommend for laundry or cleaning is Ochin Laundry, 18/6 Soi 23, Sukhumvit Road (tel. 258-4235).

Libraries The American University Alumni (AUA) runs a free public library, 179 Rajdamri Rd. (tel. 252-8170), open to foreigners and residents Monday through Friday from 8:30am to 6pm, on Saturday from 9am to 1pm. The collection of 15,000 books and 170 periodicals focuses on current developments in the United States. The National Library, located on Samsen Road (tel. 281-5212), is open Monday through Friday, 9am to 4pm; admission is free. The Siam Society, 131 Soi 21, Sukhumvit Road (tel. 258-3494), operates a library concentrating on history, art, and culture; it is open to members only. The Neilson Hays Library, 195 Surawong Rd. (tel. 233-1731), is a subscriber-supported lending institution that has a good selection of English-language books, which are available to nonsubscribers on the premises only, Monday through Friday from 9:30am to 4pm. The British Council, 428 Siam Sq., Soi 2, Rama I Road (tel. 252-6136), opens its library and information services to the public Tuesday to Friday from 10am to 7:30pm, Saturday from 10am to 5pm.

Lost Property If you have lost anything or had your valuables stolen, call the Tourist Police, Crime Suppression Division, Vorachak Road (tel. 225-7758 or 221-6206, ext. 4). We have heard several factual reports of lost items being returned to the appropriate consulate by taxi drivers or bus attendants. Call the Consular Services section of your embassy to check.

Luggage Storage Both the Domestic and International Terminals of Don Muang International Airport offer luggage storage for 25B ($1) a day—from 7am to 10pm in the Domestic Terminal, 24 hours a day in the International Terminal. Most hotels will allow you to store luggage while you're away on trips in the countryside.

Mail Information Airmail postcards to the United States cost 10B (40¢); first-class letters cost 15B (60¢) per 5 grams (rates to Europe are about the same).

Air parcel post costs 480B ($19.20) per kilogram ($8.75 per pound). Surface or sea parcel post costs 160B ($6.40) for one kilogram ($2.90 per pound). U.S. delivery for airmail usually takes a week or, in our experience, more likely two or more. An express sticker will speed things up for an additional 20B (80¢). For still faster service, try International Express Mail (EMS) at 300B ($12) for 250 grams ($21.80 per pound), delivery guaranteed within 4 days. Sea mail can take 3 to 4 months.

For shipping those special souvenirs home, take advantage of the packing service offered by the General Post Office, Monday through Friday from 8am to 4:30pm, on Saturday, Sunday, and holidays from 9am to noon. Small cardboard packing cartons cost 5B to 17B (20¢ to 70¢), with an enormous 5B (20¢) service charge.

Maps See Section 1 of this chapter.

Newspapers/Magazines There are two domestic English-language dailies, the *Bangkok Post* and *The Nation,* distributed in the morning in the capital and later in the day around the country. Both cover the fascinating and ever-changing domestic political scene, as well as offering broad-based international news from the AP, UPI, and Reuters wire services, and cost 12B (48¢). You'll also find up-to-date schedules of cultural events and movies. Both the *Asian Wall Street Journal* and the *International Herald Tribune* are available Monday through Friday in Bangkok on their day of publication (they seem to reach the provinces a day or two later).

Where and *Look East* are slick English-language monthlies that are often found on a complimentary basis in hotel rooms. Both magazines emphasize events and features about Bangkok, with lesser coverage of other Thai cities and provinces. In addition, *Time, Newsweek, The Economist, Asiaweek,* and the *Far Eastern Economic Review* are sold at newsstands in the international hotels, as well as in bookstores throughout the city.

Pets   Contact the Thai consulate in your home country before you consider bringing along a pet. Animals brought by air are allowed in with an entry permit, which can be obtained at the airport. If pets are brought in by boat, one must apply in advance to the Department of Livestock Development (tel. 251-5136) in Bangkok. In any case, all animals must have proper vaccination certificates. Rabies is common in Thailand, so make sure that the pet has had complete vaccinations. Be advised that the United States has quarantine restrictions on animals returning from Thailand.

Photographic Needs   The price of film is about on a par with what you'd pay in most American camera stores. A 36-exposure roll of print film costs about 120B ($4.80) and you'll find a full range of Fuji and Kodak film throughout the country. The light is very bright, so an ultraviolet or sky-light filter and lower-speed film (ASA 25–100) are advisable. Keep your exposed and unexposed film in a cool place. For the plane, it's a good idea to put all film in your carry-on luggage and to have it inspected by hand rather than allow it to pass through an X-ray machine. (We've never fully believed the FILMSAFE signs on the X-ray machines.)

Fast photo-processing labs are found throughout the city and country, offering adequate quality at low prices. Ask the concierge at your hotel for a recommendation.

If your camera needs repair, inquire at the concierge's desk in your hotel for a reputable shop. There are several on Silom Road that offer major-brand cameras for sale and also provide repair service. However, most tourists will be in Bangkok too short a time to allow for repairs. Photographic equipment prices are no bargain here, due to high import tariffs.

Police   The Tourist Police (tel. 1699 or 221-6206-10) are a branch of the Police Department whose assignment is tourist assistance. They speak English, are open 24 hours, and deal with problems ranging from stolen purses to settling disagreements between tourists and Thais to assisting car-accident victims. You should call them in any emergency rather than dialing the police emergency number (see also "Emergencies," above). There are branches of the Tourist Police in major cities throughout the country.

Post Office   The General Post Office (GPO), a large institutional building behind a black iron fence, is on New Road (tel. 233-1050), between two major hotels, The Oriental and the Royal Orchid Sheraton. Telegraph and telephone service are also available here, in the north end of the building. GPO hours are 8am to 8pm Monday through Friday, 8am to 1pm on Saturday, Sunday, and holidays. Express-mail hours are 8:30am to 3:30pm Monday through Friday, 9am to noon on Saturday.

The poste restante window is on the left as you enter. For those unfamiliar with this wonderful service, it is comparable to General

Delivery in the United States. You can receive mail addressed to you here, c/o Poste Restante, GPO, Bangkok. You need either a valid passport or an ID card to claim your mail, and you must sign a receipt and pay 1B (4¢). Hours of operation are generally the same as for the post office.

Stamp collectors will want to stop by the Philatelic Promotion Center, open Monday through Friday from 9:30am to 5:30pm.

See "Mail Information," above, for rates and other information.

Radio/TV You can listen to English-language programming on Radio Thailand at 97 on the FM band daily from 6am to midnight. Classical music can be heard on FM 101.5 daily from 9:30am to 11:30pm, presented by Chulalongkorn University.

Television channels include 3, 5, 7, 9, and 11, which offer some English-language programming. Check the *Bangkok Post* or *The Nation* for listings. It's a rare hotel that doesn't offer English-language movies daily.

Religious Services For English-language **Catholic** services, contact the Holy Redeemer Roman Catholic Church, 123/19 Soi Ruam Rudee 5, off Wireless Road (tel. 256-6305), or the 19th-century Assumption Cathedral, 23 Oriental Lane, east of The Oriental (hotel) (tel. 234-8556). **Anglican Episcopal and Ecumenical** services are held at Christ Church, 11 Convent Rd., between Silom Road (at Patpong) and Sathorn Road (tel. 234-3634). There are **Jewish** services at the Jewish Association of Thailand, Soi Sai Pan 2, off Soi 22, Sukhumvit Road (tel. 258-2195), and at the Bossotel Inn. For those who are kosher, contact the Jewish Association for food recommendations.

Restrooms Except at temples and tourist sites, public toilets are a rarity in Bangkok, but you'll find no difficulty using restaurant or hotel restrooms. Most restaurants and all hotels above the budget level will have Western-style toilets. Most wats, some shops, some restaurants, and many budget hotels will have Asian toilets (a hole in the floor with foot pads on either side). They are usually clean but offer major difficulties for the handicapped. Near the toilet is a water trough with a small ladle; use the ladle and water for flushing the toilet. There may be some toilet paper, but it's best to carry your own supply. Dispose of the paper in the wastebasket usually provided.

In some lodgings you may find an Asian shower—a square sink and a ladle. Pour (cold) water over yourself, soap up, and rinse with another ladle of water. Try it, you'll like it.

Safety Whenever you're traveling in an unfamiliar city or country, stay alert. Be aware of your immediate surroundings. It's your responsibility to be aware and alert even in heavily touristed areas.

In general, Bangkok is a safe city. There is a low incidence of direct personal crime—muggings or robberies—but there are specific areas where pickpocketing and bag-snatching are problems. The Bangkok public buses are infamous for skilled and ingenious pickpockets, and the overnight trains and long-distance buses are equally treacherous. If you must ride the Bangkok public buses, pay very close attention to your belongings at all times, keeping valuable possessions in front of you (don't keep a wallet, for example, in a back pocket).

It's advisable to keep all important documents, including your passport, and valuable jewelry in your hotel's safe-deposit box. Carry a photocopy of your passport.

Be careful with credit cards. Make sure you destroy carbons and keep all receipts. Be suspicious of any prolonged period when your credit card is away from you.

A Special Warning: Though the Thai people are deservedly famous for their warm and hospitable ways, you must be wary of strangers who offer to guide you, take you to shop (especially a jewelry shop), or buy you food or drink. This is most to likely occur near a tourist attraction like the Grand Palace, and you will find it hard to resist a con man's friendly greeting and seeming concern. This kind of forward behavior is simply not normal for the average Thai.

There are rare exceptions, but most likely these new "friends" will attempt to swindle you in some way. This often takes the form of trying to persuade you to buy jewelry or gems at "bargain" prices—items that you will later find to be nearly worthless. This is a big problem in Bangkok (and elsewhere in Thailand), and difficult to avoid. Also beware of anyone inviting you to their home, then offering to show you a famous Thai card game. You *will* lose. If you are approached about such schemes, call the Tourist Police immediately.

Last, but not least, for those who contemplate bringing a "companion" to their hotel room, be advised of the danger of food or drink laced with sleeping potions. There are many reports of such incidents, with victims waking up two days later to find their valuables gone.

Shoe Repair   Break that heel descending Wat Arun? There are many shoe-repair shops along New Road and lower Silom Road, near The Oriental (hotel), and along Sukhumvit Road. Try Siam Bootery, 292–4 Sukhumvit Rd., (tel. 251-6862). Most department stores and shopping malls have a "Mr. Minit" counter for shoe repairs. Better yet, ask your hotel concierge to arrange for the repair.

Taxes   Rooms and services at hotels are taxed at 7%. Meals at hotels and restaurants are taxed at 7% VAT, though some restaurants include the tax in the price. There is no general sales tax. There is an airport departure tax of 20B (80¢) for domestic flights and 200B ($8) for international flights.

Taxis   See Section 2 of this chapter.

Telephone/Telegrams/Telex   The main government telephone office occupies a separate building on the grounds of the General Post Office, on New Road between The Oriental and the Royal Orchid Sheraton, and is open daily for 24 hours. This office is for international calls. The procedure for making a call is as follows: book your call by filling out a form at one of the desks, specifying the telephone number you wish to call and an approximate length for your call; take the form to the cashier and pay; wait until you are called to a booth. The cost of a person-to-person call to North America is 250B ($10) for 3 minutes; station-to-station calls are 200B ($8) for 3 minutes, 60B ($2.40) per each additional minute. Collect or credit-card calls can be made without an extra fee. There are also telephone/telegraph offices at both terminals at Don Muang International Airport, open from 7am to 10pm in the Domestic Terminal, 24 hours in the International Terminal. You can utilize the "Home Country Direct" service of AT&T, Sprint, or MCI from most hotels and from special phones in the airports and some train stations. This allows you to dial a special number for your long-distance service and charge the call to your calling card. Hotel surcharges still apply, but the overall cost will generally be less than if you dial direct. The access code for AT&T's USA Direct is 011-999-11111; for Sprint Express, 0012-99-13877; for MCI's Call USA, 001-999-12001. These numbers may change, so check with your carrier before you depart.

At all hotels, there are surcharges on international calls, usually 25% to 40% (occasionally much higher, check with the hotel operator before dialing). A credit-card or collect call carries a service charge, typically 160B ($6.40). A call of more than 4 minutes will usually be cheaper on a credit-card or collect billing.

Local calls can be made from any red public pay telephone. Calls cost 1B (4¢) for 3 minutes, with additional 1B coins needed after hearing multiple beeps on the line. You will find private pay telephones in hotel lobbies, shops, and restaurants. These usually cost 5B (20¢) and require that you push a button on the instrument when you hear the other party pick up. Don't miss the *free* public phone booths in both the departure lounge and baggage-claim area of the Domestic Terminal of the airport.

There are also new silver (the old ones were blue) long-distance telephones in strategic places throughout Bangkok, such as at the airport (both terminals). These can be used for either local or domestic long-distance calls, at rates from 6B to 18B (25¢ to 75¢) per minute. You will need a pile of 5B coins and can observe your running total on the meter, putting in more coins as needed. From 6 to 10pm there is a 50% discount on these rates; from 10pm to 7am, a 67% discount. At the airport you can get change from the Airport Information booth. You cannot make domestic long-distance calls from the overseas telephone offices anywhere in the country. You'll find certain shops offering long-distance calls. Charges are usually only slightly higher than the official rate, but ask first.

For information within the Bangkok metropolitan area, dial 13; for the provinces, 183.

Telegraph services are offered in the telephone and telegraph office of the General Post Office, open daily for 24 hours, including fax service and telegram restante service. The same services (except for telegram restante) are offered at the telephone and telegraph offices at Don Muang International Airport. A fax to the United States costs about 350B ($14) and must be prepared on the official form. Every hotel offers normal fax service as well.

Time Zones Bangkok and all of Thailand are 7 hours later than Greenwich mean time (GMT). During winter months this means that Bangkok is exactly 7 hours ahead of London, 12 hours ahead of New York, 15 hours ahead of Los Angeles. Daylight saving time will add 1 hour to these figures.

Tipping If a service charge is not added to your restaurant check, a 10% to 15% tip is appropriate. In small noodle shops, a 10B (40¢) tip may be added if the service is particularly good. Airport or hotel porters expect tips of 20B (80¢) per bag. Taxi drivers do not expect tips. But carry small bills, as many cab drivers either don't have, or won't admit to having, small change.

Transit Information Note the following: Thai Airways International (tel. 233-3810, international reservations; 280-0070, domestic reservations; 535-2081, airport), Bangkok Airways (tel.

229-3456, reservations), air-conditioned buses going north (tel. 279-4484), air-conditioned buses going south (tel. 435-1199), Hua Lampong Railroad Station (tel. 223-7461 or 223-0341), and Tourism Authority of Thailand (tel. 226-0060 or 226-0072).

Water Even though Bangkok's tap water is treated, we advise you to be cautious about it. Good health while traveling begins with good water. All hotels will include bottled water in the room. Most restaurants serve bottled or boiled water and ice made from boiled or purified water, but always ask to be sure. Ask the assistant manager of your hotel for advice. Outside of Bangkok, drink only bottled water.

If you are traveling with a small child, it is extremely important that you serve him or her only purified water. It's readily available at small shops everywhere, in town and in the country, for 10B (40¢) per bottle and up. Drink lots of it—it's the best antidote to the heat.

3. NETWORKS & RESOURCES

The **American Women's Club of Thailand,** 33 Rajdamri Road (tel. 252-9948; fax 252-1689), is more oriented toward long-term visitors rather than tourists. To quote their president: "The AWC was organized for the purpose of promoting friendship in the American community and emphasizing friendship and cooperation with Thai women through social, cultural, and philanthropic activities."

4. MOVING ON—TRAVEL SERVICES & SYSTEMS

TRAVEL AGENTS

Bangkok has an array of travel agents that provide everything from local tours to cut-rate international airline tickets. **Sea Tours Company** (tel. 251-4862) and **World Travel Service** (tel. 233-5900), with branch offices in nearly every major hotel, offer a full range of travel services, including booking international and domestic airline tickets, arranging hotels and tours at other destinations in Thailand, and organizing tours of Bangkok, both customized and packaged. They can also provide a car with driver for your stay in Bangkok.

Where Travel Service, 27 Ngam Dupli, Rama IV Road (tel. 286-7274 or 287-1439; fax 02-287-1439) opposite the Malaysia Hotel, is a reputable bucket shop (discount travel center) we have used since 1981 with good results. (Open Monday to Friday, 9am to 5pm, Saturday until noon) Cheap tickets have their price. The tickets are usually highly restricted, with severe penalties for cancellation or changes. Check the conditions that apply to any discounted ticket before purchasing.

Be very careful of storefront bucket shops, particularly in the Khao San Road area. There have been several instances of ticket agencies disappearing, leaving customers holding worthless tickets.

READERS RECOMMEND

Beware of Bucket Shops. *"You may wish to note the continuing problem of ticket scams (particularly on Khao San Road); per this article from* The Nation *'. . . By all accounts the "agency" has been doing a roaring trade, prices have been at rock bottom level for the last three weeks, effectively building up a short term swell in trade and boosting their "cash only" intake well above its normal level. Then, without warning, the agent vanished leaving in his wake a group of tourists who had paid over their savings in return for the promise of airline tickets to destinations all over the world. . . . This instance of fraud on tourists would seem to be something of a trend.'"*
—Lemuel Morgan, Vice Consul, British Embassy, Bangkok.

TRAVEL BY PLANE

Bangkok has become a major hub for airline travel in Southeast Asia, with over 50 airlines offering connections. Domestic service is provided primarily by Thai Airways, serving numerous cities throughout the country. Rapidly growing Bangkok Airways is the sole carrier flying between Bangkok and Ko Samui, with connections on to Phuket, and also offers daily service to Hua Hin. As of 1993, Bangkok Airways was planning service from Bangkok to Trat.

Here are a few useful airline addresses and telephone numbers:

- Thai Airways (domestic), 6 Larn Luang Rd. (tel. 280-0070)
- Thai Airways International 485 Silom Rd. (tel. 233-3810); airport office (tel. 535-2081)
- Bangkok Airways, 140 Pacific Place Building, Sukhumvit Road (tel. 253-4014 or 229-3465)
- United Airlines, on 9th floor of Regent House, Rajdamri Road (tel. 253-0558)
- Delta Airlines, on 7th floor of Patpong Building, 1 Surawong Rd. (tel. 237-6838)
- British Airways, on 2nd floor of Charn Issara Tower, 942/81 Rama IV Rd. (tel. 236-0038)
- Garuda Indonesia Airways, 27th floor, Lumpini Tower, 1168 Rama IV Rd. (tel. 285-6470)
- Pakistan International Airlines, 52 Surawong Rd. (tel. 234-2961)
- Qantas Airways, Charn Issara Tower, 942/51 Rama IV Rd. (tel. 237-6269)
- Singapore Airlines, on 12th floor of Silom Center Building, 2 Silom Rd. (tel. 236-0440)
- Canadian Airlines International, 6th floor, Maneeya Center, 518/5 Ploenchit Rd. (tel. 251-4521)
- Continental Airlines, 4th floor, Charn Issara Tower, 924/126 Rama IV Rd. (tel. 237-6145)
- Northwest Airlines, 4th floor, The Peninsula Plaza, 153 Rajdamri Rd. (tel. 254-0789)

TRAVEL BY TRAIN

The Thai rail network is extremely well organized, connecting Bangkok with major cities throughout the country. All trains to and from the capital stop at **Hua Lampong Railroad Station,** at the intersection of Rama IV Road and Krung Kasem Road. For current schedules and fares, contact the reservation and information office (tel. 223-7010 or 223-7020), open weekdays from 8:30am to 6pm, on weekends and holidays from 8:30am to noon. Some travel agents also provide reservation service.

Reservations can be made up to three months in advance of traveling and should be made as far in advance as possible during the peak season (particularly for a sleeper on the overnight trains to Chiang Mai or the southern resorts).

The train station has a money-exchange booth open daily from 8am to 6:30pm. The luggage storage room, charging 20B (80¢) for each piece, is open daily from 4am to 10:30pm. An information booth is open Monday through Friday from 8:30am to 6pm, on Saturday, Sunday, and holidays from 8:30am to noon.

As the station is centrally located, a metered taxi will cost no more than 100B ($4) to most hotels; a tuk-tuk will be no more than 70B ($2.80).

Warning: On trains, pay close attention to your possessions. Thievery is common on overnight trips.

TRAVEL BY BUS

Thailand has a very efficient and inexpensive bus system, highly recommended for budget travelers and short-haul trips. Be aware of the distinctions between air-conditioned and non-air-conditioned buses: air-conditioned buses cost more, but are significantly more comfortable, make fewer stops, and therefore offer a shorter trip. There are also fancier, more comfortable VIP buses, operated by private companies, which offer even more comfortable seats, serve sodas and snacks, and sometimes torture you with overloud Thai disco music.

There are three bus stations, each serving a different part of the country. All public buses to the southern peninsula depart from the Southern Bus Terminal, on Pinklao-Nakhonchaisi Road, west of the river over the Phra Pinklao Bridge from the Democracy Monument (tel. 435-1199 or 435-1200). Service to the east coast (including Pattaya) originates at the Eastern Bus Terminal, on Sukhumvit Road past Soi 63 (tel. 392-9227 or 391-9829). To the northern, northeastern, and northwestern areas, buses leave from the Northern Bus Terminal, Phaholyothin Road, just west of the airport freeway near the Chatuchak Weekend Market (tel. 279-4484). To confuse matters further, private companies serve various points of the country with buses originating at their offices. Consult the concierge or travel agent at your hotel for advice.

As all stations are far from most hotels, take a taxi or tuk-tuk. Public buses also make easy connections to certain areas of town. Ask at the information counter at the bus terminal.

Warning: When traveling by long-distance bus, pay close attention to your possessions. Thievery is common, particularly on overnight buses.

TRAVEL BY CAR

We don't recommend driving yourself in Bangkok, but outside the city it's an option for those willing to risk the left side of the road. You can rent a car, with or without driver, through Avis, 2/12 Wireless Road (tel. 255-5300). In 1994 self-drive rates started at 1,300B ($52) per day or 7,800B ($312) per week for a Toyota Corolla or Nissan Sunny, plus modest (300B to 500B [$15 to $20]) drop-off fees for one-way trips. A Volvo 740 GL with driver cost 2,700B ($108) per day, plus 5B (20¢) per kilometer over 200 kilometers (124 miles), and 250B ($10) per hour beyond 9 hours. There is also a living allowance charge for the driver on overnight trips. Prices include insurance.

Sea Tours Company and World Travel Service can also arrange cars with drivers, sometimes at lower rates. There are many local car-rental agencies for self-drive cars. Make sure their prices include insurance and carefully check the condition of the car. If you have a breakdown on the road, you will have wasted precious vacation time and saved no money.

Driving rules are as follows:
1. Always drive on the left side of the road.
2. Maximum speed limit for cars inside a city limit is 60kmph (36 m.p.h.); outside a city limit, 80kmph (48 m.p.h.).
3. Give the right-of-way to vehicles coming from main roads.
4. There is no turning on a red light.
5. Slow down through school zones and around hospitals.
6. If involved in a traffic accident that causes injury or property damage, notify the police.
7. Never operate a vehicle if under the influence of drugs or alcohol.

CHAPTER 4

BANGKOK ACCOMMODATIONS

1. **ON THE RIVER**
 • **FROMMER'S SMART TRAVELER: HOTELS**
 • **FROMMER'S COOL FOR KIDS: HOTELS**
2. **HISTORIC BANGKOK—NEAR THE GRAND PALACE**
3. **THE BUSINESS DISTRICT**
4. **THE SHOPPING/ EMBASSY AREA**
5. **AROUND THE RAILROAD STATION**
6. **NEAR THE AIRPORT**

If you checked the annual surveys of the world's great hotels, you'd certainly find Bangkok well represented. We're of the opinion that, if you can afford it, you should take the opportunity to stay in one of these grand establishments. Fortunately, Bangkok offers a rich variety of choices in all price categories, and compared with similar facilities in Europe, even the most expensive hotels represent good value.

Given the tremendous traffic problems and the size of the city, we suggest you read Section 1 of Chapter 3 carefully before selecting a hotel. Choose the location based on how you plan to spend your time in Bangkok. Tourists will have priorities different from those of business travelers. Unfortunately, few of Bangkok's world-renowned upper-crust hotels are located in the heart of the sightseeing zone, near the Grand Palace. Yet each part of the city has its own appeal for first-time visitors.

In the high-season months, December through February, you must make reservations well in advance for the very expensive and expensive hotels, and even for the popular guesthouses, or you may find yourself with no room at the inn.

We heartily encourage budget travelers to consider vacationing in the low season, when discounts—in what has recently become an overbuilt city—range from 25% to 60%! The most deluxe hotels disguise their "discount rates" in valuable packages including free breakfast, river views, room upgrades, airport transfers, and other perks, which at The Oriental last season amounted to 30% off the Christmas peak rates. We stayed at the very comfortable Amari Boulevard and had our huge tower room discounted from $125 to $40 as part of their "Super Bonanza" package! It's true that low seasons exist because it's the hot or rainy time of year, but there are such bargains to be had!

Accommodations listings are organized by price range within each area of the city. The star symbol indicates our special favorites, and the dollar sign, what we consider to be best-value choices.

The hotels falling into the very expensive category are all world-class deluxe hotels, with prices starting at 5,200B ($208) per night for a double. Several are near the Chao Phraya River, though you'll also find them in the Business District and in the Shopping/

Embassy Area. Here you will enjoy the highest levels of service and luxury.

The expensive category includes hotels considered first class—still luxurious, but at a level slightly below that of the deluxe hotels in the service area as well as in decor. There are good values to be found here, and in every neighborhood. Prices range from 2,500B ($100) to 4,700B ($188) for doubles.

Moderate hotels fall short of these luxurious standards but are still quite comfortable and well staffed. Most have pools, color TVs, restaurants, room service, and laundry service. Prices here will range from 1,450B ($58) to 2,500B ($100) for doubles, and if you look carefully, you can find very good value without sacrificing creature comforts.

For the more budget-conscious tourist, Bangkok offers a few good low-cost lodgings in each neighborhood. Our inexpensive category includes the prices from 500B to 1,250B ($20 to $50), while the budget category covers housing that costs less than 500B ($20).

The cheapest budget area is Khao San Road, north of the Grand Palace. This is a street of side-by-side guesthouses, some as cheap as 60B ($2.40) per person for a small fan-cooled partitioned room, with bath and Asian toilet down the hall. We appreciate not only the camaraderie shared by the backpacking crowd in these guesthouses but also the community bulletin boards that offer advice to fellow travelers about cheap fares, restaurants, and potential ripoffs on the road.

For a little more money, about 500B ($20) per night, two can find a better value, to our way of thinking, in less Spartan housing. You can expect a clean, simple fan-cooled room with private bathroom, but don't look for a private TV, swimming pool, or minibar.

As we went to press in the spring of 1994, three new deluxe hotels were under various stages of construction, all on Bangkok's most prized real estate, the banks of the Chao Phraya River. However, these new palaces will be on the Thonburi side, accessible by bridge and possibly private boat to Bangkok's major sights. From north to south, they are the Chao Phraya Sofitel Bangkok, bound to be a culinary as well as an architectural landmark in the prestigious French chain; the Ritz Carlton, on a site opposite The Oriental, and likely to rival its venerable competition with top-notch service; and the stately Peninsula, breaking ground across from the Shangri-La, and certain to excel in old-world style and grandeur.

Note: Unless otherwise noted, all prices listed are subject to 7% government tax and 10% service charge.

1. ON THE RIVER

This is one of our favorite areas. The river hotels have the priceless view of, and easy access to, the fascinating Chao Phraya River. But view and access don't come cheaply, so expect to pay the highest prices at the three centrally located facilities. For less money you can go up or down river (and soon, across-river!) to hotels that are less convenient but provide their own boat transportation. There are also two lower-priced choices for budget travelers.

VERY EXPENSIVE

THE MENAM HOTEL RIVERSIDE, 2074 New Rd., Yan-nawa, Bangkok 10120. Tel. 02/289-1148. Fax 02/291-9400. Telex 87423 TH. 688 rms, 39 suites. A/C MINIBAR TEL TV **Directions:** 1.5km (1 mile) south of Sathorn Bridge, off New Rd.

$ Rates: 5,100B ($204) single; 5,450B ($218) double; from 8,400B ($336) suite. AE, DC, MC, V.

For a large hotel, The Menam offers a fair amount of charm—there is an unpretentious, comfortable air about the whole place. The good news is the riverside venue; the less good news is that it's downriver from areas where most tourists roam, about 10 minutes by cab south of the Sathorn Bridge. This leaves the traveler with lengthy bus or taxi trips to the major tourist attractions. However, if you're adventuresome enough to try the riverboats (and we recommend that you do), the location can work to your advantage. The hotel offers hourly shuttle boats to either The Oriental (hotel) or the River City Shopping Complex, or you can walk a block up New Road and hop on one of the Chao Phraya Express Boats to go almost anywhere on the river (see Section 2 of Chapter 3).

The hotel is popular with tour groups, drawn by its relatively reasonable riverfront prices. Deluxe riverview rooms are nicely appointed, with colorful Chinese murals for headboards and marble-tiled bathrooms. The style and view set these accommodations well apart from the less appealing (but 10% cheaper) cityview standard rooms, which feel a bit worn. The pool is large, though screened from the river by the Riverview Terrace Barbecue. As with any major hotel, you must book at least one month in advance for high-season travel (Dec–Mar).

Dining/Entertainment: The Chinese luncheon buffet at Menam Tien is very popular, and buffet fans could then move on to the evening seafood buffet at the Riverside Terrace Barbecue. Classic French fare is offered at La Brasserie. In addition to standard fare, the 24-hour coffee shop has a Japanese Corner, offering a wide array of Japanese foods at lunch and dinner.

Services: 24-hour room service, concierge, limousine service, babysitting, laundry service.

Facilities: Swimming pool, health club, business center, beauty salon and barbershop, shopping arcade.

THE ORIENTAL, 48 Oriental Ave., Bangkok 10500. Tel. 02/236-0400, or toll free 800/526-6566. Fax 02/236-1937. Telex 82997 ORIENTAL TH. 394 rms, including 34 suites. A/C MINIBAR TEL TV **Directions:** On riverfront off New Rd.

$ Rates: 7,200B–8,700B ($288–$348) River Wing single, (8,700B ($348) Garden Wing single; 7,500B–9,200B ($300–$368) River Wing double, 9,200B ($368) Garden Wing double, from 10,800B ($432) suite. AE, DC, EC, MC, V.

In a field of intense competition for the ultimate in luxury and service, The Oriental has managed to find the right balance between up-to-date facilities and tradition. Part legend, part reality, it stands tall on the banks of the Chao Phraya River as one of Bangkok's finest hotels. The original hotel was established in the 1860s by two Danish sea captains soon after King Rama IV (Mongkut) reopened Siam to world trade. The Oriental has since added three buildings—the first in 1876; the larger, more modern pair in 1958 and 1976—which have played host to a glittering

FROMMER'S SMART TRAVELER: HOTELS

1. Although many hotels belong to international reservations networks (such as Utell and SRS), it's often possible to improve upon the published rates at the larger hotels by reserving through a Bangkok travel agent (see Chapter 3). Lower rates often include airport transfers and continental breakfast.

2. Ask your local travel agent about saving by combining hotel reservations with your air tickets (through Thai Airways packages, for example).

3. If asked, hotels will lower their off-season rates by as much as 25% to 60%, or will include breakfast, an item that can save a considerable amount of money. Bargain over the phone if you feel uncomfortable doing it in person.

4. Avoid major holiday periods (see Chapter 2). Rooms are more difficult to find in these periods.

5. If you plan to travel in high season—mid-December through February, you must reserve your accommodations well in advance. Even the low-budget guesthouses book up early in these crowded months.

6. Compare twin-bed and double-bed room rates. Twin rates are sometimes higher in lower-priced hotels.

7. Seek out the best of the hotels in the moderate and budget categories. A moderately priced hotel will have basic comforts, even though it will lack the luxurious details of bigger hotels.

roster of Thai and international dignitaries, celebrities, and writers such as Joseph Conrad, Somerset Maugham, and Noël Coward. Jim Thompson, of Thai silk trade fame, even served briefly as the hotel's proprietor.

It would be inaccurate to describe The Oriental merely as a hotel—it offers the kind of facilities that lead some to spend their Bangkok stay exclusively within its confines (not that we suggest you do this). For example, those who wish to learn more about Thai cuisine can attend the Thai Cooking School. The shopping arcade and in-house restaurants offer a wide range of quality options, and there is an evening classical dance concert. Daily lectures and demonstrations cover a wide swath of Thai culture. Farther afield, the boats *Oriental Queen I* and *Oriental Queen II* make daily river runs up the Chao Phraya to the ancient capital of Ayutthaya and to the Royal Summer Palace at Bang Pa-In.

Not to rest on its considerable laurels, the hotel has recently undergone an overall upgrade. We visited each wing, the new Library, and the restaurants and were impressed by the tastefully redecorated interior. However, its the level of service that distinguishes The Oriental from the other riverfront hotels; time and again, we hear from travelers about some particular nicety that made their stay remarkable. (Our favorite is from a New Yorker, who told us that when he was diagnosed in Malaysia with malaria, he immediately flew to Bangkok and checked in at The Oriental, where the superb staff nursed him for the six weeks he was confined to bed.) Of course, others differ; some guests have found that The Oriental's vaunted staff doesn't treat everyone in the same gracious way.

Though not for everyone, the legendary Oriental remains extremely popular, and reservations should be made as far in advance as possible.

Dining/Entertainment: Among the many food options we highly recommend lunch or dinner in The Normandie (see Section 1 of Chapter 5), high tea in the Authors' Lounge (3:30 to 6pm daily), the healthy breakfast buffet on the Verandah, and the Terrace's evening barbecue. The China House has a fantastically expensive (by no means universally admired) Cantonese menu. Equally regarded for its high prices and less-than-perfect food is Lord Jim's, The Oriental's seafood outlet. Also on the premises is the recommended Bamboo Bar (see Section 3 of Chapter 9).

Services: 24-hour room service, concierge, complimentary welcome fruit basket, limousine service, babysitting, house doctor, and laundry service.

Facilities: No-smoking floors, two swimming pools, health club, tennis and squash courts, beauty and fitness spa, business center, cooking school, beauty salon and barbershop, shopping arcade, daily boat excursions.

ROYAL ORCHID SHERATON HOTEL & TOWERS, 2 Captain Bush Lane, Siphya Rd., Bangkok 10500. Tel. 02/ 234-5599, or toll free 800/325-3535. Fax 02/236-8320. Telex 84492 ROYORCH TH. 701 rms, 70 suites. A/C MINIBAR TEL TV
Directions: Next to River City Shopping Complex.
$ Rates: 5,300B–5,500B ($212–$220) single or double; 6,700B ($265) Towers single or double; 9,000B ($360) suite. Extra person 600B ($24), 950B ($38) in Towers. AE, DC, EC, MC, V.

The Royal Orchid, like its downriver neighbors The Oriental and the Shangri-La, overlooks the magnificent Chao Phraya River, and according to us, it offers the best view of all the major riverfront hotels. It's ideal as a base for shopping or sightseeing, and is adjacent to the River City Shopping Complex (there's actually a connecting walkway) and the Siphya Express Boat Pier. The rooms are spacious, pastel-hued, and trimmed with warm teakwood, lending a refined and distinctly Thai ambience to your stay. All in all, a good package.

However, to us the Royal Orchid feels like a fancy, but not luxurious, group hotel. Perhaps it's the guests crowding its too small lobby, or maybe it's that slightly less-than-well-maintained hallway, or the mediocre service and food in its pleasant coffee shop. If you're in search of the ultimate riverside hotel, you might go elsewhere.

The more pricey Sheraton Towers, a hotel within a hotel on the 26th through 28th floors (with its own check-in desk and express elevator), offers more ornate decor and a higher level of service; Towers suites, for example, have personal fax machines in the sitting rooms, and all rooms are manned by butlers on 24-hour call.

Dining/Entertainment: The Royal Orchid boasts eight major food outlets, including such cuisines as Japanese, Indian, Italian, Thai, grill, and generic Western. Bravo for their kids' menus! The Thara Thong Thai restaurant is the most attractive, both commanding a lovely view of the river and set in a gorgeous room resplendent with teak, bronze, and celadon. In the evening, there is a low-key performance of Thai classical music. The Captain Bush Grill, on the same floor, is very popular with Western guests for its well-prepared prime rib.

Services: 24-hour room service, concierge, complimentary welcome tea (Towers only), house doctor, limousine service, babysitting, laundry service, jogging shuttle to Lumpini Park.

Facilities: No-smoking floors, swimming pool, health club, sauna, children's pool and playground, tennis courts, business center, beauty salon and barbershop, shopping arcade.

SHANGRI-LA HOTEL, 89 Soi Wat Suan Plu, New Rd., Bangkok 10500. Tel. 02/236-7777, or toll free 800/359-5050. Fax 02/236-8579 or 212/986-3699. Telex 84265 SHANGLA TH. 868 rms, 60 suites. A/C MINIBAR TEL TV **Directions:** Overlooking Chao Phraya River, adjacent to Sathorn Bridge, with access off New Rd. at south end of Silom Rd.

$ Rates: 5,400B–6,800B ($216–$272) single, 6,000B–7,400B ($240–$296) double, 7,500B–8,200B ($300–$328) Krung Thep Wing; from 9,600B ($384) suite. AE, DC, MC, V.

The glitzy Shangri-La, on the banks of the Chao Phraya, boasts acres of polished marble, a jungle of tropical plants and flowers, and two towers that offer breathtaking views of the river. Though thoroughly modern, the Shangri-La has an opulence that harks back to the august hotel palaces of the late 19th century.

All rooms overlook the Chao Phraya and are decorated with lush carpeting, teak furniture, and marble bathrooms; their amenities include flowers, slippers, hairdryers, safes, and tea and coffee makers. Most of the deluxe rooms on the higher floors have either balconies or small sitting rooms, making them closer to junior suites. We think these are a particularly good value for on-the-river upscale accommodations, especially when compared with the higher-priced Horizon Floor's business-oriented accommodations. For such an enormous place, the level of service and facilities is surprisingly good.

The superluxurious Krung Thep Wing adds another 17-story, riverview tower to the grounds, as well as a restaurant, riverside swimming pool, and breakfast lounge. After passing through the flower-filled atrium signifying the Krung Thep's own entry, guests register in their superlarge rooms, surrounded by colorful Thai paintings and meters of glistening Thai silk. Deluxe features include a separate shower stall, twin sinks, and bidets in the huge marble bathrooms. Small balconies overlook the Sathorn Bridge and busy Chao Phraya River. The full-size, one-bedroom junior suites (12,000B/$480), with a dining area and 1½ baths, are a particularly good value for families. Larger suites include private fax machines, Jacuzzis, living rooms, and even more opulent Chinese decor.

We'd suggest the livelier main building for tourists, groups, and families, and the quieter Krung Thep Wing for those seeking a respite from Bangkok's busy byways, or just a sojourn in luxury.

Dining/Entertainment: Extravagance means 11 separate dining facilities, including the riverside Coffee Garden and Menam Terrace (which offers a nightly barbecue dinner); the popular Shang Palace for Chinese food (see Section 1 of Chapter 5), and one of Bangkok's prettiest settings for Thai cuisine, Sala Thip (see Section 1 of Chapter 5), housed in two teakwood pavilions sitting right by the active riverside. The new Club Restaurant has nightly music. The hotel's river cruiser, the *Ayutthaya Princess*, motors up the Chao Phraya to Ayutthaya daily and makes a 3-hour dinner cruise on Sunday.

FROMMER'S COOL FOR KIDS:
HOTELS

Most of the moderate and expensive hotels have pools, a guaranteed plus for the kids, though none are especially oriented for children.

Hilton International *(see p. 83)* The Hilton has Bangkok's best pool, large and shallow and set in a lush 8-acre tropical garden. Tennis courts (and instruction) are also available.

Bangkok Christian Guesthouse *(see p. 81)* This more moderately priced hotel has a large lawn where kids can play and a warm family atmosphere.

Siam Inter-Continental *(see p. 86)* Dozens of gregarious ducks, swans, geese, pelicans, and peacocks roaming this hotel's huge grounds. The rolling terrain is also dotted with caged tropical birds, fish ponds, Thai pavilions, and a (rusty) slide and swing set.

Services: 24-hour room service, concierge, house doctor, limousine service, helicopter transfer, babysitting, laundry service.

Facilities: No-smoking floor, two swimming pools, health club, tennis courts, squash courts, business center, beauty salon and barbershop, shopping arcade.

EXPENSIVE

ROYAL GARDEN RIVERSIDE, 257/1–3 Charoen Nakorn Rd., Thonburi, Bangkok 10600. Tel. 02/476-0021. Fax 02/476-1120. 394 rms, 26 suites. A/C MINIBAR TEL TV

Directions: On the Thonburi side of the Chao Phraya River, near the Krung Thep Bridge, 15 minutes by boat from River City.

$ Rates: 4,300B–4,800B ($172–$192) single; 4,800B–5,000B ($192–$200) double; from 6,000B ($240) suite. AE, DC, MC, V.

This city resort is the newest of the riverfront hotels, a luxuriously sprawling complex on the banks of the Chao Phraya a few miles downstream from its nearest competition. You can leave the urban jangle of Bangkok behind as you board the hotel boat at River City for the short ride. The three wings of the hotel surround a large swimming pool set in a garden by the river. The lobby is dramatic, marble-clad, and soaring. Rooms are comfortable and modern, with pale cream walls and pink and blue fabrics, tastefully decorated and fully equipped with all the amenities. If you don't mind the boat ride (and we don't), it's a good choice. Boats go to and from River City every half hour, from early to late.

Dining/Entertainment: They go for the big international names—Trader Vic's Polynesian Restaurant and Benihana Japanese-American Steak House, as well as their own Garden Café (Thai and international cuisine), the Rice Mill Chinese Restaurant, and the Market Restaurant for beef and seafood.

Services: 24-hour room service, concierge, limousine service, babysitting service (arranged with advance notice).

Amari Airport Hotel **56**
The Amari Boulevard **50**
Amari Watergate Hotel **58**
The Atlanta Hotel **42**
Bangkok Center Hotel **14**
Bangkok Christian
   Guesthouse **31**
Bangkok YWCA **34**
Bel-Aire Princess **43**
Bossotel Inn **16**
Buddy Guesthouse **6**
City Lodges **52**
Comfort Inn **51**
Dusit Thani **32**
Dynasty Inn **45**
Golden Dragon Hotel **55**
Golden Horse Hotel **11**
Grand China Princess Hotel **7**
Grand Hyatt Erawan Bangkok **57**
Happy Inn **44**
Hilton International
   at Nai Lert Park **41**
Holiday Inn Crowne Plaza **26**
Hotel Majestic Palace **9**
Krung Kasem Sri Krung Hotel **13**
Landmark Hotel **47**
Lek Guesthouse **4**
Malaysia Hotel **35**
The Mandarin Bangkok **29**
Manhattan Hotel **53**
Manohra Hotel **25**
The Menam **21**
Le Méridien Président **39**
The Montien **30**
New Peninsula Hotel **23**
Nith Charoen Hotel **5**
Novotel **36**
The Oriental **19**
Peachy Guesthouse **2**
P.S. Guesthouse **3**
The Regent, Bangkok **38**
River View Guest House **15**
Royal Garden Riverside **10**
Royal Hotel **8**
Royal Orchid Sheraton
   Hotel & Towers **17**
Royal Princess Hotel **12**
Royal River Hotel **1**
Ruamchitt Travelodge **49**
Shangri-La Hotel **20**
Siam Inter-Continental **37**
Siam Orchid Inn **40**

The Somerset **54**
The Sukhothai **24**
Suriwongse Tower Inn **22**
Swan Hotel **18**
Tai-Pan Hotel **48**
Trinity City Hotel **27**
Uncle Rey's Guesthouse **46**
Wall Street Inn **28**
YMCA Collins
   International House **33**

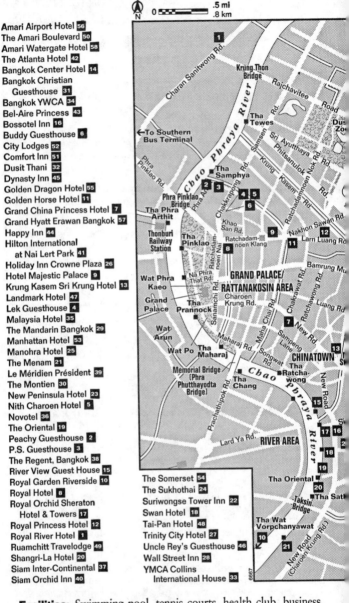

Facilities: Swimming pool, tennis courts, health club, business center, beauty salon and barbershop, shopping arcade.

ROYAL RIVER HOTEL, 670/805 Charansanitwong Rd., Bangplao, Bangkokonoi, Bangkok 10700. Tel. 02/433-0200. Fax 02/433-5880. Telex 22048 RORIVER TH. 444 rms, 14 suites. A/C MINIBAR TEL TV **Directions:** On a small lane north of Rajchavitee Rd., west of the Krung Thon Bridge
$ Rates: 2,760B–3,840B ($110–$154) single; 3,100B–4,200B

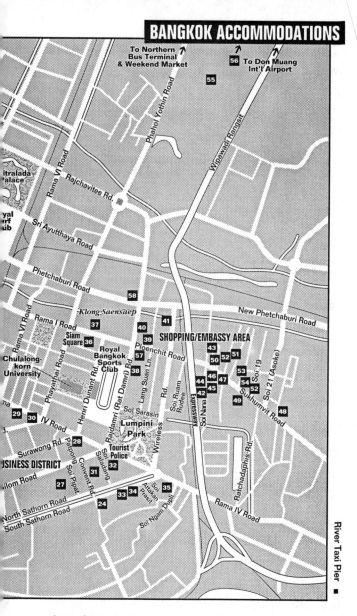

BANGKOK ACCOMMODATIONS

To Northern Bus Terminal & Weekend Market

56 To Don Muang Int'l Airport

55

Phahol Yothin Road

Wipawadi Rangsit

Rama VI Road

Rajchavitee Rd.

itralada palace

yal urf ub

Sri Ayutthaya Road

Phetchaburi Road

58

New Petchaburi Road

Klong Saensaep

Rama I Road

37

40 41

SHOPPING/EMBASSY AREA

Siam Square 36

39

Ploenchit Road

Rama VI Road

Royal Bangkok Sports Club

57

43

Chulalong-korn University

38

50 52 51

53

Henri Dunant Rd.

Lang Suan Ln.

44 46 47

54

na

29 30 IV Road

Rajdamri (Rat Damri) Rd.

42 45

52

Sukhumvit Road

48

Phayathai Road

Soi Ruam Rudee

49

Soi 19

Soi 21 (Asoke)

Sol Sarasin

Lumpini Park

Wireless Rd.

Expressway

Soi Nara

Ratchadapisk Rd.

28

Tourist Police

Surawong Rd.

Papono Convent Rd.

Salaoaeno

32

River Taxi Pier ■

USINESS DISTRICT

31

ilom Road

27

Convent Rd.

Soi Pipat

33 34

24

Soi Attakan Prasit

35

Rama IV Road

North Sathorn Road

South Sathorn Road

Soi Ngan Dupli

($124–$168) double; from 6,800B ($272) suite. Extra bed 480B ($19). AE, DC, MC, V.

It's a fairly long journey upriver to this northernmost of the river hotels—just north of the Krung Thon Bridge—but the Royal River offers free shuttle boats every other hour for the 20-minute ride to the River City Shopping Complex. (Don't even think about a taxi to this part of town.) There is an express-boat stop nearby for the short ride to the Grand Palace Area, but the major sights are close enough that a taxi ride would also be comfortably short.

The pool is so small that it would pass for a Jacuzzi at some other hotels, and we've never seen a less inviting pedestrian access (probably because few guests enter by foot, though the traditional neighborhood is quite interesting for a casual stroll). With these caveats, consider the Royal River for the good value of its riverview accommodations. The superior and deluxe rooms have an elegant Asian deco air, comfortably large balconies look down on the passing river traffic. Standard rooms, though well priced, are often worn and a tad shabby, victims of the group turnover that provides the bulk of this establishment's clientele.

Dining/Entertainment: Like most river hotels, this one has a Riverside Terrace with both a barbecue buffet and a menu offering international and Thai cuisine. The Natee Thong Restaurant specializes in Thai food, served buffet style at lunch. The Fang Nam Coffeehouse and Restaurant offers a wide range of choices.

Services: 24-hour room service, concierge, limousine service, babysitting, laundry service.

Facilities: Swimming pool, health club, business center, beauty salon and barbershop, shopping arcade.

MODERATE

BOSSOTEL INN, 55/8-9 Soi Charoen Krung 42/1, New Rd., Bangkok 10500. Tel. 02/235-8001. Fax 02/237-3225. 39 rms, 7 minisuites. A/C MINIBAR TEL TV **Directions:** Off New Rd., on Soi 42, on way to Shangri-La Hotel.

$ Rates: 1,075B–1,350B ($43–$54) single; 1,350B–1,600B ($54–$64) double. AE, MC, V.

Situated in the shadow of Bangkok's giants in the hotel world, this is one of those places that escape most budget travelers. It's not on the water and there isn't a view to speak of, but the spiffy, renovated new wing, in particular, warrants consideration.

Many of the guests are long-term visitors, and interestingly, quite a few are Orthodox Jews in the jewelry trade. This explains why, on our last visit, we discovered that the lobby restaurant served the only kosher food in Bangkok (see Section 6 of Chapter 5). The large rooms are Spartan, but up-to-date; facilities include a small business center and laundry service. The Bossotel's renovated wing (behind the slick glass entrance) is a better value than the older wing above the restaurant.

We'll let readers Ted and Dee Slosek from Pleasanton, California speak: "We had a delightful stay at the Bossotel. The room was spacious, clean, and comfortable—a good value for the price and only a few steps away from the Shangri-La and the Chao Phraya River. We found the staff to be pleasant, cordial, efficient, and helpful. The friendly greetings, care, and service we experienced here stood above any other of our entire stay in Bangkok."

INEXPENSIVE

RIVER VIEW GUEST HOUSE, 768 Soi Panurangsri, Songwat Rd., Sanjao Josuekong, Taladnoi, Bangkok 10100. Tel. 02/234-5429. Fax 02/236-6199. 44 rms. **Directions:** About 500 yards southeast of railroad station, between the intersection of Songwat and New Rds. and the river.

$ Rates (including tax and service): 255B ($10.20) single with fan; 515B ($20.60) double with fan; 770B ($30.80) single or double with A/C. MC, V.

As you might gather from the address, this special place deep in the heart of Chinatown, only 5 minutes from the railroad station, and a stone's throw from the river, is difficult to find! We stayed there 4 days during our last visit and grew to love the views of the river and a neighboring Chinese temple, but we're not sure we could find it again. Half of this guesthouse's appeal is the friendly staff; the other half is wandering through the neighboring sois, lanes, and labyrinthine alleys, asking everyone to point the way. There's a lot of variety in the quality, upkeep, and views from each room, so look first if you're lucky enough to arrive when there's more than one room open. However, breakfast in the eighth-floor restaurant, overlooking temples and the busy Chao Phraya, is truly special for everyone. How can you find it? Arrange with the airport taxi desk to explain the address to your driver, or have someone write it out for you in Thai; then, as soon as you get there, grab one of the River View Guest House business cards and keep it with you.

SWAN HOTEL, 31 Soi Charoen Krung 36, New Rd., Bangkok 10500. Tel. 02/234-8594. 72 rms. A/C (62 rms) TEL **Directions:** 2 sois north of The Oriental, off New Rd.

$ Rates (including tax and service): 425B ($17) single with fan, 650B ($26) air-conditioned single; 550B ($22) double with fan, 775B ($31) air-conditioned double. No credit cards.

Two budget travelers we met in Nepal discovered the Swan. The pool is large, there is a luggage checkroom as well as laundry service, and only 10 spacious guest rooms are without air-conditioning—all have toilets and showers, but with limited hot-water hours. Our only gripe is that many of the rooms, though clean, are worn and shabby. Look first before committing to a room, and check out the rear wing. If it meets your standard, you've found one of the few acceptable low-cost accommodations smack in the middle of Bangkok's Gold Coast.

2. HISTORIC BANGKOK — NEAR THE GRAND PALACE

Since our last visit, one new Chinatown hotel and several renovations have made staying in this part of town a real possibility. Most major tourist attractions are located here, making sightseeing by foot feasible and taxi rides mercifully short. There are fewer restaurant choices than in other areas, but for budget travelers, the widest range of lowest-price accommodations is found here.

EXPENSIVE

GRAND CHINA PRINCESS HOTEL, 215 Yaowaraj Rd., Samphantawongse, Bangkok 10100. Tel. 02/224-9977. Fax 02/224-7999. 133 rms, 22 suites. A/C MINIBAR TV TEL **Directions:** Corner off Ratchawong Rd., just south of New Rd.

$ Rates: 2,280B–2,400B ($91.20–$96) single; 2,520B–2,640B ($100.80–$105.60) double; from 6,000B ($240) suite. Extra bed 550B ($22). AE, DC, MC, V.

The hotel we, and many tourists, have been waiting for—luxurious yet affordable, close to many attractions, and only a five-minute walk from Ratchawong Pier and the Chao Phraya ferry system. Built amid the bustling shophouses and businesses of colorful Chinatown, the Grand China Princess begins 10 stories above a shopping arcade and Chinese restaurant. Rooms are modern, yet gracefully Oriental and very comfortable, with the amenities found in much more expensive hotels. The suites are especially roomy, and decorated in muted tones of rose and gray. The 25th floor features Bangkok's first revolving lounge, with spectacular views over the city and Chao Phraya River. Other facilities include a coffee shop, whose lavish buffet breakfast (200B/$8) is a real bargain; a fitness center; business center; and Chinese banquet restaurant.

ROYAL PRINCESS HOTEL, 269 Larn Luang Rd., Bangkok 10100. Tel. 02/281-3088. Fax 02/280-1314. Telex TH 87688 PRINCES. 165 rms, 5 suites. A/C MINIBAR TEL TV **Directions:** East of Wat Saket

$ Rates: 3,900B–4,300B ($156–$172) single; 4,300B–4,700B ($172–$188) double; from 7,800B ($312) suite; 4,800B–5,100B ($192–$204) Princess Club Rooms. Extra bed 700B ($28). AE, DC, MC, V.

⭐ Completed in 1989, this gem more than lives up to the high standards of the Thai Dusit Hotel family, and we recommend it to travelers whose main interest is the sights of old Bangkok. It's a 10-minute taxi ride to either the Grand Palace or the Vimanmek Mansion Museum, and though the area lacks the diversity of Western dining choices found in the Shopping/Embassy Area or the Business District, proximity to tourist attractions and the original flavor of this old neighborhood more than compensate.

Public spaces are wall-to-wall marble and bustling with activity, yet the scale is intimate. Rooms are very tastefully appointed in muted blues and grays, with marble bathrooms fully stocked with amenities. Higher-priced deluxe rooms have balconies overlooking the tropically landscaped pool, while the superior rooms of the same style look out over the neighborhood.

Dining/Entertainment: Food service here encompasses a plethora of riches, starting with the superb Cantonese cuisine of The Empress (see Section 2 of Chapter 5). The Mikado offers fine Japanese cuisine in a garden setting, with Piccolo providing Italian specialties. The Princess Café serves both Asian and Western food, with a sumptuous Thai buffet available at lunch.

Services: 24-hour room service, concierge, turndown service, limousine service, babysitting, laundry service.

Facilities: Swimming pool, business center, exercise room.

MODERATE

GOLDEN HORSE HOTEL, 5/1–2 Damrongrak Rd., Bangkok 10100. Tel. 02/280-1920. Fax 02/280-3404. 130 rms. A/C MINIBAR TEL TV **Direction:** North side of Klong Mahanak, near Wat Saket.

$ Rates: 1,350B ($54) single; 1,550B ($62) double. MC, V.

This small hotel is conveniently located just 1 block from the main Thai Airways International office and near the city's major tourist attractions. Because of Golden Horse's popularity with economy-minded tourists and small groups, the staff is helpful and ready to answer any questions. The marble lobby has seating areas and newspapers for guests, as well as a large restaurant serving moderately priced Thai food, plus some Chinese and continental favorites. Minibars and televisions grace the nondescript rooms, all simply furnished but well maintained. Higher-floor, south-facing rooms even have a view of nearby Wat Saket, the golden *chedi* on the mount.

HOTEL MAJESTIC PALACE, 97 Ratchadamnoen Klang Rd., Bangkok 10200. Tel. 02/280-5610. Fax 02/280-0965. 60 rms, 5 suites. A/C MINIBAR TEL TV **Directions:** Near Democracy Monument.

$ Rates: 1,680B ($67.20) single; 2,150B ($86) double; 3,600B ($144) junior suite. MC, V.

Bangkok's oldest hotel, built by King Rama V over 80 years ago in a grand Thai interpretation of colonial Victoriana, has been recently renovated to its former glory. Though not as flashy or convenience-filled as many of the new hotels, the Majestic Palace has a mature elegance that will please old Asia hands and those on sentimental journeys. The high-ceilinged marble lobby, with bay windows and a shrine to His Highness, reminds you that this property is still in the hands of the royal family.

The friendly management offers compact pastel-toned rooms with carved teak headboards, pink-marble bathrooms with hair-dryers, cozy seating areas, and sepia photos of old Bangkok. The corner junior suites have writing desks, as well as larger sitting areas, and they overlook Bangkok's Champs-Elysées. (Request an avenue-facing room both for the view and for the size. Double-glazed windows blunt the traffic noise.)

Dining/Entertainment: The glass-enclosed café looks out onto the avenue and serves moderately priced Thai, Chinese, and continental cuisine.

Services: 24-hour room service, concierge, limousine service, laundry service.

ROYAL HOTEL, 2 Ratchadamnoen Klang Rd., Bangkok 10200. Tel. 02/222-9111. Fax 02/224-2083. Telex 84252 ROYALTHO TH. 130 rms. A/C MINIBAR TEL TV **Directions:** 2 blocks east of National Museum.

$ Rates: 1,150B ($46) single; 1,560B ($62.40) double. AE, MC, V.

The venerable Royal, near Thammasat University and a 5-minute walk from the Grand Palace, is perfect for budget-minded sightseers.

The hotel's glitzy lobby, with polished marble floors, chandeliers, and massive modern white Corinthian columns, was a field hospital during the May 1991 democracy demonstrations. Now, it's again abuzz with guests from around the world. The simpler old wing's large staircase and other architectural details date from the art deco era. Other aspects of the Royal harken back to the 1950s, so that the overall effect is of an architectural pastiche that would make Robert Venturi proud.

Clean, kitschy (pink ruffled polyester Chinese bedspreads) doubles in the old wing have high ceilings and are quite spacious. Request a room that faces away from the noisy street. The nondescript new wing has comfortable, already-worn accommodations that are usually presold to group tours. Many of these rooms overlook the small pool. Facilities include a multinational-cuisine restaurant, an inexpensive 24-hour coffee shop, a tour desk, and several shops off the lobby. The reception desk can help arrange babysitters.

BUDGET

BUDDY GUESTHOUSE, 137/1 Khao San Rd., Banglamphu, Bangkok 10200. Tel. 02/282-4351. 40 rms. **Directions:** Between Chakkra Phong Rd. and Tanao Rd.
$ Rates (including tax and service): 120B ($4.80) single; 240B ($10) double. No credit cards.

This is not our number-one choice, but if everything else is fully booked, try this popular spot. Satisfied guests have told us that their tiny rooms were clean (the place was full and management wouldn't let us in for an inspection) and that all have private toilets and shower stalls. There's a ground-floor snack bar that serves cheap meals and provides ample opportunity for swapping travelers' tales.

LEK GUESTHOUSE, 125–127 Khao San Rd., Banglamphu, Bangkok 10200. Tel. 02/281-2775. 20 rooms (all with common bath). **Directions:** Near Chakkra Phong Rd.
$ Rates (including tax and service): 100B ($4) single; 175B ($7) double. No credit cards.

What distinguishes the Lek from its neighbors in a row of guesthouses is that it's slightly more dependable. The accommodations are as basic as can be—small partitions, all with fans—but most guests we spoke with felt that the proprietor and family work hard to make guests feel at home. The place has a safe for storing valuables, a simple roof terrace, free luggage storage for guests who have checked out, laundry facilities, and a few balconies. For a quiet night, request a room away from the street.

NITH CHAROEN HOTEL, 183 Khao San Rd., Banglamphu, Bangkok, 10200. Tel. 02/281-9872. 25 rms. A/C **Directions:** Between Chakkra Phong Rd. and Tanao Rd.
$ Rates (including tax and service): 385B ($15.40) single or double; 435B ($17.30) triple. No credit cards.

⑤ Set back from busy Khao San Road, this well-maintained guesthouse is a good choice if you're willing to pay a higher price for a quieter and cleaner place. We liked it for the fresh coat of paint, the higher moral tone, and the friendly staff. All rooms even have a simple cold-water Asian bath, as well as a toilet and shower.

PEACHY GUESTHOUSE, 10 Phra Arthit Rd., Banglamphu, Bangkok 10200. Tel. 02/281-6471. 35 rms. **Directions:** 1 block from Phra Arthit Express Boat Pier.
$ Rates (including tax and service): 110B ($4.40) single with fan; 155B ($6.20) double with fan. No credit cards.

This large, comfortable guesthouse is one of the most popular for the price. Rooms are stacked in a U-shaped block around a courtyard where breakfast and snacks are served. Large, bright rooms are Spartan but clean, most with ceiling fans. Communal toilets and cold-water showers on each floor are kept very clean. Peachy also has a funky lounge on each floor where fellow travelers can hang out. This place serves a budget crowd more mature than that found in the Khao San Road guesthouses—Peace Corps and UNICEF workers, as well as families.

P.S. GUESTHOUSE, 9 Phra Sumeru Rd., Chanasongkrom Pranakorn, Bangkok 10200. Tel. 02/282-3932. 50 rms.
Directions: 2 blocks from Phra Arthit Express Boat Pier.
$ Rates (including tax and service): 110B ($4.40) single; 165B ($6.70) double. No credit cards.

Near the Peachy Guesthouse, with a city-view roof garden, the P.S. is another in the Spartan but clean category. The small rooms barely give you walking space around the twin beds, but there are fans, screened windows, storage lockers, and washed linens for each, as well as scrubbed-clean toilets and cold showers down the hall. Rooms start on the second floor, above the simple Evergreen Restaurant. You'll find the higher floors and klong-view rooms to be quieter. The extra perk here is cheap in-house laundry plus the Washy Mashy Laundromat across the street, where a full load costs only 85B ($3.40) if you do it, 115B ($4.60) if they do.

READERS RECOMMEND

Shanti Lodge, Si Ayutthaya Rd. (Tel. 02/281-2497).
"The Peachy Guesthouse was always full so I went to the Merry V. right next door. It had a public restaurant/hanging-out space downstairs and a more clean-cut, somewhat older crowd. But I heard about guesthouses in the National Library area, and a South African couple I met (professors both) loved the Shanti Lodge, off Sri Ayutthaya Road, just west of Sam Sen Road. It has vegetarian food and they thought it had a wonderful atmosphere, very clean and very cheap." —Ariel Zeitlin, New York, NY.

3. THE BUSINESS DISTRICT

VERY EXPENSIVE

DUSIT THANI, Rama IV Rd., Bangkok 10500. Tel. 02/236-0450. Fax 02/236-6400. Telex TH 81170. 487 rms, 33 suites. A/C MINIBAR TEL TV **Directions:** At corner of Silom Rd., opposite Lumpini Park.
$ Rates: 6,300B ($252) single or double; 8,000B ($320) Landmark single or double; from 12,000B ($480) suite. Extra bed 1,200B ($48). AE, DC, MC, V.

Gurgling lobby fountains, exotic flower displays, and a poolside waterfall cascading through dense foliage make this top-rated hotel a welcome retreat at the end of a day's business appointments or sightseeing. Dusit Thani literally means "town in heaven."

Luxurious, well-lit rooms are adorned with Thai arts and architectural details, and use traditional materials such as mutmee silk and teakwood. The Landmark Tower rooms are extremely large and include butler service; complimentary daily fresh fruit, flowers, and English-language newspapers; bathrobes and slippers; hairdryers; and large baths and separate massage showers. Complimentary breakfast and drinks are available to guests in the Landmark Lounge.

Dining/Entertainment: Among the hotel's nine restaurants, the Mayflower and the Benjarong are ranked among the finest restaurants in Bangkok (see Section 3 of Chapter 5). The top-floor French-cuisine Tiara Restaurant has a sensational view over the city. The popular Pavilion Coffeeshop, with fine international buffets and "light" cuisine, and the Chinatown Restaurant are lesser-priced establishments. There are also a steak house, a new Vietnamese restaurant, and Japanese eateries; the latter especially popular with businessmen. Bubbles Videotheque draws a high-class local crowd as well as guests.

Services: 24-hour room service, concierge, house doctor, limousine service, babysitting, laundry/valet.

Facilities: Fitness center with gymnasium, tennis and squash courts, attractively landscaped swimming pool, business center, barbershop and beauty salon, shopping arcade, bakery/gourmet shop.

THE SUKHOTHAI, 13/3 Sathorn Rd., Bangkok 10120. Tel. 02/287-0222. Fax 02/287-4980. 146 rms, 76 suites. A/C MINIBAR TV TEL **Directions:** South of Rama IV Rd. next to the YMCA.

$ Rates: 5,200B–6,600B ($208–$264) single or double; from 9,000B ($360) suite. Extra bed 700B ($28). AE, DC, MC, V.

The stunning new Sukhothai, a property of the prestigious Beaufort Group from Singapore, brings unexpected luxury to a noisy, busy locale better known for the neighboring low-budget YWCA and YMCA hostels. Nonetheless, once you've left Sathorn Road behind for one of the Sukhothai's five white pavilions, peace reigns supreme. The hotel's Thai minimalist aesthetic bathes visitors in a welcome, if studied, serenity. Every design element contributes to a heightened sense of drama throughout. The broad, colonnaded public spaces are decorated with mud- and olive-toned silk panels, woven to fit this unique space. Bronze metalwork is brushed a dull black, so as not to clash with the redbrick stupas and sculpture that quietly accent black-tiled wading pools. Terra-cotta friezes, stupa-shaped wall sconces, and celadon ceramics and tiles evoke memories of the ancient kingdom of Sukhothai. The work of master designer Ed Tuttle (maestro of Phuket's Amanpuri and Bali's Amandari resorts), it is truly quite beautiful.

Guest-room pavilions overlook lotus ponds inspired by the gardens of the Sukhothai era. Teak and cinnabar-accented rooms strive for the latest in luxury: reclining chaises, butler service, electronic DO NOT DISTURB signs and automatic doorbell override, two full-size teak closets, separate shower stall in granite bathrooms, personal fax machines installed on request, and terraces with the Garden Suites. Though gorgeous design is the Sukhothai's most obvious attribute, guests commend its excellent service and assured sense of privacy.

Dining/Entertainment: There are many stylish dining venues. The less formal Colonnade (is coffee shop a wild misnomer?) is most popular at Sunday brunch, when local jazz bands play while guests cruise the deluxe international buffet (500B/$20). The exterior Terrazzo serves *nuova italiana* under big Japanese umbrellas by the pool; formal French fare is dished up at lunch (Monday to Friday only) or dinner (nightly) in La Noppamas's elegant silver and beige dining room. Celadon is the gourmet Thai restaurant, housed in a pavilion perched above a water garden.

Services: Room service, 24-hour butler service, concierge, house doctor, limousine service, babysitting, laundry.

Facilities: Olympic-size swimming pool, health club, two squash and one tennis court, business center, Guerlain beauty salon, upscale shopping arcade where reproductions of some of the hotel's design motifs are sold.

EXPENSIVE

HOLIDAY INN CROWNE PLAZA, 981 Silom Rd., Bangkok 10500. Tel. 02/238-4300. Fax 02/238-5289. Telex 82998 HIBKK TH. 726 rms, 28 suites. A/C MINIBAR TEL TV **Directions:** On Silom Rd., 1 block above New Rd.

$ Rates: 3,800B–4,800B ($152–$192) single, 5,275B ($211) Executive Club singles; 4,300B–5,300B ($172–$211) double, 6,000B ($240) Executive Club Crowne double; from 7,200B ($288) suite. Extra person 600B ($24). Children under 19 stay free in parents' room. AE, DC, MC. V.

If you've never been to a Holiday Inn outside the United States, you're in for a shock, and this from the company that promises "no surprises."

The entrance to the gleaming white-marble lobby is on the second floor, isolated from the street noise and traffic of busy Silom Road (it's only a short walk to the Shangri-la Hotel and The Oriental). The lobby links the Holiday Inn's two towers.

Rooms in the Plaza Tower represent an excellent value. The most distinctive aspect of their design is the oversized porthole windows that look out over the city. Although the rooms are less spacious than those in the Crowne Tower, high ceilings make the space feel quite large. A soothing gray-and-white color scheme and quality amenities give the impression of deluxe accommodations, but at a standard-room price. The Crowne Tower offers up-to-date, high-end quarters worthy of nearly any hotel in Bangkok. Our deluxe king room had a large walk-in closet, a marble bathroom with glassed-in corner shower (and separate bath), and all of the amenities one associates with the best in town. Although few rooms have a genuine river view, the upper-floor rooms do command a fine panorama from their angled bay windows.

Managing the facilities is a genuinely helpful and good-humored staff (we had a hilarious incident with a jammed safe that brought an army of technicians to solve the problem, reminding us of the Marx Brothers' *Monkey Business*). And, if you have children under 19 and can stand to room with them, they stay free.

Dining/Entertainment: One of Bangkok's better breakfast buffets is served in the Window on Silom restaurant. In the afternoon the hotel serves a lovely high tea in the Orchid Lounge. Lunch and dinner are well prepared in the Thai Pavilion, and an evening drink at the Cheers Pub makes a welcome end to a tiring day (see Section 3 of Chapter 9). The Tandoor (see Section 3 of Chapter 5) is a Moghul kitchen that turns out fine vegetarian and tandoori dishes.

Services: 24-hour room service, concierge, complimentary welcome tea, limousine service, babysitting, laundry service.

Facilities: Swimming pool, health club, tennis courts, business center, beauty salon and barbershop, shopping arcade.

THE MANDARIN BANGKOK, 662 Rama IV Rd., Bangkok 10120. Tel. 02/234-1390. Fax 02/237-1620. Telex TH 87689. 400 rms. A/C MINIBAR TEL TV **Directions:** East of Si Phraya Rd.

$ Rates: 3,200B–3,700B ($128–$148) single; 3,500B–4,000B ($140–$160) double; 6,600B ($264) suite. Extra bed 480B ($19.20). AE, DC, MC, V.

The Mandarin, a property of the Dutch Golden Tulip Hotels Group, is a glitzy full-service hotel convenient to the sights. Though perhaps better known in Bangkok for its nightclub (wildly popular with locals on weekends) than for its rooms, accommodations here are clean, modern, and spacious, done in a luminous white-and-gray color scheme. Double-pane windows cut down on street noise. Rates vary with size and decor, but all rooms represent good value. European tour groups give the place an international flavor, especially in the lively lobby, whose decor combines velvet-upholstered reproductions of Asian and European antiques with polished-brass doors and glittering chandeliers. The hotel's pool is small, often shrouded in shade, and noisy from the nearby traffic.

Dining/Entertainment: The queen of Bangkok cocktail lounges is the Nile Night Club (see Section 2 of Chapter 9). It and the 24-hour coffee shop (also with live bands!) are open nightly, but the real action takes place on weekends.

Services: 24-hour room service, concierge, limousine service, babysitting, laundry service.

Facilities: Small swimming pool, business center, beauty salon and barbershop, shopping arcade.

MANOHRA HOTEL, 412 Surawong Rd., Bangkok 10500. Tel. 02/234-5070. Fax 02/237-7662. Telex TH 82114. 242 rms, 8 suites. A/C MINIBAR TEL TV **Directions:** Between New Rd. and Mahesak Rd.

$ Rates: 2,650B–2,900B ($106–$116) single or double; from 4,800B ($192) suite. Rollaway bed 600B ($24). AE, DC, MC. V.

The bright and fetching Manohra Hotel, a 5-minute walk from The Oriental (hotel) and the Chao Phraya River, is a modern, quiet oasis with a pleasant coffee shop overlooking this busy street. The glass- and stone-sheathed lobby faces a small indoor swimming pool, contributing to the glitzy appearance of the public spaces. Guest rooms, on the other hand, are rather dimly lit and tend to be smaller than those in other first-class hotels. However, they have a full range of amenities and are often booked by European tours.

THE MONTIEN, 54 Surawong Rd., Bangkok 10500. Tel. 02/233-7060. Fax 02/236-5219. Telex TH 81160. 460 rms, 40 suites. A/C MINIBAR TEL TV **Directions:** Near Patpong.

$ Rates: 4,800B–6,725B ($192–$269) single; 5,275B–7,200B ($211–$288) double; from 9,600B ($384) suite. AE, DC, EU, MC, V.

Like many of the first-class tourist hotels that are attempting to break into the Bangkok business market, The Montien is really two facilities in one. The first caters to its traditional clientele—mainly Australian groups, who occupy the lower floors of one of the hotel's two wings, with its dark-teak hallways and bright, pleasant rooms. The other wing has been thoroughly upgraded and renamed the Executive Club, with dark teak giving way to bleached wood, gray granite, and matching gray carpet. The elegantly furnished Executive Club commons, adjoining the business center, serves complimentary continental breakfast and, in the evening, free drinks. The new decor and near-Patpong location have, apparently, lured Japanese businesspeople to The Montien. Whether the hotel justifies the additional 40% is up to you, but we were impressed with the fine facilities and services in the upgraded wing.

Unique in Bangkok is the hotel's Montientong Theater, where Thai and international plays are produced. And if that's not enough to sway you, how about the 20 in-house fortune-tellers, who offer their prognostications on the mezzanine level for approximately 350B ($14) per reading and are widely consulted by Bangkok residents.

Dining/Entertainment: The Montien has an in-house bakery and good French and Chinese outlets. Our favorite (and popular on Bangkok's social scene) is the Jade Garden Cantonese restaurant.

Services: 24-hour room service, concierge, complimentary welcome tea, house doctor, limousine service, babysitting, laundry service, fortune-telling.

Facilities: Swimming pool, health club, tennis courts, business center, beauty salon and barbershop, shopping arcade, theater.

NEW PENINSULA HOTEL, 295/3 Surawong Rd., Bangkok 10500. Tel 02/234-3910. Fax 02/236-5526. Telex 84079 PENNINHO TH. 110 rms. A/C MINIBAR TEL TV **Directions:** Near Mahesak Rd.

$ Rates (including service): 2,400B–2,750B ($96–$110) single; 2,600B–3,000B ($104–$120) double; 4,200B–5,400B ($168–$216) suite. AE, DC, M, V.

The best of the "New" chain—including the neighboring New Fuji and the sorely neglected New Trocadero—really is almost new. That is to say, it was redone in 1990 and now features a small outdoor pool with an adjacent beer garden and soothing waterfall.

The rooms are small, basic, but well maintained, if not brightly opulent. At night the lobby-level Krua Thep Restaurant comes alive with local bands performing to a very young and appreciative local clientele; the music plays from 9pm to 1am (keep the hours in mind if you're a light sleeper). Judging from the listed price, we think there are better values in the neighborhood; but if you're stuck, bargain a little, and the New Peninsula becomes an acceptable choice.

TRINITY CITY HOTEL, 425 Silom, Soi 5, Bangkok 10500. Tel. 02/231-5050. Fax 02/231-5417. 110 rms, 4 suites. A/C MINIBAR TEL TV **Directions:** 2 blocks east of Silom Rd. on Soi 5.

$ Rates: 2,500B ($100) single; 2,800B ($112) double; 3,200B ($128) suite. Extra bed 350B ($14). AE, DC, MC, V.

At the quiet end of "Can't Keep Your Money" Lane (famous among Bangkokians for its many and various bargains), you'll find the most pleasant small mid-price hotel in town. It has the marble lobby and tastefully furnished rooms of a large hotel, with the intimacy of a smaller European establishment. The staff is charming, friendly, and helpful. The 24-hour coffee shop has good food and service at very reasonable prices; there's a supermarket a few doors up and several nearby restaurants. The rooftop swimming pool in an adjacent tower, a fitness center, beauty shop, massage and sauna, together with easy access to both the Silom Road business and shopping activity and the river, make this top o' the class for both comfort and convenience.

MODERATE

YMCA COLLINS INTERNATIONAL HOUSE, 27 S. Sathorn Rd., Bangkok 10120. Tel. 02/287-1900. Fax 02/287-1966. Telex 72185 BHMCA TH. 258 rms, 3 one-bedroom suites. A/C TEL TV **Directions:** 4km (2.5 miles) south of Rama IV Rd.

$ Rates (plus 7% tax; no service charge): 1,300B–1,600B ($52–$63) single; 1,450B–2,000B ($58–$80) double; 2,800B ($112) suite. AE, MC, V.

⭐ This is a good value in the moderate price range, with no compromise in comfort. Imagine a modern nine-story hotel with sparkling, homey rooms, a 75-foot swimming pool, and multiethnic restaurant service, all tucked into a quiet lane off Sathorn Road, near the Dusit Thani hotel and the Business District. Both staff and clientele are very friendly. The Y's front desk offers copy, fax, telex, and secretarial services, and our friends Joan and David claim that the Rossukon Restaurant has the most delicious and varied buffet in town, at a bargain price. All rooms have private showers. A new wing houses another restaurant, gym, and 120 more-deluxe rooms featuring TVs, minibars, and full bathtubs, though at higher prices. Families should note that this YMCA even has one-bedroom suites—a Bangkok best buy.

SURIWONGSE TOWER INN, Executive House Building, 410/3-4 Surawong Rd., Bangrak, Bangkok 10500. Tel. 02/235-1206. Fax 02/237-1482. 80 rms. A/C MINIBAR TV TEL **Directions:** Between New Rd. and Mahesak Rd.

$ Rates: 1,450B–1,700B ($58–$68) single; 1,500–1,800B ($60–$72) double; from 4,000B ($80) suite. Extra bed 250B ($10). AE, MC, V.

This establishment is difficult to find because it comprises the 14th to 18th floors of the modern Executive House condominium tower, in a cul-de-sac off of noisy Surawong Road. Don't be put off—it's a good value for families who will make use of its oversize rooms (formerly apartments), with their small balconies (great Chao Phraya views), well-kept bathrooms, and simple, eclectic international modern furnishings. That each room offers its unique odd leatherette armchair, wall-to-wall carpeting, flower-print bed linens, parquet floors, or mirrored bar area only contributes to the residential feeling exuded here. Although worn in a homey way, the Suriwongse Tower is well maintained, with a nice staff and a small coffee shop on the ground floor.

WALL STREET INN, 37/20–24 Surawong Rd., Soi Surawong Plaza, Bangkok 10500. Tel. 02/233-4164. Fax 02/236-3619. 75 rms. A/C MINIBAR TEL TV **Directions:** Between Surawong Rd. and Silom Rd., around corner from Patpong Rd.

$ Rates: 2,000B–2,800B ($80–$112) single; 2,300B–3,100B ($92–$124) double. Rollaway bed 500B ($20). AE, DC, MC, V.

This six-floor hotel, tucked in a Japanese restaurant–lined street near the modern Wall Street Tower Building, is an efficient operation quite popular with Japanese and European businesspeople on a budget. The lobby is small and bustling, with a very active coffee shop adjacent to the check-in desk. The compact guest rooms are fairly dark (even those with windows have no view to speak of), but they are quite clean and are fitted with a full range of amenities. With 24-hour room service, limousine service, babysitting, laundry service, and a business center, the Wall Street Inn offers many big-hotel advantages at a moderate price.

INEXPENSIVE

BANGKOK CHRISTIAN GUESTHOUSE, 123 Saladaeng, Soi 2, Convent Rd., Bangkok 10500. Tel. 02/233-6303. Fax 02/237-1742. 36 rms, 1 suite. A/C TEL **Directions:** 1 block east of Silom Rd., off corner of Convent Rd.

$ Rates (including breakfast): 770B ($30.80) single; 1,150B ($46) double. Extra person 350B ($14). No credit cards.

This tranquil two-story guesthouse, originally a Presbyterian missionary residence, was converted in the late 1960s into a lodge with a "family atmosphere of Christian concern," operated by the Church of Christ in Thailand. Large recently refurbished accommodations are simple but spotless. The nicest rooms are on the second floor overlooking the large lawn with its sitting area, goldfish pond, and teak pavilion. You'll also find a grandma-style lounge, a library, a cheap restaurant (meals by reservation only) and a friendly young staff. There's a definite Christian atmosphere here, and it's so comfy, in fact, that it's usually booked four to six weeks in advance; so plan ahead.

BANGKOK YWCA, 13 Sathorn Rd., Bangkok 10120. Tel. 02/286-3310. 46 rms (10 with shared bath). A/C **Directions:** 100 yd. south of Rama IV Rd.

$ Rates (including tax and service): 680B ($27.20) single; 820B ($32.80) double. Rooms with common shower 50B ($2) less. No credit cards.

The venerable YWCA has come of age, offering clean, simple rooms to women, men, and couples. It would be hard, if not impossible, to top this Y for value. There is a pool, beauty salon, tour desk, and common TV lounge. To top it off, there is a canteen/snack bar and a cozy, very popular full-service restaurant where two can dine for less than 225B ($9). Did we forget to mention the YWCA Cooking School, or the Sri Pattana Thai Language School? A solid value for short- or long-term visitors.

MALAYSIA HOTEL, 54 Soi Ngam Dupli, Rama IV Rd., Bangkok 10120. Tel and fax 02/287-1457. 120 rms. A/C MINIBAR TEL TV **Directions:** On small soi south of Rama IV Rd., east of Sathorn Rd.

$ Rates (including tax and service): 600B ($24) single; 725B ($29) double. AE, MC, V.

The Malaysia was Bangkok's best-known budget hotel for years, after being immortalized in Tony Wheeler's *Southeast Asia on a Shoestring*. Though it still plays host to some round-the-world backpackers, who rely on its once-famous bulletin board to communicate with friends and explore the scene, it has embraced the ubiquitous tour group (mainly Yugoslavian) and installed a courteous uniformed lobby staff. The hotel even supplies soap and towels to the freshly painted but still shabby rooms. The Malai Coffee Shop's continental breakfast is still a bargain, but be sure to avoid a room above the (late) nightclub.

4. THE SHOPPING/EMBASSY AREA

This wide-ranging area covers the hotels on either side of Sukhumvit/Ploenchit/Rama I Road. Many of the major shopping centers and stores are found here. The river is not so far away, but the taxi ride to the Grand Palace Area can be more than an hour at peak traffic times.

From the many choices in this top-dollar price range, three world-class hotels now vie for your patronage. The youngest candidate, the Grand Hyatt Erawan, is big and splashy and sure to impress. The low-rise, friendly Hilton International offers the prettiest pool and gardens and the best food in town. The luxurious Regent, Bangkok prides itself on understated elegance and impeccable service. Each has its devotees, and you won't go wrong at any of them. See below for more details.

VERY EXPENSIVE

GRAND HYATT ERAWAN BANGKOK, 494 Rajdamri Rd., Bangkok 10330. Tel. 02/254-1234. Fax 02/253-5856. Telex 20975 HYAT BKKTH. 362 rms, 38 suites. A/C MINIBAR TV TEL
Directions: Corner of Rama I Rd.
$ Rates: 5,900B–6,500B ($236–$260) single or double; 7,200B ($288) Regency Club single or double; from 9,000B ($360) suite. Extra bed 700B ($28). AE, DC, MC, V.

A grand hotel has risen anew at the site of Bangkok's famed Erawan shrine, the bustling, open-air temple dedicated to the four-headed Brahma, Tan Thao Mahaprom. Beyond the portal guarded by two bronze Erawans, dozens of banyan trees dapple the light pouring into a four-story atrium lobby. The air is filled with the sounds of waterfalls and gurgling goldfish ponds. Modeled after the residential gardens of a Thai mansion, it's just part of the grandness at the aptly named new Hyatt.

Although it aims to lure expense-account business travelers (the brochure even claims that the hotel's proximity to the shrine may bring luck in business!), the Hyatt Erawan is a luxurious choice for all travelers. The works of dozens of contemporary Thai artists grace hallways and spacious rooms, where earth-toned silks, celadon accessories, antique-finish furnishings, parquet floors, Oriental rugs, large bathrooms, and city views abound. The three Regency Club levels feature a lounge for continental breakfast, day-long coffee and tea service, cocktails, butler service, and private entertainment units with a library of CDs and videos. Suites include additional amenities such as pantries for entertaining, Jacuzzis, a sauna with built-in TV, and in the Presidential Suite, another grand—a baby grand piano!

In addition to the facilities one expects from a five-star hotel, there is a delightful fifth-floor pool terrace, where a waterfall tumbles down a rocky wall into a full-size hot tub. The teak Sala Thai, surrounded by fountains, is used for cocktails, and the casual, fan-cooled café services pool guests and health club members.

Dining/Entertainment: The pleasant lobby restaurant features a grand buffet at breakfast, lunch, and dinner, as well as a continental à la carte menu and a high tea. Spasso is the Hyatt's trendy Italian bistro cum jazz bar, a popular local hangout (see Section 4 of Chapter 5). The stunning high-style deco Chinese Restaurant is a gourmand's delight and worthy of a special trip (see Section 4 of Chapter 5). The basement shopping arcade features a pastry and cappuccino parlor.

Services: 24-hour room service, concierge, limousine service, house doctor, babysitting, laundry.

Facilities: Swimming pool, large health club with jogging track, tennis and squash courts, business center, beauty salon and barbershop, rooftop heliport, shopping arcade.

HILTON INTERNATIONAL AT NAI LERT PARK, 2 Wireless Rd., Bangkok 10330. Tel. 02/253-0123. Fax 02/253-6509. Telex 72206 HILBKK TH. 306 rms, 37 suites. A/C MINIBAR TEL TV **Directions:** Between Ploenchit Rd. and New Phetchaburi Rd.

$ Rates: 5,300B–5,800B ($212–$232) single; 5,900B–6,600B ($236–264) double; from 10,800B ($432) suite. Garden room 600B ($24) extra. Executive Floor: 6,600B ($264) single; 7,200B ($288) double. Extra person 1,200B ($48). AE, DC, MC, V.

Set in lushly landscaped Nai Lert Park, near the British and American embassies, this tropical paradise is something of a mixed blessing—you will sleep far from the madding crowd, but you may find the taxi ride to the river or tourist sights a minor nuisance (though the brave will ride the convenient klong boat to the Grand Palace Area). However, after a long day of business or sightseeing, returning to the peaceful tranquillity of the Hilton has the very comfortable feeling of returning home. The airy atrium lobby, distinctly Thai-modern in design, is at once elegant and friendly. With its classic teak pavilion and open garden views, it ranks as one of the great public spaces in Bangkok.

The spacious guest rooms all have bougainvillea-draped balconies, the most preferred (and expensive) of which overlook the free-form pool and parklike grounds. Handsome Thai cotton prints cover the comfortable rattan armchairs. All-marble bathrooms feature not one but two bathrobes (one light cotton, one heavier terrycloth), slippers, and hairdryers. Fruit baskets greet all newcomers, and treats of candy, Thai sweets, sushi, or cakes arrive unexpectedly at your door.

The fifth floor is dedicated to busy executives who don't mind the premium price for amenities such as complimentary continental breakfast, drinks served in the private lounge, and 24-hour butler service. The Hilton's professional and friendly staff is a decided plus on all floors and especially accommodating to our energetic toddler. The Hilton offers periodic special-rate weekends, which include rooms and meal packages at a very attractive price.

Dining/Entertainment: Food service is outstanding and very good value. The so called "coffee shop," Suan Saranom, is really a grand dining area overlooking the garden. Though serving both Thai and continental dishes, it has, for many years, been voted the best Thai restaurant in a Bangkok hotel. (It also serves up the champion breakfast buffet in all of Thailand.) The elegant Ma Maison offers excellent French cuisine at reasonable prices and ranks among the top Western restaurants in the city (see Section 4 of Chapter 5). Completing the offerings are Genji Restaurant, a Japanese country inn (see Section 4 of Chapter 5); a cozy lobby bar; and an evening poolside grill. On Sunday the sumptuous brunch buffet includes lots of balloons, and pool privileges for parents and children alike.

Services: 24-hour room service, concierge, limousine service, house doctor, babysitting, laundry service.

Facilities: World-class swimming pool, fitness center with tennis and squash courts, business center, beauty salon and barbershop, shopping arcade.

LANDMARK HOTEL, 138 Sukhumvit Rd., Bangkok 10110. Tel. 02/254-0404. Fax 02/253-4259. Telex TH 72341. 360 rms, 55 suites. A/C MINIBAR TEL TV **Directions:** Between Soi 4 and Soi 6.

$ Rates: 5,800B–6,400B ($232–$256) single; 6,000B–6,700B ($240–$268) double; from 8,400B ($336) suite. Extra bed 720B ($28.80). AE, CB, DC, MC, V.

If you can tear yourself away from the myriad shops and restaurants on the first 9 floors of this contemporary glass tower, you'll find attractive rooms on the next 20 floors. The more spacious corner deluxe rooms, with dueling grand views, teak trim, and pastel-upholstered sitting areas, are the best value. Night owls will appreciate the video text system, which connects the TV monitor to a keyboard in every room and a computer in the business center, displays phone messages, transmits faxes, accesses airline schedules and databases, and allows you to track your hotel account. It's a minor amenity, but fun just the same. Don't be seduced by the "Studio Room" rate, which for less money will give you a room without windows.

Dining/Entertainment: You can start at the top of the tower and eat your way down through seven restaurants, beginning with the Rib Room Grill on the 31st floor, with its grand views toward the distant river and a menu matching its name. On the same floor is the Hibiscus Room, an elegant Thai and seafood restaurant with views over the Sukhumvit Area. Farther down the tower, you can sample KiKu No Hana Restaurant (Japanese), Nipa (Thai), Sui Sian Restaurant (Chinese), the Atrium (continental buffet), and the 24-hour street-level Greenhouse, a popular night munching spot for hungry locals.

Services: 24-hour room service, concierge, limousine service, babysitting (with notice), doctor (on call), laundry service, safe in room.

Facilities: Pool with sun deck and bar, Jacuzzi, health club, squash court, 24-hour business center, beauty salon and barbershop, shopping arcade.

NOVOTEL BANGKOK, Soi 6, Siam Sq., Bangkok 10330. Tel. 02/255-6888. Fax 02/255-1824. Telex TH 22780. 393 rms, 36 suites. A/C MINIBAR TEL TV **Directions:** In Siam Sq., off Rama I Rd.

$ Rates: 4,900B ($196) single; 5,400B–6,200B ($216–$249) double; from 7,000B ($283) suite. Extra bed 600B ($24). AE, DC, MC, V.

Elegant and opulent, this slickly built high-rise hotel represents one of this French chain's best places to stay. The entrance, with a mountain of granite and marble plus expansive glass walls, has been designed on a grand scale. The public-room decor contrasts gray stone with soft-pink leather-upholstered sofas and chairs. The pastel tones carry over into the guest quarters, where rooms are spacious and fully equipped. Among our favorite facilities are the 18th-floor no-smoking suites and the full-featured business center that overlooks the kidney-shaped pool. Novotel's fitness center is as slick as the lobby. The hotel's location isn't ideal for visiting Bangkok's traditional tourist sites, but if you're in town on business or prefer being in one of Bangkok's better shopping areas, the Novotel is a very fine choice.

Dining/Entertainment: The Pastel Lounge (what else could they call it?) serves a delicious continental breakfast and afternoon tea; in the evening, there is a string quartet. Chinese, Thai, seafood, and Western food is available in the hotel's other dining outlets.

Services: 24-hour room service, concierge, house doctor, limousine service, babysitting, laundry service.

Facilities: No-smoking floor, swimming pool, health club, business center, bakery, beauty salon and barbershop.

THE REGENT, BANGKOK, 155 Rajdamri Rd., Bangkok 10330. Tel. 02/251-6127. Fax 02/253-9195. Telex 20004 REGBKK TH. 400 rms. A/C MINIBAR TEL TV **Directions:** South of Rama I Rd.

$ Rates: 5,400B–7,800B ($216–$312) single or double; from 9,600B ($384) suite. AE, DC, MC, V.

The starkly modern Regent, Bangkok feels like home to all who have sampled this chain's other deluxe accommodations in the United States or Asia. The cavernous lobby, with its high ceilings and vast mural depicting 200 years of Bangkok history, constantly hums with activity and is always colorfully decorated for the festival of the season. The impeccable service begins at the registration desk, where guests are greeted. They are then whisked off to complete check-in in their rooms. Complimentary Chinese tea soon follows, joining the fruit basket and box of chocolates.

An air of luxury pervades each room, with amenities such as cotton robes, slippers, a scale, and an umbrella tucked in the plush, carpeted dressing area off the tiled bath. Cool pastel-upholstered couches and armchairs invite windowside lounging, especially if your room overlooks the verdant Royal Bangkok Sports Club and Race Track. The recently built cabanas, with double doors opening onto a landscaped lawn and teak lounge chairs overlooking the pool, evoke a nouvelle grandeur with colonial overtones. For royalty or the high-dollar executive, the ninth-floor Rajadamri Suite is one of the most elegant in town. A private dining room, a huge sitting room, seven bedrooms, and a manorial library provide all that you would expect for 43,000B ($1,720) a night.

Dining/Entertainment: We found the lobby dining area a bit too exposed for a casual dinner, but it's great for tea, at 180B ($7.20), accompanied by the sounds of a string quartet from the balcony above. La Brasserie's indoor booths and outdoor café tables are better for relaxed dining; the international-cuisine buffet lunch, at 360B ($14.40), is very popular in this upscale shopping district. The informal Spice Market is many foreigners' favorite Thai restaurant in the city (see Section 4 of Chapter 5). The Regent Grill is the hotel's premier spot for continental fare, featuring California cuisine in an L.A.-slick setting (see Section 4 of Chapter 5). The intimate bar, decorated with the watercolors of Thai artist Suchart Wongthong, offers evening piano music.

Services: 24-hour room service, turndown service, complimentary welcome tea, concierge, house clinic, limousine service, eight-passenger mobile office, babysitting, laundry/valet, complimentary shoeshine and necktie cleaning.

Facilities: Pool and health club (with sauna), business center, beauty salon and barbershop, gourmet bakery and deli, shopping arcade.

SIAM INTER-CONTINENTAL, 967 Rama I Rd., Bangkok 10330. Tel. 02/253-0355. Fax 02/253-2275. Telex TH 81155 SIAMINT. 400 rms. A/C MINIBAR TEL TV **Directions:** Across from Siam Square.

$ Rates: 4,000B–5,200B ($160–$211) single; 4,300B–5,500B ($172–$220) double; from 8,400B ($336) suite. AE, DC, MC, V.

Set in 26 acres of parkland—part of the Srapatum Royal Palace estate—the Siam Inter-Continental represents an island of calm in frenetic Bangkok. A gracious driveway leads to a massive Eero Saarinen–inspired clamshell-shaped lobby, which overlooks the well-landscaped property. As might be imagined with such enormous grounds, the Siam Inter-Continental offers some of the best outdoor sports facilities of any hotel in Bangkok. Groomed jogging trails, lit tennis courts, and golf (minicourse and driving range) are among the more popular options. The hotel's small aviary and zoo are popular with children.

A 1993 renovation has spruced up the rooms and public spaces of the sprawling ranch-style complex. Pastel carpets and dark Chinese-style furniture provide a rich, pleasing ambience. The Club Inter-Continental wing is the two-story equivalent of an "executive" floor, with slightly smarter furnishings and free breakfast and drinks in the private lounge. The least expensive, "standard" rooms in the one contemporary Tower Wing had not been renovated as of our visit.

Dining/Entertainment: The all-you-can-eat buffet lunch at Similan, the Inter-Continental's Thai and seafood restaurant, is excellent quality and good value at 375B ($15).

Services: 24-hour room service, concierge, complimentary welcome tea, house doctor, limousine service, babysitting, laundry service.

Facilities: Swimming pool, sports center, business center, beauty salon and barbershop, shopping arcade, and bakery.

EXPENSIVE

THE AMARI BOULEVARD, 2 Soi 5, Sukhumvit Rd., Bangkok 10110. Tel. 02/255-2930. Fax 02/255-2950. Telex TH 84033 AMARIBV. 300 rms, 15 suites. A/C MINIBAR TEL TV **Directions:** North of Sukhumvit Rd on Soi 5.

$ Rates: 3,300B–4,500B ($134–$180) single; 3,600B–5,000B ($144–$200) double; 6,600B ($264) one-bedroom suite. Extra bed 600B ($24). AE, DC, EU, MC, V.

Since the completion of a glass-and-steel tower that seems to lean back against the original hotel, the modern Boulevard appears more elegant than ever. The glamorous Krung Thep wing adds 137 spacious rooms in contemporary muted tones, featuring full granite bathrooms and terrific city views. The larger corner deluxe rooms are especially striking, with separate shower stalls, two seating areas, and a desk. The original wing, with mahogany-paneled hallways and attractive balconied rooms, is now sold at the lowest prices and is an even better value. When we stayed there, the links between the original building, with, its small pool and restaurant, and the new wing, with its coffee shop and common lobby but separate elevators, remained confusing. Yet, despite the erratic service, when rooms are discounted 40% to 60% in the low season, this is a very good value.

Dining/Entertainment: The Peppermill Restaurant serves an array of international cuisine, including Thai, Japanese, and vegetarian dishes.

Services: 24-hour room service, concierge, complimentary fruit basket, limousine service, babysitting, laundry service.

Facilities: Swimming pool, health club, business center, beauty salon and barbershop, shopping arcade.

AMARI WATERGATE HOTEL, 847 **Phetchaburi Rd., Pratunam, Rajthevi, Bangkok 10400. Tel. 02/252-7843.** Fax 02/255-5707. 575 rms. A/C MINIBAR TV TEL **Directions:** North of World Trade Center, between Pratunam (Watergate) Market and City Centre Shopping Arcade .

$ Rates: 4,000B ($160) single; 4,400B ($176) double; from 6,000B ($240) suite. AE, DC, MC, V.

The new flagship of the Amari Hotel chain wasn't quite finished at our last visit, but we managed a preview of this attractive tower. It's in the middle of Bangkok's busiest and biggest shopping area, near two expressways, and less than an hour from the airport—close, these days. The lobby is spacious and the rooms are large and certain to be luxurious.

Dining/Entertainment: You'll not want for variety—Thai, Chinese, Japanese, Vietnamese, and Italian restaurants are planned, as well as Henry J. Bean's Bar and Grill, a 24-hour coffee shop, bakery, lobby bar, and pool bar.

Services: 24-hour room service, concierge, limousine service, babysitting, laundry, house doctor.

Facilities: Swimming pool with Jacuzzi, kiddie pool, heath club, squash courts, business center, beauty salon and barbershop, shopping arcade.

BEL-AIRE PRINCESS, 16 **Soi 5, Sukhumvit Rd., Bangkok 10110. Tel. 02/253-4300.** Fax 02/255-8850. Telex 20672 BELAIRE. 160 rms and suites. A/C MINIBAR TV TEL **Directions:** North of Sukhumvit Rd. on Soi 5.

$ Rates: 3,400B–4,100B ($136–$164) single; 3,700B–4,400B ($148–$176) double; from 6,000B ($240) suite. Extra person 700B ($28). AE, DC, MC, V.

This is a fine midsized hotel on a quiet soi off bustling Sukhumvit Road, one of the cousins in the highly acclaimed Princess chain. The name is an homage to the famous luxury hotel in Los Angeles, and the mural behind the desk is some idealized version of the gardens of that hotel. Rooms are spacious and tastefully appointed. The small health club, rooftop pool, and good location add to the appeal.

Dining/Entertainment: The California Café continues the underlying theme of the hotel, with solid continental fare. The Tiffin Room is the more elegant eatery.

Services: 24-hour room service, concierge, limousine service, babysitting (with notice), laundry.

Facilities: Rooftop swimming pool, health club, business center.

LE MERIDIEN PRESIDENT, 135/26 **Gaysorn Rd., Bangkok 10330. Tel. 02/253-0444,** or toll free 800/543-4300. Fax 02/253-7565. Telex TH 81194. 373 rms. A/C MINIBAR TEL TV

Directions: Near intersection of Rama I Rd. and Rajdamri Rd.

$ Rates: 3,600B–4,600B ($144–$184) single; 4,100B–5,400B ($164–$202) double; from 6,600B ($276) suite. AE, DC, MC, V.

Part of the Méridien chain, this group-tour-oriented hotel has undergone extensive renovation. The gray-marble lobby now has a welcoming and homey ambiance (a far cry from some Bangkok hotels with their impressive, though cold, decor). The newer suites are more sumptuously appointed than the compact, attractive rooms, with pale-wood paneling, tasteful pastel furnishings, and the usual panoply of luxury amenities. As in other Méridien hotels, many of the guests are French, and the renowned Gallic culinary sophistication may explain why the dining rooms here are among the top choices in Bangkok.

Dining/Entertainment: The Fireplace Grill (see Section 4 of Chapter 5) is considered one of Bangkok's best Western dining rooms. Cappuccino rates as one of Bangkok's better coffee shops; desserts are excellent.

Services: 24-hour room service, concierge, complimentary welcome tea, house doctor, limousine service, babysitting, laundry service.

Facilities: Swimming pool, health club, business center, beauty salon and barbershop, shopping arcade.

THE SOMERSET, 10 Soi 15, Sukhumvit Rd., Bangkok 10110. Tel. 02/254-8500. Fax 02/254-8534. Telex 72361 SOMRSET TH. 76 rms, 5 suites. A/C MINIBAR TEL TV **Directions:** 1 block north of Sukhumvit Rd.

$ Rates: 2,900B ($116) single; 3,200B ($128) double; 5,400B ($216) suite. AE, DC, MC, V.

It's surprising to find a Best Western affiliate on a quiet lane off Sukhumvit Road, but don't be misled by any chain stereotypes, for this is a fine little hotel. Lobby and rooms are tastefully done with lots of marble and cool pastels. The 24-hour business center, eager-to-please service, and the small, intimate scale make this a good business traveler's choice in this price range.

Dining/Entertainment: The Kensington Café is an above-average coffee shop serving a variety of international dishes.

Services: 24-hour room service, concierge, limousine service, babysitting (with notice), laundry service.

Facilities: Swimming pool, health club, business center.

TAI-PAN HOTEL, 25 Sukhumvit Soi 23, Bangkok 10110. Tel. 02/260-9888. Fax 02/259-7908. Telex 20540 TAIPAN TH. 139 rms, 11 suites. A/C MINIBAR TV TEL **Directions:** 1 block north of Sukhumvit on Soi 23.

$ Rates: 2,900B–3,400B ($116–$136) single; 3,100B–3,600B ($124–$144) double; from 6,000B ($240) suite. Extra bed 600B ($24). AE, DC, MC, V.

Known by shoppers for the excellent luncheon buffet at its coffee shop, Tai-Pan is within walking distance of Rasi Sayam, L'Arcadia, and several other boutiques. Opened in 1991, this modern white tower rises above a quiet soi in a neighborhood that's perfect for shoppers, decorators, and those in the fashion industry. The attentive staff, and guest housing in bright, carpeted rooms with comfortable seating areas and city views, guarantee a pleasant stay. With all the facilities you'd expect from a more expensive hotel, this is a good value.

Dining/Entertainment: Excellent coffee shop with bargain buffet breakfasts and lunches. Great Thai and continental food.

Services: 24-hour room service, limousine service, babysitting, laundry.

Facilities: Small swimming pool, exercise room, business center.

MODERATE

MANHATTAN HOTEL, 13 Soi 15, Sukhumvit Rd., Bangkok 10110 Tel. 02/255-0166. Fax 02/255-3481. Telex TH 87272. 200 rms, 3 suites. A/C MINIBAR TEL TV **Directions:** Just north of Sukhumvit Rd., near Ambassador Bangkok.

$ Rates: 1,450B ($58) single; 1,700B ($68) double. AE, DC, MC. V.

We New Yorkers hesitate to put you in a hotel of this name, especially one with a popular, inexpensive coffee shop named The Broadway. But this newly modern high-rise is surprisingly attractive, with rooms that are spacious and quietly tasteful. Plus, it has features you'd pay more for elsewhere—pool, friendly lobby bar, nightclub with live bands, and its own Four Seasons Restaurant. This top value is even busier since their write-up in the *New York Times*!

SIAM ORCHID INN, 109 Soi, Rajdamri Rd., Bangkok 10330. Tel. 02/255-3140. Fax 02/255-3144. 40 rms, 3 suites. A/C MINIBAR TEL TV **Directions:** Across from World Trade Center.

$ Rates: 1,300B–1,600B ($52–$64) single; 1,600B–1,800B ($64–$72) double; 2,100B ($84) suite. Extra person 350B ($14). AE, DC, MC, V.

This is not a luxury establishment, though it was built during Bangkok's late-1980s boom. Guest rooms are Spartanly furnished and lighting is of the fluorescent variety. However, we found the friendliest hotel staff in town, and the location is pretty good for those on a frugal businessperson's or shopper's budget. Add to these virtues a comfortably furnished lobby and coffee shop and a larger-than-average offering of services in this price category, and the Siam Orchid emerges as a moderately priced alternative worth consideration.

INEXPENSIVE

CITY LODGE, Soi 9 Sukhumvit, Bangkok 10110. Tel. 02/253-7705. Fax 02/255-4667. 28 rms. A/C MINIBAR TV TEL **Directions:** Corner of Sukhumvit and Soi 9.

$ Rates: 1,140B ($45.60) single or double. MC, V.

Budget-watchers will do well by the two small, spiffy City Lodges. Both the newer Lodge on Soi 9 and its nearby cousin, the older, 35-room City Lodge on Soi 19 (tel. 02/254-4783; fax 02/255-7340) provide clean, supercompact rooms with simple, modern decor. Each has a pleasant coffee shop (facing the bustle on Sukhumvit at Soi 9; serving Italian fare on Soi 19), a small but friendly staff, and privileges at the rooftop swimming pool at the more deluxe Amari Boulevard Hotel on Soi 5. All three belong to the Amari Hotels and Resorts Group. No frills here, but still a lot of comfort for your money.

COMFORT INN, 153/11–14 Soi 11, Sukhumvit Rd., Bangkok 10110. Tel. 02/251-0745. Fax 02/254-3562. Telex

22418 COMFORT TH. 36 rms. A/C MINIBAR TEL TV **Directions:** North of Sukhumvit Rd., opposite Swiss Park Hotel.

$ Rates: 1,250B ($50.40) single or double. AE, MC, V.

This small hotel has clean and compact rooms, very simply furnished but with a warm, homey feel. The friendly staff and quiet but convenient location on Soi Chaiyod recommend it. A 5% discount is offered for stays of a week or longer, 10% for a month or more.

DYNASTY INN, 5/4–5 Soi 4, Sukhumvit Rd., Bangkok 10110. Tel. 02/252-4522. Fax 02/252-9930. 55 rms. A/C TEL TV **Directions:** South of Sukhumvit Rd., opposite Nana Hotel

$ Rates (including tax and service): 1,000B–1,200B ($40–$48) single or double. Extra person 350B ($14). AE, MC, V.

Although the larger Nana Hotel is just across the street, this small hotel with its teak-walled lobby, gentle Thai staff, and well-kept rooms presents a much warmer welcome. Ask for a third-floor room overlooking Soi 4—it's much brighter.

RUAMCHITT TRAVELODGE, 11/1 Soi 10, Sukhumvit Rd., Bangkok 10110. Tel. 02/251-0284. Fax 02/255-1372. 72 rms. A/C FRIDGE TEL TV **Directions:** Near end of Soi 10, south of Sukhumvit Rd.

$ Rates (including breakfast): 1,375B ($55) single; 1,500B ($60) double. Extra person 300B ($12). Student and senior-citizen discounts available. AE, MC, V.

This scrubbed-clean, matter-of-fact hotel, with its large, simply furnished rooms and sparkling new all-tile bathrooms, is a real find in this popular neighborhood. The atmosphere is quiet and friendly, with a lobby coffee shop that seems made for lounging.

BUDGET

THE ATLANTA HOTEL, 78 Sukhumvit Soi 2, Bangkok 10110. Tel. 02/252-1650. Fax 02/255-2151. 60 rms. TEL TV **Directions:** 1 long block south of where Ploenchit becomes Sukhumvit Rd.

$ Rates: 360B ($14.40) single with fan; 480B ($19.20) double with fan; 600B ($24) single with A/C; 720B ($28.80) double with A/C. No credit cards.

This fine old suburban hotel has seen better days, and that's one of its many charms. Among previous guests we've met, some praise it, some hate it, but all have at least one story about its special services and quirky staff. It's considered home by many, and, though homelike, it's more than a little eccentric. Some of the rooms are homely, the fan-only rooms have no hot water, some are up several flights of stairs, but there's atmosphere to spare. We were initially drawn to the hotel by a letter from its proprietor, Dr. Charles Henn, who wrote: "The Atlanta has a unique charm and character, and an inimitable atmosphere . . . not perfect—far from it—but it has a mystique." Though put off by the worn exterior and bewildered by its facilities, we left agreeing with Dr. Henn's description, and were completely won over.

HAPPY INN, 20/1 Sukhumvit Rd., Soi 4, Nanatai, Bangkok, 10110. Tel. 02/252-6508 or 255-6794. Fax 02/255-6794. 10 rms. A/C TEL TV **Directions:** South of Sukhumvit Rd., beyond Rajah Hotel.

$ Rates (including tax and service): 600B ($24) single or double. No credit cards.

The name seems to match the place, and although the rooms are plain and simple, the staff is all smiles (with a smattering of English). The basics are here—air-conditioning, showers, TVs, minifridge, twin beds— but nothing extra, not even an elevator. Still, if everything else is full, you'll find this location convenient. Cheap food stalls are found throughout the neighborhood.

UNCLE REY'S GUESTHOUSE: 7/10 Soi 4, Sukhumvit Rd., Bangkok 10110. Tel. 02/252-5565. 24 rms (all with bath). A/C TEL **Directions:** In cul-de-sac off Soi 4 opposite Nana Hotel.

$ Rates (including tax and service): 400B–500B ($16–$20) single or double. No credit cards.

Its convenient and quiet location makes this family-run inn a good value. Decent-sized rooms—all quaintly named—are simply furnished but include armoires and small writing desks. Attached bathrooms include bathtubs with Danish showers. If you take one of the cheaper rooms, you'll get a good workout on the way up the two or three flights of stairs.

READERS RECOMMEND

Golden Palace Hotel, *15 Soi 1, Sukhumvit Rd.* *"When I showed up at the Hotel Atlanta, I found they didn't take credit cards. Being Sunday and the King's birthday, the banks were closed and the ATM in the Northern Bus Terminal was broken. Fortunately, down the block was the Golden Palace Hotel, which was in the same general category, had a swimming pool, charged only 100B more per night, and took credit cards!"* —Ariel Zeitlin, New York, NY.

---

5. AROUND THE RAILROAD STATION

As with most cities, the area around the Hua Lampong Railroad Station is not what you would call idyllic. But if you're going to be in Bangkok only one night and it's more convenient to stay near the station, here are two moderately priced choices.

MODERATE

BANGKOK CENTER HOTEL, 328 Rama IV Rd., Bangkok 10500. Tel. 02/238-4848. Fax 02/235-1780. Telex 72067 BACENHO TH. 250 rms. A/C MINIBAR TEL TV **Directions:** 2 blocks east of Hua Lampong Railroad Station.

$ Rates (including service, plus 7% tax): 1,800B ($72) single; 1,600B–1,800B ($64–$72) double. Extra bed 300B ($12). AE, DC, MC, V.

It's a basic businessperson's hotel—a plain, functional place set back from the busy, clamorous thoroughfare. Rooms, though not fancy, are comfortable. A lunchtime buffet in the scenic rooftop ballroom is supplemented by a popular Chinese restaurant downstairs, open for both lunch and dinner. Night owls can sample the Centre Club Disco or the 24-hour coffee shop.

BUDGET

KRUNG KASEM SRI KRUNG HOTEL, 1860 Krung Kasem Rd., Bangkok 10100. Tel. 02/225-0132. Fax 02/225-4702. 129 rms (all with bath). A/C TEL TV **Directions:** Just across street from Hua Lampong Railroad Station.

$ Rates (including tax and service): 600B ($24) single; 650B ($26) double; 1,075B ($43) triple. No credit cards.

This is the best budget choice for cross-country train travelers. The quieter, back-facing rooms have small balconies and city views, air-conditioning, private toilets, and Asian showers, as well as a high standard of cleanliness. Each of the seven floors has a luggage locker, handy for storing that extra baggage during an up-country expedition. Business travelers and neighborhood vendors like the Valentine Coffee Shop's inexpensive Thai/Chinese fare.

6. NEAR THE AIRPORT

Don Muang International Airport is so far from the center of Bangkok that we recommend staying in the area only if you have connecting flights.

EXPENSIVE

AMARI AIRPORT HOTEL, 333 Choet Wudhakat Rd., Don Muang, Bangkok 10210. Tel. 02/566-1020. Fax 02/566-1941. Telex TH 87424 AIRHOTL. 434 rms. A/C MINIBAR TEL TV **Directions:** Across highway from airport's International Terminal. Walkway from terminal leads over freeway to hotel.

$ Rates: 3,900B–5,000B ($156–$200) single; 4,000B–5,400B ($160–$216) double; 6,000B ($240) suite. Extra person/bed 950B ($34). AE, DC, MC, V.

This is the fanciest, the closest, and, if budget is not a concern, the best of all choices near the airport. It's connected by an overpass to the International Terminal, from which you can take a free shuttle to the Domestic Terminal 1 kilometer (.6 mile) away. There is also a free shuttle bus to and from the airport. It's a short walk to the Don Muang Railroad Station, where many, but not all, trains to and from the north stop en route to and from Bangkok's Hua Lampong Railroad Station. For those wanting to pop into the city, there's a 60B ($2.40) shuttle bus that runs regularly to Ploenchit Road in the heart of Bangkok's shopping district.

But the Amari Airport Hotel is so comfortable that you may not want to go anywhere. It's got a new, superefficient Executive Floor with extra services, plus all the facilities you'd expect from a first-class hotel, plus a recurring aeronautical theme. Flight arrival and departure information scrolls across monitors in the lobby. Spacious deluxe rooms are decorated in soothing pastel colors and, better still, the windows are soundproofed. There's a Ladies Only Floor and a few special-access rooms for the handicapped. Although expensive, this hotel tries to give you your money's worth.

Note: Short-staying transit passengers waiting for a flight will appreciate the hotel's 3-hour ministay package. For 550B ($22) per single or 600B ($24) per twin room (inclusive of tax and service charge), guests can use not only the room but also the pool, the health club, and other hotel facilities. The offer is strictly limited to the hours between 8am and 6pm daily.

Dining/Entertainment: Airbridge Café, the Bel-Air Grill, the Zeppelin Coffee Shop (open 24 hours), and a Thai restaurant.

Facilities: Swimming pool, health club, shopping arcade.

INEXPENSIVE

GOLDEN DRAGON HOTEL, 20/21 Ngarm Wongwan Rd., Bangkok 11000. Tel. 02/589-0130. Fax 02/589-8305. Telex 82133 NGDTEL TH. 120 rms. A/C TEL TV **Directions:** 10km (6 miles) or 15 minutes south of Don Muang International Airport.

$ Rates (including tax and service): 1,150B ($46) single; 1,400B ($56) double. AE, MC, V.

For travelers-in-transit, this is the best—and a relatively inexpensive—alternative to the luxurious but pricey Amari Airport Hotel. Rooms are simple but clean, though the Hardest-Mattress-in-Thailand Award must go to this establishment. There are a pool and a basic restaurant, and best of all, it's only a 15 to 20-minute drive to the airport.

READERS RECOMMEND

Promenade Hotel, *Sukhumvit, Soi 8.* "*We found another hotel called the Promenade. It is a Comfort Inn, recently opened, with rooms for 1,200B ($48) per night. They come with cable television and a large, American-style bath. The Indian management is a bit quirky, but the rooms are first-class and well soundproofed. We will definitely return.*"—*John D. Connelly, Chicago, Il.*

CHAPTER 5

BANGKOK DINING

1. ON THE RIVER
• FROMMER'S SMART TRAVELER: RESTAURANTS
2. HISTORIC BANGKOK—NEAR THE GRAND PALACE
3. THE BUSINESS DISTRICT
• FROMMER'S COOL FOR KIDS: RESTAURANTS
4. THE SHOPPING/ EMBASSY AREA
5. CHINATOWN
6. SPECIALTY DINING

Thai food is among the finest in Southeast Asia and, some would argue, in the world. Bangkok offers a delightful variety of Thai restaurants, ranging from simple noodle stands to elegant dining rooms offering "royal" or "palace" cuisine. It's so reasonably priced that even in the fanciest Thai establishment you'll have a hard time spending more than $30 for two! Because the task of ordering can be daunting, we offer some advice in the cuisine section of Chapter 1.

If you're here more than a few days, you will undoubtedly need a break from Thai spices. Never fear, for the city offers a spectacular array of fine European, Chinese, and other Asian dining spots, which are generally more expensive than those catering to locals, but still a bargain compared with the same meals back home.

You'll even find the familiar fast-food outlets that you thought you left behind—McDonald's, Kentucky Fried Chicken, Burger King, Pizza Hut, Dunkin' Donuts, and more. For fast food Thai style, there are street vendors all over the city where the brave can graze, or the more hygienic food courts in many shopping malls, where you can easily sample a wide range of Thai treats.

We've organized this section first by neighborhood, then by price, with restaurants listed alphabetically. Don't be shy about trying unfamiliar cuisines! That's one reason why you came to Asia. And allow time to cross town for a special meal. The traffic congestion is usually reduced in the evening, and taxis are cheap and plentiful. We highly recommend the few restaurants that offer Thai classical dance performances as part of the evening. The dinner cruises on the Chao Phraya River, though not the ultimate in Thai cuisine, are also a special treat. These last two categories are listed below, under "Specialty Dining" (Section 6), along with the fast-food outlets in town.

1. ON THE RIVER

EXPENSIVE

THE NORMANDIE, in The Oriental, 48 Oriental Ave. Tel. 236-0400.

Cuisine: FRENCH. **Reservations:** Required. **Directions:** Off New Rd., overlooking river.

$ Prices: Appetizers 375B–1,025B ($15–$41); main courses 575B–1,450B ($23–$58); menu dégustation 2,500B ($100). AE, DC, MC, V.

Open: Lunch daily noon–2:30pm; dinner daily 7–10pm.

The Normandie represents the apex of formal dining in Thailand, both in price and quality. Set atop the renowned Oriental, with commanding panoramic views of Thonburi and the Chao Phraya River, this ultraelegant hotel dining room has recently emerged from a 25,000,000B ($1 million) renovation decked out in stunning, champagne-colored silk and gold brocade. In keeping with our more modest times, two excellent-value fixed-price lunches (500B/$20 and 575B/$23) have been added to a new menu with lower prices overall. At our visit, the superb menu dégustation began with prawns served on a bed of watercress, and included a risotto with red snapper and clams, a melt-in-your-mouth lamb with mushrooms and basil, assorted imported cheeses, a chocolate mousse, and a refreshing chilled fruit soup with ice cream. The chefs so-called menu découverte (3,800B/$152) also features a variety of wines by the glass, selected to enhance the fine seasonal cuisine.

We found the service a bit on the formal side, but this is only a minor quibble in what is obviously a superior culinary event. Reservations are a must, as the dining room is relatively small.

MODERATE

SALA THIP, In Shangri-La Hotel, 8 Soi Wat Suan Plu. Tel. 236-7777.

Cuisine: THAI. **Reservations:** Recommended. **Directions:** Overlooking Chao Phraya River, adjacent to Sathorn Bridge.

$ Prices: Appetizers 110B–175B ($4.40–$7); main courses 150B–400B ($6–$16). AE, DC, MC, V.

Open: Dinner Mon–Sat 6–10:30pm; High-season Sun buffet dinner 6–10:30pm.

Located on the river terrace of the Shangri-La Hotel, Sala Thip is arguably Bangkok's most romantic Thai restaurant. Classic music and traditional cuisine are superbly presented under one of two aged carved-teak pavilions perched over a lotus pond, or at outdoor tables that overlook the Chao Phraya. (For those who crave a less humid environment, we suggest reserving a table in one of the air-conditioned dining rooms.) Although the food may not inspire aficionados, it is skillfully prepared by one of the few women chefs in town. We find the airy spring rolls, kuai tiao phad thai (broad rice noodles), and roast duck with vegetables achieve divine heights in this wonderful setting.

**FROMMER'S SMART TRAVELER:
RESTAURANTS**

1. If you can't eat Thai food at the extremely hot (spicy) level served outside the major tourist centers, inform the waiter that you want it "*Mai phet; farang*"—"Not spicy; foreigner." If you forget to add the "*farang*," the chef may assume you're a Thai diner with a subtler palate rather than a foreigner who's serious about the request.

2. Splurge on a Thai or Chinese feast rather than on gourmet continental fare. These are the least expensive cuisines throughout the country (and usually better prepared).

3. There's no need to save those fresh fish and lobster specials for the beach resorts, because most seafood is shipped to Bangkok, where competition keeps prices lower.

4. Thai food is served family style, so the greater the number of diners, the cheaper the meal and the greater the variety. Main-dish orders are often priced according to size: small (two portions), medium (four to six), or large (six or more).

5. The traditional Thai breakfast of khao tom (a bland rice soup served with pork, chicken, crab, or fish, vegetables, an egg, and several condiments for flavor) is cheaper at most hotels than a continental or American breakfast, and it provides more sustenance for a morning of sightseeing.

6. The food courts in the major department stores are the cheapest places to eat.

7. "*Mai sai phong chu rod*" means "Please don't add MSG." Thais use a lot of it. Most chefs know it by its Japanese brand name, *Ajinomoto*. At all but the finest restaurants, it's usually premixed with seasonings and sauces, but it never hurts to ask.

8. If you want an alcoholic beverage with your meal, Thai beer is the best value, because imported beer, liquor, and wine are extremely expensive.

SHANG PALACE, in Shangri-La Hotel, 89 Soi Wat Suan Plu. Tel. 236-7777.
   Cuisine: CHINESE. **Reservations:** Recommended in evenings and on weekends. **Directions:** Off New Rd., near The Oriental (hotel).
$ Prices: Appetizers 300B–950B ($12–$38); main courses 150B–2,400B ($6–$96). AE, DC, MC, V.
   Open: Lunch daily 11:30am–2:30pm; dinner daily 6:30–10:30pm.
A smiling gold Buddha presides over the colorfully decorated Shang Palace, a Chinese restaurant popular with both hotel guests and Thai businesspeople (who really appreciate gourmet Chinese cooking). At lunch and dinner, the kitchen turns out a wide range of Cantonese à la carte specialties, including the usual shark's-fin, duck, and very pricey bird's-nest offerings, as well as an enormous number of seafood and meat main courses. At lunch only, the Shang Palace also serves delightful, inexpensive dim sum; among our favorites are crispy scallop dumplings, shrimp balls, and chicken spring rolls served by the plate, with three to six pieces per portion.

THANYING, 10 Pramuan Rd. Tel. 236-4361.
  Cuisine: THAI. **Reservations:** Recommended. **Directions:**
  1½ blocks south of Silom behind the Holiday Inn Crowne Plaza.
$ Prices: Appetizers 85B–145B ($3.40–$5.80); main courses 180B–
  425B ($7.20–$17). AE, MC, V.
  Open: Daily 11am–11pm.

Even by our first visit in 1987, the stately Thanying had, for many years, been an old-world restaurant favored by petty royalty and an aging wealthy class. Excellent Imperial cuisine from the recipes of King Rama VII's time were artfully presented and slowly savored by the gracious, but fast disappearing, social elite. As Bangkok's market economy took off and created rich young tigers, Thanying fell out of favor. Too fussy. Too old-fashioned. Too slow. Now, those bored with too casual, too new, and too fast restaurants, have become an appreciative clientele. Traditional favorites include red curry with roast duck, fried chicken in pandanus leaves, fresh fish with tamarind and mango sauce, and the fluffy, delicately spiced catfish salad. A slightly more casual branch at the too new World Trade Center shopping complex on Rajdamri Road (see Section 4 in this chapter) has helped revive this classic dining room's popularity with the young.

BUDGET

**HIMALI CHA CHA RESTAURANT, 1229/11 New Rd.
Tel. 235-1569.**
  Cuisine: INDIAN. **Directions:** On side street off New Rd., corner of Surawong.
$ Prices: Appetizers 50B–150B ($2–$6); main courses 50B–200B
  ($2–$8). 300B ($12) minimum for credit cards. MC, V.
  Open: Lunch daily 11am–3:30pm; dinner daily 6–10:30pm.

This place comes with lots of stories. Cha Cha, the graying chef and proprietor, was on Lord Mountbatten's staff in India. He then cooked for the diplomatic corps in Laos, and after that country's fall, he came to Bangkok to open this restaurant in 1980. You'll find him in attendance at the cash register nightly. House specialties include three-darbesh curry, vegetable kofta curry, and palak paneer, all extremely flavorful and well prepared. The Indian thali plates are our favorites. Two people can taste a sampling of seven dishes, with bread and rice, for 425B ($17) for the vegetarian thali and 550B ($22) for the meat thali. Vegetarians will enjoy the wide selection of other meatless offerings. All who dine here will enjoy the friendly atmosphere.

2. HISTORIC BANGKOK—
NEAR THE GRAND PALACE

MODERATE

**THE EMPRESS, in Royal Princess Hotel, 269 Larn Luang
Rd. Tel. 281-3088.**
  Cuisine: CHINESE. **Reservations:** Recommended. **Directions:**
  West of Krung Kasem Rd.
$ Prices: Appetizers 115B–215B ($4.60–$8.60); main courses 115B–
  1,000B ($4.60–$40). AE, DC, MC, V.

Open: Lunch daily 11:30am–2:30pm; dinner daily 6–10:30pm.

⭐ The high-style mint-and-jade padded banquettes are jammed at lunch with government officials, upscale tourists taking a break from nearby sightseeing, and local businessmen all savoring a selection from the 20 or so dim sum choices. The fresh steamed, fried, and boiled morsels (mostly seafood) provide an inexpensive midday break. Former prime minister Chatichai Choonhaven prefers a Cantonese banquet menu at lunch, including the tart abalone salad, bird's-nest soup, chicken and black mushroom soup, and the whole steamed fish of the day. Even the lesser-priced fare is delicious and artfully presented. We liked the tender, moist tea leaf–smoked duck, steamed bean curd stuffed with minced prawns, and sautéed seasonal vegetables with crabmeat sauce. This is one restaurant where you can't go wrong.

KANIT RESTAURANT, 68 Ti Thong Rd. Tel. 222-1020.
   Cuisine: CONTINENTAL. **Reservations:** Recommended for dinner. **Directions:** Just west of Wat Suthat.
$ **Price:** Appetizers 105B–300B ($4.20–$12); main courses 200B–575B ($8–$23). AE, DC, V.
   Open: Mon–Sat 11 am–11pm.

We discovered this refined and relaxed eatery on a hot afternoon while mapping out our "Wat's What" walking tour (see Section 1 of Chapter 7). The shaded facade and cold-drinks list beckoned us, and inside we found a moody dark-wood interior, an ambitious menu that includes French and Italian specialties; a fine wine list with lots of California varietals; and a wide sampling of snacks, teas, and coffees.

Kanit serves flavorful and original Western main courses minus the hype and glitziness found in most hotel dining rooms. Among the better dishes that we tried: "Pizza Gulf of Siam," with shrimp, mussels, and clams; rib-eye steak with coriander seeds and fresh Brazilian red-pepper sauce; and spaghetti with prawns and herb butter. Desserts are French-inspired. Service is efficient and friendly.

INEXPENSIVE

KALOANG HOME KITCHEN, 2 Sri Ayutthaya Rd. Tel. 281-9228.
   Cuisine: THAI. **Reservations:** Required for boat tables only. **Directions:** North of National Library, overlooking Chao Phraya River.
$ **Prices:** Main courses 60B–300B ($2.40–$12). AE, MC, V.
   Open: Daily 11am–11pm.

⭐ For ambience alone, this riverside café overlooking the Royal Yacht Pier has become John's favorite Thai restaurant in Bangkok.

Street vendors selling quick-fried bananas and frilled squid line the narrow entrance to Kaloang Home Kitchen. When you arrive, you face two separate dining areas. The first is a covered wooden pier set with simple outdoor furniture, while adjacent to it is a retired wooden boat that contains about 10 small tables. We just loved sitting at the head of the boat, commanding a vista of the quiet river and taking in a cool breeze. Nearby, kids play in the water, swimming next to the royal family's private boats, and across the way are several lovely colonial-style villas.

We supped on yam paduk fu (a salad of roasted catfish whipped into a foam, then crisply and deliciously fried), horseshoe-crab curry with pineapple and coconut, sam lee fish with mango, and chicken marinated in an unknown (to us) Thai liquor. All are highly recommended and inexpensive. In fact, some of the better food that we sampled did not appear on the menu, so inquire about daily specials. If you have the patience to hunt this one down, don't miss this off-the-beaten-tourist-track experience.

MAJESTIC HOUSE, In Hotel Majestic Palace, 97 Ratchadamnoen Klang Rd. Tel. 280-5610.
   Cuisine: AMERICAN/THAI/CHINESE/ITALIAN. **Directions:** Near Democracy Monument.
$ Prices: Appetizers 75B–145B ($3–$5.80); main courses 75B–300B ($3–$12). MC, V.
   Open: Daily 7am–2am.
Here is one place bound to accommodate nearly all tastes. Imagine a single restaurant that offers hamburgers, tom yam kung, chicken with cashews, and spaghetti alla bolognese—served in a spacious air-conditioned haven overlooking one of Bangkok's busiest thoroughfares. Speaking of thorough fare, we were not only impressed with the breadth of the menu but equally delighted to find good quality cuisine. The Chinese dishes were by far the most impressive and are well recommended.

BUDGET

MARIA RESTAURANT, 50–52 Building 4, Ratchadamnoen Klang Rd. Tel. 221-5211.
   Cuisine: CHINESE/JAPANESE. **Directions:** Near Wat Saket in Chalerm Thai Theater Building.
$ Prices: Appetizers 40B–75B ($1.60–$3). No credit cards.
   Open: Lunch daily 11am–2pm.
For a super lunchtime bargain, we suggest a stop at the Maria Restaurant, a completely local favorite where authentic and tasty dim sum appetizers are brought to your table on a rolling cart and served in bamboo steamers. The noisy single dining room is cavernous and clean, though a tad on the dark and dingy side, and you'll likely be the only tourists in a sea of government workers.

SORN DAENG RESTAURANT, 78/2 Ratchadamnoen Klang Rd. Tel. 224-3088.
   Cuisine: Thai. **Directions:** On Democracy Monument traffic circle.
$ Prices: Appetizers 100B–150B ($4–$6); main courses 100B–375B ($4–$15). No credit cards.
   Open: Daily 10am–10pm.
Sorn Daeng, one of the city's oldest restaurants and long a casual hangout for government workers and mid-level army officers, is now gussied up with white linen and ruffled tablecloths. We found it a bit too formal but did enjoy an excellent Thai spring roll. Among our other favorites: papaya salad, beef or chicken with basil leaves and chili, hot-and-sour chicken, and fried morning glory in oyster sauce.

TAKIANG, 62 Chakrphatiphong Rd. Tel. 281-2837.
   Cuisine: THAI. **Reservations:** Not required except for large groups. **Directions:** Near Ratchadamnoen Klang Rd.
$ Prices: Main courses 50B–110B ($2–$4.40). No credit cards.
   Open: Lunch daily 11am–2pm; dinner daily 4–11pm.
The atmosphere at Takiang (meaning literally "The Lamps") is almost better than the excellent Thai fare. Behind a nondescript facade with only a Thai name on the sign beneath the canopy, you'll

find a cozy teak-trimmed series of rooms lit by the warm glow of dozens of table lamps, chandeliers, wall sconces, and overhead fixtures. To the gentle Thai tunes of the resident pianist, specials like steamed seafood in coconut curry, fish or shrimp tom yam soups, ground-beef- and tomato-filled omelets, and light, crispy, stuffed chicken wings will send you happily to the nearby (10-minute cab ride) Grand Palace Area. The place is a little hard to find, so ask for help at the Thai Airways office around the corner at 6 Larn Luang Rd.

3. THE BUSINESS DISTRICT

EXPENSIVE

BENJARONG, in the Dusit Thani Hotel, Rama IV Rd. Tel. 236-0450.
   Cuisine: THAI. **Reservations:** Recommended. **Directions:** Corner of Silom Rd.
   $ Prices: Appetizers 100B–265B ($4–$10.60); main courses 120B–550B ($3.60–$22). AE, MC, V.
   Open: Dinner daily 6–10:30pm.
This classy dining room, named for the exquisite five-color pottery once reserved exclusively for the use of royalty, is one of the few places where you'll want to dress up. Benjarong prides itself on offering the five basic flavors of Thai cuisine (salty, bitter, hot, sweet, sour) in traditional "royal" dishes. The illustrated menu encouraged us to start with the unusual kratai chom suan, (delicate cakes of jellied pork); followed by gung pao nam pla wan (grilled lobster with tamarind sauce); pra ram long song (an unusual beef tenderloin, baked and served with morning glory greens—one of Kyle's favorites—and a peanut/coconut/curry paste); and mee krob chao wang (crisp-fried vermicelli with bean curd, decorated with a papaya and bean sprout "daisy" that was the most artistically presented dish of all.) The kong wan is an ornate selection of typical Thai desserts, light but odd, sweet, and very satisfying.

MAYFLOWER, in Dusit Thani Hotel, Rama IV Rd. Tel. 236-0450.
   Cuisine: CHINESE. **Reservations:** Required. **Directions:** Corner of Silom Rd.
   $ Prices: Appetizers 300B–950B ($12–$38); main courses 200B–8,000B ($8–$320). AE, DC, MC, V.
   Open: Lunch daily 11:30am–2:30pm; dinner daily 6:30–10:30pm.
This coolly elegant gold-toned dining room has some stunning Chinese food at the highest prices in town. If you can afford to try some of China's more exotic delicacies, the menu lists nine varieties of shark's-fin soup and more than half a dozen each of abalone and swallow's-nest dishes. (The shark's-fin soup in brown sauce is particularly good.) The Peking duck, served in several courses, is outstanding—really crisp skin followed by rich, moist meat wrapped in thin pancakes. Beef, prawn, pork, crab, bean curd, noodle, chicken (more affordable at 225B to 500B [$9 to $20]), and more exotic pigeon and turtle dishes round out the menu.

MODERATE

KIKUSUI, 133 Pan Rd., Silom. Tel. 234-6687.
Cuisine: JAPANESE. **Directions:** East of Silom Rd.
$ Prices: Appetizers 145B–280B ($5.80–$11.20); main courses 95B–700B ($3.80–$28). AE, MC, V.
Open: Lunch daily 11:30am–2pm; dinner daily 5:30–10pm.

The focus at this small, simple Japanese country inn is solely on the food. The expert sushi chefs work with only the freshest fish: fish roe and yellowtail tuna imported from Japan, as well as Thai abalone, snapper, and tuna. Sushi platters of 10 artfully arranged pieces cost from 275B to 600B ($11 to $24) depending on the fish selected. Kikusui also specializes in grilled fish (we especially like the eel) and in beef shabu-shabu (traditional stew).

SHANGARILA, 154/4–5 Silom Rd. Tel. 234-9147.
Cuisine: CHINESE. **Reservations:** Recommended for large parties. **Directions:** South of Rama IV Rd.
$ Prices: Appetizers 25B–220B ($1–$8.80); main courses 60B–700B ($2.40–$28). AE, DC, MC, V.
Open: Daily 11am–10pm.

Shangarila is a glitzy, crowded, Shanghai-style restaurant. The decor is bright and splashy, with a carp pond taking up part of the downstairs dining room. The fine food is inexpensive, well prepared, and more interesting than at many casual Chinese eateries.

The traditional beggar's chicken is stuffed with mushrooms and baked in a thick clay coating. Peking duck, peppery Shanghai dumpling soup, and the fresh seafood dishes (especially crab) are among our favorites. The crisp mille-feuille-style Shanghai spring rolls are light as air.

The Grand Shangarila, with its 15 chandeliers on the ground floor, is a larger version of the original, with the same menu, at 58/4–9 Thaniya Rd., in Thaniya Plaza, off Silom Road (tel. 234-0861).

SILVER PALACE, 5 Soi Pipat, Silom Rd. Tel. 235-5118.
Cuisine: CHINESE. **Reservations:** Recommended. **Directions:** Just east of Silom Rd. on Soi Pipat.
$ Prices: Appetizers 150B–300B ($6–$12); main courses 150B–600B ($6–$24). AE, DC, MC, V.
Open: Dim sum lunch daily 11am–2pm; dinner daily 6–10pm.

Edith Tai's Silver Palace is one of Bangkok's slickest Hong Kong–style restaurants. You enter a warm, elegant dining room furnished with lovely Chinese bentwood chairs.

The diverse and imaginative menu features extensive and delicious duck, seafood, and shark's-fin choices. Favorites include braised duck with eight-jewel (vegetables and condiments) rice, subtly flavored drunken prawns, and asparagus with crabmeat in a light sauce. A large and truly succulent whole roast pig is sometimes devoured by as few as three diners. Some complex dishes—the excellent Peking duck, as well as phu thew chang and other shark's-fin specialties—require advance notice. And don't miss the exotic seasonal specials! Mrs. Tai personally lends a gracious touch to the service.

TANDOOR, in Holiday Inn Crowne Plaza, 981 Silom Rd. Tel. 238-4300.
Cuisine: INDIAN. **Reservations:** Recommended. **Directions:** Silom Rd. 1 block north of New Rd.

Banana Leaf 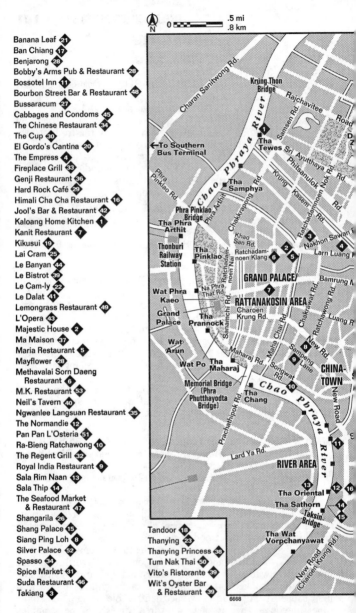 21
Ban Chiang 17
Benjarong 28
Bobby's Arms Pub & Restaurant 28
Bossotel Inn 11
Bourbon Street Bar & Restaurant 48
Bussaracum 27
Cabbages and Condoms 45
The Chinese Restaurant 34
The Cup 30
El Gordo's Cantina 20
The Empress 4
Fireplace Grill 33
Genji Restaurant 36
Hard Rock Café 29
Himali Cha Cha Restaurant 16
Jool's Bar & Restaurant 42
Kaloang Home Kitchen 1
Kanit Restaurant 7
Kikusui 19
Lai Cram 25
Le Banyan 44
Le Bistrot 39
Le Cam-ly 22
Le Dalat 41
Lemongrass Restaurant 49
L'Opera 43
Majestic House 2
Ma Maison 37
Maria Restaurant 5
Mayflower 28
Methavalai Sorn Daeng Restaurant 6
M.K. Restaurant 53
Neil's Tavern 40
Ngwanlee Langsuan Restaurant 35
The Normandie 12
Pan Pan L'Osteria 51
Ra-Bieng Ratchawong 10
The Regent Grill 32
Royal India Restaurant 9
Sala Rim Naan 13
Sala Thip 14
The Seafood Market & Restaurant 47
Shangarila 26
Shang Palace 15
Siang Ping Loh 8
Silver Palace 52
Spasso 34
Spice Market 31
Suda Restaurant 46
Takiang 3

Tandoor 18
Thanying 23
Thanying Princess 38
Tum Nak Thai 50
Vito's Ristorante 39
Wit's Oyster Bar & Restaurant 39

$ Prices: Set menus from 350B–500B ($14–$20). AE, MC, DC, V.

Open: Lunch daily noon–2:30pm; dinner daily 6:30–11pm.

Perhaps because of its Indian ownership, the Holiday Inn Crowne Plaza's elegant Moghul dining room is considered one of the city's better venues for northern Indian cuisine. The authentic tandoor and clay ovens ensure that every chicken, prawn, or lamb tandoori dish is baked to perfection after a long bath in fragrant spices and yogurt. Other favorites served within different set menus are the

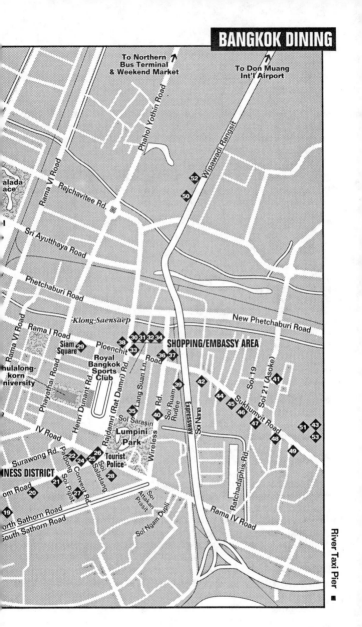

To Northern
Bus Terminal
& Weekend Market

To Don Muang
Int'l Airport

Phahol Yothin Road

Wipawadi Rangsit

alada
ace

Rama VI Road

Rajchavitee Rd.

52

50

Sri Ayutthaya Road

Phetchaburi Road

New Phetchaburi Road

Klong-Saensaep

Rama I Road

Rama VI Road

Siam
Square

29

Ploenchit

38

30 31 32 34
33

SHOPPING/EMBASSY AREA

hulalong-
korn
niversity

Phayathai Road

Royal
Bangkok
Sports
Club

Road

36 37

Henri Dunant (Rat Damri) Rd.

Lang Suan Ln.

Rd.

39

42

Sol 19

Sol 21 (Asoke)

41

Rajdamri (Rat Damri) Rd.

Soi Ruam
Rudee

44

45

Sukhumvit Road

46

35

Sol Sarasin

40

Expressway

Soi Nana

51

43

53

IV Road

26

Lumpini
Park

Wireless

48

49

Surawong Rd.

24

25

Tourist
Police

NESS DISTRICT

22

Convent Rd.

Sol
Saladang

Patpong Soi Pipat

28

Ratchadaphisk Rd.

m Road

20

27

21

Soi
Attakan
Prasit

Rama IV Road

19

orth Sathorn Road

South Sathorn Road

Soi Ngam Dupli

River Taxi Pier ▪

lamb cooked in poppy seeds, spicy lobster masala, and garlic naan
(a light pita bread).

INEXPENSIVE

BANANA LEAF, Basement Level, Silom Complex, Silom
Rd. Tel. 231-3124.
Cuisine: THAI. **Reservations:** Not required. **Directions:** Base-
ment level of shopping mall.

$ Prices: Appetizers 55B–75B ($2.20–$3); main courses 60B–180B ($2.40–$7.20). No credit cards.

Open: Daily 11:30am–9:30pm.

If you're ready to drop from shopping around Silom Road, you can't beat this clean, brightly lit place for fast, good, and inexpensive Thai food. Decor is not its strong suit, but authentically spiced delicacies like baked crab with glass noodles and spicy beef salad more than compensate for the ambience. In the evenings, Banana Leaf is packed with locals who stop for a quick bite on their way to the mall or its movie theaters.

BAN CHIANG, 14 Sriviang Rd. Tel. 236-7045.

Cuisine: THAI. **Reservations:** Recommended. **Directions:** 1 block east of Holiday Inn Crowne Plaza, ¹/₂ block north of Surasak Rd.

$ Prices: Appetizers 60B–110B ($2.40–$4.40); set menu for two 700B ($28), for four 1,050B ($42). MC, V.

Open: Daily 11:30am–10:30pm.

Like some other fine Bangkok restaurants, this is a traditional Thai house that has been converted into a restaurant. Ban Chiang's well-prepared Thai standards are attuned to international tastes, and the place is extremely popular with local expatriates. We liked the chicken hoh mok (minced chicken, basil, and coconut milk soufflé presented in a banana-leaf cup) and the lightly fried cuttlefish tempura. The set menu is a solid introduction to Thai cuisine's subtle blend of tastes, and includes a spicy prawn tom yam soup, local crab spiced and served in a crabshell, and a tangy sweet-and-sour pork. Ban Chiang is a safe bet if you're a bit shy about "getting burned" at your first Bangkok Thai meal.

BOBBY'S ARMS PUB & RESTAURANT, 114/1–2 Silom Rd. Tel. 233-6828.

Cuisine: BRITISH. **Reservations:** Not required. **Directions:** Top of ramp to parking garage, northernmost street of Patpong (no. 2) between Silom Rd. and Surawong Rd.

$ Prices: Appetizers 60B–180B ($2.40–$7.20); main courses 120B–350B ($4.80–$14). AE, DC, MC, V.

Open: Daily 11am–1am; Sun 8–11pm (Dixieland music).

Anglo-food-philes will enjoy this boisterous British pub with its typical offerings of fish-and-chips, shepherd's pie, roast beef with Yorkshire pudding, and steak-and-kidney pie. Hearty lunch specials, draft beer, and other, less pub-ish offerings will also satisfy the carnivores among us. Sunday evenings are popular for the Dixieland band, while quieter singers and musicians entertain the largely expatriate crowd on other nights.

BUSSARACUM, 35 Soi Pipat 2, off Convent Rd. Tel. 235-8915.

Cuisine: THAI. **Reservations:** Recommended. **Direction:** Between Silom Rd. and Sathorn Rd.

$ Prices: 50B–200B ($2–$8); main courses 95B–240B ($3.80–$9.60). AE, DC, MC, V.

Open: Lunch daily 11:30am–2pm; dinner daily 5:30–10:30pm.

Bussaracum is a traditional favorite with Thais hosting foreigners, for the fine food and the classical royal decor. At this tranquil teak-paneled sanctuary with its linen tablecloths, the Thai menu is changed every month. Bussaracum's rhoom (minced pork and shrimp in egg-net wrapping) was the favorite appetizer of King

---

Ⓕ **FROMMER'S COOL FOR KIDS: RESTAURANTS**

Thai food, with its exotic spices and Chinese-style presentation, may not be the favorite cuisine of most Western kids, but there are some basic dishes that will appeal to all youngsters: spring rolls (similar to egg rolls), fried chicken, fried rice, noodles.

Any restaurant on the river will be interesting to children. The parade of passing boats is endlessly fascinating. Try the riverside restaurants at the Shangri-La, Oriental, Menam, or Sheraton Royal Orchid Hotels, or the Kaloang Home Kitchen. For adventure or an even better river view, try one of the dinner cruises. However, the kids may get restless during the formal parade of courses.

MBK (Mah Boon Krong) is one of the major shopping malls that contains a food court offering a diverse range of Thai foods. The kids can cruise the food stalls and buy only what they want to sample.

Suan Saranom, the more-than-coffee-shop at the Hilton International, serves a sumptuous Sunday buffet with lots of balloons and special attractions for children. Pool privileges at the best pool in Bangkok come with the meal, and clowns are sometimes on hand to entertain the little ones.

Tum Nak Thai is another entertaining open-air dining experience with a huge menu, roller-skating waiters, and a nightly classical Thai dance program.

Rama II. Saengwa (cold shrimp salad served in a squash gourd) is an unusual dish, one that complements their noteworthy tom yam soup and gaeng kari gai hang (special chicken curry). Allow the helpful staff to make suggestions, and finish the meal with bauloy sarm see (a dessert of taro and pumpkin in coconut milk).

EL GORDO'S CANTINA, 130/8 Silom, Soi 8. Tel. 237-1415.

Cuisine: MEXICAN. **Reservations:** Recommended for large parties. **Directions:** On Soi 8 off Silom Rd.

$ Prices: Appetizers 35B–120B ($1.40–$4.80); main courses 100B–360B ($4–$14.40). AE, MC, V.

Open: Mon–Sat 11am–1am; Sun 5pm–1am.

Ron's from Texas, so don't expect a rave review of this cantina's "Tex Mex Special" platter of nachos, quesadillas, and tacos. But the food's pretty good and we managed to finish an "El Suprema," self-described as the "Mount Everest of Food"! After this hearty sampling of almost every item on the menu, we can guarantee you'll have quenched that yearning for chips 'n salsa. The brick walls, Corona beer, cozy family-style tables, suspended sombreros, and C & W band add a kitschy Mexican flair to this small and jovial place.

LE CAM-LY, No. 1 Patpong Bldg., 2nd floor, Soi Patpong 1-2, Surawong Rd. Tel. 234-0290.
  Cuisine: VIETNAMESE. **Reservations:** Recommended at dinner.
  Directions: Corner of Surawong Rd. and Patpong 1 Rd., south of Rama IV Rd.
$ Price: Appetizers 80B–125B ($3.20–$5). AE, DC, V.
  Open: Lunch daily 11:30am–2pm; dinner daily 6–10pm.

This is sister restaurant to the popular Le Dalat (see "The Shopping/Embassy Area" later in this chapter), serving similar excellent food while lacking the other's lovely garden setting. Indeed, Le Cam-Ly is slightly more businesslike, as befits its neighborhood, and concentrates on a wide selection of small dishes. As at Le Dalat, we love the bi guon (spring rolls with herbs and pork), as well as the salads, pork ribs, and noodles.

BUDGET

LAI CRAM, Thaniya Plaza Building, 2nd floor, Thaniya Rd. Tel. 231-2117.
  Cuisine: THAI. **Directions:** Between Silom Rd. and Surawong Rd. near Rama IV Rd.
$ Prices: Appetizers 60B–180B ($2.40–$7.20); main courses 110B–175B ($4.40–$7). AE, DC, MC, V.
  Open: Lunch daily 10am–2pm.

The upholstered banquettes, marble floors, and modern art in this restaurant hardly suggest Thailand, but the extensive authentic menu (14 soups, 40 rice or noodle dishes, and much more) compensates for the surroundings. As at other Thai restaurants favored by locals, you might want to tone down the spices here. Lunch specials include homok hoi (steamed ground mussels cooked in coconut milk on the half shell) and croket kai kub hed sod (chicken croquettes with fresh mushrooms). There are two other branches: at Soi 23, Sukhumvit Road (tel. 258-2337), and at Laksi Plaza, Soi 49, Sukhumvit Road (tel. 392-5864).

4. THE SHOPPING/EMBASSY AREA

EXPENSIVE

FIREPLACE GRILL, in Le Meridien President, 135/26 Gaysorn Rd. Tel. 253-0444.
  Cuisine: CONTINENTAL. **Reservations:** Required. **Directions:** Near intersection of Rama I Rd. and Rajdamri Rd.
$ Price: Appetizers 145B–800B ($5.80–$32); main courses 350B–1,050B. AE, DC, MC, V.
  Open: Lunch Mon–Sat noon–2:30pm, Sun noon–2:30pm, dinner Mon–Sat 7–10:30pm.

This is one of the city's most intimate hotel restaurants, where formal meals are served in a dark-wood and rough-hewn-birch dining room. At our visit, the Chef's Menu Dégustation featured seafood: curried oyster salad, oysters on the halfshell, and a tournedos of dorado in a caviar-based sauce. Friends who are lucky enough to live in Bangkok year-round rave about the rich pâté de fois gras and the exotic tempura of squid, mullet, and asparagus; others covet the rack of lamb served with gnocchi and the grill's famed grilled meat and fish main courses. And don't even think about saving calories on the dessert!

GENJI RESTAURANT, in Hilton International, 2 Wireless Rd. Tel. 253-0123.

Cuisine: JAPANESE. **Reservations:** Recommended, required for a tatami room. **Directions:** In Nai Lert Park.

$ Prices: Appetizers 60B–300B ($2.40–$12); main courses 85B–1,000B ($3.40–$40); set dinners 700B–2,000B ($28–$80). AE, DC, MC, V.

Open: Lunch daily noon–2:30pm; dinner 6:30–10:30pm.

To our tastes, this is one of the best Japanese restaurants in Bangkok—no great shock, as it's located in a great hotel that caters to a Japanese clientele. If you go to Genji for lunch, you'll likely discover a roomful of Japanese businesspeople, which we take as a good sign for sushi eaters. Lunch served from the set menu is not only delicious but also a great value. For as little as 180B ($7.20) you can have a complete meal. The Executive Special Lunch, at more than thrice the price, is also an excellent value for an extremely well prepared and presented five-course meal. The sushi, something that we always question in warm-water locations, is either imported from Japan or utterly fresh from the morning market.

At dinner, there are both set menus and an enormous selection of à la carte dishes. Aside from the excellent sushi, sashimi, and makisushi, we sampled several robust hot-pot concoctions made with a rich broth, fresh vegetables, and a variety of fish and seafood; you can also find a Kobe beef shabu-shabu at the high end of the price range. A lengthy list of grilled meat and fish courses, as well as a multitude of noodle dishes, rounds out the menu. We would be remiss if we didn't mention the highly imaginative Japanese drink menu, which includes 12 separate cocktails made with sake. What can you say about a sake martini, a sake tonic, or a samurai rock?

We also love the quiet, casually stylish setting, with windows overlooking the Hilton's lush garden. The service by beautifully kimonoed women is friendly and attentive, making even sushi novices feel quite welcomed.

LE BANYAN, 59 Soi 8, Sukhumvit Rd. Tel. 253-5556.

Cuisine: FRENCH. **Reservations:** Recommended. **Directions:** 1 block south of Sukhumvit Rd.

$ Prices: Appetizers 200B–650B ($8–$26); main courses 300B–1,100B ($12–$44). AE, MC, V.

Open: Lunch Mon–Fri noon–2pm; dinner Mon–Sat 7–10pm.

In the same league as the French restaurants in the deluxe hotels, this local favorite serves fine Gallic fare on a quiet Sukhumvit soi. A spreading banyan tree on the edge of the gardenlike grounds inspires the name. Dining rooms are warmly furnished: sisal matting on the floors, stunning Thai carvings, old photos, and prints of early Bangkok adorning the white-clapboard walls.

The cuisine is classically French with Thai touches. The most popular house special is pressed duck for two: baked duck is carved and pressed to yield juices that are combined with goose liver, shallots, wine, and Armagnac or calvados to make the sauce.

The sliced meat is lightly sautéed, and when bathed in the sauce, creates a sensational dish. Other fine choices include rack of lamb à la provençal and salmon with lemongrass. All are served with seasonal vegetables and can be enjoyed with one of the reasonably priced wines. A friendly and capable staff helps make this a memorable culinary evening.

LE BISTROT, 20/18 Ruam Rudee Village. Tel. 251-2523.
   Cuisine: FRENCH. **Reservations:** Recommended. **Directions:** Behind U.S. embassy, off Ploenchit Rd.
$ Price: Appetizers 125B–400B ($5–$16); main courses 335B–700B ($13.40–$28). AE, DC, MC, V.
   Open: Lunch Mon–Fri 11:10am–2:30pm; dinner daily 6:30–10pm.

Long a favorite of the embassy and business crowd, this quiet room will appeal to those who are bored with gilt and colored mirrors. Indeed, we are soothed by Le Bistrot's pale decor, intimate booth seating, and sparkling-crystal and linen table settings. The menu is decidedly non-nouvelle. On our last visit we sampled cream of asparagus soup, curried steamed mussels, baby clams smothered in garlic butter, and rabbit in casserole with a red-wine sauce. At lunch, there are lighter main courses such as salade niçoise, a choice of seven pâtés, steaming gratinée onion soup, and pigeon rôti. It may not be au courant, but Le Bistrot is still one of the very best.

MA MAISON, in Hilton International, 2 Wireless Rd. Tel. 253-0123.
   Cuisine. CONTINENTAL. **Reservations:** Recommended at lunch, required at dinner. **Directions:** In Nai Lert Park.
$ Prices: Appetizers 125B–350B ($5–$14); main courses 450B–1,050B ($18–$42); menu dégustation 1,600B ($64); set menu 1,200B ($48). AE, DC, MC. V.
   Open: Lunch daily noon–2:30pm; dinner daily 6:30–10:30pm.

★ If the *Bangkok Post* had polled us, we would have voted Ma Maison Bangkok's best continental restaurant. They didn't ask us, but other readers have come to the same conclusion. The food is superb, the service attentive but unpretentious and the pastel and bleached-wood decor soothing and gracious. If you're on a budget and want to try Ma Maison, go for the fixed-price lunch for a very reasonable 650B ($26).

Although the menu has changed several times since we first visited, it still retains its French orientation. One can enjoy a classic succulent sliced breast of duck with pan-fried reinette apples or oven baked rack of lamb with rosemary sauce among the selection of highly imaginative dishes. For dessert we sampled several excellent fruit pastries, foregoing the tantalizingly creamy sweets. A fine wine list rounds out the menu, but be careful: The French varieties, in particular, are wildly expensive.

Apparently the king and queen, who rarely dine in public outside of state ceremonies, have graced the restaurant with their royal presence, as have many dignitaries. If it's good enough for them . . .

NEIL'S TAVERN, 58/4 Soi Ruam Rudee. Tel. 256-6874.
   Cuisine: STEAK/SEAFOOD. **Reservations:** Required on weekends. **Directions:** Behind U.S. embassy off Ploenchit Rd.
$ Prices: Appetizers 125B–300B ($5–$12); main courses 350B–1,000B ($14–$40). AE, DC, MC, V.
   Open: Lunch Mon–Sat 11:30am–2pm: dinner daily 5:30–10:30pm.

For over two decades the expatriate community has relied on smartly decorated Neil's Tavern, behind the embassies on Wireless Road, for American-style steak and seafood. Though the dress is casual, you'll find the place full of diplomats and businesspeople in jackets and ties.

Nearly everything about Neil's will make an American in Bangkok feel at home. Surf-and-turf, charcoal-broiled filet (with burgundy sauce), and cobalt-blue Phuket lobster (the closest thing this side of Tonga to a Maine lobster, at about $32) are prepared in a style that's reminiscent of a similar establishment we visited in suburban Omaha—they've even gone so far as to import beef from the United States. Dinner includes salad, baked potato, garlic bread, and vegetable. For dessert, try the chocolate cake.

THE REGENT GRILL, in The Regent, Bangkok, 155 Rajdamri Rd. Tel. 251-6127.

  Cuisine: CONTINENTAL. **Reservations:** Recommended. **Directions:** South of Rama I Rd.

$ Prices: Appetizers 150B–400B ($6–$16); main courses 300B–850B ($12–$34). AE, DC, MC, V.

  Open: Lunch Mon–Fri noon–2:30pm; dinner daily 6:30–11pm.

The Regent Grill dining room, best described as well landscaped—a Thai/California touch—is a treat at lunch when the light pours in, bathing the slickly done room in warm tones. The menu is equally sunny. Daily specials often combine Thai ingredients with those from Mexico or Italy. This cross-cultural dining experience originated at the Regent Beverly Wilshire in Los Angeles, lending a certain California-cuisine aura to the grill's inventive bill of fare. At a recent lunch we had vegetable salad with a tart coriander dressing, creamy corn bisque with rock lobster, and grilled plakapong with caper mayonnaise. There is a two-course set lunch at a very reasonable 450B ($22). Dinner delights include lobster cream soup with lemongrass, angel-hair pasta with Thai basil and tomato sauce, and surf-and-turf U.S. prime rib served with a tiger prawn. As with almost all first-class Bangkok restaurants, watch out for surprisingly high wine prices. A bottle of average-quality wine runs about 850B ($34).

MODERATE

BOURBON STREET BAR & RESTAURANT, 29/4–6 Soi 22, Sukhumvit Rd. Tel. 259-0328.

  Cuisine: CAJUN. **Reservations:** Not required. **Directions:** Behind Washington Theater.

$ Prices: Appetizers 85B–125B ($3.40–$5); main courses 90B–450B ($3.60–$18). AE, MC, V.

  Open: Sun–Fri 7am–1am, Sat 7am–1:30am.

This is a longtime favorite among expatriates for New Orleans–style Southern cooking. Though the food will not overwhelm those who have tasted New Orleans' best, there is some Southern comfort to be found in the tasty spicy Cajun gumbo, blackened redfish, steak, barbecue (chicken, pork, and ribs), and pecan pie. And you won't find a purer American bar scene in Bangkok—white-tile floors and red tablecloths, with a classic belly-up-to-the-bar bar.

THE CHINESE RESTAURANT, in the Grand Hyatt Erawan, 494 Rajdamri Rd. Tel. 254-1234.

  Cuisine: CHINESE. **Reservations:** Recommended. **Directions:** Corner of Ploenchit Rd.

$ Prices: Appetizers 50B–100B ($2–$4); main courses 145B–1,800B ($5.80–$72). AE, DC, MC, V.

Open: Lunch daily 11:30am–2:30pm, dinner daily 6–10:30pm.

Style and substance are harmoniously wed in this ultraelegant, ultragourmet Cantonese restaurant. Three of Hong Kong's best-known chefs were lured to the Erawan and given free reign to delight customers with the likes of exotic shark's-fin dumpling soup (delicate shreds of shark's fin in a rich broth), delicious pigeon and ham steamed in lotus leaves (moist and a bit salty), scallop and bean curd soufflé (delightfully light and subtle), and a crispy chicken and shrimp dipped in tangy lemon sauce. Of course, we also sampled many of their lighter-than-air dim sum, including some imaginative vegetable and seafood combinations wrapped in seaweed, instead of the typical rice flour pastry. A delightful gastronomic experience in a high-style Shanghai deco-inspired dining room. A real treat!

HARD ROCK CAFE, 424/3–6 Soi 11, Siam Sq. Tel. 251-0792.

Cuisine: AMERICAN. **Reservations:** Not required. **Directions:** In the back side of Siam Sq., opposite the Siam Inter-Continental Hotel.

$ Prices: Appetizers 60B–160B ($2.40–$6.40); main courses 140B–425B ($5.60–$17). AE, MC, V.

Open: Daily 11am–2am.

Yes, it's for real. This is an authentic Hard Rock Café, with the same blue-and-white checkered tablecloths, gold records on the wall, guitar-shaped bar, and even the same menu. You'll forget you're in Bangkok when you peruse the menu, though the traffic on the way home will bring you back down. There are the burgers, the barbecue chicken and ribs, the pulled-pork pig sandwich, fajitas, fries, and more. There is also a nightly band upstairs, usually rock and roll. It's not our thing, but it's a touch of home.

L'OPERA, 53 Soi 39, Sukhumvit Rd. Tel. 258-5606.

Cuisine: ITALIAN. **Reservations:** Recommended at dinner. **Directions:** 1 km (.6 mile) north of Sukhumvit Rd.

$ Prices: Appetizers 120B–260B ($4.80–$10.40); main courses 120B–390B ($4.80–$15.60). AE, DC, MC, V.

Open: Lunch daily 11am–2pm; dinner daily 6–11pm.

The decor is so familiar—exposed brick walls, Chianti bottles covered with candlewax, checkered tablecloths, framed Italian photographs—you'll forget you're in Thailand. L'Opera serves wonderful pasta, veal, grilled meats, pizza, and local seafood prepared Italian style. The homemade gelati and the Italian-crooner Muzak will only enhance the feeling that you're back home in your local Italian joint.

PAN PAN L'OSTERIA, 6–6/1 Soi 33, Sukhumvit Rd. Tel. 258-9304.

Cuisine: ITALIAN. **Reservations:** Not required. **Directions:** Just north of Sukhumvit Rd.

$ Prices: Appetizers 75B–115B ($3–$4.60); main courses 135B–280B ($5.40–$11.20). AE, DC, MC, V.

Open: Daily 10am–11pm.

This is still one of Bangkok's favorite trattorias for casual fare, with two locations. The original L'Osteria has moved into a new tinted-glass and stucco home whose bright balconied dining room provides a fashionable setting for good pastas, passable pizzas, salads, gelati, and Italian coffees. The second outlet, Pan Pan Capri, showing its age but conveniently located, offers the same menu, at 45 Lang Suan Rd. (tel. 252-7104).

THE SEAFOOD MARKET & RESTAURANT, 388 Sukhumvit Rd. Tel. 258-0218.

Cuisine: SEAFOOD. **Reservations:** Recommended for large parties. **Directions:** Corner of Soi Asoke (Soi 21).

$ Prices: Approximately 225B–575B ($9–$23). AE, DC, MC, V.

Open: Daily 11am–midnight.

The Seafood Market & Restaurant is a cross between the consummate tourist restaurant and an American-style supermarket: low ceilings, long, cool fluorescent lighting, shopping carts, and checkout lines. The three-story neon marquee proudly boasts, "If it swims, we have it!" Below it, the open-air kitchen appears reckless and wild, outdoing even Benihana. Inside, you walk to the rear to choose your fish, fresh vegetables, or bounteous fruits (all sold by the pound), and select from the imported wine and liquor choices. Food consultants (not waiters) will tell you how your fish selection is best cooked (grilled, steamed, or fried, and with or without Thai seasoning). Though its spices are distinctly Thai, the restaurant will especially please those who seek out the freshest foods and don't mind paying a premium for them.

SPASSO, in the Grand Hyatt Erawan, 494 Rajdamri Rd. Tel. 254-1234.

Cuisine: ITALIAN. **Reservations:** Recommended at dinner. **Directions:** Corner of Ploenchit Rd.

$ Prices: Appetizers 120B–265B ($4.80–$10.60); main courses 195B–525B ($7.80–$21). AE, DC, MC, V.

Open: Lunch daily 11:30am–2:30pm, dinner daily 6–10:30pm.

Since great word of mouth first drew us to this classy trattoria in the Erawan's arcade, we didn't mind finding a mobbed bar and jovial crowd waiting outside. That's because the popular, hip, young Spasso really pays off with surprisingly good food and even better company. After an authentic caponata (eggplant salad, here served with goat cheese), and minestrone, Ron tried the gnocchi with pesto sauce and John had the Thai-style fusilli with chilis and shrimp. Thin-crust pizza fans will find a dozen combos, all made with fresh ingredients and baked in a brick oven. Ciao-down before the local bands start at 9pm, when the dancing bodies make it hard to think about food.

SPICE MARKET, in the Regent, Bangkok, 155 Rajdamri Rd., Tel. 251-6127.

Cuisine: THAI. **Reservations:** Recommended. **Directions:** South of Rama I Rd.

$ Prices: Appetizers 85B–250B ($3.40–$10); main courses 125B–500B ($5–$20). AE, CD, DC, EU, MC, V.

Open: Lunch daily 11:30am–2:30pm; dinner daily 6:30–11pm.

Many contend that the Spice Market is the city's finest pure Thai restaurant. The theatrical decor reflects the name: burlap spice sacks, ceramic pots, and glass jars set in dark-wood cabinets around the dining area playfully re-create the mercantile feel of a traditional Thai shophouse. The food is artfully presented, authentically spiced, and supremely delicious, though the chef understands how to temper spices to your palate. Among the better dishes are khao tang na tung (deep-fried crispy rice with minced-pork dip), kaeng phed ped (duck curry with fried swordfish), kai hor bai toey (a chicken dish), pla dook thord foo (deep-fried cat-fish), and pla jaramet sarm rod (a whole pomfret in a spicy sweet-and-sour sauce). The adventurous might want to try traditional Thai herbal potions, available here (as in local herb shops) for those seeking qualities like long life and potent sexuality. It's a special place to entertain, though slightly pricey by local standards.

THANYING PRINCESS, 5th floor, World Trade Center, Rajdamri Rd. Tel. 255-9838.

Cuisine: THAI. **Reservations:** Not required. **Directions:** In Isetan Department Store, 5th floor.

$ Prices: Appetizers 85B–145B ($3.40–$5.80); main courses 180B–425B ($7.20–$17). AE, MC, V.

Open: Daily 11:30am–10pm.

The original austere Thanying (see Section 1 of this chapter) has been joined by a casual but still-elegant branch at the hopping WTC. The excellent Imperial cuisine that Thanying's royal chef helped revive is here served in a sitting parlor straight out of *The King and I*. Under the somber eyes of several Thai oil portraits, well-dressed diners may peruse an extensive menu of soups, salads, eight different dips and pastes, and unique main courses fit for royalty. There are even separate menu categories for pork, wild pork, and pork rib dishes. This is as good a choice for shoppers who shun fast-food courts as for those with an interest in sampling complex and subtle cuisine.

VITO'S RISTORANTE, 20/2–3 Ruam Rudee Village. Tel. 251-9455.

Cuisine: ITALIAN. **Reservations:** Recommended. **Directions:** Behind U.S. embassy, off Ploenchit Road.

$ Prices: Appetizers 145B–435B ($5.80–$17.40); main courses 145B–500B ($5.80–$20). AE, MC, V.

Open: Lunch daily 11:30am–2:30pm; dinner daily 6–11pm.

Ebullient chef Gianni Favro greets newcomers to Vito's with genuine enthusiasm. He's justly proud of the trattoria-style display of delicious antipasti: mushrooms, baked eggplant, peppers, salads, olives, and other assorted appetizers. Although there are many fresh pastas, Gianni recommends his northern Italian specials such as scallopini of veal, grilled meats or fish, and the particularly tasty frutta di mare made with excellent locally caught shrimp and lobster.

WIT'S OYSTER BAR & RESTAURANT, 20/10–11 Ruam Rudee Village. Tel. 251-9455.

Cuisine: BRITISH. **Directions:** On Ruam Rudee Rd., south of Rama IV Rd.

$ Prices: Appetizers 110B–1,000B ($4.40–$40); main courses 200B–600B ($8–$24). AE, DC, MC, V.

Open: Daily 11:30am–midnight.

Wit's is a refreshing bit of Thai-style old England in the middle of the Embassy District. The decor is fancy and soothing without being stuffy, with walls of hunting green and etchings hanging everywhere. The food is authentic, tasty, and interesting. We enjoyed a perfect fish-and-chips, juicy London mixed grill, a plakapong (fish) en papillote, and delicate ravioli in mushroom sauce. Wit, the Thai proprietor, spent several years in London and has a picture of his young self with the young queen to show for it!

INEXPENSIVE

THE CUP, 153 Peninsula Plaza, 2nd floor, Rajdamri Rd. Tel. 253-9750.
Cuisine: CONTINENTAL. **Directions:** Between Regent and Erawan hotels.
$ Prices: Appetizers 35B–125B ($1.40–$5); main courses 125B–325B ($5–$13). AE, DC, MC, V.
Open: Mon–Sat 11am–6pm.

Although a variety of main courses, including excellent daily specials, is available, most visitors appreciate The Cup for its European-style tearoom ambience and its soothing lilac and paisley-print decor. We can't deny that we enjoy savoring a good cappuccino and fastidiously crafted pastries while studying the street life from big picture windows. But our favorite aspect of life at The Cup is its policy, prominently posted: "Please Refrain from Using Mobile Phones in the Dining Room."

JOOLS BAR & RESTAURANT, Soi 4, Sukhumvit Rd. Tel. 252-6413.
Cuisine: BRITISH PUB FOOD. **Reservations:** Not required. **Directions:** Just south of Sukhumvit Rd.
$ Prices: Appetizers 75B–240B ($3–$9.60); main courses 125B–360B ($5–$14.40). No credit cards.
Open: Daily 9am–1am.

If you're in the Sukhumvit area and crave some old-fashioned pub food, this is a decent little spot for beer and some fish-and-chips, a burger, "snake and pygmy" pie, or even roast beef with Yorkshire pudding. Decor is cute, with white curtains and red-and-white-checked tablecloths. American rock and roll will help you feel right at home. At night the bar is crowded with local Anglos and Anglophiles.

LE DALAT, 47/1 Soi 23, Sukhumvit Rd. Tel. 258-4192.
Cuisine: VIETNAMESE/FRENCH. **Reservations:** Recommended at dinner. **Directions:** 1km (.6 mile) north of Sukhumvit Rd.
$ Prices: Main courses 100B–135B ($4–$5.40). AE, DC, MC, V.
Open: Lunch daily 11am–2:30pm; dinner daily 6–10pm.

We appreciate Le Dalat both for its fine food and for its lovely setting. The restaurant is casual, understated, and quietly elegant. The menu is prepared by Vietnamese-trained Thai chefs, and we enjoyed bi guon (spring rolls with herbs and pork) for starters, followed by chao tom (pounded shrimp placed on ground sugar cane in a basket of fresh noodles) and cha ra (fresh filet of grilled fish). If the weather is accommodating, you'll enjoy dining in the gracefully landscaped outdoor garden.

LEMONGRASS RESTAURANT, 5/1 Soi 24 Sukhumvit Rd. Tel. 258-8637.
Cuisine: THAI. **Reservations:** Required for dinner. **Directions:** Off Sukhumvit Rd.
$ Prices: Appetizers 30B–100B ($1.20–$4); main courses 100B–450B ($4–$18); set menus 450B–1,200B ($18–$48). AE, DC, MC, V.
Open: Lunch daily 11am–2pm; dinner daily 6–11pm.

The Lemongrass, located in a converted Thai house decorated in a homey pastiche of Asian styles, runs a kitchen that turns out consistently delicious food, although to our tastes the dishes have been overly tailored to the restaurant's enthusiastic foreign clientele.

Opinions vary, but we find their spices and ingredients border on the bland. Offsetting this is a helpful and knowledgeable staff, with most waiters speaking enough English to guide you through the menu of Thai classics. Among our favorite dishes are gai yang pak panang (richly sauced grilled chicken on coconut sticks), chili-stuffed pork, sumptuous lemongrass chicken, Burmese-style pork curry, and tom yang kung (spicy sweet-and-sour broth flavored with large fresh shrimp and ginger shoots).

NGWANLEE LANGSUAN RESTAURANT, Soi Lang Suan, at Ploenchit Rd. Tel. 250-0936.
   Cuisine: CHINESE/THAI. **Reservations:** Not required. **Directions:** Across street from north side of Lumpini Park.
   $ Prices: Appetizers 35B–115B ($1.40–$4.60); main courses 75B–210B ($3–$8.40). No credit cards.
   Open: Daily 11am–11pm.

This open-air courtyard eatery came to our attention when it was noted as being a favorite of the Oriental Hotel Cooking School's top instructor. We found a lively place crowded with Thais; one where a lack of spoken English was remedied by a photo display of the most popular dishes, coded by number. Everyone around us was having a great meal from the huge selection of fresh seafood and vegetables available, but we found it difficult even to get served. Perhaps we would have done better in one of the two air-conditioned dining rooms. In any case, the dinner that finally came was delicious, and certainly bargain-priced.

BUDGET

CABBAGES & CONDOMS, 10 Soi 12, Sukhumvit Rd. Tel. 251-5552.
   Cuisine: THAI. **Reservations:** Recommended for dinner. **Directions:** .5km (.3 mile) south of Sukhumvit Rd.
   $ Prices: Appetizers 55B–80B ($2.20–$3.20); main courses 95B–210B ($3.80–$8.40). AE, MC, V.
   Open: Daily 11am–10pm.

This may be the only restaurant in the world where population control is the theme, but that's only natural, since it's affiliated with the Population Development Association (PDA), a well-known organization working on this issue in Thailand. Have a drink in the Vasectomy Bar, then take a seat in the Condom Room. Don't be misled by the whimsical theme elements—this is a very popular eatery serving excellent food. Try the yam tung yang, aka condom salad (prawns and chicken on Shanghai noodles), or the chaw muang (chicken and onions steamed in dough), or perhaps the sam lee dad deao (deep-fried cottonfish in a spicy sauce). Don't leave without information about the PDA's work, and make a donation if you like their approach.

M.K. RESTAURANT, 47 Soi 39, Sukhumvit Rd. Tel. 260-1988.
   Cuisine: CHINESE. **Directions:** About 1km (.6 mile) north of Sukhumvit Rd.
   $ Prices: Appetizers 25B–65B ($1–$2.60); main courses 35B–175B ($1.40–$7). AE, MC, V.
   Open: Daily 10am–10pm.

This two-level dining room with picture windows overlooking a quiet lawn in a residential neighborhood invites a leisurely meal. Until noon, 20 different dim sum offerings are served in portions of three, four, or five pieces. The rest of the day is devoted to a large variety of noodle dishes, illustrated in a colorful photo-menu. Our English friend, Glenda, liked the egg noodles stir-fried with duck so much that she ordered a second helping! What draws so many Thais (and kids!) to M.K. is the sukiyaki—a Japanese stockpot kind of dish where you cook ingredients in a pot at your table, adding your own seasonings. The M.K. chain has branches in Central Chidlom and the Silom Complex, and is still growing!

SUDA RESTAURANT, 6–6/1 Soi 4, Sukhumvit Rd. Tel 252-2597.
   Cuisine: THAI. **Directions:** 1 short block south of Sukhumvit Rd.
$ Prices: Main courses 35B–150B ($1.40–$6). No credit cards.
   Open: Daily 11am–midnight.

This is one of those basic restaurants where only the food matters. Style is not the point here, though the place has its own charm—it's an open-air, high-ceilinged room with overhead fans cooling the local crowd (mostly Thais and expatriates), which spills out onto the sidewalk. The menu relies on good, solid, well-prepared Thai cuisine with Chinese overtones. We started with a big bowl of tom yam kai (coconut milk soup with chicken), then moved on to grilled yellowfin tuna with cashew nuts and roasted curry paste, then fried squid with vegetables over rice. You could also dive into the fried fish with three-flavor sauce. In the bang-for-the-baht sweepstakes, Suda could just be the winner.

5. CHINATOWN

There are few, if any, large Chinese restaurants in the Chinatown area other than in the hotels. Locals eat at small food stalls or tiny hole-in-the-wall places. We've listed a few restaurants that are part of our Chinatown walking tour (see Section 2 of Chapter 7), all on the fringes of the area.

INEXPENSIVE

RA-BIENG RATCHAWONG, 292–8 Ratchawong Pier, end of Ratchawong Rd. Tel. 222-8679.
   Cuisine: THAI. **Directions:** *By Boat:* Take Chao Phraya Express Boat to Ratchawong (also spelled Rajawongse) Pier, get off and walk to left (north) end of pier. *On Foot:* Walk to end of Ratchawong Rd. and enter restaurant on right side of pier.
$ Prices: Appetizers 60B–180B ($2.40–$7.20); main courses 60B–215B ($2.40–$8.60).
   Open: Dinner daily 5pm–2am.

In this simple Thai restaurant with a world-class view of the river, the decor is nothing fancy but the food is good and inexpensive. Despite the new management, little English is spoken, so point and pray and you'll be fine. We loved the steamed whole garoupa with chili sauce, but those with more sensitive palates should stick with milder dishes like mixed vegetables.

SIANG PING LOH, in the Grand China Princess Hotel, 8th floor, 215 Yaowaraj Rd. Tel. 224-9977.
   Cuisine: CHINESE. **Reservations:** Recommended. **Directions:** Corner of Ratchawong Rd.
$ Prices: Appetizers 90B–200B ($3.60–$8); main courses 110B–1,600B ($4.40–$64). AE, DC, MC, V.
   Open: Lunch daily 11:30am–2:30pm; dinner daily 6:30–10:30pm.

At last, a high-quality mid-upscale restaurant in Chinatown. We've looked for years now for this type of establishment and it's here in the newly opened Grand China Princess. Dishes range across the spectrum of Cantonese, Szechuan, and Tae Chew cuisines. The lotus carpet and dark furniture lend a lush, exotic air to the place. Downstairs, on the ground floor, the hotel is opening a tea/coffee bar, which will also offer traditional Chinese potions to the local trade and daring travelers.

BUDGET

ROYAL INDIA RESTAURANT, 392/1 Chakraphet Rd. Tel. 221-6565.
   Cuisine: INDIAN. **Directions:** On a small soi off Chakraphet Rd., south of Sampeng Lane on western edge of Chinatown.
$ Prices: Appetizers 6B–25B (25¢–$1); main courses 25B–60B ($1–$2.40). No credit cards.
   Open: Daily 9am–10pm.

You'll have to work at finding this tiny, charming Indian restaurant, but it's worth the journey. The northern Indian cuisine is well prepared and dirt cheap. Vegetarians will find solace in the few dozen dishes just for them.

6. SPECIALTY DINING

DINNER WITH THAI DANCE

SALA RIM NAAN, on Thonburi side of Chao Phraya River, opposite The Oriental (hotel). Tel. 437-6211.
   Cuisine: THAI. **Reservations:** Required. **Directions:** Take free shuttle boat from The Oriental's pier.
$ Prices: Buffet lunch 350B ($14); fixed-price dinner 950B ($38) adult, 800B ($32) children. AE, MC, V.
   Open: Lunch daily noon–2pm; dinner daily 7pm (dance performance at 8:30pm).

As you would expect from the Thai restaurant of The Oriental, this is one of Bangkok's special dining spots. Guests sit on pillows at low tables in the glittering bronze-trimmed, teak-and-marble main hall and dine on finely crafted Thai dishes. Readers complain about the food, but everyone loves the ambience. In the evening, classical dancers from Bangkok's Department of Fine Arts perform a 1-hour show of royal dances of the Sukhothai and Ayutthaya periods, as well as various folk dances. Lunch is served buffet style, with no performance. You can take the free shuttle from the dock behind the Authors' Wing of The Oriental, or ferry pickups can be arranged from other hotels. Check with your concierge.

TUM NAK THAI, 131 Ratchadaphisek Rd. Tel. 274-6420.
   Cuisine: THAI/CHINESE. **Reservations:** Recommended for large groups. **Directions:** 1.6km (1 mile) north of New Phetchaburi Rd. on Ratchadaphisek Rd., which is parallel to airport freeway.
$ Prices: Appetizers 50B–90B ($2–$3.60); main courses 75B–200B ($3–$8). AE. MC. V.
   Open: Daily 11am–11pm; dance performance 8–9:30pm.

Tum Nak Thai has long billed itself as the largest restaurant in the world, with tables for 3,000. Roller-skating waiters with minicomputers ferry orders to and from 33 far-flung dining pavilions (tell your host you want a table near the stage). Tum Nak Thai has a huge menu, with specialties from Thailand's major regions. The food is good, if hardly Bangkok's best, but we enjoyed the traditional dancing and the overall spectacle of the place.

   In total defiance, the recently opened Royal Dragon Restaurant swept the 1994 *Guiness Book of World Records* title with 32,000 square meters of Chinese pagodas, Confucian temples, and boat-style seating for 5,000! If you enjoy this Thai-style extravaganza, try Chinese cuisine on roller skates and let us know what you think.

READERS RECOMMEND

Royal Dragon Restaurant. *"I believe it's actually the largest restaurant in the world, located at the foot of the Bangna-Trad Expressway. A wonderful time when dining with friends. Everything you select is from live aquariums. Prices are quite reasonable; most of the staff is on roller skates. It's a good time and quite worth mentioning!"*—Tonya Mathis, Portland, Ore.

Green Mango, *Surawong Road. "We found a wonderful restaurant right across from the Tawana Ramada called the Green Mango. It is in a house with a garden, and bills itself as featuring classical Thai cuisine. We had dinner there a couple of nights, spending about $24 for two including tips, drinks, more food than we could eat, and dessert. It is a peaceful oasis in the middle of a noisy part of town, the food is inspired and service excellent. Also, they have their own herb garden, which they were delighted to show us."*—John D. Connelly, Chicago, Ill.

DINNER CRUISES ON THE CHAO PHRAYA

The two most widely recommended cruises are offered by **Loy Nava** (tel. 437-4032 or 233-4195) and **Sun Moon Shine Tour** (tel. 448-0211) Loy Nava's twice-nightly cruises begin at the River City Pier between 6 and 8pm in the high season only. Sun Moon Shine's excursions run according to demand and are available for private charter. The boats are either lavishly converted rice barges or luxury vessels similar to those that travel up to Ayutthaya. Both companies offer a mixed Thai and Western buffet, and in some cases there is music to accompany the meal.

   A dinner cruise can be booked through Sea Tours (tel. 251-5240) or by any major hotel, while reservations on the Sun Moon Shine boats should be made directly with the company's office, 603/1 Arun Amarin Rd. Your concierge can also make this booking. Each company charges approximately 720B ($28.80), including food and transfers.

KOSHER

BOSSOTEL INN, 55/12–14 Soi Charoen Krung 42/1, New Rd. Tel. 235-8001.
    Cuisine: KOSHER. **Directions:** Off New Rd., on way to Shangri-La Hotel.
$ Prices: Buffet 250B ($10). AE, MC, V.
    Open: Dinner daily 6–9:30pm.

Where do Bangkok's finest five-star hotels turn when they're asked to cater a kosher wedding? The kosher kitchen of the Bossotel's plain, informal coffee shop (formerly the Tina Tower Inn Restaurant) handles all such requests, as well as turning out a nightly repast for the hotel's many Israeli guests. The food is prepared under the supervision of Rabbi Jeremy Mizrachi; multiethnic buffets range from barbecue to vegetarian, and from Israeli to Persian. Occasionally the spread includes Thai noodles or an Indian curry, but at our visit offered a tasty tabouleh salad, Israeli diced tomato and cucumber salad, rice pilaf, vegetable and spinach strudel, and an eggplant salad. As of early 1994, the Bossotel Inn served the only kosher food in Bangkok, although this may change in the future (contact the Jewish Association; see "Religious Services" under "Fast Facts" in Chapter 3).

HEALTH FOOD

We didn't find a single strictly vegetarian restaurant in Bangkok, so if you find one, please write to us. We usually recommend that you stick with Chinese, Indian, and Japanese restaurants, most of which offer choices of nonmeat appetizers and main dishes.

However, at our most recent visit, we found that many of the top hotels were offering new "health food," "spa cuisine," "low-fat," and "light" menus. For example, the Dusit Thani has added several vegetarian and low-cholesterol items to their coffee shop and continental restaurant menus; the Grand Hyatt Erawan's Pool Terrace restaurant serves light Thai-style fare to health club members as well as hotel guests; The Oriental is recommending specially prepared low-calorie dishes available in all of their restaurants to guests at their fantastic new health and beauty spa; the Hilton International's grand buffets are staffed by a chef who will custom-make an egg-whites-only omelet, pasta with just a hint of olive oil and garlic, or grilled lean meat or fish.

HIGH TEA

In our opinion, the ritual of high tea is one of the greatest legacies of the British Empire. We love its civilized atmosphere, an opportunity to sample goodies between meals, and the cool and relaxing break it provides in a busy day. The Chinese insist that hot tea (which encourages perspiration) is the most cooling and revitalizing fluid on hot days. After reveling in the tea ceremonies at the following hotels, we couldn't agree more.

GRAND HYATT ERAWAN, Garden Lounge, 494 Rajdamri Rd. Tel. 254-1234.

Cuisine: HIGH TEA. **Reservations:** Not required. **Directions:** Corner of Ploenchit Rd.

$ Prices: Snacks 55B–150B ($2.20–$6). AE, MC, V.

Open: High tea daily 2:30–7pm.

The Erawan's soaring colonnaded atrium, filled with trees and tinkling ponds, makes the Garden Lounge a popular shopper's halt at teatime. As a soothing, classical trio beckons all to enter, diners choose from several blends of tea (80B/$3.20) and an à la carte selection of muffins, scones, meat pies, sandwiches, and ice creams. We always feel less guilty about taking a tea break when the sweets are part of a fixed package, but this is a particularly soothing and special place for a break.

HILTON INTERNATIONAL, Lobby Lounge, 2 Wireless Rd. Tel. 253-0123.

Cuisine. HIGH TEA. **Reservations.** Recommended on weekends.

Directions: Between Ploenchit and New Phetchaburi Rd.

$ Prices: High tea 175B ($7). AE, MC, V.

Open: High tea daily 2:30–5:30pm.

Our favorite high tea for its superb pastries and delicate tea sandwiches, the Hilton's elegant and intimate lounge is also the perfect place to snack and talk. Three-tiered silver servers bearing scones, pastries, and tea sandwiches are as proper as the bone china, linen, and chamber music performed by a classical trio. Excellent value, and a lovely way to while away the afternoon.

SHANGRI-LA HOTEL, Main Lobby, 89 Soi Wat Suan Plu. Tel. 236-7777.

Cuisine: HIGH TEA. **Reservations:** Not Required. **Directions:** On the Chao Phraya River, with street access from the south end of Silom Rd.

$ Prices: High tea 250B ($10). AE, MC, V.

Open: High tea daily 3–6pm.

If a huge buffet of delectable pastries, candies, Thai sweets, puddings, cakes, crêpes, and tasty sandwiches on fresh-baked rolls doesn't faze you, rush to the opulent high tea spread at this comfortable, riverview lounge. One of the riverfront's better food values, an afternoon with the Shangri-La's string quartet provides welcome respite from the city's heat and congestion.

FAST FOOD

The world may drive Japanese cars and watch videos on Japanese TVs and VCRs, but when it comes to fast food in Bangkok, the Americans reign supreme. You'll feel right at home with the wide array of familiar menus and will find the prices comparable to those back home.

In the Siam Square shopping complex and on Rama I Road between Phayathai Road and Henri Dunant Road, there is a long row of fast-food outlets. Among them: **Kentucky Fried Chicken, McDonald's, A & W Family Restaurant, Pizza Hut, Shakey's,** and **Dunkin' Donuts.** Several cinemas that screen American films are found in this area, so you can combine a movie with a Big Mac, side of fries, and crispy apple turnover.

On Ploenchit Road, east of Sogo Department Store and the corner of Rajdamri Road, you'll also find McDonald's and Pizza Hut, as well as **Swensen's**. In the Business District, you'll find further Pizza Hut and McDonald's branches in the C.P. Tower, 313 Silom Rd. The World Trade Center boasts Mr. Donut and K.F.C. Most fast-food restaurants are open weekdays from 9 or 10am to 10pm, on weekends until 11pm or midnight.

For authentic Thai fast food, try the **Mah Boon Krong Food Center** on the sixth floor of the M.B.K. Shopping Center, at the corner of Rama I Road and Phayathai Road. This is our favorite Thai fast-food outlet, offering a vast trove of Thai and Chinese specialties at astonishingly low prices—50B to 75B ($2 to $3) is a princely sum here. Most of the take-out food, packaged in Baggies, is destined for the modern, on-the-go Thai household—giving rise to the somewhat sexist name "the plastic housewife"—but there are also clean booths and tables for those who wish to dine "al shopping mall." One can order small amounts of food here, making M.B.K. an ideal place for the single traveler or for families who want to sample a wide variety of tastes. The ordering system is unusual: buy food coupons from the vendors; take each dish from one of the trays and pay (cafeteria style) with your coupons; cash in excess coupons for change. M.B.K. is one of the best examples of how contemporary Thai families combine local and Western styles.

There are several large new supermarkets as well as smaller food courts and international fast-food outlets in the basement of Silom Complex on Silom Road, on the fifth floor of the World Trade Center on Rajdamri Road, and on the lower level of the New Road shopping complex between Soi 50 and Soi 46.

Lovers of tradition should note that on almost every corner in Bangkok, you'll find a food stand serving simple and inexpensive fare. You must be careful what you eat, making your own judgment about the freshness of the food and the hygiene of the stand. We've survived and even thrived on freshly cooked hot food, but as always, we must warn you—caveat eater.

CHAPTER 6

WHAT TO SEE & DO IN BANGKOK

- **SUGGESTED ITINERARIES**
1. **THE TOP ATTRACTIONS**
- **DID YOU KNOW . . . ?**
- **FROMMER'S FAVORITE BANGKOK EXPERIENCES**
2. **MORE ATTRACTIONS**
3. **COOL FOR KIDS**
4. **ORGANIZED TOURS**
5. **SPORTS & RECREATION**

Few capitals in Southeast Asia have as much to offer as does Bangkok. From its colorful and fascinating klongs to its incredible Buddhist wats, from a wide range of exotic sports (kick boxing, kite fighting, beetle fighting) to a variety of interesting and unusual excursions, Bangkok has a bounty of sightseeing opportunities.

A tour of Bangkok's waterways or a visit to its many wats not only offers compelling attractions but also gives the visitor a rewarding experience of Thai life and culture.

SUGGESTED ITINERARIES

IF YOU HAVE 1 DAY   Tour the Grand Palace, Wat Phra Kaeo, and Wat Po. Have a massage (possibly as part of a walking tour). After lunch, hire a long-tail boat for a Thonburi klong tour. At night, enjoy a Thai dinner with dance performance (see Section 6 of Chapter 5).

IF YOU HAVE 2 DAYS   Spend Day 1 as outlined above. On your second day, take a boat to Wat Arun, then tour the National Museum. After lunch, go shopping. After dinner, walk through the Patpong district.

IF YOU HAVE 3 DAYS   Spend Days 1 and 2 as outlined above. On the morning of your third day, take our Chinatown or Thonburi walking tour, with stops for more shopping. In the afternoon, take a tour of Jim Thompson's House (museum).

IF YOU HAVE 5 DAYS OR MORE   Spend Days 1 through 3 as outlined above. On day 4, take a boat trip to Ayutthaya and the Bang Pa-In Summer Palace. On your fifth day, you might hire a car or join a tour to the Floating Market at Damnoen Saduak. Visit Wang Suan Pakkard in the afternoon.

1. THE TOP ATTRACTIONS

BANGKOK'S WATERWAYS

The history of Bangkok was written on its waterways, which have always been the essential focus of the city's life. When the 18-century capital was moved from Ayutthaya to Thonburi, and then across the river to Bangkok, King Rama I built a canal (now called Klong Ong Ang and Klong Banglamphu) that created Ratanakosin Island out of the large bend in the river, to strengthen the defensive position of the Grand Palace. Other klongs were added, these becoming the boulevards and avenues of the city. Boats were the primary means of transportation, with horse-drawn travel reserved for royalty.

Like Ayutthaya before it, Bangkok became known as the Venice of the East. Sadly, many of its klongs have been paved over in the last decade or so. But the magnificent Chao Phraya River (which means River of Kings) continues to cut through the heart of the city, separating the early capital of Thonburi from today's Bangkok. On the Thonburi side, the klongs still branch off into a network of arteries that are relatively unchanged as the centers of neighborhood life.

Boats of all sizes and shapes ply the Chao Phraya River day and night. Ferries run up, down, and across the water, transporting commuters to work, kids to school, and saffron-robed monks to temple. Elegant rice barges pull mountains of rice, gravel, sand, lumber, and vegetables, as well as carrying the countless families who make them their homes.

The strangest, most frequently seen boat on the river is the *hang yao* (long-tail water taxi), a long, thin, graceful vessel powered by an automobile engine connected by a long, exposed shaft (tail) to the propeller. The exposed engine is balanced on a fulcrum mount, and muscular boatmen move the entire motor-and-shaft assembly to steer the boat—an amazing feat of strength and balance, especially at 30 knots. These water taxis carry passengers throughout the maze of klongs and are a vital element in supplying Bangkok with fresh food from upriver farms and fresh fish from coastal villages.

For an intimate glimpse of traditional Thai life, we urge you to explore the waterways. You'll see people using the river to bathe, wash their clothes, and even brush their teeth (a habit not recommended to Westerners). Floating kitchens in sampans serve rice and noodles to customers in other boats. Men dance across carpets of logs floating to lumber mills. Wooden houses on stilts spread back from the banks of the river and klongs, each with its own spirit house perfumed with incense and decked out with flowers and other offerings.

The best way to see the waterways is to travel as many Thais do—by boat. The Chao Phraya Express Boat ferries are our favorite mode of transportation in Bangkok. The air is clean, the scenery fascinating, and the price is right (see "Getting Around" in Chapter 2). But to get closer to the everyday pattern of Bangkok life, you have to leave the river and explore the klongs.

There are several approaches to touring the klongs. Both Sea Tours Company and World Travel Service offer standard group tours: the basic canal tour is organized around the so-called Floating Market in Thonburi, but it's become so touristy and crowded that we can't recommend it. Instead, to really see the waterways, take either a rice barge cruise or a canal tour that is devoted to just that. Some tours explore the canals north of the city on the west bank, where the signs of urban sprawl are less visible.

Better yet, charter a hang yao for about 300B to 400B ($12 to $16) an hour—expect to negotiate the price. You'll find boats for hire at any pier, or you can make arrangements through your hotel concierge. Beware of independent boat operators who offer to take

DID YOU KNOW . . . ?

- The full name of the capital city is Krung Thep, Maha Nakorn, Amorn Ratanakosindra, Mahindrayudhya, Mahadilokpop Noparatana Rajdhani, Burirom, Udom Rajnivet Mahastan, Amorn Pimarn Avatarn Satit, Sakkatuttiya Vishnukarm Prasit, which translates as "The city of gods, the great city, the residence of the Emerald Buddha, the impregnable city (of Ayutthaya) of God Indra, the grand capital of the world endowed with nine precious gems, the happy city, abounding in enormous palaces that resemble the heavenly abode where reigns the reincarnated God, a city given by Indra and built by Vishnukarm."

- There are more than 100,000 mobile phones in use in Bangkok.

- The island of Ko Samui exports more than two million coconuts to Bangkok each month.

you to the Floating Market or to souvenir or gem shops. Take more time and ask to explore Klong Bangkok Noi and Klong Bangkok Yai, with a stop at the Royal Barge Museum on the way back.

A more leisurely way to see the klongs (our favorite) is to travel on one of the local long-tail water taxis that depart from almost every Chao Phraya Express Boat Pier. Try the Ratchawong (also spelled Rajawongse) Pier, where you can climb into any long-tail boat that is filling up and ride up Klong Bangkok Yai, across the river in Thonburi. The fare is a paltry 5B (20¢) and you can ride until you want to turn back; then get off and catch the next return boat. We enjoyed a stop at the spectacular temple complex of Wat Pak-Nam. Ask the driver to point it out and wander among the myriad buildings of the wat. You'll see few Westerners here. The Maharaj Pier is a good spot to catch a boat into Klong Bangkok Noi, where you could jump off at the Royal Barge Museum on your way back. Try this serendipitous approach and enjoy the rich window into life afforded by Bangkok's klongs. It's a unique experience.

If you've got the time, take a day to visit the more original Floating Market at Damnoen Saduak (about 80km [50 miles] southwest of Bangkok in Ratchaburi Province); see Section 3 of Chapter 10. In this narrow klong, women in woven bamboo hats sell fruit, vegetables, chili paste, rice, and noodles from their small, canoelike boats. All the tour operators offer this as a half-day trip unto itself, or combined with a stop at the Rose Garden Country Resort for a full-day excursion. You can also take a public bus from the Southern Bus Terminal. However you go, start early to see the best of it.

GRAND PALACE, Na Phra Lan Rd. Tel. 222-8181, ext. 40.

One of King Rama I's earliest accomplishments was to move the capital from Thonburi to a more defensible site at a bend in the Chao Phraya River on the opposite bank. The site he picked was then the center of the Chinese community, which was moved south to an area called Sampeng, the current Chinatown.

Rama I had the capital built in the exact image of the destroyed Ayutthaya. The construction of the Grand Palace and Wat Phra Kaeo was the first phase of his grand goal, though both were added to and rebuilt in subsequent reigns.

The palace as it appears today was greatly influenced by Western architecture, including colonial and Victorian motifs. Anna—tutor to the son of Rama IV and the central figure in the musical *The King and I*—lived here. The royal family moved to the Chitralada Palace after the death of King Ananda in 1946, but it was here, in 1981, that General Chitpatima attempted to overthrow the government in an unsuccessful coup.

As you enter the palace gate, built in the 1780s, you'll see the **Pavilion for Holy Water,** where priests swore loyalty to the royal family and purified themselves with water from Thailand's four main rivers. Nearby is a lacquered-wood structure called the **Amporn Phimok Prasad** (Disrobing Pavilion), built for the king to conveniently mount his palanquin for royal elephant processions (most of the time it served as a kind of elephant parking lot).

Also nearby is the **Chakri Maha Prasad,** designed as a royal residence for Rama V by Western architects, to commemorate the centenary of the Chakri Dynasty. The king's advisers urged him to use Thai motifs to demonstrate his independence from growing Western influence: the Thai temple-style roof rests physically and symbolically on top of an Imperial Victorian building. This Thai-Victorian structure contains the ashes of members of the royal family on the third floor, the throne room and reception hall on the main floor, and a collection of weapons on the ground floor.

The whitewashed stone building nearby now serves as the **Funeral Hall,** though it was originally the residence of Rama I and Rama II. The corpse of a deceased royal figure is kept here for a year before it is cremated in a nearby field. On the four corners of the roof are Garuda figures ("vehicles" for the Hindu god Rama) symbolizing the king, who is thought to be a reincarnation of Rama. The garden was rebuilt under Rama IV in the 1860s, and the highlight here is a section that reproduces the landscape of a Thai mountain-and-woods fable; here the coming-of-age ceremonial cutting of the Thai princes' knots took place.

Also in the Grand Palace is the **Forbidden Quarters,** or harem building (no one other than the king was allowed to enter), where the king's wives lived. Close by is the **Amarin Vinichai Prasad** (Coronation Hall), built by Rama I and added to by subsequent kings. Today this building is used, like the palace in general, only for coronations, royal weddings, and state events, and it is here that the king makes his most grand appearance.

Admission: 125B ($5). Price includes Wat Phra Kaeo, as well as admission to the Vimanmek Palace (near the National Assembly) and to the Coin Pavilion. The ticket booth is on the north side of the complex.

Open: Daily 8:30am–noon and 1–3:30pm; most individual buildings are closed to the public except for special days proclaimed by the king. **Directions:** Near Sanam Luang. Take Chao Phraya Express Boat to Chang Pier, then walk east and south.

WAT PHRA KAEO, within grounds of grand palace. Tel. 222-8181, ext. 40.

⭐ Probably no Thai shrine is as revered as Wat Phra Kaeo, or, as it is commonly known, the Temple of the Emerald Buddha. Part of the Grand Palace complex, it is surrounded by walls over 2 kilometers (1¼ miles) long and contains some of the finest examples of Buddhist sculpture, architecture, painting, and decorative craft in the country.

Central to the wat is the **Emerald Buddha** itself, a rather small dark statue made of green jade ("emerald" in Thai refers to intense green color only, not to the gemstone) that sits atop a huge gold altar. This very revered image was discovered inside a *chedi* (a pointed dome-shaped stupa housing a Buddha relic) in Chiang Rai when a bolt of lightning struck the monument in 1434. Some historians believe that the Buddha was sculpted around that time, attributing it to the Chiang Saen school; others believe that it was produced in Sri Lanka. The reigning king of Chiang Mai, at that time the most powerful state in the north, tried to bring the Buddha to his own city, but on three separate occasions the elephant that was to transport the statue stopped at the same spot in the crossroads in Lampang. Never one to cross the determined spirit of the Buddha, the king built a monumental wat at that spot in Lampang, where the statue remained for 32 years.

A more dogged monarch, King Tiloka, insisted that the Emerald Buddha be brought to Chiang Mai. There it was placed in a chedi at Wat Chedi Luang until 1552, when the new ruler of Chiang Mai, King Chaichettha, took the peripatetic Buddha to the Luang Prabang. Some 12 years later, the statue was moved again, this time to Vientiane, Laos, where it stayed for 214 years, until Rama I brought it back to his capital at Thonburi after his successful campaign in Laos. In 1784, when the capital was moved across the river to Bangkok, Rama I installed the precious figure in its present shrine.

The Buddha, like all others in Thailand, is covered in a seasonal cloak, changed three times a year to correspond to the summer, winter, and rainy months. The changing of the robes is an important ritual, performed by the king, who also sprinkles water over the monks and well-wishers to bring good fortune during the upcoming season.

The Emerald Buddha is housed in an equally magnificent **ubosoth,** used by monks for important religious rituals. The interior walls are decorated with late-Ayutthaya–style murals depicting the life of the Buddha, the steps to enlightenment, and the Buddhist cosmology of the Worlds of Desire, Form, and Nonform. The cycle begins with the birth of the Buddha, which can be seen in the middle of the left wall as you enter the sanctuary, and the story continues counterclockwise. Also note the exquisite inlaid mother-of-pearl work on the door panels.

The surrounding portico of the ubosoth is an example of masterful Thai craftsmanship. On the perimeter are 12 open pavilions, built during the reign of Rama I. The portico galleries across from the ubosoth contain painted murals depicting stories from the *Ramakien,* the Thai version of the Hindu epic *Ramayana.* The pastel and gold-leaf works require repainting every five years or so; it's likely you'll see a restorer working somewhere in the galleries.

Subsequent kings built more monuments and restored or embellished existing structures. Among the most interesting of these are the **three pagodas** to the immediate north of the ubosoth, representing the changing centers of Buddhist influence: the first, to the west, is Phra Si Ratana Chedi, a 19th-century Sri Lankan–style stupa housing ashes of the Buddha; in the middle is Phra Mondop (the library), built in Thai style by Rama I and known for its excellently crafted Ayutthaya-style mother-of-pearl doors, its bookcases containing the *Tripitaka* (sacred Buddhist manuscripts), its human- and dragon-headed *nagas* (snakes), and its statues of Rama kings;

Dusit Zoo ❷

Giant Swing ❶❻

The Grand Palace ❶❷

Kamthieng House ❷❺

Lak Muang ❶❶

Lumpini Boxing Stadium ❷❹

Lumpini Park ❷❸

Magic Land ❷❻

Mini-Playland ❷❾

National Museum ❽

Rajdamnern Stadium ❺

Red Cross
    Snake Farm ❷❷

Royal Bangkok
    Sports Club ❷❶

Royal Barge Museum ❼

Royal Turf Club ❹

Jim Thompson House ❶❾

Queen Sirikit National
    Convention Center ❷❼

Vimanmek Mansion
    Museum ❶

Wang Suan Pakkard ❷⓿

Wat Arun ❶❸

Wat Benchamabophit ❸

Wat Bovornivet ❻

Wat Mahathat ❾

Wat Phra Kaeo ❶❶

Wat Po ❶❹

Wat Saket ❶❼

Wat Suthat ❶❺

Wat Traimit ❶❽

World Ice Skating Center ❷❽

and to the east is the Royal Pantheon, built in Khmer style during the 19th century and now open to the public for one day in October to commemorate the dynasty of the first Rama kings.

To the immediate north of the library is a **model of Angkor Wat,** the most sacred of all Cambodian shrines, constructed by King Mongkut as a reminder that the neighboring state was under the dominion of Thailand.

To the west of the ubosoth, near the entry gate, is a black-stone **statue of a hermit,** considered a patron of medicine, before

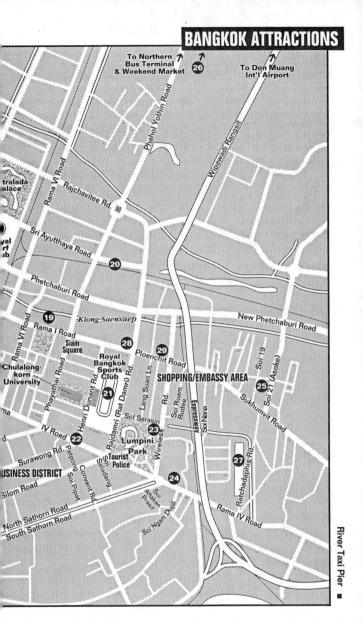

whom relatives of the ill and infirm pay homage and make offerings of joss sticks, fruit, flowers, and candles.

Scattered around the complex are statues of elephants, thought to represent independence and power. Thai kings went into battle atop elephants, and it is customary for parents to walk their children around an elephant three times to bring them strength. Rub the head of one of the statues for good luck (and notice how smooth it is from millions of superstitious palms).

Admission: Included in ticket to Grand Palace, 125B ($5).

Open: Daily 8:30am–noon. **Directions:** Take Chao Phraya Express Boat to Chang Pier, then walk east and south.

WAT PO, Maharat Rd. Tel. 222-0933.

⭐ Wat Po, the Temple of the Reclining Buddha (also called Wat Phra Chetuphon), was built by Rama I in the 16th century and is the oldest and largest Buddhist temple in Bangkok. A 15-minute walk south of the Grand Palace entrance, the compound is divided into two sections by Chetuphon Road: the northern area contains the most important monuments, and the southern portion is where resident monks live.

Most people go straight to the enormous **Reclining Buddha** in the northern section. More than 140 feet long and 50 feet high, it was built during the mid-19th-century reign of Rama III. The statue is brick, covered with layers of lacquer, plaster, and always flaking gold leaf; the feet are inlaid with mother-of-pearl illustrations of 108 "auspicious" signs of the Buddha.

Outside, the grounds contain 91 chedis, four *viharns* (halls), and a *bot* (the central shrine in a Buddhist temple). Most impressive, aside from the Reclining Buddha, are the four main chedis dedicated to the first four Rama kings and, nearby, the library. Wat Po is among the most photogenic of all Bangkok sights, so don't forget your camera and film.

Of the major temples in Bangkok, Wat Po is one of the most active. It is considered Thailand's first public university, with many of the monuments explaining principles of art, religion, science, and literature. Visitors still drop satang pieces in 108 bronze bowls—corresponding to the 108 auspicious signs of the Buddha—for good fortune and to help the monks keep up the wat.

Visitors are encouraged to learn about traditional Thai massage and medicine at the Traditional Medical Practitioners Association center. Although we enjoyed a fabulously restorative Thai medical massage here—90B ($3.60) for 30 minutes, 150B ($6) for an hour—those with sensitive muscles may prefer to abstain and watch instead.

Admission: 10B (40¢).

Open: Daily 8am–5pm; massages offered until 6pm. **Directions:** Near Chao Phraya River, 1km (.6 mile) south of Grand Palace.

WAT ARUN, west bank of Chao Phraya river, opposite Thien Pier.

⭐ The 260-foot-high Khmer-inspired tower, the centerpiece of the Temple of Dawn, rises majestically from the Thonburi side of the Chao Phraya, across from Wat Po. This religious complex served as the royal chapel during King Taksin's reign (1809–24), when Thonburi was the capital of Thailand.

FROMMER'S FAVORITE BANGKOK EXPERIENCES

Boat Trips on the Chao Phraya River This is our favorite way of getting around. The Chao Phraya Express Boats are cheap, fast, and provide the best view of Bangkok. For a more serendipitous experience, charter a long-tail boat from any of the express boat piers (or arrange through your hotel) and take a tour of Klong Bangkok Yai or Klong Bangkok Noi. Better yet, go farther north and explore the more rural klongs near Nonthaburi.

An Evening Drink at a Riverfront Hotel Try the outdoor bars at The Oriental, The Shangri-La, Menam, or Royal Orchid Sheraton.

A Massage at Wat Po After a visit to the remarkable reclining Buddha, pause for an hour or so and enjoy the best value in traditional Thai massage at the massage school at Wat Po.

A Walk Through Chinatown Arise early and explore the back lanes and markets of Chinatown, an area of unchanged ethnic diversity.

A Tour of the Jim Thompson House or Wang Suan Pakkard Both of these museums offer a glimpse of old Thai-style houses, though Jim Thompson merged Western amenities with Thai grace in his klong-side residence. Suan Pakkard is a delightful example of the pure Thai house, with an extensive collection of Thai ceramics and sculpture.

Shopping at the Patpong Night Market This stretch of Sin City has been overrun by stalls hawking ersatz Western jeans, luggage, sunglasses, videotapes, and watches.

Shopping at the Chatuchak Weekend Market It's a long haul to get there, but worth the effort. There are acres of stalls selling everything you can imagine from all parts of the country. Don't miss it. Buy Nancy Chandler's "Map of Bangkok" for a good guide to its layout.

Originally only 50 feet high, the tower was expanded to its current height during the rule of Rama III (1824–51). The exterior is decorated with floral and other decorative motifs made of ceramic shards donated to the monastery by local people, at the request of Rama III. At the base of the complex are Chinese stone statues, once used as ballast in trading ships, gifts from Chinese merchants.

You can climb the central *prang* (tower), but be warned: The steps are treacherously large and steep, and are even more precarious on the descent. If you go up, notice the caryatids and the Hindu gods atop the three-headed elephants. The view of the river, Wat Po, and the Grand Palace is well worth the climb. Be sure to walk around the back of the tower to the monks' living quarters, a tranquil world far from the bustle of Bangkok's busy streets. Although it's called the Temple of Dawn, we suggest a late-afternoon visit.

Admission: 5B (20¢).

Open: Daily 8:00am–5:30pm. **Directions:** Take water taxi from Tha Thien (pier near Wat Po) or cross Phra Pinklao Bridge and follow river south on Arun Amarin Rd.

NATIONAL MUSEUM, Na Phra That Rd. Tel. 224-1333.

⭐ The National Museum, a 15-minute walk north of the Grand Palace and the Temple of the Emerald Buddha, is the country's central treasury of art and archeology (32 branches are located throughout the provinces). Some of the museum's many buildings are themselves works of art.

The current museum was built as part of the Grand Palace complex when the capital of Siam was moved from Thonburi to Bangkok in 1782. It was called the Palace of the Front and was the home of the Wang Na—the Prince of the Palace to the Front, who was the brother of Rama I and his appointed successor (he died before Rama I). There was also a Prince of the Palace of the Rear. The position of princely successor was eventually abolished and the Wang Na buildings became space for the museum. Thammasat University, the College of Dramatic Arts, and the National Theater were also built on the royal grounds, along with additional museum buildings.

To see the entire collection (which we recommend), plan on at least 3 hours, starting with the Thai History and the Prehistoric Galleries in the first building. If you're rushed, go straight to the **Red House** behind it, a traditional 18th-century Thai building that was originally the living quarters of Princess Sri Sudarak, sister of King Rama I. It is furnished in period style, with many pieces originally owned by the princess.

Another essential stop is the **Phutthaisawan Chapel,** built in 1787 to house the Buddhist figure Phra Buddhasihing, brought here from its original home in Chiang Mai. It's an exquisite example of Buddhist temple architecture.

From the chapel, work your way back through the main building of the royal palace to see the gold jewelry (some from the royal collections) and the Thai ceramics (including many pieces in the five-color Bencharong style). The Old Transportation Room contains ivory carvings, elephant chairs, and royal palanquins. There are also rooms of royal emblems and insignia, stone carvings, wood carvings, costumes, textiles, musical instruments, and Buddhist religious artifacts.

We loved the collection of royal funeral chariots, but connoisseurs of fine art and sculpture will spend most of their time in the newer galleries at the rear of the museum compound. Gallery after gallery is filled with both Thai and Pre-Thai sculpture (including some excellent Mon work), as well as Hindu and Buddhist images from the provinces.

Admission: 25B ($1).

IMPRESSIONS

Bangkok is stuck as thick with pagodas as a duff with plums.
—CROSBIE GARSTIN, *THE DRAGON AND THE LOTUS,* 1928

The royal Wat is not a wat but a city of wats . . . there are structures made of tiles and encrusted with strange tile flowers . . . and small ones rows of them that look like the prizes in a shooting gallery at a village fair in the country of the gods.
—SOMERSET MAUGHAM, *THE GENTLEMAN IN THE PARLOUR,* 1930

Open: Wed–Sun 9am–4pm. English-language tours: Thai Art and Culture, Tues 9:30am; Pre-Thai and Thai Art, Thurs 9:30am (call the museum or TAT or check newspaper for current schedule). **Directions:** About 1km (.6 mile) north of Grand Palace.

2. MORE ATTRACTIONS

JIM THOMPSON'S HOUSE, Soi Kasemsan 2. Tel. 215-0122.

Jim Thompson was a New York architect who served in the OSS in Thailand during World War II and afterward settled in Bangkok. He single-handedly revived Thailand's silk industry, employing Thai Muslims as skilled silk weavers and building a thriving international trade around what had been a cottage industry. Thompson mysteriously disappeared in the Cameron Highlands of Malaysia in 1967. Despite extensive investigations, the case has never been resolved.

His legacy was substantial, both as an entrepreneur and collector. Thompson's traditional Thai wooden house contains a sumptuous display of Khmer sculpture, Chinese porcelain, Burmese wood carving (in particular, a 17th-century teak Buddha), and antique Thai scroll paintings.

Thompson's training as an architect paid off handsomely, if his house is any measure of his skill. It comprises six linked teak and *theng* (harder than teak) wood houses from northern Thailand that were rebuilt according to Thai architectural principles but with Western additions (such as staircases and window screens). In some rooms the floor is made of Italian marble, but the panels are pegged teak. The house slopes toward the center to help stabilize the structure (the originals were built on stilts without foundations). The house overlooks a klong that was once home to Thompson's first weavers (long since gone). Still, the densely landscaped garden is a lovely spot, especially on a hot day.

To buy silk from the Jim Thompson Silk Company retail shop, head for the intersection of Surawong Road and Rama IV Road, where you'll find a busy high-priced establishment selling the finest materials. (We do find the clothes somewhat old-fashioned.)

Admission: 125B ($5), 40B ($1.20) students. Profits support local charities.

Open: Mon–Sat 9am–4:30pm. **Directions:** At the end of a small soi off Rama I Rd., opposite National Stadium.

WANG SUAN PAKKARD, 352 Sri Ayutthaya Rd. Tel. 245-4934.

One of our favorite places in Bangkok is Wang Suan Pakkard, or Palace of the Cabbage Garden. This nontouristy site was the home of Princess Chumbhot of Nagara Svarga. Five 19th-century teak houses were moved from Chiang Mai in 1952 and rebuilt in a garden on a private klong, separated by a high wall from the tumult of Bangkok's streets. The Lacquer Pavilion (actually an Ayutthaya house, moved here in 1958) was a birthday present from the prince to the princess.

The princess was an avid art collector and one of the country's most dedicated connoisseurs—credited with having partly financed the excavations at Ban Chiang in 1967. There is an entire room of objects from that site, including pottery and jewelry, surpassed only by the collections in the National Museum. The balance of the collection is diverse, with Khmer sculpture, ivory boxes, perfume bottles, niello ware, and wonderful prints by European artists depicting their image of Siamese people before the country opened to the Western world. There is a fabulous Buddha head from Ayutthaya, as well as a royal barge, and be sure to ask to see the pavilion housing the princess's collection of Thai and Chinese ceramics—it's exquisite.

The gift shop offers ceramics that are a mix of real and reproduction pieces. We urge caution on the buyer, though the prices are quite reasonable.

Admission: 60B ($2.40), including tour of grounds and collections.

Open: Mon–Sat 9am–4pm. **Directions:** East of Phayathai Rd.

VIMANMEK MANSION MUSEUM, 193/2 Rajchavitee Rd., Dusit. Tel. 281-6880.

Built in 1901 by King Chulalongkorn the Great (Rama V) as the Celestial Residence, this large and beautiful teakwood building was only recently restored, then reopened by Queen Sirikit as a private museum housing a collection of the royal family's memorabilia. The highly recommended hour-long tour takes you through a series of apartments and rooms (81 in all) in what is said to be the largest teak building in the world. Highlights are the Trophy Room, the king's working room, and the ivory items in the library. Now the Abhisek Dusit Throne Hall has been renovated to display a collection of Thai handcrafts made by members of SUPPORT, Queen Sirikit's Foundation for the Promotion of Supplementary Occupations and Related Techniques. Nine buildings north of the mansion display photographs, clocks, fabrics, royal carriages, and other regalia. In addition, Thai classical dance and martial arts performances are given twice daily, at 10:30am and 2pm.

Admission: 75B ($3); 125B ($5) with ticket to Grand Palace and Wat Phra Kaeo.

Open: Daily 9:30am–4pm. **Directions:** Opposite Dusit Zoo, north of National Assembly.

ROYAL BARGE MUSEUM, Klong Bangkok Noi, Thonburi. Tel. 424-0004.

If you've hired a long-tail boat on the Chao Phraya River, stop by this unique museum housing the royal barges. These elaborately decorated sailing vessels, rowed by up to 60 men, are used by the royal family on state occasions or for high religious ceremonies. The king's barge, the *Suphanahong*, is decorated with red-and-gold carvings of fearsome mythological beasts, like the Garuda or the dragon on the bow and stern. If you can't make it to the royal barges, there is a smaller display of barges at the National Museum, near Wat Phra Kaeo.

Admission: 15B (60¢).

Open: Daily 8:30am–4:30pm. **Directions:** Take taxi over Phra Pinklao Bridge, or hire boat from Maharaj Pier or any other Express Boat Pier.

WAT MAHATHAT, Na Phra That Rd. Tel. 221-5999.

This temple is still much in use as a Buddhist center of meditation and study, known for its overwhelming amulet, talisman, and traditional-medicine market on the periphery of the temple precincts. Each Sunday hundreds of worshipers squat on the ground, magnifying glasses in hand, studying tiny images of the Buddha, hoping to find the one that brings good fortune. (The newer amulet market is part of Wat Rachanada, off the intersection of Mahachai Road and Ratchadamnoen Klang Road, across from the Golden Mount at Wat Saket.)

Inside the wat is a center for Vipassana meditation of the Buddhist University, with some programs for English-speaking guests. Inquire at the Section 5 office for more information. Wat Mahathat itself is one of Bangkok's oldest shrines, built to house a relic of the Buddha.

Admission: Free.
Open: Daily 9am–5pm. **Directions:** Na Phra That Rd. near Sanam Luang Park, between Grand Palace and National Museum.

LAK MUANG [City Pillar Shrine]. Sanam Chai Rd.
The City Pillar is a diminutive though delightful shrine, said to be inhabited by the spirit that protects Bangkok. Rama I placed a stone pillar—perhaps harking back to the Hindu custom of installing a lingam (phallic symbol) at the center of Siva temples—to mark the site of the city's guardian soul. Lak Muang was recently renovated and though it isn't on most tourist itineraries, many locals pay tribute to the shrine. There is often Thai classical dancing performed (a little before noon) to amuse the spirit.

Admission: Free.
Open: Mon–Fri 8:30am–4:30pm. **Directions:** .5km (.3 mile) northeast of Grand Palace, southeast corner of Sanam Luang.

WAT BENCHAMABOPHIT, Sri Ayutthaya Rd. Tel. 281-2501.
Wat Benchamabophit (Marble Wat), an early 20th-century temple designed by the half-brother of Rama V (King Chulalongkorn), is the most modern of Bangkok's royal wats. Unlike the older complexes, it has no truly monumental viharn or chedi dominating the grounds. Many smaller buildings reflect a melding of European materials and designs with traditional Thai religious architecture. The courtyards are made of polished Carrara marble. Walk inside the compound, beyond the main bot, to view the many Buddhas that represent various regional styles. During the early-morning hours, monks chant in the main chapel—sometimes so intensely that it seems as if the temple were going to lift off.

Admission: 10B (40¢).
Open: Daily 8am–5pm. **Directions:** South of National Assembly, near Chitralada Palace.

WAT BOVORNIVET, Phra Sumein Rd.
Although few visitors bother to come to this quiet retreat opposite the old town wall, we find it rewarding. You can wander along the paths between the monks' quarters and the waterways, used by the king for water-purification experiments. Many kings were monks here, including Prince Mongkut (later King Rama IV), who served as abbot for 14 years. Of the two Buddhas inside the bot, the smaller one in front was cast in bronze in Sukhothai in 1257 to celebrate the country's liberation from Khmer rule. Several murals depict foreigners in Thailand—the English at a horse race, American missionaries disembarking, and Germans prospecting for minerals.

Admission: Free.

Open: Daily 8am–5pm. **Directions:** North of Ratchadamnoen Klang Rd., near Democracy Monument.

WAT SUTHAT, Sao Chingcha Sq. Tel. 222-0280.

The huge teak arch in front is all that remains of the original Giant Swing, which was used until 1932 to thank Siva for the bountiful rice harvest and to ask for the god's blessing on the next. The Minister of Rice, accompanied by hundreds of Brahman court astrologers, would lead a parade around the city walls to the temple precincts. Teams of men would ride the swing on arcs as high as 82 feet, trying to grab a bag of silver coins with their teeth. The swing ceremony has been discontinued, but the thanksgiving festival is still celebrated in mid-December after the rice harvest.

The temple is among the oldest and largest in Bangkok and was built by Rama I—he carved one of the viharn's doors. It houses a beautiful 14th-century Phra Buddha Shayamuni that was brought from Sukhothai. The wall paintings for which it is known were done during Rama III's reign. Outside the viharn stand many Chinese pagodas, bronze horses, and figures of Chinese soldiers.

Admission: 10B (40¢).
Open: Daily 9am–5pm. **Directions:** Near intersection of Bamrung Muang Rd. and Ti Thong Rd.

KAMTHIENG HOUSE, 131 Soi Asoke. Tel. 258-3491.

Like Wang Suan Pakkard, the 19th-century Kamthieng House, on the grounds of the Siam Society headquarters, is a teak house transplanted from Chiang Mai (in the 1960s). The collection here was organized with financial help from the Asia and Rockefeller Foundations, and is oriented toward ethnographic objects illustrating the culture of everyday life.

Many agricultural and domestic items are on display, but we were drawn to the exhibits about the northern hill tribes; if you plan to trek through this area, you would particularly enjoy this small but informative collection. We also enjoyed walking through the grounds, which are landscaped like a northern Thai garden.

The Siam Society supports an excellent library and gallery at the same location, concentrating on regional culture. It also publishes scholarly texts on Thai culture.

Admission: 40B ($1.60); students free.
Open: Tues–Sat 9am–noon and 1–5pm. **Directions:** North of Sukhumvit Rd. on Soi 21.

WAT TRAIMIT, Traimit Rd.

Wat Traimit (Temple of the Golden Buddha) houses one of the most astonishing Buddhas—10 feet high, weighing over 5 tons, and said to be cast of solid gold. This powerful image has such a reflective polished finish that its edges seem to disappear. The seated statue was supposed to have been cast during the Sukhothai period, though it looks strangely robotic.

Its story is as fantastic as its appearance. During a storm not long ago, water soaked a large stucco Buddha (believed to be from Ayutthaya) that was being temporarily stored. The stucco cracked and pieces flaked away, revealing gold underneath. The protective exterior is thought to have disguised the Buddha during the Burmese invasions of the 18th century. Pieces of the stucco are on display in a case to the left of the Buddha.

Admission: 10B (40¢).
Open Daily 9am–5pm. **Directions:** At intersection of Krung

Kasem Rd. and Charoen Krung Rd. (a continuation of Rama IV Rd.), near train station, walk southwest on Traimit Rd. and look for school with playground; wat is up flight of stairs overlooking school.

WAT SAKET, Ratchadamnoen Klang and Boriphat Rds.

Also known as the Golden Mount, Wat Saket is easily recognized as the temple atop a 78m (254ft.) tall hill near the pier for Bangkok's east-west klong ferry. Begun in the late 18th century during the reign of Rama I, this temple is most interesting for the vista of old Rattanakosin offered from its stucco "hill" (a breathtaking, but short, walk uphill). The golden chedi is open to visitors and contains some relics of the Buddha.

Admission Free.

Open: All day for the view; chedi open 9am–5pm.

RED CROSS SNAKE FARM, 1871 Rama IV Rd. Tel. 252-0161.

For a short, entertaining, and enlightening show, stop by the Red Cross Snake Farm (the Queen Saovabha Memorial Institute) in the heart of Bangkok, opposite the Montien hotel. Established in 1923, the farm was the second facility of its type in the world (the first was in Brazil). There are slide shows and snake-handling demonstrations on weekdays at 10:30am and 2pm; on weekends and holidays at 10:30am. You can watch and cringe (we did) as the handlers work with deadly cobras, banded kraits, and green pit vipers. They also demonstrate the milking of venom, stockpiled as an antidote for those bitten by poisonous serpents. If you want a souvenir, the Thai Red Cross will inoculate you against such maladies as typhoid and cholera, then sell you a medical guide.

Admission: 100B ($4).

Open: 8:30am–4:30pm. **Directions:** At corner of Rama IV Rd. and Henry Dunant Rd.

DUSIT ZOO, Rama V Rd. and Rajchavitee Rd. Tel. 281-0000.

The Dusit Zoo (also called Khao Din Wana) is in a lovely park between the Chitralada Royal Palace and the National Assembly. Besides admiring the many indigenous Asian animals (including royal white elephants), you can rent paddleboats for the pond. Children love riding the elephants while tired parents sit at one of the zoo's cafés under broad shade trees.

Admission: 10B (40¢).

Open: Daily 8am–6pm.

LUMPINI PARK, at corner of Rama IV Rd. and Rajdamri Rd.

This large park is good for walking and getting away from the city bustle. During the spring months you'll find lots of kite flying here, and you can even buy your own and join the fun. Or you can rent

---

IMPRESSIONS

One cannot avoid contrasting the size and costliness of the sacred edifices with the meanness of the city in other respects. The houses are small and rude, and the streets in general nothing more than footpaths, overgrown with bushes, bamboos, and palms . . .
—MALCOM, 1838

paddle- or rowboats to take out on the pond in the northwest corner of the park; the boat concession is open daily from 6am to 7pm, charging 30B ($1.20) per half hour plus a 90B ($3.60) deposit. There are a small restaurant and a snack stand near the boat pond.

QUEEN SIRIKIT NATIONAL CONVENTION CENTER, Ratchadaphisek Rd., off of Rama IV Rd. Tel. 229-3000.

The stunning QSNCC (as it's popularly known), christened in August 1991, is the venue for many new exhibits and art shows open to the public. At our visit, an International Travel Show (with interesting photo exhibits highlighting different provinces of Thailand) was followed by a huge philatelic exhibition. Watch the *Bangkok Post* or *The Nation* calendar of events to see what's happening. It's also become the pivotal point for Bangkok's fastest-growing neighborhood, along Ratchadaphisek Road.

Admission: Free.

Open: Call for the schedule of each show. **Directions:** Just south of Sukhumvit Rd. at Soi 21.

3. COOL FOR KIDS

IN BANGKOK

Look under Sections 1 and 2 of this chapter for fuller information about the following:

Dusit Zoo *(see p. 135)* All the fun of a zoo is found in this quiet and lushly landscaped park with a pond (paddleboats are available for rent). On weekends and holidays you'll sometimes find circus performances.

Bangkok's Waterways *(see p. 121)* A trip down a Bangkok klong in a long-tail boat is a treat for kids of all ages, as well as an interesting experience of local life.

Lumpini Park *(see p. 135)* Good for a walk, a paddleboat ride, or watching kite flying in the spring.

Ice Skating (see p. 139) Indoors at the World Trade Center shopping mall, this is a favorite pastime of Thai teens. See Section 5 of this chapter for more information.

MINI-PLAYLAND, 5th floor, Central Department Store, Ploenchit Rd. Tel. 255-6955.

After you've tried all the better-known sights, head for the main branch of this fine department store. The entire fifth floor is devoted to kids' clothes, toys, baby supplies (including a wide range of European, American, and Thai disposable diapers), and a mini-playland. There's a small enclosed play area with climbing toys, slides, plastic toy houses, and other fun stuff. A Lego table seating four is set with hundreds of sample blocks; model trains are running; there's a speedway for miniature race cars, a water table filled with aqua toys, video games and monitors showing movies, and best yet—lots of other kids to play with. Great rainy-day activity.

Admission: Free.

Open: Daily 10am–9pm. **Directions:** At the corner of Chidlom Rd. near the Hilton and Grand Hyatt Erawan hotels.

MAGIC LAND, 72 Phaholyothin Rd. Tel. 513-1731.

This is your basic amusement park with a Ferris wheel, roller coaster, game areas, and even a dinosaur exhibit.

Admission: Entrance 125B ($5); 250B ($10) includes all rides.

Open: Daily 10am–6pm. **Directions:** Near Central Plaza Hotel. Tell your taxi driver you want to go to Daen Neramit (Thai name for Magic Land).

OUT OF TOWN

For more on these attractions, see Chapter 10.

Rose Garden Country Resort *(see p. 183)* With its diverse range of activities, from swimming to cultural shows, this place is fun for all members of the family.

Samutprakarn Crocodile Farm *(see p. 183)* Good crocodile wrestling and trained-animal show.

Samphran Elephant Ground and Zoo *(see p. 184)* Kids will enjoy the elephant shows, crocodile wrestling, magic acts, and more.

Siam Park *(see p. 185)* This wonderful (especially on a hot day!) water park is only an hour away from the city.

4. ORGANIZED TOURS

There are numerous travel agencies offering local tours. Two of the largest are **Sea Tours Company** (tel. 251-4862) and **World Travel Service** (tel. 233-5900), both of which have branch offices in nearly every international hotel and can arrange custom tours as well as offering the standard packages. Typical tours and rates: Temples Tour, 550B ($22); Grand Palace and Emerald Buddha Temple Tour, 600B ($24); Floating Market Tour, 475B ($19); Boat and Barge Cruise, 650B ($26); Jim Thompson's House and Suan Pakkard Palace, 600B ($24); River Kwai Tour, 950B ($38); *Oriental Queen* Ayutthaya Tour, 1,300B ($52); Rose Garden, Thai Village, and Show, 475B ($19); and Damnoen Saduak Floating Market and Rose Garden, 1,000B ($40). Some of these tours have a two-person minimum. Children under 12 pay half price on most tours.

See "Bangkok Waterways" in Section 1 of this chapter for information on boat tours.

Two of our favorite aspects of Thai culture—Bangkok's waterways and Thai cuisine—are combined in an imaginative tour organized on request by **Asian Overland Adventures/The Thai House,** a local travel company. Participants take a 1-hour cruise by long-tail boat deep into Bangkok's back klongs, then arrive at a traditional Thai teak house where ingredients have been assembled for a basic cooking class. After a day of studying, watching, chopping, and sampling class efforts, you're transported by boat 22km (13 miles) back to the city. The fee in 1993 was 1,850B ($74) with a two-person minimum. Contact The Thai House reservation office (tel. 280-0740; fax 662/280-0741) for information on week-long cooking classes and homestay programs.

5. SPORTS & RECREATION

SPECTATOR SPORTS

COCK, BEETLE & FISH FIGHTING These are the spectator sports of Thailand's gamblers, though not easily found by tourists. Besides the more familiar battling cocks, Siamese fighting fish and large-horned beetles are the dueling pugs in these bouts. You can buy the combatants at some markets! Also, children train crickets for fighting and arrange bets; check the marketplaces, especially the Chatuchak Weekend Market.

HORSE RACING Few cities in the world offer easier access to horse racing. There are two elegant tracks in the heart of town: the private **Royal Bangkok Sports Club,** on Henri Dunant Road, opposite Chulalongkorn University, north of Rama IV Road (tel. 251-0181); and the **Royal Turf Club,** just south of the Chitralada Palace on Phitsanulok Road. Races start each Sunday at 12:10pm on an alternating schedule. At our visit, admission to each track was 125B ($5), and betting began at 50B ($2) on a win-place basis only.

KITE FIGHTING A favorite Bangkok sport is kite fighting, a team event with sponsors and prizes. The sport is seasonal, extending from February through April, and it's held in the city's main parks. Even if you aren't part of a team, you can buy a colorful *chula* (male) or *pukpao* (female) kite and just send it flying into the sky. The two major sites are **Sanam Luang** or **Pramane Grounds,** just north of Wat Phra Kaeo; and **Lumpini Park,** at the corner of Rama IV Road and Rajdamri Road.

TAI CHI Though tai chi is actually Chinese, this stretching and exercise regimen is practiced in Thailand by Chinese and Thai alike. You'll have to get up early in the morning to watch (or participate). **Lumpini Park,** at the intersection of Rama IV Road and Wireless Road, is a center of tai chi.

THAI BOXING We are big fans of this sport and heartily recommend it either to boxing fans or to travelers with a genuine interest in Thai culture. It's a combination of karate and Western boxing in which the fighters (who wear Western-style gloves) are allowed to kick their opponents as well, even in the head. There are two major stadiums for boxing: **Lumpini Stadium,** on Rama IV Road, east of the park of the same name (tel. 280-4550 or 252-8765), and **Rajdamnern Stadium,** on Ratchadamnoen Nok Road (tel. 281-4205 or 281-0879), near the TAT office. Admission ranges from 175B ($7) to 1,200B ($48). Bouts begin at 5pm at Rajdamnern and 6pm at Lumpini, and go on well into the evening. There are fights at one or the other every night of the week. Call the TAT office (tel. 226-0060) or the stadiums for the current schedule.

RECREATION

GOLF Golfing in Thailand has rapidly come of age. Japanese and Thai investors have brought in world-class designers to build stunning new courses, many of them a short drive from the heart of

Bangkok. Greens fees range from 1,000B ($40) on weekdays to 2,500B ($100) on weekends; clubs can be rented from 400B ($16). The sport is wildly popular, so reservations should be made well in advance. Some courses require a deposit in advance of the play date. Ask your hotel concierge to help arrange your game.

Navatanee Golf Course, a top-rated course designed by the famous Robert Trent Jones, and site of the 1975 World Cup, is in the eastern suburb of Bangkapi, at 22 Mu 1, Sukhaphiban 2 Road (tel. 376-1031 or 376-1034).

Rose Garden Golf Course is close to the Rose Garden Country Resort cultural center, so the family can enjoy that experience while others tee off. It is located on the way to Nakhon Pathom, 45 minutes southwest of town (tel. 253-0295).

Krungthep Kritha, also known as **Huamak Golf Course,** is a challenging course, located about a half hour east of Bangkok, at 516 Krungthep Kritha Rd., Hua Mak, Bangkapi (tel. 374-6063).

ICE SKATING Though probably not the first must-try activity on any athlete's list, ice skating has taken Bangkok (particularly its youth) by storm! On the top floor of the highly entertaining and futuristic WTC shopping mall is an indoor rink where hundreds wait for the beginning of each session. You can join the fun by renting skates there and hitting the ice, or take a private lesson with an Olympic skater for a whopping 1,800B ($72) per hour! Avoid the bargain Family Session (Saturday 4:30 to 6:30pm, when four skate for 150B [$6]), which is mobbed with novices and potentially dangerous. And you'll be glad to know there's a stiff fine for bringing hockey gear onto the premises.

The **World Ice Skating Center,** eighth floor, World Trade Center, Rajdamri Road off of Ploenchit Road (tel. 255-9500), charges 130B ($5.20) per session including skates. At our visit, 3- or 4-hour sessions with half-hour ice-cleaning breaks were scheduled on Sunday through Friday from 10am to 9pm and on Saturday from 11:30am to 9pm.

SCUBA DIVING The best scuba diving in the country seems to be among the islands off Pattaya and in the waters off the island of Phuket. See Section 2 of Chapter 11 for more information about Pattaya. Call the TAT or write for their brochure about diving around Phuket and at other aquatic destinations.

TENNIS While several of the international hotels have their own tennis courts, there are also two convenient tennis centers.

Central Tennis Club, Soi Attakarnprasit, is found off Sathorn Road (tel. 286-7202 or 391-8824). Fees: 7am to 6pm, 50B ($2) per hour; 6 to 10pm, 90B ($3.60) per hour.

The other center is **Sawadii Soi Sawadii,** Sukhumvit Road between Soi 29 and Soi 31 (tel. 258-4502). Fees: 7am to 6pm, 60B ($2.40) per hour; 6 to 11pm, 100B ($4) per hour.

CHAPTER 7

STROLLING AROUND BANGKOK

1. WAT'S WHAT
2. CHINATOWN
3. THONBURI

Our favorite way to explore any city is on foot. However, we've found that walking is not particularly inviting in many parts of Bangkok. The dense traffic creates so much pollution and noise that strolling down the major streets (in Thai, *thanons*) can be a trying experience.

We've designed three interesting walking tours that avoid some of these problems and provide explorations of three older Bangkok neighborhoods via smaller back streets (*sois*).

Even though any walking trip in Bangkok will inevitably become a hot experience, keep in mind that you'll be entering religious buildings and will need to dress modestly (in other words, no tank tops or shorts). You should also carry bottled water with you, as it's not always easily available in some of these areas. Carry small baht bills or change to use for contributions at the wats (10B [40¢] is appropriate).

The directions for these routes are sometimes complicated, but don't hesitate to ask for guidance if you lose the way.

WALKING TOUR 1 — WAT'S WHAT

Start: Wat Saket.
Finish: Maharaj Pier.
Time: Approximately 2 hours, not including tours of Wat Po and the Grand Palace complex, shopping, or snack stops.
Best Times: Weekends or weekdays in the cooler early morning.
Worst Times: Midday heat and late afternoon (the Grand Palace closes at 3:30pm).

Our "Wat's What" tour is designed to serve as an introduction to many of Bangkok's best-known Buddhist shrines. The walk is centered in Rattanakosin or "old Bangkok," that is, the original part of the city, although many of the buildings and neighborhoods are anything but old. What you will get on this stroll is a view, some shopping, excellent sightseeing, good food, a dose of exercise, and—if you're up for it—a traditional herbal massage.

FROM WAT SAKET TO RATCHADAMNOEN KLANG ROAD
The tour begins at the base of:

1. **Wat Saket,** along Thanon Boriphat, which runs parallel to Mahachai on the other side of one of the city's older klongs (in fact, if you take a klong boat, get out at the Wat Saket stop). Thanon Boriphat is lined with woodworking shops and lumber yards, and the curious will, like us, stick their heads into the shops to garner a view of wood carvers and craftspeople fashioning intricately worked architectural elements. The stairs at Wat Saket (also known as the Golden Mount, built in the late 18th century during Rama I's reign) wind around the base of the massive structure and lead up to the top. (Did you remember to wear a hat and sunscreen? It's always hot up here.) There is a 5B (20¢) admission fee, ostensibly for a chance to look out over the city (the relics inside are of little aesthetic or spiritual importance) and, in our case, to map out the balance of the walking tour. Proceed to the windows on your left as you enter the observatory room. Immediately in front and below is Wat Ratchanada; to the right are the four pillars of the Democracy Monument; farther away and to the left are Wat Suthat and the Giant Swing; and even more distant are the spires of the Grand Palace and Wat Po.

   After descending the winding staircase and ramp, find your way back out to Thanon Boriphat, and turn right, crossing over Klong Mahanak; veer left, then turn left (crossing over the klong again) and proceed straight to:

2. **Wat Ratchanada** (Temple of the Metal Castle). Prior to crossing the street to the wat, pay special attention to vehicles careening in all directions at high speed; the stroll from Wat Saket should take about five minutes. This may be your first time at a Buddhist wat, so explore but don't dawdle, as there are many more (and more interesting) wats to discover.

   Wat Ratchanada is on:

3. **Ratchadamnoen Klang Road,** the Champs-Elysées of Bangkok. (It really was patterned after Paris's most famous boulevard!) Walk west (left as you exit the wat) along the wide street toward the Democracy Monument. The buildings along this long stretch of road, built in the 1920s and 1930s, were the first major integration of contemporary European city planning and architecture in Bangkok, a previously haphazard sprawl of klongs, bridges, and roads; after negotiating the traffic, you can judge which system works better. Along this span you'll find three:

REFUELING STOPS They are **Maria Restaurant** in the Chalerm Thai Theater Building, for delicious and cheap dim sum; **Majestic House,** in the Hotel Majestic Palace on the opposite side of the street, for substantial snacks; and **Methavalai Sorn Daeng Restaurant,** farther down (just opposite the Democracy Monument) for inexpensive Thai food. (See Section 2 of Chapter 5 for details on these restaurants.)

FROM THE DEMOCRACY MONUMENT TO WAT MAHA-THAT After snacking, pay a visit to the:

4. **Democracy Monument,** built to honor the establishment of the modern Thai form of parliamentary monarchy (which these days is under some strain). This spot is popular for picture taking.

   There's an enormous traffic circle that revolves around the Democracy Monument; navigate this (if you can) and backtrack a bit up Ratchadamnoen Klang Road and turn right on:

5. **Dinso Road,** which quickly becomes **Ti Thong Road.** We like this street a lot for its lively local shops: gold vendors, food stalls, bakeries and florists, supplier of Buddhist religious articles, and discount-tape sellers.

   Ease on down Dinso Road/Ti Thong Road. Your goal is:

6. **Wat Suthat** and the **Giant Swing,** located about 3 blocks down from Ratchadamnoen Klang Road, at the corner of Bamrung Muang Road. Take some time to explore Wat Suthat, built over a 27-year period during the reign of Rama III (1824–51). Set in the city's most intriguing temple grounds, the complex is a wonderful and typical mélange of colors, smells, shapes, and textures.

REFUELING STOP Feeling hungry, are we? Just a step across the street from the west gate is the fine **Kanit Restaurant,** where East meets West on your palate and everyone goes home happy; good for a drink, snack, or sumptuous feast. (See Section 2 of Chapter 5 for details.)

Continue several blocks along Ti Thong Road, making a right turn on Ratchabophit Road to:

7. **Wat Ratchabophit.** The road leading down to the wat is another good one for shops (there is also a noisy school with a legion of uniformed students). The temple is elaborately decorated and nicely maintained: walk in and explore the inner sanctum. Pay particular attention to the mother-of-pearl inlaid door and the hand-painted tiles in this European-influenced complex (it may remind some of the Marble Wat).

   Continue along Ratchabophit Road until it dead-ends into a klong. Cross over the footbridge, and on your right is a much-venerated:

8. **Pig** (sculpture, that is), occupying a prominent position atop a rock tableau. The street opposite this porcine beauty is Saranrom Road; take it to:

9. **Wat Ratpradit,** which will be on your left, behind a fairly discreet gate. This certainly isn't a well-known place (probably why we like it, snobs that we are), but you can be among the wat cognoscenti in saying that you've been here, too. Check it out! It's full of neighborhood life, and kids like to hang out here to play wild games of table tennis.

   After demonstrating your paddle proficiency, exit on Saranrom Road and turn left, continuing for a few blocks, which will cleverly deposit you at the rear of the Grand Palace on Sanam Chai Road. But that is for later, our goal is Wat Po, so turn left on Sanam Chai Road (we suggest walking on the cooler, garden side) and continue for several blocks, make a right on Chetuphon Road and, voilá, you'll be at:

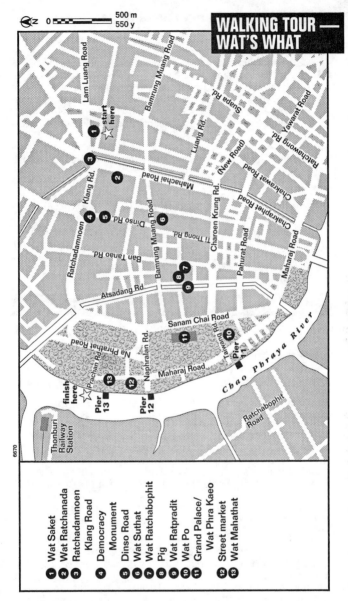

500 m
550 y

1 Wat Saket
2 Wat Ratchanada
3 Ratchadamnoen
    Klang Road
4 Democracy
    Monument
5 Dinso Road
6 Wat Suthat
7 Wat Ratchabophit
    Pig
8 Wat Ratpradit
9 Wat Po
10 Grand Palace/
    Wat Phra Kaeo
11 Street market
12 Wat Mahathat

10. Wat Po (about 15 minutes from Wat Ratpradit). We won't go into details about Wat Po here (you can find them in Section 1 of Chapter 6), but this is the much-ballyhooed stop for those in need of a good herbal massage, Thai style (open daily 8am to 5pm; 100B [\$4] per half hour). Oh, and don't miss the bottoms of the feet of the reclining Buddha (you'll see what we mean when you circumnavigate the wat's most famous attraction).

After exiting Wat Po, work your way to Maharaj Road, running parallel to the Chao Phraya River, turn right, and—if you're so inclined and have the time—enter the gates to the:

11. **Grand Palace/Wat Phra Kaeo** (Temple of the Emerald Buddha, housing Thailand's most sacred Buddha) complex. (If you want to include this as part of the walking tour, we suggest allocating a good 2 hours.)

Continue north along Maharaj Road to Bangkok's most thriving:

12. **street market** for amulets and other trifles; we particularly like the The Tha Chang fruit and vegetable market on the pier of the same name. The final stop is:

13. **Wat Mahathat,** located on Na Phra That Road, which runs parallel to Maharaj Road. To find it, turn right on Naphralan Road and veer left on Na Phra That Road; Wat Mahathat will be a little farther on, abutting the vast green known as the Pramane Ground, or Sanam Luang (at the right time of year, April or so, you may see some mean kite flying/fighting here). This is one of Bangkok's oldest wats and of vast educational significance, as it contains the country's leading Buddhist teaching center.

WALKING TOUR 2 — CHINATOWN

Start: White Orchid Hotel, 490–421 Yarawat Rd. (tel. 225-8243).

Finish: Ratchawong Pier, end of Ratchawong Road at the Chao Phraya River.

Time: Approximately 2 hours, not counting spontaneous shopping sprees.

Best Times: Weekdays 9am to 5pm; Saturday 9am to noon.

Worst Times: Saturday afternoon, all day Sunday.

Chinatown is one of the densest and richest ethnic neighborhoods in Bangkok. The Chinese community was originally located on the site of the Grand Palace, but was forced to relocate when Rama I chose to build his new capital there in the 18th century. This tour is a walk through several shopping areas, each offering a special category of goods, with side visits to several Chinese and Thai temples. The path is slightly convoluted, so you'll have to follow the directions closely. If you get lost, don't be shy about asking for help.

FROM THE WHITE ORCHID HOTEL TO THE CHAO PHRAYA RIVER Turn right out of the front door of the White Orchid Hotel, then right again onto Thanon Plaeng Nam. (The parallel street to the left of the hotel is Thanon Texas, but don't ask us why!) Continue up Plaeng Nam (enjoy the nice costume shop on your left), then cross Thanon Charoen Krung (New Road) and move to the left-hand sidewalk and follow the street as it veers diagonally left and becomes Thanon Phlapphlachai. Walk a short block passing a new Chinese temple, until the street angles right at Wat Kanikapol and a small lane, Thanon Yommarat Sukhim, intersects at a 90° angle to the left. An even smaller lane, Trok Issarahuphap, leads off to the extreme left. Walk a block down this left-most route, but look first at the:

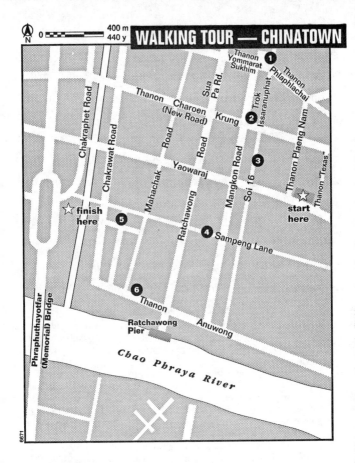

- **1** Chinese funerary shops
- **2** Neng Noi Yee
- **3** Soi 16
- **4** Sampeng Lane
- **5** Wat Chakrawat
- **6** Fine wooden house

1. corner shop on the left, the first of many on this soi that sell Chinese funerary supplies and objects. Paper models of worldly items ranging from books to credit cards and portable phones are cremated with the deceased to ensure comforts of this world on the journey to the next.

After a block, turn right on Thanon Charoen Krung (New Road), and about 50 meters (55 yd.) later turn right into a fantastic Chinese Buddhist temple:

2. Neng Noi Yee. Explore the temple with respect and refrain from taking pictures in the inner shrine, where people are praying. Go to the rear chambers and you'll pass two large temple guardians on the left before finding a trio of gold Buddhas and an assembly of statuary monks. A quiet garden with monks' quarters lies to the rear left but should be left unexplored. As you go out toward New Road, notice the distinctive Chinese architecture above the courtyard entrance.

Turn left and return to the small lane of the funerary shops, cross New Road, then continue down the lane, whose street sign on the right-hand (it's Soi 21 on the left-hand) side reads:

3. Soi 16. You'll pass countless shops selling a staggering array of foodstuffs. On the left you will quickly come to the entrance of a small temple. Explore the side lanes to the left, where meats and seafood are cleaned and prepared, but return to Soi 16 or you'll lose the trail. Beware of motorcycles that brave the crowded walkway.

Continue down Soi 16 and cross busy Yaowaraj Road. Continue down the small street, wider here, until it narrows, then turn right into the teeming shopping world of:

4. Sampeng Lane, also known as Woi Wanit I. (There are no signs here to guide you, however, so ask for help if you're worried.) Walk as far as you like down Sampeng Lane. You'll pass stores selling fabrics, sarongs, shirts, toys, accessories, and more. At the corner of Mangkon Road, the first side lane, there is a colorful gold shop housed in a typical old-style wooden building.

As you continue west, Chinese shops give way to those of Indian textile merchants. Cross busy Ratchawong Road, then continue on Sampeng Lane on Mahachak Road, a small but well-traveled lane just past the shops at no. 148 and no. 175 Sampeng Lane. Turn left on Mahachak Road and walk about 100 yards and turn right past Perupon Textiles (no. 550) through a small ornate gate that leads to:

5. Wat Chakrawat. (If you miss Mahachak Road, you'll come to the busy Chakrawat Road, where you can turn left and left again into the wat.) Entering the wat, you'll find on your left a crocodile pond, behind which is an old *chedi*, surrounded at its base by long rows of Buddhas. The older temples in the complex are being restored and, like Wat Arun, are covered with mosaics of broken china, donated by local people in another century. On the side of the compound opposite the crocodile pond, there is a wonderful rocky grotto with many small shrines and chedis. On the lower wall of the grotto, there is a haunting ghostly Buddha image.

After resting in the tranquillity of the wat, return to Mahachak Road, turn right, and walk to the busy Thanon Anuwong, at the far end of the wat complex. Turn left onto Thanon Anuwong and walk to Ratchawong Road, passing a:

6. fine wooden house, no. 17–19, with a tree growing into its walls. Turn right onto Ratchawong Road and walk to the Chao Phraya River, where you can catch an express boat. Note that the left part of the dock is for the express boats and the center for the cross-river ferries. You must pay 1B (4¢) to enter the Ratchawong Pier.

Note: This tour can also be done in reverse order, starting at the Ratchawong Pier.

REFUELING STOPS The best and most appropriate stop for a Chinatown tour is **Siang Ping Loh,** the top eatery in the new Grand China Princess Hotel. (See Section 5 of Chapter 5 for details.) As you leave the narrow passage of Soi 16, turn right on Yaowaraj Road, and walk to the major intersection at Ratchawong Road. Across the street is the Grand China Princess (the restaurant is on the eighth floor). On the ground floor, you'll find a nice coffee/tea shop serving Chinese pastries. Resume the tour by walking down Ratchawong Road (to the right) to Sampeng Lane, about 100 yards down, and enter to the right.

If you'd prefer to end the Chinatown tour with Indian food, steer a course for the **Royal India Restaurant,** 392/1 Chakraphet Rd. (See Section 5 of Chapter 5 for details.) To get there, you'll need to continue on Sampeng Lane (with a detour for Wat Chakrawat) past Chakrawat Road, to Chakraphet Road, where Sampeng Lane ends. Turn left and, after about 100 meters (110 yd.), turn left at a sign pointing the way to the Royal India.

WALKING TOUR 3 — THONBURI

Start: Saphan Phut Express Boat Pier.
Finish: Thien Express Boat Pier, opposite Wat Arun, near Wat Po.
Time: Allow approximately 2½ hours, not including exploration of Wat Arun.
Best Time: Early morning or late afternoon.
Worst Time: Midday.

This tour starts with a walk over the Chao Phraya River to a fascinating wat, circles a Portuguese Catholic church, continues through an old local neighborhood into an impressive wat complex, goes across a klong by small boat, and ends at the soaring Wat Arun, Temple of the Dawn.

FROM SAPHAN PHUT EXPRESS BOAT PIER TO WAT ARUN Starting at the Saphan Phut Express Boat Pier, near the Pak Klong Talaat Market in Chinatown (see Chapter 3, "Getting Around"), walk over the upriver side of the Memorial Bridge. Pause in the middle and look upriver (northwest), where you will see the "high" points of your journey—the soaring chedis, the elegant temple rooftops, and the cross of the Church of Santa Cruz.

At the far side of the bridge, walk down the steps and continue to the right on the curved drive, past several food shops and across a small lane (Thanon Thesaban Soi 1), and go another 60 feet before turning right into:

1. **Wat Prayunrawonsawat** (Wat Prayun). This complex of temples and buildings was built during the reign of Rama III by a powerful local family. It is totally dominated by the

immense chedi, but look first to your right as you enter to find Turtle Mount, a gnarled grotto of small shrines and stupas that rise out of a small pond. As you circle the mount (Buddhists go clockwise), you'll see the hundreds of turtles that give this grotto its name. You can buy bread (10B [40¢]) or papaya (20B [80¢]) to feed the creatures, but don't forget to get a stick to put the food on, as the turtles have developed a taste for tourist fingers. Enter the temples reverently, after removing your shoes. Near the temple shop, you can leave a donation toward a new temple roof.

Continue straight through the complex, past the giant chedi on your right, then turn right as you pass through the gate, after passing a small graveyard on your left. Continue down the small lane, noticing the fine old wooden houses on your left. Turn left onto the small street (Thanon Thesaban Soi 1), then cross it and turn right into a small walkway past the parking lot and go toward the:

2. **Church of Santa Cruz,** also known as the Temple of Chinese Monk's Quarters, for reasons unknown. The original church was established on this site by the Portuguese community during the reign of King Taksin (1767–82) and was named after a crosslike piece of wood that washed ashore at the site. The first Portuguese came to Thailand in the 16th century as part of their exploration effort in Southeast Asia. Eventually, a minor colony developed here, though there is little presence of that nationality today. The present church was built in the early 20th century with an interior incorporating both Western and Chinese elements. Unfortunately, it's open only for daily masses (delivered in Thai). Sunday masses are held at 6am, 8:30am, and 5pm; those on other days, at 6am and 7pm (tel. 465-0930 or 466-7009.)

You might want to explore the labyrinth of walks through the:

3. **old Portuguese neighborhood** adjacent to the church and admire the fine wooden houses there. Please respect the privacy of the residents, who are not accustomed to tourists in their neighborhood. Most of the paths here end at a small klong, but there *is* a route that will lead back to a small street to continue the tour. Kudos to those who find it, but most will want to retrace their steps to the church and to Thanon Thesaban Soi 1, then turn right onto that street and right again on the first street, Soi Wat Kalaya, and continue until they come to:

4. **Wat Kalaya Namit.** This is a complex of decaying buildings, the largest of which contains a huge seated Buddha in the subdued Mara pose. The statue is sometimes lit only by a feeble fluorescent light, but wait for your eyes to adjust and you'll find it very impressive and moving. You can purchase candles for the altar from the desk on the right. As always, remove your shoes and show proper reverence for the worshipers. The beggars outside the door will approach you on both your entrance and exit, but give only to those you believe are worthy.

Walk to the river and inspect the:

5. **rice barges** that are home to people who work them. (For a short detour, turn right on the walkway and you'll come to another interesting neighborhood and a cross-river ferry dock.) To continue the tour, turn left at the river and walk until you

★ **finish here**

Chao Phraya River

Triphet Road

Chakraphet Rd.

Thanon Wang Doen

Klong Wat Arun

Saphan Phut Pier

★ **start here**

Phraphuthayotfar (Memorial) Bridge

⑤
④
⑥ Soi Wat Kalaya

Klong Bangkok Yai

② ③

Thanon Thesaban Soi 1

①

Thanon Thesaban 2

Thanon Thesaban 3

Itsaraphap Road

Pracha Tipok Rd.

Somdejchaophraya Rd.

Chaokrungthon Rd.

Cross-River Ferry Pier ■

BANGKOK

Thonburi Area

① Wat Prayunrawonsawat
② Church of Santa Cruz
③ Old Portuguese neighborhood
④ Wat Kalaya Namit
⑤ Rice barges
⑥ Klong Bangkok Yai
⑦ Wat Arun

come to a series of homes and shops that specialize in recycling cooking-oil cans.

6. Klong Bangkok Yai runs next to these shops, and you'll soon come to a small dock where you can hail a small long-tail boat to cross the klong. The fare should be 2B (8¢) but you'll be charged 5B (20¢). (You can also reach the dock by returning to the street from Wat Kalaya Namit and walking until it dead-ends at the klong.)

After crossing the klong, you'll find another Buddhist compound. Turn left before the temples and walk past the school buildings up to the main road. Novice monks may try to practice English with you as you pass their quarters. Turn right past the school, then left at a white wall (behind which sits Vichai Prasit Fortress), then right again at Klong Wat Arun. Walk until this small lane joins the larger street, Thanon Wang Doen, and follow it as it curves to the right and leads to the walls of:

7. **Wat Arun** with its recognizable large chedi. Turn right into the Wat Arun complex and make your way past the monks' quarters and other buildings to the river, where you can find refreshments and the entrance to the wat.

The cross-river ferry dock is found on the upriver side of Wat Arun, where you can connect with the Thien Express Boat Pier. Cross over and return to your hotel, or walk from the Thien Pier inland to Wat Po and the Grand Palace. If you're going straight to the Grand Palace, take an upriver boat to the Chang Pier, one stop away.

REFUELING STOPS There are no proper restaurants within the tour. You may find an occasional vendor selling sodas around the temples, but it's best to take along some bottled water, then head for one of the river restaurants after the tour. We like **Kaloang Home Kitchen** (north of the National Library, near the Tewes Pier), easily accessible from the river. (See Section 2 of Chapter 5 for details.)

CHAPTER 8

BANGKOK SHOPPING

1. THE SHOPPING SCENE

2. SHOPPING A TO Z

It may not have Hong Kong's or Singapore's reputation for shopping, but Bangkok will dazzle you with shops and markets ranging from primitive to ultrachic. Even the most world-weary shopper will find unusual high-quality goods at extremely reasonable prices.

1. THE SHOPPING SCENE

The Tourism Authority of Thailand (TAT) publishes the *Thailand Shopping Guide*, which offers sound advice on what to purchase and which markets to visit. If you do encounter problems with merchants, you can contact the Tourist Police (tel. 221-6206-10), who may be able to help you resolve the situation.

Most shops are usually open from 10am to 6pm six days a week. Variations in these hours are noted for some of the shops below.

GREAT SHOPPING AREAS & MARKETS There are many shopping areas in Bangkok; plan your itinerary with a map (once again we recommend Nancy Chandler's, which is known as "The Market Map and Much More"). One of the main issues in planning your shopping routes is traffic. Try to concentrate your efforts in one area—say, Sukhumvit Road—and spend your day exploring it, leaving another area for another day.

Most major hotels have **shopping arcades,** in many cases with respectable, quality shops, though their prices are often much higher than those in less upscale neighborhoods. The best arcades, in our opinion, are those at The Oriental (don't miss the diminutive stall with the model Thai and Chinese ships; one of our favorites!) and The Regent, Bangkok. Goods of similar price and quality are found at the high-end **malls,** particularly at River City Shopping Complex, next to the Royal Orchid Sheraton. The World Trade Center, Sogo Shopping Center, Charn Issara Tower, Peninsula Plaza, and Central Department Store have displaced Siam Square and the nearby Mah Boon Krong Center as the city's leading malls; all of these are centrally located in Bangkok's shopping district.

READERS RECOMMEND

Shopping Tip "*I should like to sound a note of caution about buying goods to be shipped home, based on our experience with buying rattan from Manila Furniture in Sukhumvit Road. We selected items from Manila's 'catalogue' (a selection of photo-articles on rattan furniture cut from Western magazines!) and agreed on a price for the furniture and, separately, a price for shipping and insurance. When we got home we received a letter from the shipping company demanding 100 pounds sterling for ocean freight charges because the furniture had been sent Freight on Board. Looking again at our receipt we saw it had the letters F.O.B. written on it. These letters meant nothing to us at the time we bought the furniture so we had disregarded them—much to our cost. To give Manila Furniture their due, the furniture was made exactly how we wanted it and of good quality, but having paid twice for shipping it was no cheaper than buying it in London.*"
—Philip M. Bates, London, U.K.

Specific streets or areas are also known for excellent shopping. Among these are the **Chinatown streets off Sampeng Lane,** where one finds the so-called **Thieves' Market,** the **Pahurat Cloth Market,** and a million and one **notions stands,** the compact **Bangrak Market,** behind the Shangri-La Hotel; **Sukhumvit Road,** with its upscale antiques and handcrafts shops, as well as bookstores; **Silom Road** and **Surawong Road,** between The Oriental and Lumpini Park; **Thewet Market,** the wholesale flower outlet off Samsen Road; and the huge **Weekend Market** at Chatuchak Park.

It used to be that Charoen Krung Road (New Road) and the smaller outlet roads near The Oriental were lined with antiques shops. There are still a few in this congested area; however, some of the finest shops have moved to the notable **River City Shopping Complex,** creating Bangkok's greatest concentration of high-end antiques galleries. In this great sampling of Thai antiques, you're certain to find something to your taste, but the River City shops are, like the Monogram stores, among the most expensive in the city.

PRICES We've quoted prices in U.S. dollars, as is the custom in many, if not most, upmarket shops. Remember that nearly all shops will negotiate, so don't be shy about asking for a discount or "your best price." If they don't want to haggle, they'll politely inform you that their prices are fixed. Go get 'em!

2. SHOPPING A TO Z

ANTIQUES

Note: Certain items, such as antiques and Buddha images, cannot be taken out of Thailand legally, and Thai Customs is extremely vigilant on this point. Also, there are many well-crafted fake antiques sold at prices equal to those of originals; if you plan to buy an expensive item, make sure the dealer is reputable, and willing to take the object back (and return your money) if you discover that it's not the genuine article.

L'ARCADIA, 12/2 Soi Sukhumvit 23. Tel. 259-9595.

This is a little gem of a shop with very good antique furniture (mostly from Myanmar/Burma), crafts, carved teak architectural ornaments, and older folk art pieces. We particularly admired an early 20th-century Burmese four-poster bed, surely a striking centerpiece for any bedroom, which cost 28,000B ($1,120).

ELEPHANT HOUSE, 67/12, Soi Phra Phinit, Soi Suan Plu, Sathorn Rd. Tel. 286-5280.

This is a mecca of great taste specializing in medium-quality and high-priced Thai and Burmese antiques, quasi-antique or used pieces, and furniture. We were most attracted to the basketry, lacquerware, and early 20th-century photographs of Thailand. Branch: River City Shopping Complex (tel. 237-0077).

THE FINE ARTS, Sukhothai Hotel, Shop No. 4, 13/3 S. Sathorn Rd. Tel. 287-0222.

An expensive but fine collection of terra-cotta pieces, Buddhist statuary, woven fabrics from the region, and one-of-a-kind objects grace the shelves of this small boutique in the ultrastylish Sukhothai Hotel. One of the shop's distinctive offerings is a collection of folk-art religious posters on cloth from Cambodia (about $250); another is the line of terra-cotta reproductions of Sukhothai-era art and architectural elements (beautiful 18-by-24-inch tiles for $880) created by decorators to grace the hotel. Open: Daily 10am–6pm.

THE GOLDEN TRIANGLE, River City Shopping Complex, Room 301, 23 Yotha Rd. Tel. 237-0077.

⭐ This simply decorated gallery, quite unlike anything else in River City, if not in all of Bangkok, is known chiefly for its excellent-quality hill-tribe artifacts. It reminds us more of the fine shops in Chiang Mai than do most outlets in Bangkok. Come to think of it, The Golden Triangle carries some merchandise that's better than what's found in Chiang Mai itself! Silver jewelry from 20 to 100 years old, clothing made from authentic hill-tribe textiles, trading beads, and various musical instruments are among the highlights. We fell in love with a wonderfully beaded Akha headdress that ran a cool $5,760. Although there are many high-priced items, canny shoppers might be tempted by hand-embroidered fabric samples for $45 to $80; cast-brass souvenir bells for $44 to $86; and large antique bells for $140. These quintessentially northern crafts are part of a private collection of antiques culled by Ms. Sumiko Chotikavan, the shop's keenly qualified owner. One of the best in Thailand. Open: Daily 11am–7pm.

THE HEIGHT, River City Shopping Complex, Suite 354, 23 Yotha Rd. Tel. 237-0077, ext. 354.

Also known as Piak Padungsiriseth (for its owner), The Height is best visited for its excellent old mutmee silk, pottery, and statuary. Khun Piak also makes intricate miniature boats to order. However, for good-quality older silk, you can't do much better than this specialty boutique. Open: Daily 10am–6:30pm.

HUM ANTIQUES, River City Shopping Complex, Suite 361–362, 23 Yotha Rd. Tel. 237-0077, ext. 362.

This is yet another River City antiques shop with a few nice

THAILAND

★ Bangkok

Bangrak Market ❼
Chinatown shops ❹
Flower Market ❿
Oriental Arcade ❻
Pahurat Cloth Market ❷
Patpong Night Market ⓯
Peninsula Plaza ⓬
Pratunam Market ⓮
River City
   Shopping Complex ❺
Sampeng Lane shops ❸
Silom Road shops ❽
Sukhumvit Road shops ⓭
   (see separate map also)
Surawong Road shops ❾
Thieves' Market ❶
World Trade Center ⓫

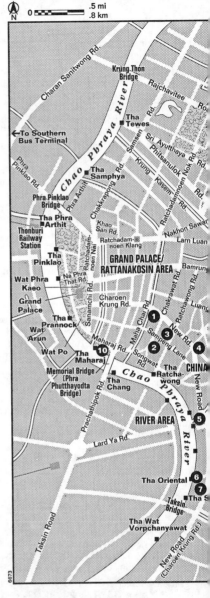

bells ($50 to $70) and a number of fine musical instruments. Hum will ship. Open: Daily 11am–7pm.

LAMPION CURIOS & ANTIQUES, River City Shopping Complex, Room 426, 23 Yotha Rd. Tel. 237-0077.
   The best things at this not-too-special antiques salon are the supposed old Lao fabrics ($24 to $52 a piece), as well as several Thai baskets and silver.

MONOGRAM I AND II, in The Oriental (hotel) and the Oriental Arcade. Tel. 236-0400, ext. 3371.

These are the oldest, and, if Elizabeth Taylor and the Reagans are to be believed, once were the finest, antiques shops in Bangkok. On our last visit we did find some gorgeous carved wooden sculpture and finely embroidered Burmese tapestries (*kalaga*) here, and the staff is wonderful, but the prices are as high as any in Bangkok. Open: Daily 9am–8pm.

NEOLD COLLECTION, 149/2–3 Surawong Rd. Tel. 235-8352.

A fine selection of new and old objects, including recently made paintings, hill-tribe shell belts ($150), 19th-century Chinese puppets ($650), a small offering of furniture, and finely crafted silver boxes. Only the rarest items may have difficulty leaving the country. Open: Mon–Fri 10am–8:30pm, Sat 10am–6pm. Branch: The Regent, Bangkok, 155 Rajdamri Rd. (tel. 250-0737).

THE OLD TIME, River City Shopping Complex, Suite 404–405, 23 Yotha Rd. Tel. 237-0077.

The Old Time is one of those places that gets better the longer you browse. Khmer stone sculptures are found intermixed with impressive 18th- to 20th-century furniture. When we last visited, our eyes were drawn to several 60- to 70-year-old baskets ($190), exquisite early 20th-century musical instruments ($770), and betelnut sets over 100 years old ($192). Open: Daily 10:30am–7pm.

PENG SENG, 942/1–3 Rama IV Rd. at Surawong. Tel. 236-8010.

After encountering so many fakes, it's a wonder to find anything genuine in the world of Thai antiques. We are hardly expert enough to judge, but those in the know assure us that the objects sold at Peng Seng are the genuine article. Located near Jim Thompson's, Peng Seng's two stories are filled with Thai and Chinese sculptures and pottery. An antique teapot or celadon bowl may cost over $1,500, but then, again, you could pay $27,000 for a 3-foot-high Khmer stone sculpture. Among the more affordable objects that appealed to us was a series of 2-foot-high carved wooden Burmese temple figures at $2,700. Peng Seng exports nearly all of its objects for sale, and can usually arrange the necessary papers for antiques. Not to be overlooked is the store's excellent selection of artbooks for sale. Open: Mon–Sat 9am–6:30pm.

PIECE OF ART LTD., River City Shopping Complex, 4th floor, Room 451, 23 Yotha Rd. Tel. 237-0077, ext. 451.

An all-purpose antiques and chatchka shop with a varied collection of silk, pottery, nice hill-tribe jewelry, and fine samples of mutmee silk. We found prices high, but a good shopper is a tough shopper; negotiate. Open: Daily 10:30am–6pm.

SAOWTHAI IKAT, River City Shopping Complex, Room 438–440, 23 Yotha Rd. Tel. 237-0077, ext. 438.

This may be the best shop for textiles in all of Bangkok, and we like to recommend it to those who prize examples of older woven fabrics. In particular, Saowthai Ikat maintains a great selection of Lao and Cambodian "antique" silk. Open: Daily 10:30am–7pm. Branch: Thaniya Plaza, Room 308, 52 Silom Rd.

BOOKS

Bangkok is blessed with a great many bookstores, many of which carry the English-language variety. We've listed two that are the best and most convenient for most travelers.

ASIA BOOKS, Peninsula Plaza, 2nd floor, Rajdamri Rd. Tel. 253-9786.

Asia Books is the country's largest English-language distributor, and one of Bangkok's best outlets for phrase books and publications

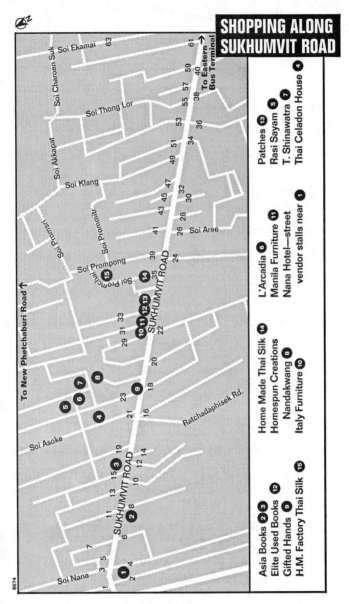

Patches **13**
Rasi Sayam **5**
T. Shinawatra **7**
Thai Celadon House **4**

L'Arcadia **6**
Manila Furniture **11**
Nana Hotel—street
  vendor stalls near **1**

Home Made Thai Silk **14**
Homespun Creations **8**
Nandakwang **8**
Italy Furniture **10**

Asia Books **2 3**
Elite Used Books **12**
Gifted Hands **9**
H.M. Factory Thai Silk **15**

Soi Ekamai
Soi Charoen Suk
Soi Thong Lor
Soi Akkapat
Soi Klang
Soi Promsri
Soi Prommitr
Soi Prompong
Soi Promchai
Soi Asoke
Soi Nana
To New Phetchaburi Road
To Eastern Bus Terminal
SUKHUMVIT ROAD
Soi Aree
Ratchadaphisek Rd.

about Asia. Open: Daily 10am–8pm. Convenient branches: 221 Sukhumvit Rd. (tel. 252-7277), Landmark Plaza (tel. 252-5456), and Thaniya Plaza (tel. 231-2106).

ELITE USED BOOKS, 593/5 Sukhumvit Rd. Tel. 258-0221.
Claiming an inventory of over 39,000 volumes—and we're not going to argue—this bookstore stocks used English, French, Japanese, and German titles, but the majority are in our mother tongue. Elite takes good-quality used books in for trade, or will buy your

books at a very low rate. Open: Daily 9am–9pm. Directions: Near Soi 33/1.

BRONZE & NICKEL

Most of the major handcrafts, silk, and jewelry shops also carry bronze (or bronze-and-nickel-alloy) flatware. We love the hand-made quality and weight of these Thai-designed sets, but be warned that ours has tarnished after repeated cleanings in the dish-washer. Decorative pieces can be coated with silicon, but this process renders them unusable for dining. We purchased a complete set for 12 at Uthai Gems (see "Jewelry," below), including every possible implement, for $150.

SIAM BRONZE FACTORY, 1250 New Rd. Tel. 234-9436.

This is one of Bangkok's larger outlets for complete bronzeware dinner sets. Before you buy, be sure to inquire whether they'll pack and ship, as it may add up to $75, depending on the number of table settings.

S.N. THAI BRONZE FACTORY, 157/33 Phetchaburi Rd. Tel. 215-8221.

This bronzeware outlet, with very competitive prices, offers complete sets, as well as bronze plate and specialty pieces. Pieces are coated upon request. Open: Mon–Sat 8am–5pm.

THAI HOME INDUSTRIES, 35 Oriental Lane. Tel. 234-1736.

This is one of the better outlets for Thai souvenirs and, especially, bronzeware, but you'll have to ignore the surly sales staff. There are many different sets available here for about $150 to $200. Be aware that such sets weigh up to 50 pounds and will have to be shipped home; expect to pay an additional $65 for postage.

CERAMICS

We aren't big fans of bencharong, especially the brightly colored variety, but we do enjoy celadon with the best of them, and the Thai designs and quality have improved steadily over the years.

PRASART COLLECTION, Peninsula Plaza, 2nd floor, 153 Rajdamri Rd. Tel. 253-9772.

This boutique features copies of antique items from the collection at the National Museum. Though not fans of bencharong porcelain, even we liked Prasart's blue-and-white and other muted color combinations. Open: Mon–Sat noon–6:30 pm.

THAI CELADON HOUSE, 8/6–8 Ratchadaphisek Rd., Sukhumvit Rd., Soi Asoke (16). Tel. 259-7744.

The Thai Celadon House displays and sells among the most attractive celadon ceramics in the city. The factory is in Chiang Mai; here is a showroom where you can order and a seconds shop with slightly imperfect goods. Open: Mon–Sat 8:30am–5:30 pm.

CLOTHING

Bangkok is internationally known for its designer look-alike fashions, clothing with famous labels that is "knocked off" at substantially lower prices than the original. Less known are the small, independent designers with their own Thai fashions that look good

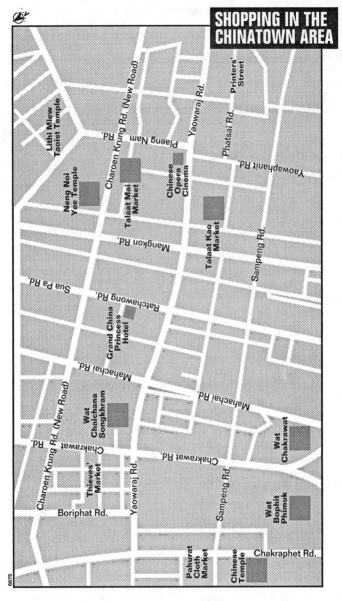

in Asia and back home. We found the quality of tailoring to vary from shoddy to outstanding, so give a careful once-over to seams and material. If you're in the market for high fashion at medium to top-end prices, we suggest heading straight to the Charn Issara Tower for everything from knockoff Matsuda ($35 for a dress shirt) to exquisite custom-made tailoring.

If you only want to buy lengths of silk or cotton, look in the "Silk and Cotton" section later in this chapter.

ART'S TAILOR, 62/15–16 Thaniya, Silom Rd. Tel. 236-7966.

This well-regarded tailor shop, primarily for men, carries a full line of wool and cotton fabrics for suits, pants, and shirts. A suit typically takes about three weeks, allowing for proper fittings and adjustments. Open: Mon–Sat 8:30am–5pm.

CENTRAL TAILOR, 182/1 Silom Rd. Tel. 234-4136.

Similar to Art's but quicker, Central is geared for the businessmen's market and can produce high-quality custom-made clothing in about one week. Open: Mon–Sat 9am–8:30pm. Directions: Near Narai Hotel.

CHOISY, 9/25 Surawong Rd. Tel. 233-7794.

This small French-owned and -operated boutique, featuring ready-to-wear and custom-made clothing, is popular within the expatriate/diplomatic community; fashions tend to appeal to an older, more conservative clientele. We appreciate Choisy's selection of silk clothing made with thinner, less stiff fabrics than found in most Bangkok shops. Off-the-rack fashions include a simple white silk blouse for $50, a midcalf-length skirt for $110, and miniskirts for $80. There is a thriving tailoring business upstairs, with well-made bespoke clothing. Open: Mon–Sat 10am–6:30pm. Directions: Just a few doors down from Jim Thompson Silk Company.

JASPAL, Charn Issara Tower, 2nd floor, 942/86 Rama IV Rd. Tel. 234-7484.

This stylish boutique features up-to-date fashions made from fabrics of varying quality (most of which come from Israel), at low to moderate prices. Open: Daily 10am–7pm. Main branches: Siam Center (tel. 251-5918), Amarin Plaza (tel. 256-9009), and others.

JULIE'S, 1279 Charoen Krung (New) Rd. Tel. 237-6592.

This is the only Bangkok clothier exclusively for women, one recommended by a writer-friend researching a travel article on custom clothing. She wrote: "The manager, Moon, is charming and efficient, and in 24 hours her shop turned out a pair of slacks for us even better cut than the original, with neatly-covered elastic stirrups, for only 400B ($16)." Open: Mon–Sat 9am–7pm.

KAI UNI-3, Charn Issara Tower, 3rd floor, 942/86 Rama IV Rd. Tel. 235-9107.

Yet another of this building's clothing boutiques offering highly styled ready-to-wear fashions at moderate prices. Open: Mon–Sat 10am–7pm. Branches: 6/10–11 Promsri I, Soi 39, Sukhumvit Rd. (tel. 392-6162), also World Trade Center and Peninsula Plaza.

NORIKO, 566 Ploenchit Rd. Tel. 251-7712.

⭐ This boutique carries some of the best-tailored ready-to-wear fashions in Bangkok. Our enthusiasm for the clothing here extends not only to its contemporary design but also to its materials: the most attractive mutmee silk and ikat cotton we found in Bangkok. Noriko offers a full line of formal and casual skirts ($180 to $225), jackets (about $200), and tops ($120 and up), all of high quality and many in smaller sizes only. Open: Mon–Sat 9am–6pm, Sun 10am–6pm. Branch: 919/1 Sukhumvit Rd. (tel. 258-7963).

PERRY'S THAI SILK CO., LTD., 60/6–7 Silom Rd. Tel. 235-3241.

This boutique features both popular ready-to-wear and custom-made clothing. Most outfits take a minimum of two to three days, and Perry's maintains a large inventory of both English and Italian fabrics. In addition to the tailoring operation, Perry's carries a line of silk products, including attractive appliqué pillows for about $12. Open: Mon–Sat 8:30am–7pm.

RIVER MARK, River City Shopping Complex, Suites 238 and 246, 23 Yotha Rd. Tel. 237-0077, ext. 238 or 246.

This and the Mark Collection (in Suite 246) are the best outlets in Bangkok for made-to-order linen clothing. It will typically take two to three days to custom-make a dress or suit, but you can expect good-quality tailoring and fine materials. River Mark also carries a large selection of cotton, silk, and wool, but head here for the large linen inventory. Open: Daily 10:30am–9pm. Branch: 1287–9 New Rd. opposite The Oriental (tel. 234-4453).

VIPAVEES, Charn Issara Tower, 2nd floor, 942/86 Rama IV Rd. Tel. 237-6154.

This boutique (formerly Rasee) for off-the-rack and custom-made clothing represents the height of quality and fashion in this center of sartorial style. Vipavees makes exquisite suits and dresses of fine fabric, with a typical suit selling for $400 to $600. Open: Daily 10am–6pm.

DEPARTMENT STORES & SHOPPING PLAZAS

Bangkok supports a mushrooming number of department-store chains. **Central** is the largest; its most accessible branches are on lower Silom Road, Ploenchit Road near the Meridien President, and off the highway near the airport, next to the Hyatt. Similar to the Central chain—and also best for buying staples such as socks, underwear, and other supplies—is **Robinson's;** the most convenient branch is at the intersection of Rama IV Road and Silom Road.

We always enjoy browsing in the perpetually crowded **Thai Tokyu** department store in the M.B.K. Shopping Center (where there is also the city's best food court; see Section 6 of Chapter 5); this is better for the spectacle of "how Bangkok shops" rather than for the merchandise. The Tokyo-based **Sogo Shopping Center,** just up the road from The Regent, Bangkok. is the city's newest and most upscale emporium; it features merchandise from both European and Asian fashion houses.

Among the city's many shopping arcades, malls, and plazas, our preference is for the **Thaniya Plaza** (Soi 4, Silom Road), the wonderful shops at the **Charn Issara Tower,** the arcade at **Regent, Bangkok,** the nearby **Peninsula Plaza arcade,** the **River City Shopping Complex,** and the arcade at the venerable **Oriental.**

DOLLS

BANGKOK DOLLS, 85 Soi Ratchatapan (Soi Mohleng), Makkasan. Tel. 245-3008.

We read about the dolls made here in the *New York Times* and were delighted to find this far-out-of-the-way "factory" where the intricately detailed figures are crafted. Traditional Thai dancers, hill-tribe figures, and playful images are the main products made and sold. Prices range from $15 to $100. Open: Mon–Sat 10am–5pm (shop), Mon–Sat 8am–5pm (factory); call ahead to make sure they're open. Directions: Call for assistance; plan on 45 to 60 minutes from center of Bangkok.

FURNITURE

It may not be practical for a few small pieces, but some sophisticated shoppers buy rooms full of well-crafted antique and newly made furniture and have them shipped back home. Teak and other hardwoods, as well as wicker or rattan, are the most popular materials. Also stroll down Sukhumvit between Sois 43 to 47 for many other shops.

ITALY FURNITURE, 527–529 Sukhumvit Rd. Tel. 258-4643.
This design and manufacturing outlet of quality wicker and rattan furniture ships to all parts of the world. A typical rattan armchair set runs $480 to $1,120, while a side table costs $64, both without shipping. To ship a cubic meter (about two chairs and a table), expect to pay around $120. Open: Mon–Sat 10am–7pm. Directions: Between Soi 29 and Soi 31.

MANILA FURNITURE, 521 Sukhumvit Rd. Tel. 258-2608.
Very similar to, and just down the street from, Italy Furniture, Manila also sells a complete line of rattan. We priced a complete living room set, including armchairs, table, and sofa, for about $720; however, you'll have to add almost twice that for packing and shipping. As at Italy, you can pick styles either from the floor or from their photo book. It typically takes about three weeks to complete an order and a minimum of one month—we say count on three to four months—to ship. Open: Mon–Sat 9am–6:30pm. Directions: Near Soi 29.

PURE DESIGN, 30 Ruam Rudee Rd. Tel. 251-5485.
If we had our druthers, we would have bought a huge pair of 200-year-old Chinese temple doors on our last visit to this fine outlet (fortunately, we were spent out). Pure Design stocks both new and old furniture (mostly teak or rattan) and is really more of an interior-design studio than a furniture warehouse. One of the more popular, and portable, objects is a silk-and-teak frame that runs approximately $150. Pure Design operates a search-and-export service for antique furniture, so if you can't find that special object, let them take a shot and send you a photograph. Open: By appointment only.

GIFTS/SOUVENIRS

We couldn't fail to mention **street vendors**. They're hardly the most reliable purveyors of goods, but you can almost always count on them for delightful souvenirs—and if you're a good bargainer, you'll get the lowest price in Bangkok. The best stalls are along Silom Road, near Silom Village, near the Nana Hotel off Sukhumvit Road, Soi 4, and in Chinatown. For many, the bustling Night Market in Patpong represents the best shopping for "counterfeit" goods in the city. Although we don't condone the purchase of pirated goods, a huge number of travelers head here to buy pirated audiotapes; most tapes are sold for about 50¢ to $1. If you buy videotapes (also in large supply), make sure that the video standard works with your machine; in most cases, you want NTSC, not PAL, tapes.

HANDCRAFTS

If you shop carefully, you'll find that Bangkok has examples of Thailand's best crafts, equal to anything found in the far-flung regions of the country and at prices that are comparable to such places as Surin, Chiang Mai, and Chiang Rai.

CHITRALADA SHOP, Chitralada Palace. Tel. 281-1111.

The royal family, in their ongoing effort to encourage production of Thai handcrafts, sponsors several stores in Bangkok under the name of the Chitralada Support Foundation. The Chitralada Shop, as well as the Hill Tribe Foundation at the Srapatum Palace, sells standard-quality Thai and hill-tribe crafts at reasonable prices. Open: Mon–Fri 9am–4:30pm. Branch: Oriental Plaza.

GIFTED HANDS, 172/18 Soi 23, Sukhumvit Rd. Tel. 258-4010.

It's difficult to find but well worth the search. Gifted Hands is the shop of Cholada Hoover, a former art teacher at the International School who wanted to find a way to help her village. What she has done is to take traditional village silver-jewelry design and incorporate it with her own glass beads for a more modern aesthetic. Working with seven associates, Ms. Hoover has developed over 600 silver-bead patterns that are then made in Surin and assembled in her Bangkok studio. Silver-bead (98% pure) and silver-accented polished-coconut earrings begin at a very reasonable $8. Bead necklaces, including some made with Ms. Hoover's handblown glass beads, are also inexpensively priced. Gifted Hands also carries the nicest nielloware jewelry (with semiprecious stones) that we've found; a nielloware necklace goes for $75 and earrings range from $10 to $100. As of our visit, the shop took cash only. Gifted Hands publishes a catalog and will ship. Open: Daily 8am–6pm. Directions: On street with Jaspal's Residence II and same soi as Shinawatra; approaching from south, it's third 172 block on right.

HOMESPUN CREATIONS NANDAKWANG, 108/3 Sukhumvit 23, Prasanmitr. Tel. 258-1962.

This is the place for textured-cotton housewares and "soft goods." Homespun features beautifully hand-spun and -woven cotton napkins and place mats in a gorgeous array of colors. Napkin prices begin at a bargain 70¢, place mats start at $1.50, and bedspreads run about $58 for a double. Open: Mon–Sat 9am–6pm, Sun 10am–5pm.

HOUSE OF HANDICRAFTS, The Regent, Bangkok, Parichart Court Arcade, 155 Rajdamri Rd. Tel. 250-0724.

This is a good outlet for a wide variety of Thai, Burmese, and Lao handcrafts and souvenirs. The store stocks hand-carved and -painted puppets and dolls, as well as other traditional Thai crafts, including fine textiles, lacquer, and mutmee. We also like the pillow-size appliqué, appliquéed baseball caps, bronze-and-rosewood flatware, and elephant-shaped celadon pitchers. Open: Daily 8am–10pm. Main showroom: 99/2–7 Moo Ban Chaiyapruek (Bang Na), Bangna Trad Rd. (tel. 316-7272). Branches: Amarin Plaza, 3rd floor, Room 36, and 496–502 Ploenchit Rd.

JADA [1969] CO., 135–135/1 Gaysorn Rd. Tel. 253-7606.

The shop carries a wide assortment of locally produced goods, but we like the Dansk-like teak housewares. Among the better items are platters, salad bowls, serving bowls, implements, and carving boards. Prices are extremely reasonable. Open: Mon–Sat 9:30am–6:30pm.

LOTUS, The Regent, Bangkok. Parichart Court, 155–157 Rajdamri Rd. Tel. 250-0732.

★ This shop, perhaps more than any other in Bangkok, reflects the best of both Asian and European design sensibilities. Along with its branches at Bangkok's Sukhothai and the Amanpuri in Phuket, Lotus is the exclusive domain of upscale tourists from America, Europe, and Asia who are attracted to the new and old objets d'art from Thailand, Burma, Indonesia, Tibet, and India collected by its European owners. The exquisite one-of-a-kind jewels and decorative objects are among the most attractive we've found anywhere in the country. Here one finds stingray-skin desk accessories, Indian ruby-encrusted animal sculptures, luscious cashmere shawls and silk scarves, silver boxes made with supreme craftsmanship, and textiles worthy of a museum. Prices are extremely high. Open: Mon–Sat 10:30am–8pm.

NARAYANA PHAND, 127 Rajdamri Rd., Pratumwan. Tel. 252-4670.

Our ace shopper, Victoria, suggests that this enormous handcrafts emporium, supported by the government, is the ideal spot to work down that long gift list before you return home. Not only is the breadth of souvenirs and goods impressive, but the quality/price relationship is of a very acceptable level. Some items that impressed us: betelnut sets and boxes, jade and semi-precious stone jewelry, mother-of-pearl, carved wood, and lacquer objects. Open: Daily 10am–8pm. Directions: North of Gaysorn Rd.

PATCHES, 591/16 Sukhumvit, Soi 33/1. Tel. 258-5057.

We like the idea of Patches more than the goods, which tend to be too traditionally early American in design and materials for our taste. Patches is the retail outlet for a women's self-help project started in the slums of Klong Toey by Catholic missionaries. Custom-made quilts of a decidedly non-Asian design (they look like what you might find in a rural American church sale!) are crafted by women from low-income families. There are a few Hmong-style products, but the main line of quilts, pillows, and table linens are of the early American variety.

It generally takes about six weeks to finish a quilt, and the shop exports to the United States. Prices are extremely reasonable. Open: Mon–Sat 8:30am–5:30pm.

RASI SAYAM, 32 Soi 23, Sukhumvit Rd. Tel. 258-4195.

★ Founded by a North American, Jonathan Hayssen, Rasi Sayam is our favorite contemporary Thai handcrafts shop in Bangkok. What Mr. Hayssen has done is to locate some of the country's best craftspeople and given them an outlet for their work. And, like others, his effort is supported by the ministry in charge of cottage industries. The geographic area covered spans as far south as Nakhon Si Thammarat and as far north as the Laotian border. Beautiful baskets, loom parts, ceramics, lacquerware, bells, wood carvings, textiles, and a myriad of other, one-of-a-kind pieces are on display in the attractively designed shop. If you're in a rush and can get to only a couple of shops, keep this one at the top of your list. Rasi Sayam is totally reliable, and will ship by UPS air. Open: Mon–Sat 9am–5:30pm.

SONG PLU, River City Shopping Complex, 4th floor, Room 425, 23 Yotha Rd. Tel. 237-0077, ext. 425.

This small boutique is best for its recently made and older baskets. Open: Tues–Sun 11am–6:30pm.

JEWELRY

Again, the best advice is BEWARE OF TOUTS! On your own, shop around at several stores before buying, so that you can compare both quality and price. We were told repeatedly by knowledgeable locals that nearly all jewelers who display their work in the best hotel shopping arcades produce fine-quality work at fair prices. Nearly all jewelry shops, even the most exclusive, negotiate, so be prepared to ask for a discount on the quoted price. We took the advice of William Warren, the *New York Times* correspondent, and read John Hoskin's *Buyer's Guide to Thai Gems* (Asia Books, 1988), an informative and entertainingly written book that even sophisticated shoppers will enjoy; it won't make you an instant expert, but you'll certainly have a better idea of what's on display in the city's reputable shops.

If you're in town to explore the wholesale market, similar to New York's West 47th Street, head for Mahesak Road, just off Silom Road. Here you'll find Thai, Chinese, Iranian, Israeli, and Indian dealers, most of whom are engaged in the import and export of colored cut stones.

ASIAN INSTITUTE OF GEMOLOGICAL SCIENCES, 484 Ratchadaphisek Rd. Tel. 513-2112.

A number of quality gem and jewelry dealers offer a certificate of identification prepared by the AIGS, a professional agency that specializes in categorizing cut stones. A typical analysis takes between 1 to 2 days and includes information about the mineral content, cut, color, and size of the loose (unmounted) stones. If you intend to purchase stones, especially expensive gems, and have the time, you should take advantage of this service, as well as attend their three-hour courses. The new AIGS headquarters is in the Rama Jewelry Center, a high-rise jewelry mart at 987 Silom Rd., near Mahesak Road.

BEE BIJOUR, Peninsula Plaza, 2nd floor, 153 Rajdamri Rd. Tel. 252-1571.

One of the better manufacturers of fashionable costume jewelry made with semiprecious stones is Bee Bijour. Although its main business is tailored to the export market, this boutique displays lines sold to the local and tourist markets as well. Open: Daily 10am–7:30pm.

BUALAAD JOAILLIER, 106–107 Peninsula Plaza, 153 Rajdamri Rd. Tel. 253-9760.

We were impressed by the fantastic stones (especially the Thai and Burmese rubies) and jewelry on display at this decidedly upmarket jewelry-design house. The quality is superb, and unlike most of the jewelry stores in Bangkok, this one eschews the current trends, preferring to base its designs on traditional motifs. We were mesmerized by an emerald necklace that ran a cool $3,400; there are many lesser-priced goodies for sale, so don't worry about our pie-in-the-sky tastes. Open: Mon–Sat 11am–6pm.

CABOCHON, Oriental Arcade, Oriental Ave. Tel. 236-6607.

This well-established and reputable boutique displays brilliant sapphire pendants (for approximately $500) and quality ruby rings accented with diamonds (for $460). As with the best shops, all of Cabochon's pieces are sold with certificates of authorization (by certified gemologists), with an offer of a refund. Open: Mon–Fri 10am–8pm, Sat 10am–6pm. Branch: Ground floor of Dusit Thani (hotel), Rama IV Rd. (tel. 233-4371).

FRANK'S JEWELRY CREATION, Peninsula Plaza, Shop No. 104, 153 Rajdamri Rd. Tel. 254-4528.

Want to shop where Elizabeth Taylor buys her jewels? Look no farther than Frank's, where you'll find displayed the city's most opulent and ornate figurative jewelry. Prices are, expectedly, among the highest around, but of course Frank's will design to your satisfaction. Open Mon–Sat 10am–6:30pm.

J.P. JEWELRY INTERNATIONAL CO., LTD., Hilton International, 2 Wireless Rd. Tel. 253-0123, ext. 8685.

This decidedly high-end shop has both the quality and the prices to match its well-heeled clientele. A lovely pearl-and-ruby necklace goes for $1,600, while an exquisite gold-and-sapphire bracelet costs $1,920. Among the lower-priced (but still costly) items is a small gold bracelet accented with a lustrous sapphire for $640. J.P. is also associated with P.T. Gems and the Royal Jewelry showroom in the Royal Orchid Sheraton. Open: Daily 10am–9pm.

JOHNY'S GEMS, 199 Fueng Nakhorn Rd. Tel. 222-1706.

Johny's Gems, in Chinatown, is one of Bangkok's oldest and largest jewelry emporiums. It enjoys a fine reputation for reliability and price, though you'll have to pick through a huge inventory to find the really good stuff. An added feature: Johny's will shuttle you gratis between the store and your hotel. Open: Mon–Sat 9:30am–6pm.

NEW UNIVERSAL, 1144–46 New Rd. Tel. 234-3514.

One of the holdouts on the diminished commercial strip along New Road, this shop next to the G.P.O. is run by the venerable Mr. Sook, who has provided good service to upscale tourists and expatriates for years. The styles tend to be fairly conventional and we found the prices to be quite fair. Open: Mon–Sat 9am–6pm.

ORIENTAL GOLD CO., LTD., 116/1 Silom Rd. Tel. 238-2715.

With a nice large selection and an easy-to-see display, Oriental Gold is a fine place to shop for unadorned gold jewelry. We liked the very simple gold braided bracelets (about $1,300), as well as the lovely gold bracelets for children ($130), priced by weight. Open: Mon–Fri 10:30am–7pm, Sat 11am–6pm.

PAA, Peninsula Plaza, No. 9, ground floor, 153 Rajdamri Rd. Tel. 253-9769.

The PAA features fabulous antique jewelry, mostly objects made of gold. Our shopper, Victoria, fell in love with a ruby-and-gold ring that sold for $340. Open: Mon–Sat 10am–6pm.

PENINSULA GEMS, The Regent, Bangkok (lobby), 155 Rajdamri Rd. Tel. 250-0720.

High-priced but good-quality jewelry is on display in this small boutique in the Regent shopping arcade. A few of our favorite things include a line of finely crafted silver picture frames and boxes ranging from $100 to $550 and an exquisite array of ruby-and-diamond rings, as well as fine sapphire rings, pendants, and earrings.

ROYAL ORCHID COLLECTION, 11 Soi Ruam Rudee, Ploenchit Rd. Tel. 255-2725.

This is a place to purchase inexpensive gifts for those back home. Their line of contemporary costume jewelry is popular. However, the specialties here are orchids and other exotic flowers that are plated with 24-karat gold and fashioned into simple jewelry. Our favorite items are a gold-plated flower-petal necklace for $20 and a pin made of orchids for $16. Open: Mon–Sat 8:30am–5pm.

SINCERE JEWELRY, 703–705 Silom Rd. Tel. 234-1241.

With a reputation for selling good-quality jewelry, the Sincere showrooms are recommended for those in search of older-style Thai and international designs as well as custom work. Directions: Opposite Narai Hotel.

TASTE JEWELERS, 292/3 Silom Rd. Tel. 234-7651.

Lots of people love marcasite jewelry, and for a wide selection of pieces—some plain and some mixed with onyx and carnelian—we recommend a visit to Taste Jewelers. Open: Mon–Sat 9am–6pm.

TOK KWANG, 224/6 Silom Rd. Tel. 233-0658.

As soon as you enter, you'll know you've come to a major, major jewelry store. Tok Kwang has been in business since the 1940s and has built a solid reputation for the town's best pearls, most of which come from Japan; an increasing number, however, are imported from Burma and Australia. A string of first-rate medium-size pearls ranges from $1,000 to $2,500. There are many more exotic varieties for prices that can only be described as astronomical. Tok Kwang also sells fine watches, diamonds, and gems. Their new branch is at The Regent, Bangkok, 155 Rajdamri Rd. (tel. 250-0735). Open: Daily 10:30am–7pm.

UTHAI'S GEMS, 28/7 Soi Ruam Rudee, Ploenchit Rd. Tel. 253-8582.

One of the most reliable jewelers in Bangkok is Uthai Daengrasmisopon. Perhaps it's his proximity to the U.S. embassy, but you'll be amazed at the number of Americans who stream in and out of his store. More impressive, though, are the number of repeat shoppers who make a stop at Uthai's their first on the Bangkok buying trail. Many come to buy from the enormous inventory of extremely well-priced, conservatively styled jewelry, but not a small number visit here for custom work or repairs—generally allow two to three days for simple items, longer for more complex work. We found lovely 1-carat sapphire rings in 14-karat-gold settings for about $225; a comparable ruby ring runs about $800. Princess rings go for $130. We were impressed with the quality and value of the gold chains here, handcrafted in 22-karat gold, and the extremely inexpensive green sapphires that Uthai crafted into real bargain earrings, rings, and pendants. He also runs a mail-order business and has a good collection of bronzeware. Open: Mon–Sat 9:30am–6pm.

WORLD JEWELS TRADE CENTER, 987 Silom Rd. Tel. 233-8388.

Mr. Ho, this shop's owner, is considered the doyen of the Bangkok gem industry, having started the Asian Institute of Gemological Sciences. Described as the "Supermarket of Gems," this is not only a fine place to look at jewelry, but one of the best inventories of cut stones in town. Prices are reasonable. Open: Mon–Fri 8:30am–5pm, and some Saturdays.

YVES JOAILLIER, Charn Issara Tower, 3rd floor, 942/83 Rama IV Rd. Tel. 233-3292.

⭐ We are unabashed fans of this boutique—arguably the most elegant in Bangkok—for its exquisitely conceived designs and exceptional quality. Yves Bernardeau, who designs nearly everything here, oversees a workshop of Thai jewelers who've been with him since he began his business 10 years ago in Silom Village. Perhaps it's his French background or his 8 years in Turkey, but Yves's best pieces (to our mind) incorporate contemporary European designs with ancient Mediterranean motifs. Accordingly, the majority of his clients are from America and Europe, with the local Thai and expatriate community just beginning to accept his unique—for Bangkok—style. Our favorite pieces are banded gold, hammered in a matte finish and featuring sapphires or rubies; most of these are of a revisionist antique style that is popular in such high-end New York stores as Barneys and Bergdorf Goodman. Yves is brilliant at made-to-order jewelry; expect three days for a ring, one to two weeks for a necklace. As for prices, we found his competitive with those in the local market and an absolute bargain in contrast to those in American boutiques; one of our favorite pieces, for example, was a 22-karat-gold ring with a fiery 2.65-carat sapphire for $3,500. Ruby earrings run about $1,500, while his Bali imported goods, in silver, are considerably less (we discovered that the wonderful Indian and Balinese jewelry at the Jim Thompson Silk Company is selected by Yves). Although Yves stocks a fine selection of stones, he will also make jewelry from loose gems and will trim them to fit his designs if necessary. All locally made jewelry with gems comes with AIGS certificates. If you're serious about buying jewelry in Bangkok, plan to stop here early. Open: Mon–Sat 10am–7pm.

READERS RECOMMEND

Venus Jewelers, 167/1–2 Wireless Rd. Tel. 252-6468.
"Venus Jewelers, located down the street from the American embassy, does a lot of business with the U.S. military and enjoys an excellent reputation, as evidenced by the huge number of business cards left by admirals, generals, and personnel of lower ranks. They have excellent service and a wide range of precious stones and settings."—Melissa Lockman, Duncannon, Pa.

LEATHER GOODS, SHOES & BOOTS

Many people leave Bangkok wearing shoes and cowboy boots made from ostrich, elephant, snake, alligator, or other exotic leather. Before planning to purchase any goods made from one of these skins, consult any office of the U.S. Customs Service for prohibited goods, lest they be confiscated upon your return. There are many shops along New Road near The Oriental and in and around Patpong that also carry clothing (inspect those seams, clasps, and zippers!), wallets (for about $14), and purses. Prices for boots range from $75 to $300.

CHAO PHRAYA BOOTERY, 116/3 Silom Rd. Tel. 234-1226.

This is another excellent outlet for shoes, boots, and a full range of leather accessories. In addition to having a large inventory, Chao

Phraya does efficient custom work (cowboy boots only); expect to have a pair made within four to five days for approximately $170, depending on the leather. One of the better bargains we encountered was a leather knapsack for $168. Although the shop carries many different varieties of skins, some are exotic species that are prohibited from import into the United States and Europe. Open: Daily 10am–9pm.

M.J. LEATHER LTD., River City Shopping Complex, 1st floor, Room 119, Yotha Rd. Tel. 237-0077, ext. 119.

We'd characterize M.J. as a producer of good-, not great-quality shoes and boots. Calf and eel skins seem to be the featured materials for men's shoes, and they can be custom-manufactured in three to five days. This is also one of the few shops in the city that will custom-make shoes for women; expect to pay $30 to $40, depending on materials. M.J. also has a variety of handbags ranging from $32 to $80, with crocodile bags running a good bit more. Open: Mon–Sat 9:30am–8:30pm; Sun 9:30am–6pm.

PATOU, Indra Shopping Center, 95/250 Rajdamri Rd. Tel. 251-3971.

Many shoe stores, such as Patou, will custom-make footwear. They also sell locally produced Charles Jourdan and other high-fashion shoes.

SIAM LEATHER GOODS, River City Shopping Complex, Room 118, Yotha Rd. Tel. 237-0077, ext. 118.

The management of this shop claims extravagantly, "Anything can be made within 24 hours." Okay! But we say that you'd best let them take a little longer and stick around yourself in case something doesn't fit exactly right. The range of shoe prices seems to be about $60 for calfskin to $320 for stingray skin, and $720 for ostrich. As usual, check with the Customs Bureau to make sure that your brand of skin is legally admissible into the United States. Open: Daily 9:30am–8:30pm. Branch: 32 Surawong Rd. (tel. 233-4521).

MARKETS

PAK KLONG TALAAT, along Chao Phraya River on Luk Luang.

Pak Klong Talaat (also called the Talaat Taywait) is home to Bangkok's cut-flower market. Huge bushels of flowers and vegetables arrive every night; buyers from around the city shop in the very early morning hours. If you're wandering around the city after midnight looking for an offbeat attraction, stop by and choose from baskets of orchids, lotus, jasmine, marigolds, and many more. You'll pay about 50B ($2) for a lovely bunch of orchids. You can also watch the flower vendors threading leis and assembling huge, colorful, intricately patterned funeral wreaths. Open: 24 hours. Directions: Located near Memorial Bridge, on Chakraphet Rd.

PATPONG NIGHT MARKET, Patpong Soi 1.

Although Patpong has been famous for its bars, neon lights, girls, sex shows, girls, massage parlors, and girls since the Vietnam War, only in the last 10 years has it become a bona fide tourist attraction. Just as the film *Deep Throat* made it acceptable for "nice" people to go to porno movies, so Patpong's Asian mystique and anything-goes sexuality became a standard stop on the "Bangkok By Night" bus tours. Then its proprietors (the land under

Patpong's many lanes is privately owned) realized what profits could be made if Patpong became an attraction for the whole family! Thus, its bustling Night Market, the direct result of closing those lanes to traffic and renting out tables to vendors of everything faux, every sound and picture pirated, every leathergood stamped with someone's initials, every Hard Rock Café T-shirt, and every handcraft or cotton clothing available to sell, sell, sell . . . Not cheap, not original, but lively. Open: Nightly after sundown. Directions: Between Silom and Surawong Rds.

PRATUNAM MARKET, along Ratchaprarop and Rajdamri Rds., north of New Phetchaburi Rd.

Pratunam is a typical Thai-style market, popular with locals for garments such as cheap jeans and men's dress shirts, cotton underwear, casual dresses, as well as fresh flowers, produce, and a number of other essentials. Some stalls are canopied, some open-air, some part of indoor malls, some tucked into corners of this consumer labyrinth, but all grouped according to goods offered. We found it fun to stroll through but overwhelming to shop in— Pratunam demands intense bargaining. Open: Daily morning–night. Directions: Around the Amari Watergate and Indra Regent hotels, in tiny lanes off, and along, both sides of Ratchaprarop Rd.

WEEKEND MARKET, Chatuchak Park.

If you're in Bangkok on a weekend, don't miss the Weekend Market, which covers a vast area with rows of stalls selling everything—fresh crabs and seafood, live fish that are scooped from tanks, dried seafood, chilies (piled high in great baskets) and other vegetables, other foods of all sorts, live chicks, orchids, clothes, blue vases and other pottery, and a host of strange items you won't know what to call. It's a great way to introduce yourself to the exotic sights, flavors, and colors of Thai life. On our last trip, the fastest-moving fashion item for the tourist trade was a patchwork mutmee silk baseball jacket; we bought one for about $20 and later saw them on the streets in New York selling for over $80. Open: Sat–Sun. Directions: Off the airport highway; up to an hour away in traffic.

SILK & COTTON

Besides those places listed below, there are also very good silk outlets in the international hotel shopping arcades. If you're looking for ready-to-wear or custom clothing, see the "Clothing" section earlier in this chapter.

ANITA THAI SILK, 294/4–5 Silom Rd. Tel. 234-2481.

This is one of Bangkok's good silk emporiums, with an emphasis on selling silk by the length. It also has gifts and a good selection of ready-to-wear items, but many people come here to buy material that is then taken to their favorite tailor shop. Open: Mon–Sat 8am–6pm.

DESIGN THAI, 304 Silom Rd. Tel. 235-1553.

Design Thai is a deliberate imitation of the Jim Thompson Silk Company, in both style and merchandise (even the building is similar). Like the higher-priced original, the store stocks a wide range of fabrics and accessories, including silk slippers ($20), jewelry boxes ($12 to $18), a good selection of purses, and a fuddy-duddy selection of ready-to-wear clothes. Our favorite item: brightly colored stuffed cotton water buffaloes for $8. Open: Daily 9am–7pm.

READERS RECOMMEND

Chatuchak Weekend Market. *"As I'm sure you know, it's a long (45-minute) taxi ride but well worth it as the bargains were irresistible and prices a fraction of the already-low downtown prices. We shipped most of the stuff back by Federal Express, which was expensive but we were advised against using the local post office. Regardless of whether you make any purchases, I'd recommend the trip on Saturday or Sunday as a unique Bangkok experience."*—Jeff Sharlach, New York, N.Y.

H.M. FACTORY THAI SILK, 45 Promchai, Soi 39, Sukhumvit Rd. Tel. 258-8766.

This lovely workshop (retail store below) may be hard to find, but it makes a good place to watch mutmee silk in the weaving stage. Silk weavers buy raw material from Isan and spin and weave clothing and upholstery-grade fabric in the private garden/home. The bulk of plain, patterned, and mutmee silk is available for sale by lengths, although there is a modest selection of clothing. One-ply mutmee runs about $16 a yard, while two-ply costs about twice that amount. Directions: Keep your eye out for a sign (it's located on side street off soi).

HOME MADE THAI SILK, 45 Soi 35, Sukhumvit Rd. Tel. 258-8766.

⭐ We also like H.M. Factory Thai Silk's retail store, Home Made Thai Silk. The quality of the silk (priced at $12 to $32 per meter—a little more than a yard) is excellent, and it's the only shop we found where you can see the material being woven. Open: Mon–Sat 8:30am–6pm.

MARIS, Hilton International Hotel, 2 Wireless Rd. Tel. 294-5906.

Though conventional, Maris is very good for such gifts as silk frames, silk jackets incorporating Burmese appliqué, paper flowers, stuffed toys, and orchid necklaces and pins, as well as made-to-order silk clothing. Open: Daily 9am–8pm.

MOTIF, 296/7–8 Silom Rd. Tel. 237-8454.

This emporium stocks a large selection of quality silk and cotton fabrics, as well as off-the-rack clothing for women. Many people come here for tailoring; expect a two- to three-day turnaround for custom work. Motif also has a housewares/gift section that includes hardwood boxes and desk accessories, lacquerware, and—our favorite—good-quality celadon dishes. Open: Mon–Sat 9am–7pm, Sun 9am–6pm (during high season only). Branches: River City (tel. 237-0077, ext. 220); Ambassador Hotel, 8 Sukhumvit Rd. (tel. 254-0444, ext. 1147).

T. SHINAWATRA, 94 Soi 23, Sukhumvit Rd. Tel. 258-0295.

Though we've visited many of this chain's branch stores, we only learned on our last trip that this outlet, the largest of all, is supplied by its own factory. There is an enormous selection of both silk and cotton, particularly in wonderful solid colors, rivaling that of all other stores (including the Jim Thompson Silk Company) for variety. *(Note:* We suggest buying upholstery-grade silk elsewhere.) One-ply plain silk runs $18 to $22 a yard, while two-ply costs $22 to $25 a yard. There is a small selection of ready-made clothes, such as silk bathrobes for about $180 and silk ties for $15. Although it's not a specialty, T. Shinawatra stocks a small line of handcrafts, including dolls, crocodile purses, and teak goodies, as well as operating a jewelry counter. Open: Mon–Sat 8:30am–6pm.

JIM THOMPSON THAI SILK COMPANY, 9 Surawong Rd. Tel. 234-4900.

It's nearly impossible to mention silk in Thailand without referring in some way to Jim Thompson (see Jim Thompson's House in Section 2 of Chapter 6), the legendary American who reestablished the modern Thai industry of silk weaving. For top-drawer goods, including finely woven cotton, Thompson's is the place—but expect to pay for the quality and know that the styles are extremely conservative. (If you do intend to buy, a skirt costs about $115; a sleeveless party dress runs $165; and a camisole is $80.) This may sound like heresy, but we have a hard time recommending the purchase of silk or cotton clothing at Thompson's. Instead, we suggest buying either silk or cotton by the yard (upholstery-grade silk, for example, runs about $44 a yard), or looking upstairs, on the second floor, at the well-designed and -crafted jewelry from India, Indonesia, and Thailand. We also like the large variety of place mats and napkins, made of cotton or silk; place mats cost about $9 in cotton, $14 in silk. Open: Daily 9am–9pm.

SILVER

CHAI LAI, Peninsula Plaza, 1st floor, Rajdamri Rd. Tel. 252-1538.

This is a great store for hill-tribe and older Thai jewelry at reasonable to high prices. We particularly admired such items as gold-bead earrings with rubies for $315 to $415; 40-year-old rings with five different varieties of blue stones; antique ruby earrings, approximately 50 years old, for $940; and a carnelian-and-silver key ring for $125. Open: Mon–Sat 11am–6pm.

CHARTERED GEMS LTD., 292 Silom Rd. Tel. 233-9320.

We came here looking for jewelry and discovered their nicely made silver products. The best values that we found in silver were a tea strainer ($80), a pair of candlesticks for $110, and a $62 salt-and-pepper set with a tray. The staff will negotiate. Open: Mon–Sat 9:30am–7:30pm.

THAI NAKORN, 79 Prachatipati Rd. Tel. 281-3526.

Again, this is a well-established shop for jewelry that we judged better for fine silver and nielloware.

CHAPTER 9

BANGKOK NIGHTS

1. THE PERFORMING ARTS

- **MAJOR CONCERT HALLS & THEATERS**

2. THE CLUB & MUSIC SCENE

3. THE BAR SCENE

4. MORE ENTERTAINMENT

Bangkok has one of the liveliest nightlife scenes in all of Asia, with a range of cultural and hedonistic activities that should satisfy anyone. Most visitors won't leave without a stroll down Patpong, the famous sex strip and Night Market, with myriad vendors and 2 blocks of bars and clubs.

At the other end of the spectrum are the programs of Thai classical dance and music held at various restaurants and performance halls. For those who want to venture deep into all aspects of local culture, what follows is a small sample of the evening's physical, intellectual, and cultural highlights.

Both the *Bangkok Post* and *The Nation* offer daily listings of cultural events and performance schedules. The Tourism Authority of Thailand (TAT) (tel. 02/226-0060) will also provide schedule information. Your hotel concierge should also be able to guide you toward the evening of your choice, particularly with tips on the latest clubs. Performance times and prices vary, but prices are always low, so get out there!

1. THE PERFORMING ARTS

MUSIC, DANCE & THEATER

NATIONAL THEATER, 1 Na Phra That Rd. Tel. 224-1342.

The National Theater (near the National Museum) presents Thai classical dancing and music, with performers drawn from the School of Music and Dance in Bangkok. Performances are generally superior to those at the tourist restaurants and hotels. There are also presentations by visiting ballet and theatrical companies. Call the TAT or the box office for the current schedule.

THAILAND CULTURAL CENTER, Ratchadaphisek Rd., Huai Khwang. Tel. 245-7711.

This is the newest and largest performance center in town, offering a wide variety of programs. The Bangkok Symphony holds forth here during its short summer season. Other local and visiting companies present theater and dance. Call for the current schedule.

MAJOR CONCERT HALLS & THEATERS

National Theater, Na Phra That Rd. Tel. 224-1342.
Thailand Cultural Center, Ratchadaphisek Rd. Tel. 245-7711.

THAI CUISINE & TRADITIONAL DANCE

Several restaurants offer classical Thai dancing with dinner, an easy and enjoyable way to sample this aspect of Thai culture. Generally, these restaurants serve a fixed-menu of Thai favorites, followed by a show. In combination, you may find neither the best food nor the best dance, but we encourage every visitor to see at least one performance. (See Section 6 of Chapter 5 for specific recommendations.)

2. THE CLUB & MUSIC SCENE

JAZZ CLUBS

BLUES-JAZZ, Soi 53, Sukhumvit Rd. Tel. 258-7747.
This little spot offers a dose of fusion jazz every night (except Sunday) after 9pm.

BROWN SUGAR, 231/20 Sarasin Rd. Tel. 250-0103.
Opposite Lumpini Park, this is a cozy but sometimes too popular bar/restaurant where the Brown Sugar Jazz Band swings every night except Sunday from 9pm to 1am. (On Sunday, a country band kicks in.) The place also serves lunch and dinner indoors or at outdoor café tables. Open: Mon–Sat 11am–1am, Sun 5pm–1am. Weekends are just too crowded for us.

ROUND MIDNIGHT PUB, 106/12 Soi Lang Suan. Tel. 251-0652.
Off Ploenchit Road, north of Lumpini Park, is a club that reminded us a bit of Santa Fe, with vines added for a tropical touch. Nightly until 9:30pm, there's a supply of American and European music with videos, then a live band mixing cool pop, soul, and funk with jazz. Popular with expatriates.

SAXOPHONE, 3/8 Phyathai Rd.
On the traffic roundabout, at the south corner of the Victory Monument, Saxophone remains a popular club. A bright and lively nightspot (open until 3am) to savor live rock bands and jazz standards.

DANCE CLUBS/DISCOS

BUBBLES, in Dusit Thani, 946 Rama IV Rd. Tel. 236-0400.
This pricey place in one of the city's top hotels attracts an older expatriate crowd mixed with high-fashion yuppies, known as "Tuppies," from Bangkok's growing middle class. A dead zone during the week, it jumps on Friday and Saturday nights.
Admission: 350–400B ($14–$16), including two drinks.

THE NILE CLUB, in The Mandarin Bangkok, 662 Rama IV Rd. Tel. 238-0230.

More of a nightclub than a disco, this extremely popular Asian-style dance club—located in one of the city's expensive hotels—is where local party animals enjoy live Thai singers and bands. Try it for a very typical Thai evening experience.

Admission: Sun–Thurs 175B ($7), Fri–Sat 325B ($13).

NASA SPACEADROME, 999 Ramkamhaeng Rd. Klongton, Klongtoey. Tel 314-4024.

This long-lived hotspot in town is way out near the eastern suburb of Huamark (taxi required). The decor matches the name, with extraterrestrial motifs (including a far-out stage show) throughout. NASA Spaceadrome's au courant Western music mix draws hordes of young Thai teenagers looking for action.

Admission: Sun–Thurs, 225B ($9), Fri–Sat 300B ($12), including two drinks.

ROME CLUB, 90–96 Soi 4, Silom Rd. Tel. 233-8836.

Our favorite (we're in our mid-thirties), this is one of the most popular discos for cosmopolitan Thais, expatriates, and visiting Westerners. Most of the local clientele is young, some straight, some gay. The marble dance floor is surrounded by video monitors and the usual array of moving lights. The Rome's quieter coffee bar across the street, providing a welcome respite from the pulsating beat, is its own scene for those who hate disco music.

Admission: Weekdays 125B ($5), including one drink; weekends 275B ($11), including two drinks.

VIBRATIONS, in the Novotel, Soi 6, Siam Sq. Tel. 225-6888.

The basement of the Novotel offers a banquet table of entertainment choices. You can dance to a disco beat at **Vibrations,** take the karaoke stage and croon your favorite tunes at the high-tech **Sensations,** or dance ballroom style at **Temptations.** All three venues are part of the Entertainment Concept at the Novotel. You can even take ballroom dance lessons at Temptations, for 300B($12) per session. Open: Daily 8pm–2am.

Admission: Vibrations, 550B ($22), which includes two drinks. Sensations and Temptations, 120B ($4.80).

ZAZA PARTY HOUSE, in the basement of the Shangri-La Hotel, 89 Soi Wat Suan, Plu. Tel. 236-7777.

This is the current hot favorite among the Thai teenage and college crowd. The DJs spin good disco/rap/classic tunes, the beat emphasized by the "body sonic" system that drives the base notes through the floor and up into your body. It's a fun place to dance or watch the scene in stylish New Mexican/Keith Haring–style surroundings. Open: Daily 9pm–2am (later is hotter).

Admission: 500B ($20), which includes two drinks.

SEX CLUBS

While the 1985 hit song "One Night in Bangkok" was actually about chess (from the musical *Chess),* the song celebrates the naughtiest aspect of life in Bangkok. Since the 1960s—and particularly since the Vietnam War—Bangkok has served as the sin capital of Asia, with sex clubs, bars, massage parlors, and prostitutes concentrated in Patpong and the so-called Soi Cowboy districts. Recent acknowledgment by the Thai government of the startling increase in HIV-positive cases has toned down some of the sex-club scene, while certain vendors have shifted their focus to younger and younger merchandise. (See "Sex" in Section 3 of Chapter 2.)

Patpong Road is perpendicular to Silom Road and Surawong Road, and its two *sois* (lanes) have long hosted an international sex street fair. A peculiar addition is the Night Market that has sprung up on Patpong Road I. You'll find families combing a sea of vendors selling everything counterfeit, from ersatz designer jeans to the latest in knock-off designer luggage to cassettes of recent pop music. This market in consumer goods has undercut the impact of the once all-too-obvious market in flesh, so you may be disappointed (or not) in Bangkok's famous sex strip. Soi Cowboy—between Soi 21 and Soi 23 off Sukhumvit Road—is a less concentrated version of Patpong. There are VD clinics in both areas, as well as many pharmacies.

It's nearly impossible to wander Patpong without a hawker approaching you with a laminated menu card, displaying the evening program at one of the numerous sex clubs. These shows are usually upstairs, sometimes above a "go-go" bar, and though they vary a bit, they usually consist of the following: "Woman smokes cigarette. Woman and razor blades. Woman opens Coke bottle. Woman and Ping-Pong balls. Woman uses chopsticks. Woman and live fish." The shows tend to be pretty routine in style, though if you've never seen one (and you probably haven't), this is the place.

Warning: Some of these shows are aboveboard, charging only for drinks. But some are simply classic clip joints where you'll be hit with an enormous bill when you leave. You should ask and ask again whether there is a cover or "show" charge before you go in. These fees can also be hidden in drink charges—a bottle of scotch might cost 2,500B ($100). Drinker beware. If you're presented with an exorbitant tab when leaving, insist on calling the Tourist Police. If this doesn't work, pay up and report the problem to the Tourist Police at their booth at the end of Patpong Road II.

At our most recent visit, the club hawkers were having a tough time tearing people away from Night Market bargains, signifying a change in public opinion that may help eliminate Bangkok's abusive sex trade.

For those who are interested in catching the act (and smart enough not to catch AIDS), try the **Limelight Bar,** the extremely loud rock scene at **Goldfingers, Lipstick,** and the better-costumed, more upscale **King's Castle III.** At all of these go-go bars, located on Patpong Soi I, you're only charged for drinks,

---

IMPRESSIONS

As Calcutta smells of death and Bombay of money, Bangkok smells of sex, but this sexual aroma is mingled with the sharper whiffs of death and money.
—PAUL THEROUX, *THE GREAT RAILWAY BAZAAR,* 1975

And then I think of Siam, which by the almost miraculous cunning of its rulers escaped enslavement by the West, only to become through liberty and propensity hardly more than a fun-fair mirror reflective of the U.S.A.
—NORMAN LEWIS, *THE CHANGING SKY,*1959

which range from 65B to 90B ($2.60 to $3.60) for a beer. Patpong Soi II now boasts mainly massage and "Turkish bath" parlors, and is a seedier proposition (no pun intended) altogether.

In Soi Cowboy, off Sukhumvit Road, between Soi 21 and Soi 23, you'll find a quieter, raunchier version of Patpong, without the dense Night Market street action and aggressive hawkers.

MASSAGE PARLORS

For a traditional medical massage, head for the school at Wat Po (see Section 1 of Chapter 6); otherwise, visit the health club at your hotel. Traditional, or "healing," massages will cost from 250B to 400B ($10 to $16) per hour, except at Wat Po, where the rate is a bargain 150B ($6) per hour.

Bangkok has hundreds of "modern," or "physical," massage parlors, which are heavily advertised and offer something not meant to relax your limbs. In physical massage, the masseuse usually employs her entire body, thoroughly oiled—a "body-body" massage. If one wishes, a "sandwich," with two masseuses, can also be ordered.

Nearly all massage parlors are organized along the same lines. Guests enter a lobby where there are a coffee shop/bar and several waiting rooms. In the latter, young Thai women wearing numbers pinned to their blouses sit on bleachers. Guests examine the women through a window and select their masseuse. Both guest and masseuse take a room in the building and typically spend between 1 and 2 hours on a massage. Rates for a physical massage start at 500B ($20). For all the variations, you're on your own.

A WORD OF WARNING

Although many of Bangkok's activities are semilicit, drugs, personal safety, and AIDS are real concerns.

Though marijuana and other controlled substances are easily available, they are not tolerated by the local authorities. The police frequently clamp down on both sellers and buyers, and ignorance is not an accepted legal defense.

Western embassies report numerous cases of tourists who are drugged in their hotel rooms by girls of the night, waking two days later to find all their valuables gone. There are a shocking number of stories about young Western travelers found dead in their hotel rooms (42 Americans in 1992) from unexplained causes. We urge caution in your dealings with strangers.

The incidence of AIDS among Thailand's commercial sex workers is alarmingly high. If you must use their services, take proper precautions. Wear condoms. (See "Health" in Section 3 of Chapter 2.)

3. THE BAR SCENE

PUBS & BARS

THE BAMBOO BAR, in The Oriental, 48 Oriental Ave. Tel. 236-0400.

The Bamboo Bar, off the lobby of this legendary hotel, is a tastefully low-key rendezvous point for older, well-to-do world travelers. After 10pm, you'll enjoy live music and singers. On Monday, a Dixieland band performs. Don't forget to stroll over to the riverside terrace afterward.

BOBBY'S ARMS, 114/1–2 Silom Rd. at Soi Patpong 2, Carpark, 1st floor. Tel. 233-6828.

A popular pub with both local and visiting Anglophiles, Bobby's Arms serves up solid English food and lively expatriate gossip. On Sundays from 8 to 11pm a Dixieland band plays, while quieter singers and musicians entertain on Friday and Saturday nights.

CHEERS PUB, In Holiday Inn Crowne Plaza, 981 Silom Rd. Tel. 238-4300.

One of our favorite bars-in-a-hotel. The regular crowd of airline crews, tourists, expatriates, and Thais from the nearby Business District gives the place a local and cheerful ambience. On our visit, a Filipino band was doing great versions of popular Western music.

HARD ROCK CAFE, 424/3–6 Soi 11, Siam Sq. Tel. 251-0792.

Yes, even here. This branch of the original chain should be filled with cheerful Tuppies and curious expatriates at it's guitar-shaped bar. After all, "Hard Rock Bangkok" T-shirts have already been sold in Thailand for years.

SPASSO, in the Grand Hyatt Erawan, 494 Rajdamri Rd. Tel. 254-1234.

Somewhere between a raucously loud, upscale Italian restaurant, a discotheque with no dance floor, and a bar with live music lies Spasso. It's fun, nightly after 9pm, when the local pop bands begin their set, and the bar's somewhat of a pickup scene before then. Of course, people waiting for tables also hang out at the long, intimately lit bar, making it a cozy and lively place.

GAY BARS

Bangkok has an active gay bar circuit. You'll find some of the raunchier clubs in the Patpong area, including those featuring male striptease shows. We always tell our gay friends to start at the central Rome Club (see Section 2 of this chapter) on Soi 4, Silom Road, find company at their coffee bar or at the popular Telephone Pub next door, and ask about the current favorite bar.

Warning: AIDS continues to spread at an alarming rate among male and female commercial sex workers.

READERS RECOMMEND

Telephone Bar, *Bangkok. "The Rome Club Disco seems to attract a very young straight crowd (maybe it was just the night we were there), the Rome Bar across the street was dead, but a place called Telephone (next door) was lively. Kind of cute actually: They had dozens of little phones around the bar identified with large numbers so you could presumably call someone you thought might be fun to talk with."*
— Jeff Sharlach, New York, N.Y.

4. MORE ENTERTAINMENT

MOVIES There are movie theaters at nearly all of the city's shopping centers and malls (such as Siam Square). Most of the main cinemas show recently released English-language films, some dubbed, others with subtitles. You'll find listings in the daily English-language newspapers. Ask your concierge to call the theater to determine whether the film is being shown in English.

For older films in English, try the **American University Alumni,** 179 Rajdamri Rd. (tel. 252-8170); and the **British Council,** 428 Soi 2, Siam Square (tel. 252-6136).

THAI BOXING We recommend that every sports enthusiast sample a Thai boxing event. You're almost guaranteed a rowdy and lively match. Two stadiums offer boxing every night of the week. (See Section 5 of Chapter 6.)

NIGHT CRUISES ON THE CHAO PHRAYA RIVER A few local boat companies offer night dinner cruises on the river. We can't vouch for the food (and can almost vouch for its mediocrity), but the experience can be relaxing and you're assured an entertaining view of the city across the water. Ask your concierge to arrange a cruise. (See also Section 6 of Chapter 5.)

CLASSES, LECTURES, ETC. There are several Western groups that offer cultural programs and film series. These are geared to expatriate nationals living in Bangkok, but tourists can also enjoy them. Among the groups:

Alliance Française (29 Sathorn Rd. Tel. 213-2122) has, like all the branches of this group, an active program of French cultural events, including films, concerts, and lectures. There are also a French-language bookstore and a library on the premises. Their new branch at Ramkhamhaeng Huamark (tel. 300-4425) also has programs.

American University Alumni Association (179 Rajdamri Rd. Tel. 252-8170) offers English-language courses, lectures, and film series. They also have a library.

British Council (428 Siam Sq., Soi 2, Rama I Rd. Tel. 252-6136). Offerings include English-language classes and lectures, as well as art, music, dance, and drama programs. Call for information or check the newspapers for schedules.

And at the **Goethe Institut Bangkok** (18/1 Soi Attakarnprasit, S. Sathorn Rd. Tel. 286-9002), you'll find German classes, films, and lectures, plus a library.

CHAPTER 10

DAY TRIPS FROM BANGKOK

1. **RIVER TRIPS TO AYUTTHAYA & NONTHABURI**
2. **BANG PA-IN**
3. **FLOATING MARKET AT DAMNOEN SADUAK**
4. **THE ANCIENT CITY**
5. **SAMUTPRAKARN CROCODILE FARM**
6. **ROSE GARDEN COUNTRY RESORT**
7. **SAMPHRAN ELEPHANT GROUND & ZOO**
8. **NAKHON PATHOM**
9. **WATER PARKS**

There are plenty of easy day trips from Bangkok. Favorites include various cruises along the Chao Phraya River to the more distant klongs and to the ancient capital of Ayutthaya, north of Bangkok (also suitable for an overnight excursion), with a stop at the Bang Pa-In Summer Palace on the way. There's also a floating market south of Bangkok that is still a tiny bit more authentic than the one in town. Culture buffs should explore the Thailand-in-miniature Ancient City, the Rose Garden Country Resort's performance-arts show, and the world's tallest *chedi* at Nakhon Pathom. For those interested in a good wildlife show, there are the Samutprakarn Crocodile Farm and the Samphran Elephant Ground and Zoo. Kids will enjoy most of these, but if they're restless, head for one of the water parks.

See the next chapter for four destinations—in addition to Ayutthaya—that are best enjoyed on overnight excursions. (However, tour operators do offer some of these as day trips.)

1. RIVER TRIPS TO AYUTTHAYA & NONTHABURI

AYUTTHAYA Several river tours venture outside Bangkok. The *Oriental Queen,* a luxurious cruise boat operated by The Oriental (hotel) (tel. 236-0400), leaves the Oriental Pier every day at 8am for Ayutthaya. Buses meet the boat in Ayutthaya for tours of the city ruins and the lovely Bang Pa-In Summer Palace. At 5pm, the buses leave for the 2-hour return trip to Bangkok. You can also reverse the trip, traveling up by bus and returning by boat. The cost is 950B ($40) per person, including lunch, tour, and full transportation.

The *Ayutthaya Princess* (tel. 255-9200) leaves at 8am daily from the Shangri-La Hotel for a similar trip, but also includes stops at several interesting wats. The price is 1,000B ($40), including lunch.

A cheaper excursion to Ayutthaya is offered by the **Chao Phraya Express Company** (tel. 222-5330). Boats leave the Maharaj Pier (off Maharat Road, north of the Grand Palace) at 8am Sunday. The Chao Phraya Express Boat tours cover the Thai Folk Arts and Handicraft Center, the Bang Pa-In Summer Palace, Ayutthaya, and the Pai Lom Temple, a sanctuary for open-bill storks (the best time to visit is from December to June). These all-day excursions are very popular with locals and cost 225B to 300B ($9-$12) each, per person, meals not included. There is no guide on the Ayutthaya tour.

For those who want to explore Ayutthaya on their own, possibly staying overnight on the way to or from the northern areas, see Section 1 of Chapter 11.

NONTHABURI For a shorter and easier river trip, take one of the Chao Phraya Express Boats (you can catch it at the Tha Chang pier) all the way up to Nonthaburi, about a half hour beyond the northern edge of Bangkok. You'll get the feeling of a smaller town, with its markets and gardens, and you can tour the colorful Klong Om.

---

2. BANG PA-IN

Only 61 kilometers (38 miles) north of Bangkok, this royal palace is usually combined with Ayutthaya on a one-day tour, although—in our view—the palace is not as interesting. If you have a choice, spend your time exploring Ayutthaya fully.

Originally, the 17th-century temple and palace at Bang Pa-In were built by Ayutthaya's King Prasat Thong. They were abandoned when Bangkok became the capital, until King Mongkut began returning occasionally in the mid-19th century. His son, King Chulalongkorn, constructed the royal palace as it is seen today.

The architectural style mixes Thai with strong European influences. The building in the middle of the lake is the Phra Thinang Aisawan Thippa-At, an excellent example of classic Thai style. Behind it, in Versailles style, are what were the king's apartments, which today serve as a hall for state ceremonies. The other building of note is the Phra Thinang Wehat Chamrun, a Chinese-style building (open to the public) where court members generally lived during the rainy and cool seasons. Also worth visiting is the Phra Thinang Withun Thatsuna, an observatory on a small island that affords a fine view of the countryside from the top.

While you're across the Chao Phraya River, the Gothic-style Wat Nivet Thamaprawat (built during King Chulalongkorn's reign) is worth seeing.

Buses leave regularly from Bangkok's Northern Bus Terminal (tel. 279-4484) and Ayutthaya's Chao Prom Market (Chao Prom Road), beginning at 6am, for Bang Pa-In.

Admission is 50B ($2), and the daily hours are 8:30am to 12:30pm and 1 to 3pm.

READERS RECOMMEND

Tour to Bang Pa-In Summer Palace. *"The tour operated by the Chao Phraya Express has an additional pickup location at the Phra Arthit ferry stop across the street from the Peachy Guesthouse. The tour is almost worthless; the hours spent floating down the river are my only fond remembrances."*—Phil Reyes, Dallas, Texas.

3. FLOATING MARKET AT DAMNOEN SADUAK

The Floating Market at Damnoen Saduak, Ratchaburi is about 40 minutes south of Nakhon Pathom, so you can combine the two sites into a one-day trip. Some tours combine the Floating Market with a visit to the Rose Garden Country Resort (see Section 6 of this chapter). If you choose to go via an organized tour, such as that offered by World Travel Service, expect to pay about 1,000B ($40).

At a real floating market, food vendors sell their goods from small boats to local folk in other boats or in klong-side homes. There are some floating markets in Bangkok that have been commercialized beyond the point of interest. Some will tout the market at Damnoen Saduak as more "authentic" than those in Bangkok: forget it. This version is about as precise a duplicate as you could imagine; however, don't let that dissuade you from going. We love this place (it's great for photographers), and you will too as long as you resist the urge to buy anything. Goods are sold at this pressurized souvenir supermarket at up to six times their normal Bangkok prices!

To do it on your own, take a bus to Damnoen Saduak from the Southern Bus Terminal on Charansanitwong Road (trip time: 2 hr.; 75B [$3]). Buses leave every 30 minutes, starting at 6am. Leave early, since market activity peaks between 8 and 10am. From the Damnoen Saduak station, walk along the canal or take a water taxi for 18B (72¢) to the market. You can also rent a nonmotorized wooden boat, for about 150B ($6) per half hour, and explore it more fully. As always, negotiate the price (and do it with gusto; this can be a rip-off activity) with the driver before you leave.

4. THE ANCIENT CITY

This remarkable museum (known as Muang Boran in Thai) is a giant model of Thailand, with the country's major landmarks built full scale or in miniature and spread over 200 acres. It has been built over the last 20 years by a local millionaire who has played out on a grand scale his obsession with Thai history.

Because it's far from the heart of Bangkok, the Ancient City is best visited by organized bus tours, though you can certainly go on your own. It's at Kilometer 33 on the Old Sukhumvit Highway in Samut Prakan province. Contact the **Ancient City Co.**, on Ratchadamnoen Klang Road in Bangkok (tel. 226-1936 or 224-1057). The company can provide you with bus-route information. All travel agents offer package tours that combine the Rose Garden Country Resort with other attractions in the area, such as the crocodile farm or the huge Buddhist chedi in nearby Nakhon Pathom.

Admission to the Ancient City is 60B ($2.50), and it is open daily from 8:30am to 5pm.

5. SAMUTPRAKARN CROCODILE FARM

When you see the flyers for the Samutprakarn Crocodile Farm, you might be intrigued, but probably not. However, we found a visit there to be a good outing for the family, a wild assortment of experiences built around a crocodile-hide business. There are 40,000 snappers in residence, ranging in size from eggs to 20-foot monsters. The sight of that many jaws is staggering. There is also the crocodile-wrestling show, the highlight of which is a trainer placing his head inside the jaws of a major croc. Wow! After the show, you can get a picture of your kid sitting on the tail of the same beast (price: 100B [$4]). You can also get Polaroids of the kid with a huge Bengal tiger, an enormous boa constrictor, and a charming chimp. There is a wonderful Chinese lion dance, an engaging elephant show, elephant rides, and a small miniature railroad. Then, there's the zoo and the store selling crocodile-skin everything. It's a 50-minute drive, but actually an entertaining half day, and the Ancient City is only 3 kilometers (2 miles) away, so a combination day is not out of the question. You'll probably want to do this on a tour, as it's a very long and expensive taxi ride. Admission is 350B ($14) for adults, 250B ($10) for children over 5. (Thais pay 40B [$1.60], but so what.) Open daily from 7am to 5pm. Crocodile wrestling on the hour, from 9am to 4pm; elephant shows on the half hour, from 9:30am to 4:30pm.

6. ROSE GARDEN COUNTRY RESORT

Besides its rose garden, this attractive if somewhat touristy resort is known for its all-in-one show of Thai culture, which includes Thai classical and folk dancing, Thai boxing, sword fighting, and cock fighting—a convenient way for visitors making only a brief visit to the country to digest some canned Thai culture. This popular spot on the typical tourist circuit is located 32 kilometers (20 miles) west of Bangkok on the way to Nakhon Pathom on Highway 4 (tel. 253-0295).

Surprisingly, the resort's restaurant is very appealing, and not expensive. It overlooks the Nakorn Chaisri River, with its islands of water hyacinths. The tom yam kung and the green curry will set your taste buds afire. The pad thai noodles are good, as is the strange-looking but very tasty pla krob salad (dried fish with tamarind sauce).

Admission to the grounds is 15B (60¢), and the show costs 200B ($8). Daily hours for the resort are 8am to 6pm, with the cultural show at 3pm. To get here, take a bus from Bangkok's Southern Bus Terminal.

7. SAMPHRAN ELEPHANT GROUND & ZOO

On one of our previous visits, this place was called a crocodile farm, but now, as the Samphran Elephant Ground and Zoo (tel. 284-1873), it has evolved into a new species. Located 1 kilometer (.6 mile) north of the Rose Garden Country Resort, in Yannawa (30km/18 miles from the city) this 22-acre complex offers a lush gardenlike environment, an entertaining elephant show, and the original thousands of crocodiles, including the world's largest white crocodile.

Admission is 225B ($9), with daily hours from 9am to 6pm. Crocodile wrestling shows are at 12:45 and 2:40; elephant show times at 1:45 and 3:30pm; and additional shows on Saturdays, Sundays, and holidays at 10:30am.

8. NAKHON PATHOM

En route to Kanchanaburi—about 60 kilometers (37 miles) west of Bangkok—the chedi of Nakhon Pathom's Phra Pathom soars like a golden bell into the sky (it's actually made of orange tiles brought from China). The world's tallest Buddhist monument (127m/413 ft.), marking the spot where Buddhism was introduced to Thailand 2,300 years ago, it is one of the country's holiest shrines. It was rebuilt at least two times: in the Khmer era and in the 19th century by King Mongkut, who visited the site when he was studying Buddhism. Take the walk all the way around the central chedi and observe the many smaller shrines and their reclined seated Buddhas. The chedi's annual festival is in November.

Air-conditioned buses leave frequently for Nakhon Pathom beginning at 6am from the Southern Bus Terminal (trip time: 1 hr; 35B [$1.40]); for additional information, contact the terminal at 435-1119.

You can also combine a day trip to Nakhon Pathom with an early morning stop at the Damnoen Saduak Floating Market, or combine it with a visit to the nearby Rose Garden Country Resort and the Samphran Elephant Ground and Zoo.

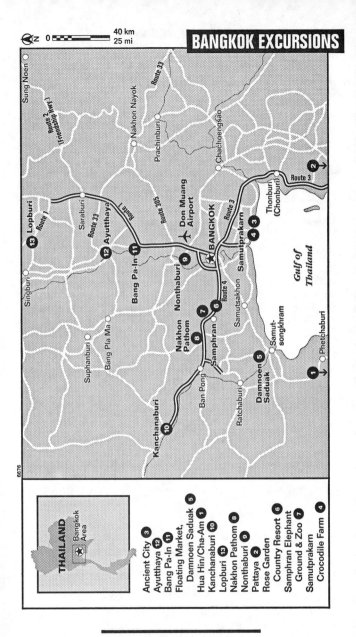

BANGKOK EXCURSIONS

40 km
25 mi

Sung Noen

Route 2 (Friendship Hwy)

Nakhon Nayok

Prachinburi

Chachoengsao

Route 33

Route 3

Thonburi (Chonburi)

Saraburi

Lopburi

Route 1

Route 33

Ayutthaya

Route 305

Lopuri

Don Muang Airport

BANGKOK

Route 3

Samutprakarn

Route 3

Bang Pa-In

Nonthaburi

Samprakarn

Gulf of Thailand

Singburi

Bang Pla Ma

Suphanburi

Nakhon Pathom

Samphran

Route 4

Samutsakhon

Samut-songkhram

Samut-songkhram

Phetchaburi

Kanchanaburi

Ban Pong

Ratchaburi

Damnoen Saduak

THAILAND

Bangkok Area

Ancient City 3
Ayutthaya 12
Bang Pa-In 11
Floating Market, Damnoen Saduak 5
Hua Hin/Cha-Am 1
Kanchanaburi 10
Lopburi 13
Nakhon Pathom 8
Nonthaburi 9
Pattaya 2
Rose Garden Country Resort 6
Samphran Elephant Ground & Zoo 7
Samutprakarn Crocodile Farm 4

---

9. WATER PARKS

If the heat and the kids have gotten to you, consider a trip to one of two water parks. The closest (and therefore the preferred) is **Siam Park (Suan Siam),** 101 Sukhapibarn 2 Rd., Bangkapi (tel.

517-0075), a 30-minute drive east of town. It's a large complex of water slides (try the Super Spiral), enormous swimming pools with artificial surf, waterfalls, landscaped gardens, playgrounds, a beer garden, and more. There is a fishing farm on the way, which the kids might also enjoy. Admission is 225B ($9) adults; 120B ($4.80) children, including rides, and the park is open on weekdays from 10am to 11pm, on weekends from 9am to 11pm. Take bus no. 26 or 27 from the Victory Monument.

Ocean World is located at Bang Saen, a beach resort on the way to Pattaya. It, too, has all the water slides you could ask for, plus pools galore, rides, restaurants, and a nearby beach. It's a 1½-hour bus ride, either on public buses from the Eastern Bus Terminal (Sukhumvit Road) or on special buses arranged through the tour operator at your hotel. Call the Ocean World office in Bangkok (tel. 399-0508) or at the park (tel. 038/383096). Admission is 100B ($4) for adults, 50B ($2) for children. Hours are 10am to 5:30pm on weekdays, 9:30am to 6pm on weekends.

CHAPTER 11

EASY WEEKEND EXCURSIONS FROM BANGKOK

1. AYUTTHAYA
2. PATTAYA
3. KANCHANABURI
4. HUA HIN/ CHA-AM
5. LOPBURI

Because of the vagaries of air travel throughout Thailand, we're recommending favorite places within driving distance of central Bangkok for anyone looking for a two- or three-day getaway. If you have three days or more and don't mind flying, we'd recommend the beaches at Phuket or Ko Samui, the historical sites at Sukhothai, or the ethnic hill tribe centers of northern Thailand for exciting side trips (see *Frommer's Thailand* for information about these destinations).

Ayutthaya, notable for its magnificent ruins, is most often visited on a day trip (see Section 1 of Chapter 10), but can be enjoyed more fully if you stay overnight. It can be reached in an hour by bus from Bangkok.

Pattaya, a fully developed beach resort, boasts anything-goes nightlife and a wide range of water sports. Kanchanaburi is a jungle-clad village on the banks of the famous River Kwai; it can be seen on a long day trip but is best experienced on an overnight excursion. Hua Hin and Cha-Am are twin seaside resorts that are family destinations. All four can be reached within 3 to 4 hours by frequent, inexpensive air-conditioned buses; all have comfortable accommodations in every price range. Lopburi, a 2-hour bus trip from Bangkok, is a historic city with a few interesting sites, often visited on the way to a tour of the Northeast.

1. AYUTTHAYA

76km (47 miles) N of Bangkok

GETTING THERE By Train There are 20 trains (tel. 223-2762) daily from Bangkok, starting at 4:30am (trip time: 1¼ hr.; 25B [$1] third class).

By Bus Twenty-five buses leave daily after 6am from the Northern Bus Terminal (tel. 279-4484) in Bangkok (trip time: 1½ hr.; 58B [$2.30]).

By Boat Tours to Ayutthaya leave from two hotels—The Oriental (tel. 236-0400) and the Shangri-La (tel. 236-7777)—or the River City Pier daily at approximately 8am (and include a stop at Bang

Pa-In). Day trips include a cruise on the Chao Phraya River and return by air-conditioned coach or vice versa (trip time: all day; 1,100B [$44]). At our visit, the *Mekhala,* a converted rice barge, sailed daily from the Menam Hotel Pier (tel. 289-1148) for an overnight cruise/tour of Ayutthaya (trip time: 1¹/₂ days; 4,800B [$192] double, including full-board accommodations, guide, and fees).

A much cheaper, self-guided boat trip can be had each Saturday at 8am, when the Chao Phraya Express Co. (tel. 225-3002) offers service from the Maharat Pier to Ayutthaya and return, via Bang Pa-In. History buffs may resent all the young Thais who come along just for an outing—we loved it.

SPECIAL EVENTS Week-long festival at the end of January, including elephant-training demonstrations and handcrafts fair.

Ayutthaya is one of the great historical highlights of any trip to Thailand. Most people take the day tour from Bangkok and are allowed about 3 hours at the sites, but for those who relish visiting archeological ruins, this ancient city justifies an overnight stay.

For 417 years (postdating Sukhothai and predating Thonburi/Bangkok), from its establishment in 1350 by King U-Thong, Ayutthaya was Thailand's capital and home to 33 kings of various dynasties. At its zenith, until the mid-18th century, when it was destroyed by the Burmese, Ayutthaya was a vast, majestic city with three palaces and 400 splendid temples on an island threaded with 35 miles of canals—a city that mightily impressed European visitors (for a depiction of Westerners in the ancient city, see the Ayutthaya-era murals in Phetchaburi).

Traces of two major foreign settlements can still be seen. Religious objects, coins, porcelain, clay pipes, and skeletons of the Portuguese (who arrived during Rama II's reign in 1511) are at the settlement's memorial building. The Japanese are remembered by a recently erected stone with an inscription and a hall and gate.

There is something hauntingly sad about Ayutthaya. In 1756, after a 15-month siege, it was destroyed by the Burmese; today every temple testifies to the hatred that drives humans to rampant and wanton destruction. Here stands a row of headless Buddhas, there a stone head lies caught in the roots of a tree. It's as if each figure were torn limb from limb. Some of the temples are still being rescued from the jungle, and more are undergoing careful excavation.

We think you'll find the architecture of Ayutthaya fascinating, especially if you've traveled around Thailand and absorbed the many important foreign influences. For those who've traveled to the Northeast, you'll recognize the Khmer influence in the design of many of the ancient wats in Ayutthaya, particularly the use of the cactus-shaped *prang* (tower). Those who've visited Sukhothai will be certain to notice the similarity of certain buildings here to those at that magnificent site. And if you've just arrived and have confined your stay to Bangkok, you might be reminded of Wat Arun (on the Chao Phraya in Thonburi) by an 18th-century structure that was built in the so-called Ayutthaya style, which is a melding of Sukhothai Buddhist influences with the Hindu-inspired Khmer style.

ORIENTATION

ARRIVING The Bangkok bus makes its last stop at the station, adjacent to the Siam Commercial Bank Building, off Chao Prom Road in the downtown area (there is another stop prior to this that lets travelers off near the bridge). Buses from Phitsanulok stop 5 kilometers (3 miles) north of town; you'll need to take a 10B (40¢) local bus into the center. A minibus from the train station into town will cost you about 20B (80¢).

CITY LAYOUT The town is encircled by water, with the perimeters defined by the Chao Phraya River on the southern and western sides, the Lopburi River to the north, and the Pasak River to the east. The main ferry pier is located on the east side of town, just opposite the train station.

GETTING AROUND

You can hire a minibus for 700B ($28) per day. Better yet, hire a long-tail or other boat to see the city the leisurely way for about 85B ($3.40) per hour. There is regular minibus service between Ayutthaya and Bang Pa-In, departing from Chao Prom Market on the road of the same name (trip time: 50 min.; 65B [$2.60]).

WHAT TO SEE & DO

AYUTTHAYA HISTORICAL STUDY CENTER, Rojana Rd. Tel. 245124.

Established in 1990 to serve as an educational resource for students, scholars, and the public, the center presents displays of the ancient city, including models of the palace and the port area, reconstructions of ships and architectural elements, and a fine selection of historical objects. There is an interesting section about the presence of foreigners in Ayutthaya. We suggest starting here for an overview of the area.

Admission: 125B ($5).

Open: Wed–Fri 9am–4:30pm, Sat–Sun 9am–5pm.

CHAO SAM PHRAYA NATIONAL MUSEUM, Rojana Rd.

This is the first of two National Museum branches in Ayutthaya. It houses impressive antique bronze Buddha images, carved panels, religious objects, and other local artifacts.

Admission: 15B (60¢).

Open: Wed–Sun 9am–noon and 1–4pm. **Directions:** 5½ blocks west of the Ayutthaya Historical Study Center (near the junction of Sri Samphet Rd.).

CHANDRA KASEM PALACE, northeast part of old city.

The other National Museum branch, the Chandra Kasem Palace, is a splendid building built in 1577 by King Maha Thamaraja (the 17th Ayutthaya monarch) for his son, who became King Naresuan. Subsequently destroyed, it was later restored by King Mongkut, who stayed there whenever he visited Ayutthaya. On display are exquisite gold artifacts, jewelry, carvings, Buddhas, and domestic and religious objects spanning the 13th to 17th centuries.

Admission: 15B (60¢).

Open: Wed–Sun 9am–noon and 1–4pm.

VIHARN PHRA MONGKOL BOPIT

Viharn Phra Mongkol Bopit is home to Thailand's largest seated bronze Buddha. It's housed in a somewhat cramped *viharn,* built in 1956 in the style of the original, which was destroyed in 1767. It was either brought from Sukhothai or copied from a Sukhothai Buddha, and was erected here in 1615 by King Ekatosarot in honor of his brother, Naresuan, who, in the 16th century, drove the Burmese from Sukhothai back into their own country, where they remained relatively peaceful for 160 years.

Directions: 7 blocks west of the Chandra Kasem Palace.

WANG LUANG, northwestern end of town overlooking Lopburi River.

Wang Luang, the old royal palace, was destroyed by the Burmese. The foundations of the three main buildings can still be made out, and the visitor can only be impressed by the size of the compound.

THE WATS

Near the old royal palace stands **Wat Phra Sri Sanphet,** originally built in 1448 as the king's private chapel (the equivalent of Wat Phra Kaeo in Bangkok) and renovated in the 16th and 17th centuries. The 17-meter (55-foot) bronze standing Buddha was originally cast in 1500 during the reign of the ninth king, Ramathipodi, and covered with gold. In 1767 the Burmese tried to melt the gold, causing a fire that destroyed the image and the temple. What remains is a replica. Nearby are three Sri Lankan–style *chedis,* built during the 15th century to enshrine the ashes of three Ayutthaya kings.

To the east of the royal palace, the prang of **Wat Phra Ram** soars into the sky. Originally built in 1369 by King Ramesuen (second king of Ayutthaya), the complex is in ruins.

Farther to the east is **Wat Mahathat** (ca. 1384). Opposite stands **Wat Ratachaburana,** built in 1424 and splendidly restored—the prangs and chedis have even retained some of their original stucco. In the two crypts, excavators have found bronze Buddha images and votive tablets, as well as golden objects and jewelry, many of which are displayed in the Chao Sam Phraya Museum. There are also murals, rows of seated Buddhas, standing disciples, and Jataka scenes (based on tales from the Buddha's former lives) in the four niches, as well as a frieze of heavenly beings and some Chinese scenes. Both remain severely damaged despite restoration.

A very large and impressive Buddha is at **Wat Phanan Choeng,** a temple built in 1324, 26 years before King U-Thong founded Ayutthaya. The image is 19 meters (62 feet) high and more than 14 meters (45 feet) from knee to knee. Adjacent to it is a small Chinese temple, a memorial to a princess who was betrothed to the king of Thailand and who committed suicide when he failed to attend her arrival.

Wat Suwan Dararam, across the river, is visited by the present royal couple when they come to Ayutthaya. It was built by Rama I. The murals and door panels depict stories from the *Ramakien.*

Wat Na Phra Mane, on the Lopburi side of the river, survived Ayutthaya's destruction and is worth visiting to see the black-stone Buddha dating from the Dvaravati period, as well as the principal Buddha fully decorated in regal attire.

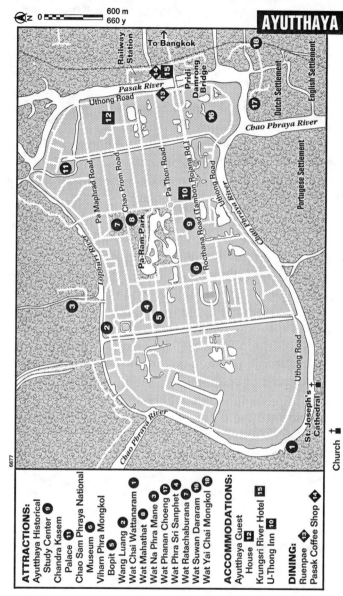

AYUTTHAYA

N 0 ——— 600 m
        660 y

To Bangkok

Railway Station

Pasak River
Uthong Road

Pridi Damrong Bridge

Lopburi River

Pa Maphrad Road

Chao Prom Road

Pa-Ram Park

Pa Thon Road

Rojana Rd.

Rochana Road (Tambol) Rojana Road

Uthong Road

Chao Phraya River

Chao Phraya River

Portuguese Settlement

Dutch Settlement

English Settlement

Uthong Road

St. Joseph's Cathedral

Church ✝

ATTRACTIONS:
Ayutthaya Historical Study Center ❾
Chandra Kasem Palace ⓫
Chao Sam Phraya National Museum ❻
Viharn Phra Mongkol Bopit ❺
Wang Luang ❷
Wat Chai Wattanaram ❶
Wat Mahathat ❽
Wat Na Phra Mane ❸
Wat Phanan Choeng ⓱
Wat Phra Sri Sanphet ❹
Wat Ratachaburana ❼
Wat Suwan Dararam ⓰
Wat Yai Chai Mongkol ⓲

ACCOMMODATIONS:
Ayutthaya Guest House ⓬
Krungsri River Hotel ⓯
U-Thong Inn ❿

DINING:
Ruenpae ⓭
Pasak Coffee Shop ⓮

Back on the main site on the other side of the river, one chedi serves as a moving reminder of the role women have often played in Thai history (in a country where they were expected to serve alongside men in war). Only a chedi and a statue remain of a temple built to commemorate Queen Suriyothai, who was killed when she intervened in a duel between her husband and a Burmese general—fought on the backs of elephants.

Don't miss **Wat Yai Chai Mongkol**, a few minutes southeast of ancient Ayutthaya. It's a well-tended temple built by King U-Thong in 1357 for meditation. The massive pagoda was built in

1592 by King Naresuan after he defeated the Burmese by killing their crown prince in single-handed combat on elephants.

A short distance from the other main temple sites (on the other side of the Chao Phraya River, west of the royal palace) is **Wat Chai Wattanaram**, which is still being restored. Roots and branches straggle around the many chedis and prangs. The overgrown complex has that haunted sense of tragedy about it—the essence of Ayutthaya. *Note:* Some sites charge 10B (40¢) admission.

WHERE TO STAY

MODERATE

KRUNGSRI RIVER HOTEL, 27/2 Rojana Rd., Ayutthaya 13000. Tel. 035/242996. Fax 035/242996. 202 rms. A/C MINIBAR TV TEL **Directions:** Northeast side of Pridi Damrong Bridge.

$ Rates: 1,675B ($67) single; 1,900B ($76) double; 4,200B ($168) suite. MC, V.

The construction of this handsome luxury hotel, close by the train station, was nearing completion at our visit. We could already see that the marble-floored lobby was cool and spacious. Rooms are uncluttered, clean, and crisp, with good-sized gray-granite bathrooms. (A number will be reserved for nonsmokers.) With 24-hour room service, a friendly staff, and many facilities, it's obviously the area's top choice.

The Krungsri has a very good coffee shop now (see "Where to Dine," below), and will have both Chinese and Japanese restaurants. Facilities include an outdoor swimming pool, health club with saunas, small bowling alley, snooker room, and beauty salon.

INEXPENSIVE

U-THONG INN, Rojana Rd., Ayutthaya 13000. Tel. 035/242236. 100 rms. A/C TV TEL MINIBAR **Directions:** In center of ancient city.

$ Rates: 900B ($36) single or double. MC, V.

The U-Thong Inn is among the best of a modest selection. Its carpeted rooms are neat and clean, and the front-desk personnel are accommodating. The hotel provides laundry service. There's also a restaurant attached and a pool.

BUDGET

AYUTTHAYA GUEST HOUSE, 16/2 Chao Prom Rd., Ayutthaya 13000. Tel. 035/251468. 10 rms. **Directions:** Just north of in-town bus station.

$ Rates: 60B ($2.40) dorm bed; 75B ($3) single; 120B ($4.80) double. No credit cards.

The former B.J. Guest House is now the domain of Mr. Hong and family, but it still offers the best of the low-budget beds in Ayutthaya. There are bicycles for rent, and a small and inexpensive garden restaurant attached to the guesthouse.

WHERE TO DINE

For real budget dining, try the small food shops near the Hua-Raw and Chao Prom markets or the informal restaurants across from the entrance to Wat Mahathat.

PASAK COFFEE SHOP, in the Krungsri River Hotel. Tel. 244333.
> **Cuisine:** THAI/CONTINENTAL. **Directions:** Northeast side of Pridi Damrong Bridge.
> **$ Prices:** Appetizers 75B–115B ($3–$4.60); main courses 115B–200B ($4.60–$8). MC, V.
> **Open:** Daily 5am–11pm.

On the first floor of the area's best hotel, this bright and airy place has marble floors and a menu more varied than that found in most coffee shops. Standard Thai dishes are carefully prepared (and not too spicy!), and Western main courses include the popular cheeseburger. The service is attentive, and at supper there's a local band.

RUENPAE, north of Pridi Damrong Bridge. Tel. 251807.
> **Cuisine:** THAI/CHINESE. **Directions:** North of ancient city.
> **$ Prices:** Appetizers 45B–100B ($1.80–$4); main courses 65B–125B ($2.60–$5). MC, V.
> **Open:** Daily 11am–10pm.

Ruenpae is a simple floating riverfront restaurant. It offers a typical Thai/Chinese menu, with such dishes as steamed fish in plum sauce, roast chicken with salt, Nanking soy cake, grilled prawns, and beef with chili. A good place to enjoy a pretty good meal after a long day of sightseeing.

2. PATTAYA

147km (91 miles) SE of Bangkok

GETTING THERE **By Plane** Pattaya International Airport is open only to charter flights from Europe and the Middle East. However, Bangkok Airways (tel. 038/603063) has four flights weekly from Bangkok (1,800B [$72]).

By Train Once a day, trains leave from Bangkok's Hua Lampong Railroad Station. Call 223-2762 in Bangkok or 429285 in Pattaya for schedule information.

By Public Bus There are more than 50 buses a day from Bangkok's Eastern Bus Terminal (trip time: 2½ to 3½ hr; 75B [$3]) and 25 buses a day from Bangkok's Northern Bus Terminal (trip time: 3½ hr.; 75B [$3]).

By Private Bus Major hotels or travel agencies often operate their own transport or can recommend private buses. Thai International Limousine Service (tel. 423140) has private car-and-driver service (trip time: 2½ hr.; 1,800B [$72]), and a minibus three times daily (trip time: 3 hr.; 225B [$9] one way) to and from Bangkok's Don Muang airport; they will pick you up from your hotel in Pattaya.

By Taxi The concierge in our Bangkok hotel negotiated with a metered-taxi driver to take us to a Pattaya resort, door to door, for 1,250B ($50). Traveling with a child and lots of luggage, this proved faster (2½ hours) and almost cheaper than the private minibus services.

By Car Take Highway 3 east from Bangkok (trip time: 2½ to 3 hr.).

SPECIAL EVENTS Festival of arts in April, with fireworks and beauty pageant. Buffalo races in Chonburi, late October.

Pattaya is not a typical beach resort, so visitors should be clear about their reasons for coming. Some come for a break from Bangkok: the verdant hills, long beach, and deep-green (though not pristine) waters of Pattaya Bay are only a 3-hour drive away. But many more of your fellow travelers have come to sample Pattaya's best-known product: sex.

Pattaya has suffered from its once-positive image as the sex playground of Southeast Asia. AIDS, environmental pollution, and lots of bad publicity have contributed to a tremendous drop in tourism. To recover, the local government is spending a lot of baht to clean up Pattaya Bay and is attempting to enforce strict new waste-management guidelines despite continuing development.

Budget travelers should only consider Pattaya or the nearby condo-land at Jomtien Beach if they are pressed for time. Both provide a convenient getaway from Bangkok, but your baht won't buy as much beach splendor as at one of the small resorts in Hua Hin/Cha-Am.

ORIENTATION

ARRIVING   All buses use the Bus Terminal on North Pattaya Road at Sukhumvit Road, a 5-minute drive from the north end of Pattaya Beach Road. Local taxis are inexpensive; the taxi stand is right outside the terminal. There is also *song tao* (shared minibus) service to Pattaya Beach Road (see "Getting Around," below).

INFORMATION   The **Tourism Authority of Thailand (TAT)** office is midway along Pattaya Beach at 241/1 Beach Rd. (tel. 038/428750; fax 038/429113). It's open daily from 8:30am to 4:30pm. The office of the **Tourist Police** (tel. 429371), next door to the tourist office, is open 24 hours.

During the life of this book, both will move to the corner of Beach Road and Soi 7 (keeping the same phone numbers) as part of a beachfront beautification program.

CITY LAYOUT   Pattaya is basically a long strip of hotels, bars, restaurants, travel agencies, and shops along Pattaya Beach Road, opposite a narrow beach overlooking Pattaya Bay. Central Pattaya (Pattaya Klang) Road bisects Pattaya Beach Road and the two streets parallel to and behind the strip, Pattaya Second Road and Pattaya Third Road. At both the far northern and southern ends of the strip are two bluffs. On the northern side is the Dusit Resort and several small hotels, and on the southern flank is the Royal Cliff Beach Resort. Farther south and east is Jomtien Beach, a 15-minute ride from town.

GETTING AROUND

BY MINIBUS   Minibuses, baht buses, or song tao (actually open-bed trucks with wooden bench seats), which cruise the major streets for passengers, are the best and cheapest form of transport. Fares within Pattaya should range from 10B to 30B (40¢ to $1.20); fares to far-flung beaches such as Jomtien run anywhere from 30B to 85B ($1.20 to $3.40). Rates are fixed by the local government, but most drivers will negotiate fiercely. Some hotels operate their own minibuses, but they charge much more for the same bumpy ride.

BY CAR   **Avis,** at the Royal Cliff Beach Resort (tel. 421421)

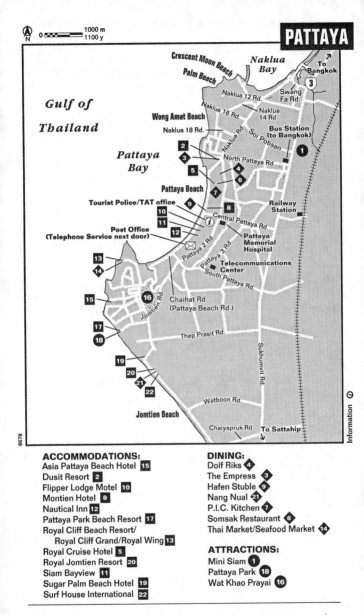

Gulf of
Thailand

Pattaya
Bay

ACCOMMODATIONS:
Asia Pattaya Beach Hotel **15**
Dusit Resort **2**
Flipper Lodge Motel **10**
Montien Hotel **8**
Nautical Inn **12**
Pattaya Park Beach Resort **17**
Royal Cliff Beach Resort/
    Royal Cliff Grand/Royal Wing **13**
Royal Cruise Hotel **5**
Royal Jomtien Resort **20**
Siam Bayview **11**
Sugar Palm Beach Hotel **19**
Surf House International **22**

DINING:
Dolf Riks **4**
The Empress **3**
Hafen Stuble **9**
Nang Nual **21**
P.I.C. Kitchen **7**
Somsak Restaurant **6**
Thai Market/Seafood Market **14**

ATTRACTIONS:
Mini Siam **1**
Pattaya Park **18**
Wat Khao Prayai **16**

or at the Dusit Resort (tel. 425611), is one of many rental-car companies offering self-drive or chauffeured cars to explore the east coast. Self-drive rates are approximately $70 per day with insurance; a car and driver costs $160, including 200 kilometers (120 miles) free. Several popular destinations have fixed rates (for example, Pattaya–Bangkok for 2,400B ($96); Pattaya–Trat for 3,600B ($144). **VIA Rent A Car**, at 215/15–18 Pattaya Second Road (tel. 426242), is a local company we liked. Their day rate for an insured, self-drive car is 900B ($36).

BY MOTORCYCLE For those who dare brave the often drunk and reckless foreign drivers in downtown Pattaya, 150cc motorcycles rent for 250B ($10) a day without insurance (ask for a helmet!). Mopeds and larger motorcycles are available from many companies along the beach strip and Central Pattaya Road.

FAST FACTS

Area Code The telephone area code for Pattaya is 038.

Bookstore A small bookstore, D.K. Book House, is near the post office, next to the Royal Garden Hotel. The Foodland and Spinny supermarkets have book corners for best-sellers.

Currency Exchange There are many independent money-changing booths around town, but bank-affiliated exchanges have better rates and often stay open 24 hours.

Medical Facilities Pattaya's medical facilities range from VD clinics to hospitals with CAT scans. The most frequently recommended centers are Pattaya Memorial Hospital, 328/1 Central, Pattaya Road (tel. 429422) and Pattaya International Hospital, Soi 4, Beach Road (tel. 428374).

Post Office The Post and Telegraph Office, between Beach Road and Pattaya Second Road on Soi Post Office (tel. 429341), is open Monday through Friday from 8:30am to 4:30pm, on Saturday and Sunday from 8:30am to noon.

Telecommunications The Telecommunications Center, South Pattaya Road (tel. 429601), is open 24 hours for overseas calls. (Many travel agents will also book long-distance calls.)

WHAT TO SEE & DO

BEACHES

The town beach, along Pattaya Beach Road, is polluted and not recommended for swimming; the beaches at the extreme ends of town are cleaner. The best choices for bathing are the **north end of Pattaya Beach** (below the Dusit Resort) and **Dong Than Beach** (at the north end of Jomtien Beach). The **south end of Jomtien Beach** is for windsurfing and sailing; it is too heavily trafficked to be safe for swimming. Though huge condos and constant construction overwhelm the Jomtien Beach community, for the moment it's still a cleaner beach than Pattaya (and almost as good as those on nearby islands) for a short holiday in the sun.

Jomtien's beaches are narrow, long, and sandy, with a line of casuarina pine trees for shade; they're easily reached by minibus (the fare is 50B [$2]).

WATER SPORTS

For water sports, most people go to nearby islands, where the sea water is cleaner. Dozens of boats will take you on day **cruises** (about 350B [$14] per person), **jetskiing** or **waterskiing** (about 1,000B [$40] per hour), or **parasailing** (350B [$14] per flight). Local fishing boats and motorboats are usually moored on the central beach stretch, near the TAT. Several beach vendors offer **Windsurfers** for rent at 450B ($18) per hour. Skilled windsurfers prefer to sail off of Jomtien Beach, where there's less boat traffic; the best winds blow northeast from November to January. Contact any of the Pattaya Beach Road travel agencies if you're interested in **deep-sea fishing;** packaged excursions, including fishing gear, usually cost 5,000B ($200) per day per boat.

Snorkeling and **scuba diving** are popular because of the area's clear waters (20–25m 65–81 ft.] average visibility), colorful coral reefs (including mushroom, lettuce, brain, and staghorn corals), and tropical fish (white- and black-tip sharks, stingrays, angelfish, and many others). Nearby Ko Larn, Ko Sak, and Ko Krok can be reached within 45 minutes by boat. There's also diving off of Ko Klung Badan, Ko Man Wichai, and Ko Rin, which are farther offshore. North of Pattaya is Ko Si Chang, famous as the summer playground of foreign ambassadors during the 19th century. Here, and off Sattahip to the south, is even better diving, at depths up to 40 meters (130 ft.).

There are several good dive shops with PADI and NAUI certified instructors we can recommend: **Seafari Sports Center,** at Soi 5, Beach Road (tel. 038/429253; fax 038/424708), is a PADI-certified school run by American expatriates Patti and Bill Burbridge. In nearby Jomtien, there's **Mermaid's Dive School,** Soi Mermaid (tel. 038/232219; fax 038/232221). **Dave's Divers Den/The Professionals** has relocated away from the beach to Moo 3, Pattaya-Naklua Road, Naklua (tel. 038/221860; fax 038/221618).

Check the certification, class schedules, equipment, itinerary, and fine print at each outfit before committing to a program. Most scuba day trips, including equipment for two dives, lunch, transportation, and dive master, cost 1,500B to 2,000B ($60 to $80) depending on your destination. Snorkeling or island-hopping day trips begin at about 450B ($18), plus 150B ($6) to rent snorkel gear. Certification courses and night dives can also be arranged.

ISLAND EXCURSIONS

Ko Larn is the largest and most popular of the nearby islands. Its main port is a long sandy beach cove facing the mainland, just a 45-minute boat ride away. Dozens of seafood restaurants and snack bars line the beach; sunbathing and eating fresh seafood are the natural pursuits. The largely uninhabited **Bamboo Island** and **Ko Man Wichai,** within an hour of Ko Larn, are suited to the deserted-tropical-island crowd. **Ko Sak** and **Ko Krok,** also popular for diving, are good fishing areas. Fishing-boat and motorboat operators moored on the main part of Pattaya Beach offer **Ko Larn** day trips for about 350B ($14) per person on a full boat, or about 1,500B ($60) for a privately chartered boat; it's 2,500B ($100) to Bamboo Island. There's lots of competition, so bargain. If you're too shy to organize this on your own, many of the beachside tour operators will sell you a ticket on their day-trip boats.

NEARBY ATTRACTIONS

WAT KHAO PRAYAI, Khao Tappraya Hill.

If you feel a need to rise above the earthly foibles of Pattaya, we can recommend a short excursion to this wat. The small temple complex offers excellent vistas, but more than that, a moment of tranquillity. Khao Prayai means "Great Buddha on the Hill," and a 10-meter-tall (32.5-ft.-tall) gold Buddha sits serenely surveying the western sea. There's also some history here—*tappraya* was the Ayutthaya-era title for "general," a name that evolved into Pattaya.

The walk up Khao Tappraya Hill will do wonders for the cardiovascular crowd. Another wat, west of Khao Prayai on a neighboring rise, can also be visited.

Admission: 10B (40¢) suggested contribution.

Open: Daily 6am–6pm. **Transportation/Directions:** Take minibus to Jomtien from Beach Road and get off on top of hill and walk up between dragon-headed columns. To drive or walk, leave town by Pattaya Second Road south, fork right after Gulf Hotel, and continue for 2km (1¼ miles) uphill. Where main road forks right to Royal Cliff Beach Resort, turn left up road guarded by two dragon-headed columns.

PATTAYA PARK, 345 Jomtien Beach Rd., Jomtien. Tel. 442300.

Though we wouldn't normally recommend Pattaya as a place to take your kids, if you find yourself there with restless children, a day at Pattaya Park's playland could save you. It's a worn, but fun, water park with a small Thai restaurant; a network of pools; several water slides, which propel you into the shallows; a narrow, clean beach; and many kinds of water-sports equipment (Windsurfers, catamarans, etc.) for rent.

Admission: 60B ($2.40) adults, 35B ($1.40) children under 120cm (4 ft.).

Open: Daily 8:30am–6pm. **Transportation/Directions:** Take minibus to Jomtien from Beach Road and get off at Pattaya Park Hotel. It's about 8km (5 miles) south of town.

MINI SIAM, 387 Sukhumvit Rd., North Pattaya City. Tel. 421628.

For those who don't have time to see all of Thailand's many wonders, this is a comprehensive tour of the country's highlights, all shown as miniature models (an example of scale: Bangkok's huge Grand Palace is waist-high). Most of Thailand's famous structures, in meticulous detail, are included. Coming in 1995: "Mini Europe," to thrill the Thai tourists who bring their kids here!

Admission: 250B ($10) adults, 125B ($5) children.

Open: Daily 9am–9pm. **Transportation/Directions:** It's 14km (8½ miles) north of Pattaya City, and can be reached by taxi (about 800B [$32] with wait) or by joining the bus tour offered by one of the local travel agents.

WHERE TO STAY

Because of Pattaya's particular industry, the hotel you choose is critical. If a good beach, clean air, and health-spa facilities sound like the perfect respite from Bangkok, choose one of the fully inclusive resorts and never leave. Otherwise, choose from any of the other hotels recommended along Pattaya Beach Road—all within a walk or brief ride of the go-go bars, beach bars, massage parlors, and private clubs.

All prices are exclusive of the 7% VAT and the 10% service charge, and do not reflect the peak-season supplement—usually 600B to 1,000B ($24 to $40) per room per night—charged by many hotels from mid-December to mid-January. (If business is bad, these fees are often waived.) During this peak period, reservations are recommended at least two weeks in advance.

PATTAYA CITY

Very Expensive

**ROYAL CLIFF GRAND, Royal Cliff Bay, Pattaya City,
20260 Chonburi. Tel. 038/250421.** Fax 038/250514. Telex
85904 CLIFFGR TH. 187 rms, 15 suites. A/C MINIBAR TV TEL
Directions: On cliff, south part of Pattaya Beach.

$ Rates: 4,300B–5,400B ($172–$216) single or double; from 10,800B
($432) suite. Extra bed 1,200B ($48). AE, DC, MC, V.

If stunning, columned public spaces with fountains, staircases, chandeliers and acres of granite mean "grand," then this newest addition to the fine Royal Cliff Beach Club Resort complex lives up to the name. Everything about the place is larger than life.

Spacious rooms in the contemporary, scallop-shaped tower have private VCRs and fax setups, as well as marble bathrooms with separate shower stalls and twin sinks. They are elegantly appointed with classic furniture and coffered ceilings in tribute to the era of King Rama V, who inspired the Victoriana/Siam design. The Royal Club on the sixth floor boasts a private spa and sun deck, as well as seven Jacuzzis for its VIP and business guests. An impressive colonnaded lobby leads down to the scenic and excellent Grand Café, whose three-story picture windows overlook the huge free-form pool and richly opulent grounds.

Dining/Entertainment: The Grand Café offers terrific continental and Thai cuisine indoors in a towering sunroom, or outdoors on a patio overlooking the gardens. Both quality and service are first-rate and prices reasonable. Guests also have access (a pleasant walk) to the many facilities at the Royal Cliff and Royal Wing hotels (see below).

Services: 24-hour room service, concierge, limousine service, babysitting, house doctor, laundry.

Facilities: Beautiful swimming pool and, as part of resort, health club, water sports, mini-golf course, business center, beauty salon and barbershop, shopping arcade, deli/bakery.

**ROYAL WING, Royal Cliff Beach Resort, Pattaya City
20260, Chonburi. Tel. 038/250421.** Fax 038/250511. Telex
85907 CLIFFEX TH. 84 executive suites, 2 presidential suites. A/C
MINIBAR TEL TV **Directions:** On cliff, south Pattaya Beach.

$ Rates: 7,700B ($308) suite; 27,500B ($1,100) presidential suite.
AE, CB, DC, EU, MC, V.

The dazzling Royal Wing is treated both by guests and its capable Swiss management as a separate entity within the impressive Royal Cliff resort. The level of service here is more personal (butlers on call 24 hours!), and the rooms are more regally furnished, than anywhere else in town.

As opulent as Bangkok's Shangri-La Hotel, the Royal Wing is the pinnacle of Hong Kong–style glitz. The lobby is white marble, with lotus bud–capped columns combining Thai and Chinese influences. Each guest is catered to personally, with butlers unpacking your luggage on arrival and beach chaise longues reserved with your own brass name plate. The large, bright, quietly tasteful rooms—decorated throughout with teak and fine pastel Thai cottons—are spaced around the breadth of the cliff. For maximum privacy, each has two balconies, draped in fuchsia or orange bougainvillea, overlooking Pattaya Bay. The free-form swimming pool is crisscrossed by small bow bridges; waterfalls add an extra exotic touch. The beach is small but uncrowded and well maintained.

Dining/Entertainment: The hotel offers daytime or romantic evening poolside dining at La Ronde, an elegant lobby bar, and the Palm Terrace for breakfast or lighter fare. The Benjarong Restaurant, with peach-colored Thai-silk upholstery and polished bleached marble floors, serves French and continental fare with a hint of Thai. Guests can try the Thai Market or Seafood Market open-air pavilion (see "Where to Dine," later in this chapter), as well as the facilities at the nearby Royal Cliff or Royal Cliff Grand.

Service: 24-hour room and butler service, concierge, limo, babysitting, house doctor, laundry, no-smoking rooms.

Facilities: Pool, Cliff Club Spa (with sauna, steam bath, and two pools), water sports, mini-golf course, tennis courts, jogging track, business center, beauty salon, barbershop, shopping arcade, deli/bakery.

Expensive

ASIA PATTAYA BEACH HOTEL, Cliff Rd., Pattaya City 20260, Chonburi. Tel. 038/250602. Fax 038/250496. Telex 85902 ASIAPAT TH. 304 rms, 10 suites. A/C MINIBAR TEL TV
Directions: On cliff above south end of beach; 3km (1.8 miles) south of town.

$ Rates: 2,300B ($92) single/double with mountain view; 2,900B ($116) single/double with water view; 5,200B ($208) family suite. AE, CB, DC, EU, MC, V.

The Asia Pattaya offers immaculate grounds, all heavily planted, and one of our favorite images, a topiary A-S-I-A in the middle of a circular driveway. The rooms are aging but well kept and have numerous amenities. Many are decorated with kitschy 1960s paneling or with leather-look furniture. The Dutch-owned Golden Tulip chain manages the resort in a friendly, homey way; European tour groups abound. The well-priced rooms and two-bedroom family suites are good value if you're looking for a well-groomed private beach, tranquillity, and relative seclusion.

Dining/Entertainment: The open-air Cliff Top Restaurant offers great views and good continental or typical Thai fare. The Neptune Disco has a popular DJ nightly, with a pretty good selection of European hits and, often, a live band.

Services: 24-hour room service, concierge, limousine service, babysitting (with notice), laundry service.

Facilities: Swimming pool, nine-hole golf course, shopping arcade.

DUSIT RESORT, 240/2 Pattaya Beach Rd., Pattaya City 20150, Chonburi. Tel. 038/425611. Fax 038/428239. Telex TH 85917. 474 rms, 26 suites. A/C MINIBAR TEL TV **Directions:** North end of Pattaya Beach.

$ Rates: 2,250B–3,150B ($90–$126) single/double with garden view; 3,750B ($150) single/double with sea view; 6,550B ($262) single/double Landmark room; from 7,200B ($288) suite. Extra bed 700B ($28). AE, DC. MC, V.

This beautifully landscaped resort offers fresh air, water sports, a good health club, and some nightlife (far from the seamier side of Pattaya). Straddling a bluff on the north end of the main beach, the Dusit has two pools and sun decks, access to two small but well-kept sandy beach coves, several dining outlets, a small shopping arcade, and newly reduced rates making it a great value!

Most of the balconied rooms overlook Pattaya Bay, but the best values are the garden view–priced rooms in Wing B, which face manicured lawns, hibiscus beds, and a side view of the sea. Tastefully modern rooms trimmed in stained woods offer all-marble bathrooms, hairdryers, and personal bathrobes. Landmark deluxe rooms have large bathrooms with separate bath and shower stalls, plus outdoor showers on their large balconies, as well as comfortable and luxurious sitting areas. We loved the Landmark Honeymoon Suite (12,000B [$480]), whose huge bathroom features a raised oval Jacuzzi tub overlooking the sea, a green silk fainting couch (what do they expect?), and a walk-in shower the size of many budget hotel rooms. If only the service matched the high-quality facilities!

Dining/Entertainment: The Dusit has several dining options, including The Empress for panoramic views and gourmet Chinese food, as well as the slow, but poolside, Bay. There is an okay coffee shop and delightful lobby lounge, the latter serving evening drinks with live musical accompaniment.

Services: 24-hour room service, concierge, limousine service, babysitting, laundry service, no-smoking rooms.

Facilities: Two outdoor swimming pools, water sports, health club (open 7am to 11pm) with daily aerobics classes, sauna rooms with TV sets, pool tables, tennis courts, squash courts, shopping arcade, beauty salon, barbershop.

MONTIEN HOTEL, 369 Moo 9, Pattaya Klang Rd., Pattaya City 20260, Chonburi. Tel. 038/428155. Fax 038/423155. Telex TH 85906. 280 rms, 20 suites. A/C MINIBAR TEL TV **Directions:** Between Beach Rd. and Pattaya Second Rd., north of Pattaya Klang Rd.

$ Rates: 3,100B ($124) single/double with ocean view; 2,600B ($104) single/double with mountain view; 4,600B ($184) deluxe room. Extra bed 500B ($20). AE, DC, MC, V.

The high-rise Montien looms above Beach Road and has perhaps the best sea and mountain vista of all the hotels on the strip. The multilevel lobby, grand and open-air, is decorated in overstuffed wicker and rattan, a style echoed in all guest rooms. The seaview ones are much brighter and airier—probably worth the splurge. The Montien offers a sprawling, well-manicured garden, large pool, tennis courts, fitness center, and several restaurants. The place buzzes with activity and gets lots of attractive young Europeans.

ROYAL CLIFF BEACH RESORT, Royal Cliff Bay, Pattaya City 20260, Chonburi. Tel. 038/250421. Fax 038/250511. Telex 85907 CLIFFEX TH. 383 rms. 324 minisuites, 127 suites. A/C MINIBAR TEL TV **Directions:** On cliff, above south end of Pattaya Beach.

$ Rates: 3,100B ($124) single/double; 4,100B ($164) minisuite; from 6,000B ($240) two-bedroom suite. AE, DC, EU, MC, V.

This is Pattaya's top family resort selection, at the southern end of town on the same garden property as the more exclusive Royal Wing and Royal Cliff Grand. It was built and upgraded in phases: the Royal Cliff Terrace building houses four terraced stories of suites with patios; the nine-story seaview hotel tower houses most of the guest rooms, including huge, perfect-for-families two-bedroom suites. Most rooms have bay views, as well as bleached wood and pastel decor; all offer spacious living quarters and terraces. If you tire of the lushly planted grounds, there's an elevator from the precipice down to the sandy beach, which is relatively clean but by most standards disappointingly small. Go for the pools, the grounds, the health club, not for the beach. The hotel has a staff of more than 1,500 waiting to serve. We found it a friendly, luxurious, and relaxing place.

Dining/Entertainment: There is an indoor/outdoor poolside coffee shop (delightful for a grand American or Thai-style buffet breakfast), as well as snack bars by the sea, in the gardens, and by the Cliff Club pool. For the evening, there's a piano bar off the lobby (for people-watching) and one in the open-air Thai Market pavilion. Restaurants include the stately up-country Grill Room, the Thai Market/Seafood Market (see "Where to Dine," below). Guests are also welcome at the exclusive Royal Wing's formal Benjarong Restaurant and the poolside La Ronde.

Service: 24-hour room service, concierge, fruit basket in suites, house doctor, limousine service, babysitting, laundry service.

Facilities: Outdoor swimming pool, Cliff Club Spa (with jogging track, sauna, steam bath, and two pools), water sports, minigolf course, tennis courts, squash courts, jogging track, business center, beauty salons, barbershop, shopping arcade, deli/bakery.

Moderate

ROYAL CRUISE HOTEL, 499 N. Pattaya Beach Rd., Pattaya City 20260, Chonburi. Tel. 038/424242. Fax 02/236-2361 (Bangkok). Telex 84204 A-ONE TH. 176 rms, 24 suites. A/C MINIBAR TEL TV **Directions:** Mid-beach, near Soi 2.

$ Rates: 2,150B–2,600B ($86–$104) single/double; from 3,400B ($136) suite. Extra bed 500B ($20). AE, DC, MC, V.

Into a cruise mode? Like the idea of a huge white cruise ship berthed among thatch-roofed bars and T-shirt stalls? If the answer is yes, try an art deco–style seaview cabin at this ultra-themed, boat-shaped hotel. Nine decks include deco signage, glass lamp bases filled with sand and coral, and hallways with portholes. There's a Le Bateau coffee shop, a nice pool and kids' playground, and a tiny weight room/mini-spa. Fun place—and you don't get seasick.

SIAM BAYVIEW, Pattaya Beach Rd., Pattaya City 20260, Chonburi. Tel. 038/423871. Fax 038/423879. Telex TH 85921. 270 rms, 16 suites. A/C MINIBAR TEL TV **Directions:** Mid-beach, at Soi 10.

$ Rates: 2,300B–2,900B ($92–$116) single/double; from 4,400B ($176) suite. Extra bed 400B ($16). AE, DC, MC, V.

This is probably the finest hotel along the middle of the Pattaya Beach strip. You enter under a flowering arbor, through a well-kept garden and take marble stairs above the fountain to reach an impressive pavilion lobby. Rooms are large, modern, and very comfortable, though furnished without distinction. However, extensive renovations had begun at our visit. Unlike its neighbors, the Bayview is relatively isolated from the nightly frazzle.

Dining/Entertainment: There are a pleasant café; Narissa, a large Asian restaurant with Thai, Chinese, and (a smattering of) Japanese dishes; and a continental restaurant. The bar off the lobby is very popular.

Services: 24-hour room service, limousine service, babysitting (with notice), laundry service.

Facilities: Swimming pool, two tennis courts, shopping arcade.

Inexpensive/Budget

FLIPPER LODGE MOTEL, 520/1 Soi 8, Pattaya Beach Rd., Pattaya City 20260, Chonburi. Tel. 038/426401. Fax 038/426403. 126 rms. A/C MINIBAR TEL TV **Directions:** Mid-beach strip, off Soi 8.

$ Rates: 850B ($34) single/double with garden view; 950B ($38) single/double with sea view; from 1,800B ($72) suite. Extra bed 150B ($6). AE, MC, V.

The best thing about the Flipper Lodge is the life-size statue of Flipper the Dolphin gracing the lobby; the second best is the price, making this the favorite budget choice in the middle of the beach strip. The decor is basic, but the older rooms are clean and the new wing looks great; the seaview rooms can't be beat. After you take a swim in the short pool (under Flipper's watchful gaze) or in the new rooftop pool, you can proceed to the attractive open-air coffee shop for some pretty good Thai and continental fare.

NAUTICAL INN, 10/10 Pattaya Beach Rd., Pattaya City 20150, Chonburi. Tel. 038/428110. Fax 038/428116. 80 rms, 2 suites. A/C MINIBAR TEL TV **Directions:** Between Soi 11 and Soi 12.

$ Rates (including tax and service): 1,100B ($44) single/double with garden view; 1,500B ($60) single/double with sea view. AE, MC, V.

The Nautical Inn is a good budget choice on the beach strip. It's a relatively new, though Spartan, facility set well back from the road. Plain tower rooms are worn, but all have sea views, while garden-view rooms surround a respectable pool. If you're staying two days or more, ask for their special reduced rates. The daily published rates are often discounted up to 50 percent in the low season.

JOMTIEN BEACH

Expensive

ROYAL JOMTIEN RESORT, 408 Moo 12, Jomtien Beach Rd., Pattaya City 20260, Chonburi. Tel 038/231350. Fax 038/231369. Telex 85934 ROYAL TH. 400 rms. A/C MINIBAR TV TEL **Directions:** North end of Jomtien Beach.

$ Rates: 2,900B–3,200B ($116–$128) single; 3,000B–3,400B ($120–$136) double; from 8,400B ($336) suite. Extra bed 600B ($24). AE, MC, V.

At home amid a cluster of stark white, contemporary condos, this newly built, 16-story tower has some of the nicest rooms along Jomtien Beach. Most featuring sea views, they're set back from the busy road and are refreshingly quiet. With lots of print fabrics, rattan-accented furnishings, and well-appointed if compact bathrooms, they are very pleasant. The lobby overlooks a good-sized pool and a landscaped sitting area. And if you've arrived in the rainy season, you can select a video to watch in your room, hit the fitness center, or head down to the eight-lane bowling alley.

Dining/Entertainment: There is a too-formal, but convenient and varied-menu, coffee shop off the lobby.

Services: 24-hour room service, taxi service, babysitting, laundry.

Facilities: Swimming pool, health club, snooker, business center.

Moderate/Inexpensive

PATTAYA PARK BEACH RESORT, 345 Jomtien Beach Rd., Pattaya 20150, Chonburi. Tel. 038/251201. Fax 038/251209. Telex 85956 PTY PARK TH. 240 rms, 24 suites. A/C MINIBAR TEL TV **Directions:** .4km (.25 mile) off road to Jomtien Beach, next to Pattaya Park water park.

$ Rates: 2,200B ($88) single/double; from 4,325B ($173) suite. Extra bed 350B ($14). AE, DC. MC, V.

This contemporary high-rise is a good place for a family beach-and-swim vacation because of the adjacent water park, with its vast pools and multiple slides. Both facilities share a good beach, where windsurfers and catamarans are available for water-sports fans. The sunny rooms can only be described as modern Spartan in decor. Standard rooms, the same price as the small cottages, may have better views but they're not as private or spacious. Family suites have two bedrooms separated only by a partition, and share one bathroom.

SUGAR PALM BEACH HOTEL, 45/16 Moo 12, Sugar Palm Beach, Jomtien, 20260, Chonburi. Tel. 038/231386. Fax 038/231889. 32 rms. A/C TEL **Directions:** North end of Jomtien Beach, just northwest of Jomtien Plaza Condos, on boardwalk.

$ Rates: 950B ($38) single/double; 1,450B ($58) single/double with sea view. AE, MC, V.

Our favorite lower-priced choice for a purely casual, beachy hotel, this place faces the quiet, clean Sugar Palm Beach and its gently lapping surf—far from the crowds on noisy Jomtien Beach Road. The simple rooms are spotless, though only two have ocean views. The Style Restaurant next door offers open-air dining on the beach, with good food and cheap prices (an American breakfast is only 80B [$3.20]).

SURF HOUSE INTERNATIONAL, 75 Jomtien Beach Rd., Jomtien 20260, Chonburi. Tel. 038/231025. Fax 038/231029. 36 rms. A/C MINIBAR TEL TV **Directions:** East end of Jomtien Beach.

$ Rates (including tax and service): 720B–810B ($28.80–$32.40) single/double. Extra bed 125B ($5). AE, EU, MC, V.

Like most Jomtien accommodations, the Surf House seems to attract a younger, more beach-loving crowd than that which frequents the Pattaya hotels. Rooms are simple and clean, with private baths, and most have balconies and water views—request a seaside room on the top floor for a good panorama of the windsurfers. Because the Surf House is separated from the beach by the busy road, we consider it a second choice to the Sugar Palm Beach Hotel.

READERS RECOMMEND

Sugar Hut (tel. 038/251686; fax 038/251689). "We generally try to get out of Bangkok on weekends and have found the Sugar Hut, inland from Jomtien Beach, to be a wonderful destination. The hotel consists of a group of traditional Thai bungalows, which are perfectly modern and comfortable, facing a large pool and gardens. The atmosphere is quiet and low key, the setting stylish and the *food quite good, at a reasonable 3,725B ($149) for two."* —Mr. and Mrs. Frederic Lucron, Bangkok.

Mermaid's Rest Beach Resort, *75/102 Moo 12, Jomtien Beach, Pattaya. Tel. 038/231907. "There is fairly new Mermaid's Rest in Jomtien Beach, with the all-famous Texas barbecue. It's a bit more upscale, with reasonable prices and a nice layout. You can receive a 40 percent discount if you dive with Mermaid's Dive School (PADI)—I had a great experience."*—Tonya Mathis, Portland, Ore.

WHERE TO DINE

EXPENSIVE

THE EMPRESS, in Dusit Resort, 240/2 Pattaya Beach Rd. Tel. 425611.

> **Cuisine:** CHINESE. **Reservations:** Recommended (request a window table).
>
> **$ Prices:** Appetizers 145B–240B ($5.80–$9.60); main courses 100B–850B ($4–$34) AE, DC, MC, V.
>
> **Open:** Lunch daily 11:30am–2:30pm; dinner daily 6:30–10:30pm.

The Dusit's reputation for fine food is upheld here, though we found the service lackluster. The rooftop setting provides a splendid backdrop for the casually elegant decor and the superlative Cantonese fare. Splurge, if you can, on stir-fried Phuket lobster with hot chili sauce, or baked crab claws with glass noodles. The seafood, though fresh and delicate, is expensive; the dim sum, simpler noodle and rice dishes, or the pan-fried duck with lemon sauce are also delicious and good value.

P.S.: The Empress has declared itself an MSG-free zone.

THAI MARKET/SEAFOOD MARKET, in Royal Cliff Beach Resort, Cliff Rd. Tel. 250421.

> **Cuisine:** THAI/SEAFOOD. **Reservations:** Recommended. **Directions:** South end of Pattaya Beach.
>
> **$ Prices:** Thai appetizers 175B–400B ($7–$16); seafood main courses (sold by weight) 300B–700B ($12–$28), average portions; Thai buffet 625B ($25). AE, DC, MC, V.
>
> **Open:** Daily 6–10:30pm.

If you've been tempted by the aromas from those tin-and-wood pushcarts parked near the beachside bars, you'll find a hygiene-guaranteed forum to sample everything right here, in this twin-sided "market." On one side of the open-air pavilion you'll find shrimp balls; garoupa steamed in banana leaves; beef, chicken, and pork satay; and many other grilled, fried, and broiled Thai standards. On the other side of the tropical bamboo bar are lobster, crab, prawn, shellfish, and many locally caught fish, all displayed on ice for your choosing. The friendly staff will help you spice your Thai food selections, or recommend different preparations for your seafood. Fresh salads and fruit round out the menu, a perfect finale for fitness buffs here on retreat.

MODERATE

DOLF RIKS, 463/77 Sri Nakorn Center, North Pattaya. Tel. 428269.

> **Cuisine:** INDONESIAN/EUROPEAN. **Reservations:** Recommended during high season. **Directions:** 1 block north of Soi 1, opposite Palladium Disco.

$ Prices: Appetizers 60B–300B ($2.40–$12); main courses 250B–450B ($10–$18); fixed-price "tourist special" 400B ($16). AE, DC, MC, V.

Open: Daily 11am–midnight.

Dolf Riks is an Indonesian-born Dutch restaurateur who's also a bit of a character. (Check out the staff's batik-aloha shirts.) His restaurant, Pattaya's oldest, remains something of a legend. Although Dolf's menu changes with his whims, he normally serves a delicious Indonesian rijstaffel as well as continental favorites. His regulars prefer the seafood in a wine-drenched broth, the Spanish garlic soup, and his fragrant ramekin Madras, an oven-baked curry ragoût. The restaurant, always a fun night out, caters primarily to Europeans.

HAFEN STUBLE, in the Nipa Lodge Hotel, Pattaya Beach Rd. Tel. 428195.

Cuisine: GERMAN. **Reservations:** Not required. **Directions:** Corner of Pattaya Klang Rd.

$ Prices: Appetizers 60B–145B ($2.40–$5.80); main courses 75B–200B ($3–$8). MC, V.

Open: Daily 11:30am–10pm.

If you've been longing for the taste of schnitzel and wurst, try this pocket of Germany on the beach. Thai girls in Heidi wardrobe serve cold steins of Anarist on tap (a new German beer), followed by platters of stout Teutonic fare. We enjoyed it as a break from Thai food, and for the convivial, pubby atmosphere.

P.I.C. KITCHEN, Soi 5, between Beach Rd. and Pattaya Second Rd. Tel. 428387.

Cuisine: THAI. **Directions:** 2 blocks north of Beach Rd.

$ Prices: Appetizers 85B–150B ($3.40–$6); main courses 100B–275B ($4–$11). AE, DC, MC, V.

Open: Daily 8am–midnight.

P.I.C. stands for Pattaya International Clinic, the medical center located directly across from the restaurant (no relation). In several lovely classic teak pavilions, you can dine in air-conditioned comfort, sit on floor cushions Thai style, or sit in an outdoor courtyard. This is the only restaurant we ate in twice! Our favorite dishes include deep-fried crab claws, spring rolls, spicy eggplant salad, mixed fried vegetables with oyster sauce, fried chicken with cashews, and steamed white snapper on a bed of vegetables, with ginger and salted prunes. Each night from 7pm to 1am, there's a live jazz show free of charge.

INEXPENSIVE

NANG NUAL, 123/24–25 Moo 12, S. Jomtien Beach Rd., Jomtien. Tel. 231548.

Cuisine: THAI/SEAFOOD. **Directions:** Mid-beach in Jomtien.

$ Prices: Appetizers 60B–140B ($2.40–$5.60); main courses 60B–300B ($2.40–$12). AE, CB, MC, V.

Open: Mon–Fri 8am–11pm, Sat–Sun 6am–11pm.

Nang Nual is an excellent lunch or dinner choice (open at breakfast, too) in the Jomtien Beach area. A Thai restaurant specializing in seafood, it is the favorite choice of Bangkok friends. A cheery fluorescent-lit blue-and-white interior is the setting for steamed butterfish with Chinese lime sauce, or the sumptuous, seasonal, grilled seafood combination. Ours had grilled prawn, a whole local lobster, and fresh crab; it varies with the catch. Freshness buffs can choose their meal from fish tanks out front. There's a less-popular branch at 214 Moo 10 in South Pattaya (tel. 428478).

SOMSAK RESTAURANT, 346/24 Moo 9, Soi 1. Tel. 428987.
   Cuisine: THAI. **Directions:** North of Beach Rd. at Soi 1.
$ Prices: Appetizers 60B–125B ($2.40–$5); main courses 75B–175B ($3–$7). DC, MC, V.
   Open: Daily 11am–1am.

This attractive restaurant is housed in a soaring Thai-style building, with chirping birds providing the background music. Among the more exotic fare, we liked the hormak pla shawn (a soufflé of minced steamed fish mixed with curry paste and served in half a coconut) and kai hor bai toey (a chicken dish). Somsak is known for its sophisticated Thai cuisine, but even a timid Anglo can find shelter in the limited continental and Chinese offerings.

FAST FOOD

Dozens of inexpensive and quick coffee shops abound along the north and south ends of Pattaya Beach Road, reminiscent to some of Las Vegas's "Eat Cheap" lit-up strip of eateries. Those nostalgic for familiar names will find **Pizza Hut, McDonald's, K.F.C.,** and even **Swensen's** amply represented.

SHOPPING

For sex-joke T-shirts and postcards, you can try the dozens of small souvenir stands tucked in between the open-air bars along Pattaya Beach Road. Branch stores of well-known Thai silk shops and jewelers (none cheaper or better than those found in Bangkok or Chiang Mai) are located on Pattaya Second and Third Roads. But for good, clean fun, try **Mike Shopping Mall,** a modern five-story mall on Pattaya Beach Road near Soi 11. The blaring P.A. system calls out bargains and activities daily from 11am to 11pm. Dozens of shops sell everything from electronics to bathing suits, furniture, groceries, and toys, all well priced. The pleasant, air-conditioned **Sie Pak Restaurant** is on the ground floor. A **Kid's Playland,** on the fifth floor next to a small food court, features a miniature carousel, amusement park rides (all 5B and 10B [20¢ and 40¢]) and a video arcade. This place really hops after sundown!

EVENING ENTERTAINMENT

Open-air and topless bars, sex shows, and massage parlors abound on Pattaya Beach Road. Most of the pickup action takes place in the clusters of outdoor bars off of Soi 8 or around Sois 14 to 17. At the raunchier go-go bars in Pattayaland (south beach strip), topless women dance on an island bar. Each wears a number and is available "after the show" for a fee. Sometimes, exuberant drinkers less than delicately place money on the bodies of their favorite dancers, demanding more. There's always more available in Pattaya, but there's other evening entertainment as well.

NIGHTCLUBS/CABARET SHOWS

Pattaya is well known for its wildly costumed and choreographed transvestite song-and-dance revues. **The Tiffany Club** (tel. 421700) and **Alcazar Cabaret** (tel. 428746), two of the most popular nightclubs, are both on Pattaya Second Road, in the northern part of Pattaya. At both clubs, three shows nightly (about an hour each) feature coy fan-waving boys in flowing silk gowns and traditional Thai costumes performing untraditional dances. Some would say "Don't miss it!" Admission is 475B ($19) or 575B ($23) for a VIP seat at Tiffany, including one drink. Here again, liquor costs can mount up quickly. Many prefer Alcazar, about 100B ($4) cheaper.

GAY BARS

Pattayaland, Sois 1, 2, and 3 (in southern Pattaya), like Soi Cowboy and Patpong in Bangkok, have many clubs catering to a gay crowd. **A Friend, Cockpit,** and **Boys Boys Boys** are some of many in Pattayaland, Soi 3, also known as "Boys Town" to locals. Ask for the latest tips at the Ambiance Hotel (tel. 424099) on Soi 3. In addition, there are several gay escort services advertised in local give-away brochures and magazines.

DISCOS

Disco Duck, in the Little Duck Pattaya Resort Hotel on Central Road (tel. 428104), is much admired by visiting Thai teenagers and "Tuppies," particularly on weekends. **Marina Disco,** in the Regent Marina Hotel (tel. 428015), offers live music most weekends to a mixed Thai and foreign young adult crowd in their 20s and 30s. Both have free entry and open from 9pm to 2am. **Palladium,** on Pattaya Second Road (tel. 424933), outshines all the other discos with its vast polished metal dance floor and hyperkinetic lighting grid. Admission is generally 250B ($10), including two drinks, higher if a well-known live band is performing (open nightly 9pm to 3am). Very popular with Thais, it also features one of the few traditional Thai massage parlors, where gentle but penetrating therapeutic massage costs 250B ($10) per hour (open daily noon to midnight).

ADULT ENTERTAINMENT

Examples of the go-go flesh trade abound in bars along Pattayaland, Soi 1, where Thai beer and a look costs about 125B ($5), though the girls work off commission and encourage clients to buy rounds for everyone. A classier act and higher prices prevail at any of the new **karaoke sing-along/hostess clubs** scattered along Pattaya Second and Third Roads. Liquor is sold: 2,000B ($80) for a bottle of Mekhong and two setups is almost the minimum.

Warning: The police frequently clamp down on drug sellers and buyers in these venues; ignorance of the law is not an accepted defense in Thailand.

Most of Pattaya's "physical" massage parlors are on Pattaya Second Road in northern Pattaya. Typically, dozens of girls with numbered signs wait to be selected by clients, who are then whisked away to private massage rooms.

Repeat Warning: Police frequently clamp down on drug sellers and buyers in these massage parlors.

All-night companionship is easy to come by, though costs mount up to club owners, security guards, etc., for in-room entertainment.

More warnings: Beware of companions bearing drinks laced with "knockout" drugs; watch your wallet; wear a condom.

3. KANCHANABURI

128km (79 miles) W of Bangkok,
65km (40 miles) W of Nakhon Pathom

GETTING THERE By Train There are two trains daily from the Bangkok Noi Station (tel. 411-3102) in Bangkok (trip time: 2½ hr.; 70B [$2.80]). Special tourist trains leave on Saturday, Sunday, and holidays, stopping for 40 minutes in Nakhon Pathom and for 30 minutes at the Bridge Over the River Kwai. A minibus will take you from Nam Tok Station to Khao Phang Waterfall, round-trip. The train continues on to Kanchanaburi for a 45-minute stop, with an overnight at the River Kwai Jungle House, and a morning excursion to the Krasae Cave Bridge, before returning to Bangkok. The trains leave in the early morning and arrive back at Hua Lampong Railroad Station in the evening of the following day. In 1993, is cost 690B ($27.60) adults, 490B ($19.60) children; reservations are recommended. A one-day version of this program is also available (340B [$13.50] adults, 290B [$11.50] children). Similar programs are offered to Erawan National Park.

By Bus Sixty nonair-conditioned buses (tel. 411-0511 for information) leave daily from Bangkok's Southern Bus Terminal (trip time, 3 hr.; 50B [$2]); 75 air-conditioned buses (tel. 414-4978) leave daily after 5:30am (trip time: 2½ hr.; 90B [$3.60]).

By Car Take Route 4 west from Bangkok.

ESSENTIALS Orientation Kanchanaburi stands at the junction where two tributaries—the Kwai Noi and the Kwai Yai—meet to form the Mae Khlong River. The bus station is around the corner from the TAT office.

Information The **TAT office** is on Saeng Chuto Road (tel. 034/511200 or 512500); it's open daily from 8:30am to 4:30pm.

Fast Facts Area code is 034. **Car (no driver) rental** is available for about 1,350B ($54) per day from B.T. Travel (tel. 511967), Saeng Chuto Road, around the corner from the TAT office. **Currency Exchange** is available at banks Monday through Friday from 8:30am to 3pm. **Laundry and dry cleaning** can be taken to White and Clean, ½ kilometer (⅓ mile) south of the TAT office. The **Tourist Police** can be reached at 512759. The **post office,** located on Saeng Chuto Road, is open Monday through Friday from 8:30am to 4:30pm, Saturday and Sunday from 8:30am till noon; there are facilities for telegrams and overseas calls, available every day from 8:30am to 10pm.

SPECIAL EVENTS The **River Kwai Bridge Festival** is a week-long celebration of the area's history with exhibitions and historical displays, cultural shows, special period train rides, daily entertainment, and a nightly sound-and-light demonstration (with fireworks donated by the Japanese government) at the end of November. There is a symbolic "bombing" of the bridge twice weekly—Saturday and Wednesday when we last visited.

The town is indelibly marked by its famous bridge, spanning the Kwai River. A visit to this site is, for some, an emotional pilgrimage to honor the suffering and heroism of the many who perished (and the few who survived) under their brutal Japanese overseers. As moving as the story is, we find the actual site a good bit less inspiring, and would recommend it only for those who are really passionate about this chapter of World War II history.

The city itself, near the bridge, is surrounded by some spectacular scenery, particularly to the north and west of town. Mountains rise in misty haze along the river; waterfalls abound as the jungle stretches away. You'll drive past fields of tapioca, tobacco, sugarcane, tamarind, mango, papaya banana, and palm. In fact, Kanchanaburi is a fine base for jumping off if you have a taste for exploring Thailand's natural areas.

We wouldn't suggest you stick around town too long; it's pretty dull and overly commercial. In other words, come to Kanchanaburi for an overnight stay to explore the area's diverse scenery or to delve into River Kwai lore. As a day trip, it's not so thrilling even when combined with stops at the Floating Market at Damnoen Saduak or the giant stupa at Nakhon Pathom.

WHAT TO SEE & DO

Before going to see the bridge itself, the main attraction, stop at the **JEATH Museum,** adjacent to Wat Chaichumpol in town. Constructed of thatch and bamboo to resemble prisoners' barracks, and filled with photographs, personal mementos, and newspaper accounts, it provides a sobering display of the suffering prisoners of war who built the bridge and the railroad. The latter, designed as a communication and supply link for the Japanese army in Burma, replaced the sea route (via the Strait of Malacca), which had been closed by the Allies. The name JEATH is an acronym of the initials of those nationalities that built the railroad—Japanese, English, American, Australian, Thai, and Hollanders.

The Japanese originally calculated that it would take five to six years to complete the 425-kilometer (264-mile) track, but they reduced that figure to 18 months for the POWs. It was finished in a year. Some 16,000 Allied prisoners—mostly British, Australian, and American—died, but even more brutal was the fate of the 100,000 Burmese, Chinese, Indians, Indonesians, Malays, and Thais who also perished during the forced labor (and were buried in unmarked graves where they dropped).

Admission is 25B ($1), and the museum is open daily from 8:30am to 5pm.

On Saeng Chuto Road in town, near the railroad station, you can stop by the **Kanchanaburi War Cemetery,** where every stone tells a story of a lost life. Many of the 6,982 graves are those of young men in their 20s and 30s who died far from home. Another 1,750 POWs lie buried at the **Chon-Kai War Cemetery,** once the site of a POW camp, and now a tranquil place on the banks of the Kwai Noi about 2 kilometers (1.2 miles) south of town.

The **Bridge Over the River Kwai** is about 4½ kilometers (2¾ miles) north of the center of Kanchanaburi. The bridge was brought from Java and assembled by POWs. It was bombed several times and rebuilt after the war, but the curved spans are the originals. You can walk across it, looking toward the mountains of Myanmar (Burma) as you go. For some it's a nerve-racking experience: Rickety railroad ties laid on an open grid allow you to see the water below. If you visit during the River Kwai Bridge Festival—usually the end of November or the beginning of December—you can also see a *son et lumière* spectacle.

We're interested in archeology and were mildly impressed by the **Ban Kao Neolithic Museum,** as well as **Prasat Muang Singha,** a Khmer site that pales in comparison to those found in the Northeast (but interesting if you don't plan to visit that region). The museum is open daily from 8:30am to 5pm; 20B (80¢) admission fee. It's located about 45 minutes north of town.

WHERE TO STAY

IN TOWN

Budget

JOLLY FROG BACKPACKER'S, Mae Nam Kwai Rd., Kanchanaburi 71000. Tel. 034/514579.

$ Rates: 60B–110B ($2.40–$4.40) single; 110B–140B ($4.40–$5.60) double. No credit cards.

The Jolly Frog has remained a clean and friendly place, located in the tourist center of town. Some rooms have toilet facilities; all are fan-cooled. The management can arrange treks and tours.

V.L. GUESTHOUSE, 18/11 Saeng Chuto Rd., Kanchanaburi 71000. Tel. 034/513546. 24 rms. A/C (in some rms)

$ Rates: 150B ($6) single or double with fan and toilet; 300B ($12) air-conditioned single or double with hot-water shower. No credit cards.

This guesthouse, across from the pricier and dirty River Kwai Hotel, is a clean, fluorescent-lit hostel. The back-facing rooms are quieter, and there is a breakfast area and laundry service. Toilets are of the Asian variety.

OUT OF TOWN

Expensive

FELIX RIVER KWAI RESORT, 9/1 Moo 3 Thamakham, Kanchanaburi 71000. Tel. 034/515061. Fax 034/515086. Telex 79802 RIVKWAI TH. 235 rms. A/C MINIBAR TV TEL **Directions:** On the banks of the River Kwai.

$ Rates: 3,600B–3,850B ($144–$154) single; 3,850B–4,000B ($154–$160) double; from 6,600B ($264) suite. Extra bed 600B ($24). Peak season surcharge (Dec 20–Jan 20) 600B ($24). Compulsory gala meals during River Kwai Bridge Week, Christmas, New Year's, Chinese New Year's 600B–1,200B ($24–$48). AE, MC, V.

Built for, but no longer managed by, the Sheraton chain, the Felix is a long, low resort tucked into the dense undergrowth surrounding the river. Rooms are spacious and filled with amenities, offering mountain and river views. Some are reserved for nonsmokers; three others have been modified for the handicapped. This is the most luxurious way to experience the River Kwai, and one sure to appeal to World War II veterans groups looking for the comforts of home.

Dining/Entertainment: The "fern bar" coffee shop offers good continental and some Thai dishes, in a very pleasant setting. The more formal Guilin Restaurant is for Chinese fare. There's also a relaxing piano bar, and a karaoke bar promised for 1994.

Services: 24-hour room service, concierge, car rental, doctor on call, Thai massage, babysitting, laundry.
Facilities: Two swimming pools, workout room, business center.

Moderate

RIVER KWAI JUNGLE HOUSE, 378 Tharua, Thamakham, Kanchanaburi 71000. Tel. 034/561052. Fax 034/561429. 15 rms. **Transport:** Management will pick up from Kanchanaburi train station.
$ Rates (including full board): 900B ($36) single; 1,800B ($72) double. V.

The River Kwai Jungle House (Ban Rim Kwae), about 40 kilometers (25 miles) west along the river from Kanchanaburi, is in a forest of mango, bamboo, and bougainvillea; turkeys and chickens peck at the dust; a couple of pet monkeys hang around for company. This primitive "hotel" is a traditional floating resort. Rattan bungalows with fans and Asian toilets float on the river, overlooking a stretch of the famed railway. The hotel conducts cave exploration, at Tamka Sae, local treks, and rafting trips. You'll need a sense of adventure and a flashlight, as the grounds are poorly lit. Contact the State Railway of Thailand (tel. 02/225-6964) for information on overnight train, tour, and accommodation packages starting at 750B ($30).

WHERE TO DINE

Note: If you're out touring the bridge at lunchtime, try the **River Kwai Restaurant** (tel. 512540) or **Sai Yok** (tel. 512702), both nearby to serve Thai and some Chinese dishes.

We want to give special mention to the **Aree Bakery** at 90–92 Prakjak Rd. (no phone), two blocks from the riverside. Sergeant Major Tanom Lonmasuarapan and wife run an American-style ice-cream shop that also serves homemade fruit pies and breakfast—what a treat!

BUDGET

PAE-BANN NOUE, Song Kwai Rd. Tel. 512326.
  Cuisine: THAI.
$ Prices: Appetizers 20B–50B (80¢–$2); main courses 35B–70B ($1.50–$2.75). MC, V.
  Open: Daily 10am–midnight.

Highlights at this riverside eatery in town are shrimp with lemongrass, steamed whole fish on lemongrass and salted prunes, beef with shredded eggplant and hot pepper, and rice noodles fried with pork, dried shrimp, and tomato sauce. Try the kuai tiew pad thai, a local variation on the famous noodle dish.

TONGNATE [Thong Nathee], Song Kwai Rd. Tel. 512944.
  Cuisine: THAI/SEAFOOD.
$ Prices: Appetizers 45B–60B ($1.80–$2.40); main courses 60B–145B ($2.40–$5.80). MC, V.
  Open: Daily 11am–11pm.

The Tongnate is a riverside restaurant with a floating dining pavilion. During the evening, there is an entertaining floor show featuring a bevy of local singers. Although the food isn't great, we suggest rice with chicken, garlic, and fresh pepper, as well as poached fresh river fish in tomato sauce.

EXCURSIONS

The surrounding area is widely known for its natural sites, especially Sai Yok National Park, and La Wa Cave, and Erawan Waterfall and National Park. The best time to visit is during the rainy season (August to October), when the waterfalls are in full flood. There is bus service to nearly every major excursion destination in the area; however, the helpful Ron at **B.T. Travel,** Saeng Chuto Road (tel. 511967), rents minivans for 1,350B ($54) per day.

Since adventure tours have become popular, this scenic area has begun capitalizing on its natural assets. The **R.S.P. Travel Center,** 271/1 Saeng Chuto Rd. (tel. 512280), organizes local jungle treks and river-rafting trips. The **V.N. Guesthouse,** at 44 Rong Heeb Oil 2 Rd. (tel. 514831), rents very basic rooms but also has good guides for budget hikes, elephant treks, and river trips. Check with the local TAT office for current rates and recommendations.

La Wa Cave is about 75 kilometers (46½ miles) from town along Route 323. **Sai Yok National Park** is about 104 kilometers (64½ miles) along the same route; its focal point is its waterfall, Sai Yok Yai, often celebrated in Thai song and verse. You can take a private boat to these two places from Pak Saeng Pier at Tam-Bon Tha-Saow. The round trip will take about 4 hours and cost about 850B ($34). Buses to Sai Yok take about 2 hours and cost only 32B ($1.30).

Just off Route 323, but farther away from town, are **Dawadung Cave** (110km [68 miles]), the **Hin Dat Hot Springs** (130km [80 miles]), and the remote three-tiered waterfall **Pha Tat.**

The most popular attraction is **Erawan Waterfall and National Park,** about 65 kilometers (40 miles) along Route 3199. The waterfall is 2 kilometers (1¼ miles) long and drops down seven tiers, creating a series of ponds and streams; it's a great bird and butterfly sanctuary, and a popular camping spot for Thais. Buses leave for Erawan from the bus terminal in Kanchanaburi on Saeng Chuto Road (tel. 511182) every 50 minutes from 8am to 4pm. The trip takes about 1½ hours and, with guide, costs 90B ($3.60). Buses to Sai Yok take about 2 hours and cost 60B ($2.40). The last bus returns to Kanchanaburi early.

Along Route 3086, 50 kilometers (31 miles) north in the Bo Phloi area, you can watch **sapphire mining.** From the roadside you'll spy the wooden framework of a winch and people filling wheelbarrows with hard lumps of earth. After washing through the mud, they may find—if they're lucky—blue or black sapphires and earn a day's living. Travel another 50 kilometers (31 miles) or so north along the same route and you'll come to the 300-meter-long (325-yard-long) **Than Lot Noi Cave** and **Traitrung Waterfall** in **Than Lot National Park.**

---

4. HUA HIN/CHA-AM

Hua Hin: 240km (149 miles) S of Bangkok

GETTING THERE   By Plane   Bangkok Airways (tel. 02/229-3456 in Bangkok) flies twice daily to Hua Hin (trip time 30 min; 1,000B [$40]) from Don Muang airport.

By Train   There are 10 trains between Bangkok and Hua Hin daily (trip time: 3½ hr. for special express), 4½ for rapid; 250B

[$10] for air-conditioned special express). The train continues south to Surat Thani (trip time: 7 hr.; 380B [$15.20]). There is also a train connection to Kanchanaburi twice daily (trip time: 6 hr.; third class is 60B [$2.40]).

By Bus   There are 22 air-conditioned buses leaving daily from Bangkok's Southern Air-conditioned Bus Terminal (trip time: 3¹/₂ hr.; 115B [$4.60]). Buses run from 5am to 10pm, leaving every 40 minutes. Nonair-conditioned buses run daily from the Southern Bus Terminal (trip time: 4¹/₂ hr.; 50B [$2]).

By Car   Take Route 35, the Thonburi-Paktho Highway. Allow 2 to 4 hours, depending on traffic.

When Thais refer to Hua Hin, what they mean is the 20-kilometer (12¹/₂-mile) strip extending from Hua Hin in the south to Cha-Am in the north. Hua Hin is an older, more developed city, with great character, while the beachfront village of Cha-Am reminds us of a cheery little Greek island town or possibly a lesser destination along the New Jersey shore. Both are jammed with people and very densely commercialized.

Hua Hin, developed in the 1920s, is actually Thailand's first beach resort. Initially favored exclusively by the royal family—they still use the Klai Kangwon ("Far from Worries") Palace in the summer—and the upper crust of Bangkok society, it was eventually visited primarily by middle-class Thai families. Although its popularity declined with the ascendence of Phuket, Ko Samui, and Pattaya, newly built grand-hotel resorts and high-rise condos have created renewed tourist interest in the area.

Bangkok's horrendous traffic problems have also made the drive south seem easier than the drive to the airport. Thus, Hua Hin is making a comeback with the upper crust—especially those looking for weekend homes.

If you can afford an unforgettable stay at the Hotel Sofitel Central, the crown jewel of Hua Hin in terms of architecture, service, and ambience, then don't miss the opportunity. If not, there are many other budget choices near Hua Hin's pier and along Cha-Am's beach that are well suited to families. Hua Hin has more charm and lots of seashell vendors, a small Night Market, and pierside dining. Cha-Am has developed right *on* the beach, so it's messier but quite lively, with street vendors, bicyclists, and discos. Any one of the more expensive resorts in either town would be restful and fun.

Try to avoid the monsoon period from November to February, when rains and high winds sometimes buffet the Gulf of Thailand coastline. (Thailand's "wet" season from June to October is much hotter, with scattered tropical storms.)

ORIENTATION

ARRIVING   Trains and buses arrive in Hua Hin. The air-conditioned bus station is located at the Sri Phetchkasem Hotel on Srasong Road, while nonair-conditioned buses stop near Chatchai Market. The railway station is on Damneonkasem Road.

INFORMATION   The **Tourism Authority of Thailand (TAT)** (tel. 032/471006; fax 032/471502) is at 500/51 Phetkasem Rd., halfway up the coastal route linking Hua Hin and Cha-Am.

Though inconvenient, they are very helpful and are open daily 8:30am to 4:30pm. The municipality of Hua Hin publishes very helpful information in a brochure available free at the Tourist Information Service Center, 114 Phetkasem Rd. (tel. 512120), near the intersection with Damneonkasem Road; open daily from 8:30am to 4:30pm.

GETTING AROUND

Both villages are small and can be walked, although many guests try an outing by *samlor*, a human-powered pedicab. Most of the larger resorts offer complimentary scheduled minivan service into town. If you want to travel between the two villages, plan on taking a local bus, *song tao* (truck taxi), motorized *tuk-tuk*, or taxi; the ride takes about 25 minutes and will run from 20B to 200B (80¢ to $8), depending on the mode of transport. You can take a water taxi from Cha-Am to Hua Hin for about 180B ($7.20).

FAST FACTS

Area Code   The telephone area code for Hua Hin/Cha-Am is 032.

Business Hours   Most shops are open from 9am to 10pm. The Night Market is open from 6pm to midnight.

Car/Minibus Rental   Avis operates a counter at the Royal Garden Resort (tel. 511881) in Hua Hin and the Dusit Resort and Polo Club in Cha-Am (tel. 520008). **Minibuses** are available for rent opposite the Chatchai Market on Phetkasem Road.

Currency Exchange   Facilities can be found on Phetkasem Road. In Cha-Am the Bangkok Bank, along the main road, is open daily from 9am to 8pm.

Laundry   Quick and cheap (32¢ for a sports shirt) laundry service is available from many of the cafés on Hua Hin's main street, or along the waterfront Naratdamri Road.

Medical Facilities   The Hua Hin Hospital, on Phetkasem Road (tel. 511743), is 4 kilometers (2½ miles) out of town.

Police   The police station can be found on Damneonkasem Road (tel. 511027).

Post Office   Together with the overseas telephone office, it is located on Damneonkasem Road.

Tours   A number of hotels offer tours in and around the area. A nonaffiliated tour company is Western Tours, located on the Hua Hin main street, at 11 Damneonkasem Road (tel. 512560).

WHAT TO SEE & DO

Most people come here to sit on a evergreen-lined **beach** or revel in the luxury of an august resort complex, but there are a few diversions (see "Excursions," below). The most compelling of these is a day trip to Phetchaburi—60 kilometers (37 miles) north—one of Thailand's oldest towns and a repository of several Ayutthaya-era artifacts and structures.

For water-sports enthusiasts, hotel owners are discouraging guests from renting jet skis or water scooters because of safety and pollution concerns. There have been a number of accidents injuring both boat drivers and swimmers (who are inadvertently run over by inexperienced drivers). Also, scooters spew fumes and excess gas into the water, and many tourists have been ripped off in gasoline or "lost or damaged" parts schemes involving credit-card deposits. (Water scooters rent for 300B [$12] per hour.) Another pollution source is the ubiquitous ponies that trot up and down the beach; they are for rent (100B or $4 per hour), but keep in mind that people swim and laze on the same stretch of sand the ponies pollute.

For golfers, there is the **Royal Hua Hin Golf Course** (tel. 511099), Thailand's first, having opened in 1924. Like the Hotel Sofitel Central, it was recently upgraded and features some wild topiary figures along the fairways. It's open daily from 6am to 6pm; clubs are available for rent.

Just 2 kilometers (1¼ miles) south of the Cha-Am Regent, down an unmarked road leading to the Rama VI Army Base, is one of the country's most sublime palaces, designed by King Mongkut, Rama VI, and completed in 1924. Known as the **Maruekkhathayawan** (or Mrigadayavan) **Palace** (Palace of Love and Hope), it is entirely made of teak and is more an open-air pavilion than a traditional European-style structure. The palace fell into a state of disrepair and has, for several years, been under renovation. For those familiar with the Thai Victorian–style Hotel Sofitel Central, the palace appears to have been designed and built in an entirely similar manner. There are English-language brochures, and it's easy enough to navigate by yourself. The palace is open daily from 8am to 4pm. Admission is by donation only.

WHERE TO STAY

Note that every hotel in the "Expensive" category charges an additional peak-season supplement of 500B to 800B ($20 to $40) per room between mid-December and late January. Conversely, hotels in every price range offer substantial discounts in the low season.

HUA HIN

Expensive

ROYAL GARDEN RESORT, 107/1 Phetkasem Beach Rd., Hua Hin 77110. Tel. 032/511881. Fax 032/512422. Telex 78309 ROGAHUA TH. 217 rms, 5 suites. A/C MINIBAR TEL TV

$ Rates: 3,600B–3,800B ($144–$152) single or double; from 8,875B ($355) suite. Extra person 600B ($24). AE, DC, MC, V.

The extremely well outfitted and maintained Royal Garden Resort is best suited to those in search of beach and sports activities. Singles and families are in evidence here throughout the year, lured principally by the amazing offering of ponds, pools, boats, golf, tennis and other racket sports, as well as the pet elephant and junglelike grounds leading down to the calm sea. The place is relatively close to Hua Hin, and there is complimentary shuttle service both into town and to the resort's sister establishment, the more traditional Thai-style Royal Garden Village. With their sea-facing views, the large, amenity-filled deluxe rooms are the best choice. There are several connecting rooms for families, and the fourth floor is for nonsmokers.

Dining/Entertainment: The Nautilus Lounge (very clubby) overlooks the pool. The Garden is a cheery coffee shop with a mixed international and Thai menu. On the beach lawn, cooled by a sea breeze, is the Italian Pavilion Restaurant (open daily 10am to 11pm), where we sampled a unique Pizza Thailandese with Thai sausage and chili.

Services: 24-hour room service, concierge, babysitting, house doctor, laundry service, Avis car rental.

Facilities: Pool, tennis, golf, fitness center, playground, zoo, beauty salon and barbershop, shopping arcade.

ROYAL GARDEN VILLAGE, 43/1 Phetkasem Beach Rd., Hua Hin 77110. Tel. 032/520250. Fax 032/520259. Telex 78314 ROGAVIL TH. 162 rms. A/C MINIBAR TEL TV **Directions:** Out of the center of Hua Hin, off the main road.

$ Rates: 3,800B–4,300B ($152–$172) single or double; 11,000B ($440) Village suite. Extra bed 700B ($28). Children under 12 free. Peak-season (Dec 20–Jan 10) supplement 500B ($20). AE, DC, MC, V.

A series of elegantly designed Thai-style pavilions make up the lobby and public facilities at the Royal Garden Village. The lobby itself is tastefully decorated with a lovely Kaliga tapestry and ornately carved teak lanterns, a warm wood floor and furniture with rose-colored cushions. Accommodations are contained within a further series of Thai-style pavilions, each one housing 12 rooms furnished with teak and rattan furniture. Superior rooms have a garden view, while deluxe rooms overlook the sand and sea. The hotel's sense of tasteful serenity is marred slightly by a seven-story concrete apartment condo that abuts one side of the property; otherwise, the setting is decidedly romantic.

Dining/Entertainment: Suan Luang is an elegant Thai restaurant serving lunch and dinner. The outdoor Rim Nam Restaurant, with a European and seafood menu, serves dinner only. An outdoor pool bar offers snacks as well as drinks.

Services: 24 hour-room service, concierge, limo service, babysitting, house doctor on call, laundry, complimentary welcome tea, and fruit basket and flowers in all rooms.

Facilities: Swimming pool and children's pool, Jacuzzi, waterskiing, parasailing, sailing lessons (4 types of boats), windsurfing, tennis, 18-hole golf course nearby, jogging track, playground, bicycles, shopping arcade.

HOTEL SOFITEL CENTRAL, 1 Damneonkasem Rd. (P.O. Box 31) Hua Hin Prachuabkirikhan 77110. Tel. 032/ 512021, or toll free 800/221-4542 in the U.S. Fax 032/511014. Telex 78313 CENTRAC TH. 146 rms, 8 suites. A/C MINIBAR TEL TV

$ Rates: 3,400B–4,400B ($136–$177) single or double; 7,200B ($288) suite. Extra person 600B ($24). AE, DC, MC, V.

The Sofitel Central, once known as the Railway Hotel, was *the* place to stay in the 1920s. With the revival of Hua Hin as a tourist destination and the renewed interest in this architectural gem in the mid-1980s (it served as the French Embassy in the film *The Killing Fields*), the restored and rebuilt hotel is not only a wonderful place to stay but a definite stop on any tour of the area. If for no other reason, go to see the well-landscaped grounds, including a 60-year-old eccentric topiary garden gone wild; huge elephants, bears, rhinos, and birds are on display. The menagerie gives way to gracious parklike grounds with an orchid and butterfly farm, wide lawns, flowering trees, and elegantly planned shrubbery. Each building has colonial Victorian-style architecture and a red-tile roof.

The spacious suites, which compromise the original hotel, are decorated with dark fans and marble baths, richly finished teak floors, and chandeliers over the sitting-room tables. Three sets of French doors lead to porches fit for elegant cocktail-parties. The high-ceilinged superior rooms in the reproduction three-story wing are built with the same quality of craftsmanship and taste found in the suites.

And across the main driveway is the unusual Villa Wing, with 42 bedrooms tucked into one- and two-unit seaside bungalows reminiscent of an Adirondacks campground. Built in the '50s, these are regulation forest green and stone gray cabins with verandas, small kitchens, cotton-covered wooden furniture, and an authentically casual and rustic feel. At 3,350B ($134) for one bedroom or 4,800B ($192) for a family-style two-bedroom, they are a terrific value; perfect for those who want privacy and a "country cabin" feeling. The Villa Wing also has its own small pool, beach access, a small playground, and a Thai restaurant with once-weekly classical dance performances.

As you can tell, we were charmed by the place, its easygoing old-world elegance, gracious staff, and adorable pet elephant. We also met the Smiths, honeymooners from London, whose entire vacation consisted of three days in Bangkok and five days at the Sofitel—they couldn't have been more pleased!

Dining/Entertainment: The Satchmo Jazz Club, the nostalgic Railway Room (done with appropriate decor), an all-purpose coffee shop and restaurant, serving ice cream, and the excellent Palm Seafood Restaurant (see "Where to Dine" later in this chapter), set in a converted greenhouse with terrific views of the sea and lots of plants, are the main dining venues. Kids will like the poolside snack bar, which sells bananas to feed the elephant, while parents will appreciate The Museum, a coffee and tea corner with a display case of original china.

Services: 24-hour room service, concierge, limo service, babysitting, laundry, complimentary welcome tea.

Facilities: Three pools (one plays Muzak underwater!), tennis courts, putting green and miniature golf, water sports, billiards, daily language or crafts lessons, beauty salon/barbershop, shopping arcade.

Inexpensive

Most of the lower-priced accommodations in Hua Hin are located in the teeming back streets between Phetkasem Road and the beach. At night, the area turns into an expatriate and tourist party zone, so expect noise.

FRESH INN HOTEL, 132 Naratdamri Rd., Hua Hin, Prachuabkirikhan 77110. Tel. 032/511389. 29 rms. A/C MINIBAR TEL TV

$ Rates: 780B ($31.20) single; 840B ($33.60) double. No credit cards.

This clean inn opened in 1990 as an adjunct to Lo Stivale, an Italian restaurant (run by Italians) that is connected via the lobby. Rooms are furnished in basic fashion, and though it's not a fancy

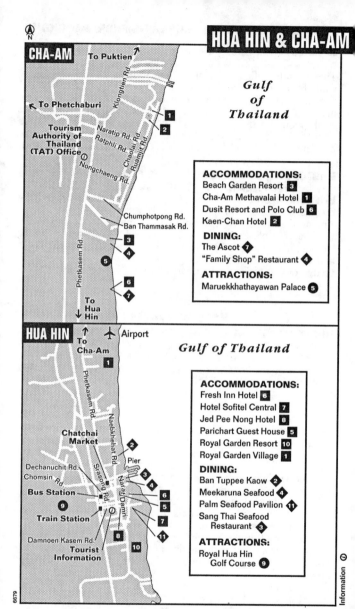

CHA-AM

To Puktien

To Phetchaburi

Klongtien Rd.

Gulf of Thailand

Tourism Authority of Thailand (TAT) Office

Naratip Rd.
Ratphli Rd.
Nongchaeng Rd.

Chaolai Rd.
Ruamit Rd.

1
2

ACCOMMODATIONS:
Beach Garden Resort **3**
Cha-Am Methavalai Hotel **1**
Dusit Resort and Polo Club **6**
Kaen-Chan Hotel **2**

DINING:
The Ascot **7**
"Family Shop" Restaurant **4**

ATTRACTIONS:
Maruekkhathayawan Palace **5**

Chumphotpong Rd.
Ban Thammasak Rd.

Phetkasem Rd.

3
4
5
6
7

To Hua Hin

HUA HIN

To Cha-Am

Airport

Gulf of Thailand

1

Phetkasem Rd.

Chatchai Market

Naebkhehat Rd.
Srisong Rd.

Pier

2

Dechanuchit Rd.
Chomsin Rd.

Bus Station

9

Train Station

Narat/Damri

3
4
6
5
7

Damnoen Kasem Rd.

Tourist Information

8
11

10

ACCOMMODATIONS:
Fresh Inn Hotel **6**
Hotel Sofitel Central **7**
Jed Pee Nong Hotel **8**
Parichart Guest House **5**
Royal Garden Resort **10**
Royal Garden Village **1**

DINING:
Ban Tuppee Kaow **2**
Meekaruna Seafood **4**
Palm Seafood Pavilion **11**
Sang Thai Seafood Restaurant **3**

ATTRACTIONS:
Royal Hua Hin Golf Course **9**

Information ⊙

6679

place, it's a good value for its nearness to the fishing pier and the beach. The restaurant, open daily from 5pm to 10pm, is intimate and, unlike the rooms, stylish. We sampled several well-prepared main dishes—including spaghetti with tomato sauce and seafood, several kinds of pizza, salad, and chicken breast with lemon—at prices ranging from 100B to 300B ($4 to $12).

JED PEE NONG HOTEL, 13/7 Damneonkasem Rd., Hua Hin, Prachuabkirikhan 77110. Tel. 032/512381. 25 rms. MINIBAR **Directions:** On main street, near the town beach.

$ Rates: 480B ($19.20) single/double with fan, 600B ($24) single with A/C; 600B–975B ($24–$39) double with A/C. No credit cards.

This recently built hotel with a Chinese flair, located about 100 yards from the Sofitel Central's elegant driveway, is so clean and well kept that it's a good choice. A bevy of family or local workers maintain the tiny garden filled with songbirds and fountains, a small pool, and the simple balconied rooms. However, many are carpeted and have air-conditioning and the higher-priced rooms have more decor and hug the pool, cabana-style. There's also a Thai seafood restaurant off the lobby and laundry service.

PARICHART GUEST HOUSE, 162/6 Naratdamri Rd., Hua Hin, Prachuabkirikhan 77110. Tel. 032/513863. 9 rms.

$ Rates: 420B ($16.80) single/double with fan; 550B–675B ($22–$27) single/double with A/C. No credit cards.

Among the low-priced alternatives along busy Naratdamri Road, we like this place. Newly built, and run by a friendly young woman, it's a modern "barefoot" guesthouse with white-tile floors and small, clean rooms. Although it's a bit worn, and the street is pretty noisy at night, the Parichart represents decent value.

CHA-AM

Very Expensive

DUSIT RESORT AND POLO CLUB, 1340 Phetkasem Rd., Cha-Am 76120, Phetchaburi. Tel. 032/520009. Fax 032/520296. Telex 78302 DRCPOLO TH. 298 rms, 10 suites. A/C MINIBAR TEL TV **Directions:** Coast Highway, 9 km (5½ miles) north of Hua Hin.

$ Rates: 4,300B–4,900B ($172–$196) single or double, 8,400B ($336) landmark double; 13,000B–27,000B ($520–$1,080) suite. AE, DC, MC, V.

In the winter of 1990, the renowned Dusit chain went a long way toward restoring Hua Hin's traditional place in high society with this lavish resort. Intended equally for the country's wealthy elite and the well-heeled foreign tourist, the Dusit combines the amenities and facilities of the best international deluxe resorts with an English country- and polo-club theme sure to appeal to the Asian taste for old-world European elegance.

Guests approach the Dusit via a long driveway running past the polo grounds, stables, and fancy Polo Club. The grandly elegant marble lobby features bronze horses, plush carpets, and seating areas hung throughout with hunting and riding oils. Hall doors have polo-mallet handles; each public area follows suit with "horsey" artwork and decor.

The large cool-blue guest rooms have pastel floral prints and burled maple and wicker furniture. Their oversize marble bathrooms boast glass-enclosed shower stalls as well as full bathtubs. The basic room rates vary with the view, although every room's balcony faces out over the lushly landscaped pool (we think it's the largest in Thailand) and the tranquil Gulf of Thailand. Landmark rooms are actually suites, with a very elegant living room (with its own Victorian fainting couch), a full pantry area, a dressing room off the huge bathroom, and even finer decor. The Princess Suite is absolutely worthy of royalty.

For all its air of formality, the resort works remarkably well for beachgoers, and those who prefer swimsuits and T-shirts to riding jodhpurs will feel right at home. Families will find a great beach with calm, shallow water, as well as a kiddie pool. Water-sports instruction is offered. There are daily demonstrations of Thai arts and crafts.

Dining/Entertainment: The Palm Court coffee shop has the best location—a huge glass pavilion jutting out over a lotus point, surrounded by the swimming pool and bougainvillea beds. Open for breakfast, lunch, and dinner, it serves Thai (excellent range of Thai breakfasts), continental, and casual snack food to pool-goers outdoors or in. The elegant Ascot (see "Where to Dine," below) and the Rim Talay seaside dining pavilion (for seafood barbecues) are open in the evenings.

Other options include a lively outdoor Italian restaurant, the San Marco (open for lunch and dinner), and the more formal and pricey Bencharong, a very fine Thai restaurant set in a teak pavilion on the grounds. Before-dinner drinks and afternoon tea (3pm to 5pm daily) can be had in the comfortable Polo Lounge on the second floor overlooking the pool; after 9pm, it becomes a jazz bar with nightly live entertainment. The large lobby lounge, the place to see the latest in European resort wear on the most elegant Thai women, is open all day and night for drinks and coffee. The Gymkhara Pub in the Polo Club, overlooking the stables and playing field, caters to the thoroughbred crowd.

Services: 24-hour room service, concierge, limo service, babysitting, house doctor, laundry, complimentary welcome fruit basket, Avis car rental.

Facilities: Fantastic outdoor pool and Jacuzzi; the Polo Club with horseback riding, weight rooms, squash courts, table tennis, billiards, sauna, and aerobics classes; tennis courts, golf and minigolf, all water sports (including scuba-diving trips to a nearby island reef), spa, business center, beauty salon/barbershop, shopping arcade on ground floor of hotel.

Expensive

BEACH GARDEN RESORT, 949/21 Phetkasem Beach Rd., Cha-Am Phetchaburi 76120. Tel. 032/471350-1. Fax 032/471291. A/C MINIBAR TEL TV

$ Rates: 2,100B–2,800B ($85–$112) single or double. No credit cards.

Located at the southern periphery of Cha-Am, this moderately priced resort is favored by European groups. The main attraction is the long sandy beach—it's clean and wide—that abuts the hotel. Facilities include an outdoor pool, two tennis courts, mini-golf, and windsurfing gear. Standard rooms have no TVs, while superior rooms have all the amenities and are on high floors with views. Between the Beach Garden and its splashy neighbor, the Regent Cha-Am (unaffiliated with the Regent International chain) are a number of fun discos and restaurants. Just south of the resort's beach is the "Family Shop" Restaurant, where they barbecue whole fish in foil (see "Where to Dine" below).

CHA-AM METHAVALAI HOTEL, 220 Ruamchit Rd., Cha-Am, Phetchaburi 76120. Tel. 032/471028. Fax 032/471590. Telex 22158 METHA TH. 115 rms, 3 suites. A/C MINIBAR TEL TV

$ Rates: 2,500B–3,000B ($100–$120) single or double. Extra person 300B ($12). AE, DC, MC, V.

This four-story terraced hotel at the north end of the beach is distinguished for its purple-and-white bougainvillea that overflows on every level. Though the deluxe rooms are enormously long and lead to flower-decorated balconies, we think the superior rooms are the better value (they, too, have balconies). All rooms have discounted low-season rates. The hotel has all of the amenities of the larger resorts, and is best for those who want to be in the heart of things.

Moderate

KAEN-CHAN HOTEL, 241/3 Cha-Am Beach Rd., Cha-Am, Phetchaburi 76210. Tel. 032/471314. Fax 032/471531. 48 rms. A/C MINIBAR TEL TV
$ Rates: 1,450B–1,800B ($58–$72) single or double. Extra rollaway bed 250B ($10). MC, V.

One year old, the beachfront Kaen-Chan, near the corner of Narathip Road, is very clean and tastefully designed. Bright rooms have bamboo furniture and a small seating area. Superior rooms (the "13" series are the largest) have views of the sea but are over the quay and quite noisy, especially in the evening. The building has an elevator, plus a small pool on the rooftop.

WHERE TO DINE

Most people will likely eat in their hotel (which is fine in Hua Hin or Cha-Am; both towns have few culinary high points), but for those who wish to venture out, we've found a few places worth sampling.

HUA HIN

Expensive

PALM SEAFOOD PAVILION, in the Hotel Sofitel Central, 1 Damneonkasem Rd. Tel. 512021.
Cuisine: CONTINENTAL. **Reservations:** Recommended. **Directions:** On waterfront end of main street.
$ Prices: Appetizers 120B–350B ($2.40–$14); main courses 120B–500B ($4.80–$20). AE, DC, MC, V.
Open: Lunch daily noon–2:30pm; dinner daily 6–10:30pm.

Dining within this plant-filled crystal pavilion is a very romantic way to start your holiday. Attentive but discreet service, beautiful table settings and linen, soothing classical music, and excellent, elegantly prepared food all contribute in pleasing harmony. The light, homemade cannelloni or tender steaks are for those who don't like seafood; we dove into a salmon consommé with tiny mushroom ravioli, fresh barracuda with fruit curry sauce, and a steamed cottonfish served with creamed spinach. As if that weren't enough, we splurged on a fluffy baked Alaska and an apple charlotte drizzled with kirsch.

Moderate

BAN TUPPEE KAOW, 7 Napkehard St. Tel. 512210.
Cuisine: THAI. **Directions:** A 35B–60B ($1.40–$2.40) *samlor* ride from center of town.
$ Prices: Main courses 125B–200B ($5–$8). No credit cards.
Open: Daily 11am–midnight.

This northern-seaside two-story green house was built in the 1920s, and since then it has been only occasionally maintained. Pom is the wonderfully hospitable young host from Bangkok, and his specialties include lemongrass shrimp with baby coconut and an intricately wrapped chicken that Pom claims only his mother can manage. As for beverages, order the tropical leaf ice "tea"; we have no idea what it's made from but we felt greatly refreshed afterward!

MEEKARUNA SEAFOOD, 26/1 Naratdamri Rd. Tel 511932.
   Cuisine: SEAFOOD. **Directions:** Near main fishing pier.
$ Prices: Appetizers 60B–125B ($2.40–$5); main courses 100B–450B ($4–$17). MC, V.
   Open: Daily 9am–11pm.

This small family-run restaurant serves fresh fish in a dining pavilion across the street, or outdoors at tables overlooking Hua Hin's main fishing pier. The menu is in English (with photographs) and we found the lack of hype—compared with that of other fish places with their hustling touts—refreshing. Among the many good dishes, we recommend steamed pomfret with plum sauce, charcoal-grilled shrimp, and the fried vegetable combination with seafood. Wear bug repellent!

SANG THAI SEAFOOD RESTAURANT, Naratdamri Rd. Tel. 512144.
   Cuisine: SEAFOOD. **Direction:** On main fishing pier.
$ Prices: Appetizers 75B–100B ($3–$4); main courses 70B–400B ($2.80–$16). AE, DC, MC, V.
   Open: Daily 9am–10pm.

Open-air dining, next to caged songbirds, is the rule at the trellis-covered, pierside Sang Thai, with fishing boats docked in front of the restaurant. Popular with locals and tourists, it also has a menu in English with photos. Among the recommended main courses are shrimp-fried asparagus, fried crab with chili paste, bean cake with fried vegetables, grilled pomfret, lobster, and charcoal-grilled prawns. Often there are seafood touts, young guys offering up to a 10% discount, roping people into the restaurant. It's really an okay place, but try to avoid visiting when a tour group is there or you might find both service and cuisine below expectations.

CHA-AM

Expensive

THE ASCOT, in Dusit Report and Polo Club, 1349 Phetkasem Rd. Tel. 280480.
   Cuisine: CONTINENTAL.
$ Prices: Appetizers 155B–400B ($6.20–$16); main courses 400B–720B ($16–$28.80). AE, DC, MC, V.
   Open: Daily 6:30pm–10:30pm.

For a taste of Hua Hin's high society, as well as a good meal in a striking setting, visit the Dusit Resort's premier restaurant. Linen, candlelight, and crystal are juxtaposed against the grand view of dramatically lit lotus ponds, palms, and crazy frangipani trees planted throughout the pool area. The chef's nightly complimentary appetizer can be followed by fresh asparagus with prosciutto, soup (such as bouillabaisse), or salad. U.S. prime sirloin, New Zealand lamb chops, or médaillon of veal are among the expertly prepared main courses, cooked to your liking. Kyle sampled the delicious seafood special, which featured grilled plakapong (a tender white fish), locally caught scallops, and huge prawns with a ginger hollandaise sauce.

Budget

"FAMILY SHOP" RESTAURANT, on the beach. No phone.
   Cuisine: THAI. **Directions:** Just south of the Beach Garden Resort.
$ Prices: Main courses 95B–120B ($3.80–$4.80). No credit cards.
   Open: Daily 8:30am–9pm.

Dining by the sea at this family-run rattan hut is a supremely rustic and casual experience. Although the menu is limited, the barbecued whole fish wrapped in foil is definitely worth sampling. If you're sunbathing on this part of beach, the place also makes an ideal barefoot snack house for those mid-meal cravings.

SHOPPING

There's nothing particularly interesting about shopping in Hua Hin or Cha-Am other than browsing the myriad seashell chatchka vendors or visiting the Night Market, located in the center of town. It's open every evening from 6pm to midnight.

EXCURSIONS

KHAO SAM ROI YOD NATIONAL PARK

Dramatic limestone caves, beaches, wondrous birds, and rarely seen mammals highlight this national park, located 20 kilometers (12½ miles) south of Hua Hin. It's not the most interesting park imaginable, but if you want to escape to a natural paradise from your luxury palace, take a trip down to **Khao Sam Roi Yod National Park.** Birdwatching is best done from December through March. There are well-marked trails leading up to Khao Daeng and Khao Chalomfang; bungalows are available for overnight stays at Tham Phraya Nakhon Cave as well as at the park headquarters.

PHETCHABURI

Phetchaburi is one of the country's oldest towns, possibly dating from the same period as Ayutthaya and Kanchanaburi, and is thought to have been settled during the Dvaravati period. After the rise of the Thai nation, it served as an important royal military city and was home to several princes who were groomed for their ascendance to the throne.

The most prominent geographic feature of the town is a series of hills. The most significant is **Khao Wang,** on which there are two monasteries (one from the Ayutthaya period), a royal palace built in 1860 by King Mongkut, and many lesser shrines and administrative buildings. We suggest starting your tour here, as there is a spectacular view of the town and its important historic monuments. Khao Wang can be visited via a walkway or, as most people do it, a tram. It operates daily from 8am to 5:30pm, with an admission charge of 30B ($1.20). The **Phra Nakhon Khiri National Museum,** at the top of the hill, on Khiri Rataya Road (tel. 425600), is open daily from 9am to 4pm. Admission is 25B ($1).

Back down in the busy streets of central Phetchaburi are several superb wats, two of which—Wat Yai Suwannaram and Wat Ko

Keo Suttharam—are decorated with murals reputed to be the only surviving paintings from the Ayutthaya period (ending in 1767) in all of Thailand.

Wat Yai Suwannaram, where the murals in the *bot* date from the latter years of the 17th century (but bear a striking resemblance to the work of contemporary folk painter Rev. Howard Finster of rural Georgia), is nearly always bypassed by tour groups. You'll have to ask for directions, and once there, you'll have to track down somebody with a key to let you in. They'll know what you're looking for when you show up! Be sure to check out the other buildings in the complex, especially the elaborately decorated and windowless *viharn*.

The other wat with miraculous paintings is **Wat Ko Keo Suttharam,** also built in the 17th century but with murals from the 1730s. These are far more representational. Of some interest to Westerners are several panels depicting the arrival in the Ayutthaya court of European courtesans and diplomats (including a Jesuit dressed in Buddhist garb). These paintings offer a keen insight into the sensibility of the artist, who obviously had little previous contact with Europeans. As with Suwannaram, you'll have to locate an abbot—or somebody with keys—to gain access to the bot.

If you want to tour a fine all-purpose wat, by all means enter the compound of **Wat Mahathat.** When we visited, there were roving musicians banging out a Buddhist beat and chanting tunes our ears were never designed to hear. The most arresting structure is the five-tiered *prang* immediately behind the central hall; each level represents an offering that is to be made according to the precepts of Thayani Buddhism.

Another favorite wat, and particularly for fans of Khmer architecture, is **Wat Kamphaeng Laeng,** thought to have been built as a Brahman shrine; like many such temples in the Northeast of Thailand, it was renovated by Buddhists to serve their very different theological traditions. Each prang honored a different Hindu deity, and when the renovation took place, the prang statues were replaced by Buddhist imagery. Unlike the brick-and-stucco construction of Thai buildings, this complex was originally built of carved sandstone, but in the renovation its appearance was greatly altered.

Phraram Ratchaniwet, a European-style palace, was built during a seven-year period (culminating in 1916) as a rainy-season retreat for Rama V. In 1918, Rama VI designated it a venue for state visits, and it must have impressed foreign dignitaries beyond comprehension, especially those who thought Thailand was unaware of Western architectural fashion. Italian and Austrian craftspeople wrought a building so magnificent in interior detail that, were it to be in Central Europe, it would be hailed a prime example of fin-de-siècle artistry. The exterior is a jumble of Post-Victorian/Central European baroque style, but don't let that put you off, for the interior is exquisite. It is also exquisitely empty, awaiting the funds to convert it into a museum. Phraram Ratchaniwet is open to the public, but it's located in the dead center of a military base, so you'd best inquire about its hours. We tried and seemingly failed to gain access, but then cajoled them into opening it up and got in; you can too, so make the effort!

If you decide to visit Phetchaburi directly from Bangkok—perhaps on your way to Hua Hin or points south—there are direct air-conditioned buses (travel time: 2 hr.; 73B [$1]) departing from the Southern Bus Terminal, as well as several daily trains. Call 223-7010 in Bangkok for more information.

Accommodations are few in Phetchaburi; you'd best move on to Cha-Am, a mere 45-minute drive south. For food, we found a delightfully local stop called **Nam Tien** (tel. 425121) at the intersection of Surin Lu Chai and Na Mai Street, about 4 blocks from Wat Mahathat. Perpetually busy, totally funky, cheap, and with great food, Nam Tien has dishes such as plajalamite tod pla (fried fish) and giao moo ra (pork dumpling soup) with very refined noodles (a house specialty and a meal in itself). It's open daily from 7am to 7pm.

5. LOPBURI

153km (92 miles) N of Bangkok,
98km (61 miles) NE of Ayutthaya

GETTING THERE By Train There is frequent train service from Bangkok (trip time: 2½ hr.; 95B [$3.80]).

By Bus There are 2 air-conditioned buses and 3 nonair-conditioned buses per hour from Bangkok's Northern Bus Terminal (tel. 279-4484)(trip time: 2¼ hr.; 45B to 85B [$1.80 to $3.40]).

By Car Take the main highway, Route 1, north past Ayutthaya on Route 32, to Singburi and turn southeast to Lopburi.

ESSENTIALS The area code for Lopburi is 036. The train station is just opposite the town gate, on the south side.

From the 10th through the mid-13th century, Lopburi served as a satellite capital of the Khmer empire. With the rise of the Thai nation in Chiang Mai, and later in Sukhothai, the Khmer were driven out of Lopburi and the ancient city was reestablished as a second capital under the suzerainty of Ayutthaya. King Narai, who was the first Thai monarch to open the country to the West, collaborated with French architects in the 1660s to rebuild the city in a Thai-European mode. Today, Lopburi's few sites reflect these many presences: Hindu-influenced Khmer-era temples, Buddhist-influenced Sukhothai-Ayutthaya structures, and Jesuit-influenced European buildings. Many travelers make it their first overnight stop on the way to exploring the Northeast, but try not to miss the annual October Banana Festival.

Like Ayutthaya, the old town is surrounded by water, principally the Lopburi River on the southern and western perimeters. Nearly all of the major tourist sites are located within the old city.

WHAT TO SEE & DO

NARAI RATCHANIVET PALACE AND SOMDET PHRA NARAI NATIONAL MUSEUM OF LOPBURI, Sorasak Rd., between Ratchadamnoen Rd. and Pratoo Chai Rd. Tel. 411456.

This Palace complex was built during King Narai's reign over a period of 12 years, circa 1666, and renovated by King Mongkut. Finds from the area as well as objects from the complex's various buildings are on display in the Somdet Phra Narai National

Museum (also known as the National Museum of Lopburi). Originally, the palace (later renovated under King Mongkut) was thought of as a reception ground for both Thai and European emissaries, and the architecture reflects both a local and a Western sensibility. For example, the Chantara Phisan Pavilion, built as a residence and Reception Hall for the king, is designed in Thai style, while the Dusit Sawan Thanya Maha Prasat building is an audience hall (where King Narai is thought to have received the Chevalier de Chaumont, Louis XIV's ambassador) that incorporates both Thai and French architectural styles, as well as a fine throne and antique mirrors imported from France. The Phiman Mongkut Pavilion was King Mongkut's Lopburi residence, designed by a Frenchman in the style popular in a 19th-century Europe, and used today to house archeological finds from the area. His harem (so to speak) was housed in the nearby Phra Pratiep, where Thai folk arts are currently on view. The grounds are filled with fascinating structures, most of them in ruins, which are worth devoting a few hours to explore.

Admission: 10B (40¢).
Open: Wed–Sun 8:30am–4pm.

PHRA PRANG SAM YOT, 200 meters from the train station.

This Hindu shrine was originally built in the Lopburi style, of stone decorated with stucco, and was converted into a Buddhist temple during the reign of King Narai. Three adjoining prangs represent the Hindu Trinity of Brahma, Vishnu, and Siva.

SAN PHRA KAN or THE KALA SHRINE, across the tracks from the station.

The original Khmer-style Brahman shrine, dedicated to the Hindu god Kala, is now best known for the hundreds of live monkeys who frolic with some carved stone ones. Cute and devilish, they steal scarves and sunglasses, grab shoulder-hung cameras, and revel in the annual December feast held at the shrine. The four-armed Buddha figure you'll see inhabits a newer temple built in the 1950s.

VICHAYEN HOUSE

Built in Lopburi as a residence for the Chevalier de Chaumont (see above) by King Narai, this estate is largely in ruins, though there is still evidence of a Catholic chapel and several residences for the ambassador and his entourage, as well as water tanks and other outbuildings.

Admission: 25B ($1).
Open: Daily 8:30am–4:30pm.

WAT PHRA SRI MAHA THAT, a block behind train station.

This shrine was probably built in the early 13th century, during the Khmer period, and later rebuilt in the Sukhothai style, with additions made during the Ayutthaya era. One prang, Prang Pathan, is finely decorated.

WHERE TO STAY

INEXPENSIVE

LOPBURI INN, 28/9 Narai Maharat Rd., Lopburi 15000. Tel 036/412300. Fax 036/411917. 134 rms. A/C MINIBAR TEL

Directions: In center of ancient city.
$ Rates: 725B ($29) single; 900B–1,450B ($36–$58) double. MC, V.
This, the largest hotel in Lopburi, is also its most fully equipped and comfortable. Like most provincial hotels found in popular stops, the Lopburi Inn is often used by tour groups and consequently suffers from wear and less-than-perfect upkeep. It's central to both sites and restaurants.

WHERE TO DINE

There are a series of typical Thai restaurants in the 200 block of Narai Maharat Road, all worth trying and of about equal quality: **Maha Sarakham** (226/7–10 Narai Maharat; tel. 411643), **Bua Luang** (229/129–32 Narai Maharat; tel. 411014), and **Anodat** (226/21 Narai Maharat; no phone).

APPENDIX

A. VOCABULARY

THAI	ENGLISH
Sawaddi (to be polite, a man would say "Sawaddi krap"; a woman would say "Sawaddi ka")	Good morning, Good evening, Good afternoon, Good night, Hello, Good-bye
Khun	Mr., Ms., Mrs.
Chai	Yes
Mai *or* Plao	No
Kun sa bai di ru?	How are you?
Sa bai di. Khopkhun	Very well. Thank you.
Khopkhun	Thank you
Chan cha pai . . .	I am going to . . .
Khun tong kan tao rai?	How much do you want?
Mak pai	Too much
Phaeng	Too expensive
Lot ra-kha noi dai mai?	Any discount?
Kao chai mai?	Understand?
Chan mai kao chai	I don't understand
Prot put cha-cha	Please speak slowly
Mai phaeng	Not expensive
Chan mai pai	No, I won't go
Prot khap cha-cha	Please drive slowly
Prot, ra-wang	Please be careful
Lieo khwa	Turn to the right
Lieo sai	Turn to the left
Khap trong pai	Drive straight on
Cha-cha	Slow down
Yut	Stop
Ra-kha tao rai?	How much is this?
Ho hai duai	Please wrap it for me
Chan sia chai	I'm sorry
Kho thot	Excuse me, pardon me
Di mak	Very good
Mai di	No good
Chok di	Good luck
Karuna *or* Prot	Please

NUMBERS

1	Nueng	13	Sip-sam	80	Paet-sip
2	Song	14	Sip-si	90	Kao-sip
3	Sam	19	Sip-kao	100	Nueng Roi
4	Si	20	Yi-sip	400	Si Roi
5	Ha	21	Yi-sip-et	600	Hok Roi
6	Hok	22	Yi-sip-song	1,000	Nueng Phan
7	Chet	25	Yi-sip-ha	10,000	Nueng Muen
8	Paet	30	Sam-sip		
9	Kao	40	Si-sip		
10	Sip	50	Ha-sip		
11	Sip-et	60	Hok-sip		
12	Sip-song	70	Chet-sip		

B. MENU SAVVY

BASIC THAI FOOD GROUPS

Khao rice
Ba mi (bakmee) egg noodles
Kuai tiao rice noodles
Woon Sen glass noodles
Phrik chili
Kai chicken
Pla fish
Goong (kung) shrimp

Nua beef
Mu (moo) pork
Pet (phet) duck
Gaeng (kaeng) curried dish
Yaam salad
Tom or gaeng soup
Khong waang snacks, appetizers

SOME FAVORITE DISHES

Tom yam goong hot-and-sour shrimp soup
Satay charcoal-broiled chicken, beef, or pork strips skewered on bamboo stick, dipped in a peanut-coconut curry sauce
Spring roll similar to egg rolls but thinner and usually containing only vegetables
Larb spicy chicken or ground-beef with mint and lime flavoring
Yaam or Salad made with nearly any ingredient as the prime flavor, with a dressing of onion, chili pepper, lime juice and naam pla (fish sauce)

Pad thai literally "Thai noodles," it includes rice noodles, large shrimp, eggs, peanuts, fresh bean sprouts, lime, and a delicious sauce
Mee krob (mi klob) crisp fried noodles with meat, seafood, and sweet-n-sour sauce
Kao soi a northern curried soup served with thin glass noodles
Tod man pla spicy, fried fish
Khao pad Thai fried rice, a simple rice dish made with whatever meat, fish, or vegetables the kitchen has on hand

RESTAURANT SAVVY

If you can't eat extremely hot (spicy) Thai food, inform the waiter that you want it "Mai phet, farang." ("Not spicy, for foreigner.")

If you react to the flavor enhancer monosodium glutamate, ask to have it deleted from your meal. "Mai sai phong chu rod" means "Please don't add M.S.G.". The Thais use a lot of it, usually pre-mixed with seasonings and sauces, but it never hurts to ask.

Use the following list to help you order in restaurants.

CURRY DISHES

THAI	ENGLISH
Kaeng mat sa man	a rich beef curry with peanuts
Kaeng ka ri	mild flavored Indian-type curry of potatoes and chicken
Kaeng kai	chicken spiced ragoût
Kaeng nua	meat spiced ragoût
Kaeng pla duk	catfish spiced ragoût
Kaeng som	fish and vegetable ragoût

SOUPS

Kaeng chut	mild-flavored vegetables, shrimp, chicken, and pork soup
Kaeng laing	typical Thai-style vegetable soup
Tom yam	chili hot and sour soup made with pork, shrimp, beef, chicken, or fish
Khao tom mu	mild rice soup flavored with pork
Khao tom pla	mild rice soup flavored with fish
Khao tom kung	mild rice soup flavored with shrimp
Kaong chut wun sen	Kaeng chut with shredded jelly added
Tom khlong	salted fish boiled with tamarind and onions

EGG DISHES

Khai luak	soft-boiled egg
Khai tom	hard-boiled egg
Khai dao	fried egg
Khai chi ao/Khai tot	plain fried omelet
Khai fu	fluffy omelet of whipped eggs
Khai tot sai mu	omelet fried with ground pork
Khai yat sai	omelet filled with meat, onions, and sugar peas

FRIED DISHES

Khao phat	fried rice
Priao wan	sweet and sour pork with vegetables

THAI	ENGLISH
Phak bung phat	Thai morning glory stem and leaf, fried
Hao kun	thin slices of shrimp eaten with Chinese syrup
Mi klob	crisp thin noodles (vermicelli) with bits of meat, shrimp, egg, and sweet-and-sour sauce
Po pai	egg roll with bean sprouts, pork, and crabmeat, not fried
Po pai tot	above egg roll, fried
Nua phat nam man hoi	fried beef with oyster-flavored sauce and green onion
Dok kalam phat mu, kung, kai, nua	fried pork, shrimp, chicken, or beef with cauliflower

RICE WITH MEAT

Khao man kai	sliced chicken served with rice mixed with chicken drippings
Khao na pet	sliced roast duck with plain rice
Khao na kai	sliced chicken with bamboo shoots and spring onions, in gravy over plain rice
Khao mu daeng	sliced cooked pork with egg and gravy over plain rice
Khao mu tot	sliced fried pork over plain rice (can be ordered with egg on top)
Khao rat na nua	fried vegetables and meat in a gravy over plain rice

NOODLE DISHES

Kuai tiao lat na	wide white noodles with meat, vegetables, and gravy
Kuai tiao haeng	white noodles
Kuai tiao nam	as above, with broth added
Kuai tiao phat Thai	thin white noodles fried with bean sprouts and foods other than meat
Kuai tiao phat si iu sai khai	noodles fried with Chinese sauce, meat, vegetables, and egg
Ba mi nam	boiled yellow noodles, meat, and broth
Ba mi haeng	same as above but without broth
Ba mi na mu (kai, pu)	fried yellow noodles and pork (chicken, crab, beef, or shrimp)
Ba mi na phak	same as above, with vegetables
Ba mi klob rat na kung	crisp fried yellow noodles and shrimp
Ba mi klob rat na mu	same as above, with pork
Bai mi klob rat na kai	same as above, with chicken

THAI	ENGLISH
Kieo nam	wonton soup
Kieo haeng	wonton with vegetables and spices

MISCELLANEOUS

Pet tun	steamed duck soup
Pla prieo wan	sweet-and-sour fried fish
Kam pu tot	fried crab claws
Kam pu nung	steamed crab claws
Kai phat phrik	fried chicken and chilies (usually spicy)
Kai yang	toasted chicken
Kai tot	fried chicken
Soup khao phot	corn soup
Hu cha lam sai pu	shark's-fin soup with crabmeat
Kung tot krob	crisp fried prawns
Sa lat nua san	roast beef salad
Pla tot	fried fish
Pla nam khao	stewed pomfret (fish) in white sauce

THAI DESSERTS

Sang kha ya	custard
Sang kha ya kha nun	jackfruit custard
Ma phrao sang kha ya	coconut custard
Fak thong sang kha ya	squash custard
Thong yib	sweet egg-petals
Thong yot	sweet egg-drops
Foi thong	sweet egg shred
Kha nom mo kaeng	egg sweet plate
Lot chong nam ka thi	rice drops in sweet coconut sauce
Kluai buat chi	banana in sweet and salty coconut cream
Luk tan chuam	palm seeds cooked in syrup
Wun whan	sweet jelly
Wun nam chuam	jellied syrup
Ta ko	gelatin with coconut cream
Khao nieo kaeo	glutinous rice cooked in coconut cream and sugar

DRINKS

Nam plao (or nam yen)	glass of water
Nam khaeng plao	glass of crushed ice
Nam khaeng sai nam cha	glass of crushed ice filled with Chinese tea
Nam ron	glass of hot water
Cha chin ron	cup of hot Chinese tea
Cha yen	iced tea with milk
Cha dam yen	iced black tea with sugar
Cha dam ron	hot black tea with sugar

THAI	ENGLISH
Cha ron	hot tea with milk
Ka fae ron	hot coffee with milk
Ka fae dam	hot black coffee with sugar
Ka fae dam mai sai nam tan	hot black coffee without sugar
Ka fae yen	iced coffee with milk
O Liang (or ka fae dam)	iced black coffee with sugar
Ko ko	cocoa
O wan tin	Ovaltine
Nam som nung khuat	a bottle of orange crush
Nom	milk

THAI FRUITS

Chom phu (Rose Apple) Many varieties. Red color, tastes sour; pink is sweet and sour; white is very sweet; green is sweet; red with white is sweet and sour. Available April to June.

Farang (Guava) Usually eaten fresh, sometimes with salt and sugar. Available year-round.

Khanun (Jackfruit) Yellow-brown in color with large seeds and thick, soft thorned skin. Boiled seeds taste like peanuts. Available year-round.

Kluai (Banana) 3 major varieties are kluai hom, kluai khai, and kluai nam wa. Kluai hom is long, fragrant; kluai khai small and round; kluai nam wa is fatter. Available year-round.

Lamut (sapodilla) Brown color, sweet taste. Available year-round.

Lamyai (Longan) Small, brown-skinned round pod, transparent white meat. Very sweet and juicy; seeds inedible. Available July to October.

Langsat Sweet-and-sour taste; seeds inedible. Available May to July.

Malako (Papaya) Yellow-brown or yellow-green rind. Sweet and fragrant pinkish-orange flesh when ripe. Raw green flesh used for spicy Thai salads. Available year-round.

Mamuang (Mango) Several varieties. Can be eaten half ripe or ripe. Popularly served during summer with sweet, glutinous rice. Available January to March.

THAI	ENGLISH
Mangkhut (Mangosteen)	Purplish, hard-rinded fruit with segmented, juicy white flesh. Available April to September.
Ngo (Rambutan)	Green and red hairy pod; transparent, sweet flesh. Available May to July.
Noi nah (Custard Apple)	Pale green fruit, segmented white flesh; seeds inedible. Available July to September.
Phutsa (Green Plum/ Crab Apple)	Small, green, plumlike taste. Available year-round.
Sapparot (Pineapple)	Green, spiny rind. Yellow sweet flesh. Available year-round.
Som (Orange)	Sweet and mildly sour varieties, available year-round.
Som oh (Pomelo)	Green rind, white pith, segmented yellow, white, or pinkish flesh. Tastes very much like grapefruit. Available October to December.
Taengmo (Watermelon)	Green rind; sweet, juicy red pulp. Available year-round.
Thurian (Durian)	Hard, yellow-brown, sharp-thorned shell. Very sweet, thick yellow flesh. Fruit has strong, pungent odor. Available March to May.

C. GLOSSARY

GENERAL TERMS

ban village
doi mountain
farang foreigner
hat beach
hang yao long-tailed water taxi
klong canal
koh island
mae nam river
muang city
soi lane, side street
thanon road
tuk-tuk/samlor three-wheeled taxis with two-cycle engines

ARCHITECTURAL TERMS

bot   central shrine in a Buddhist temple
chedi/stupa   a pointed, domed structure housing the relics of the Buddha
mondop   square-shaped structure containing a Buddha
naga   dragonlike snake figure
prang   Khmer-inspired cactus-shaped tower
viharn   large hall in a Buddhist temple used for daily rituals
wat   temple or monastery complex

D. CONVERSION TABLES

THE METRIC SYSTEM

LENGTH

1 millimeter (mm)	=	0.04 inches (*or* less than ¹⁄₁₆ inch)
1 centimeter (cm)	=	0.39 inches (*or* just under ½ inch)
1 meter (m)	=	1.09 yards (*or* about 39 inches)
1 kilometer (km)	=	0.62 mile (*or* about ⅔ mile)

CAPACITY

1 liter(l)	=	33.92 onces = 2.1 pints
	=	1.06 quarts = .26 U.S. Gallons
1 Imperial gallon	=	1.2 U.S. gallons

WEIGHT

1 gram (g)	=	.035 ounces (or about a paperclip's weight)
1 kilogram (kg)	=	35.2 ounces = 2.2 pounds
1 metric ton	=	2,205 pounds (1.1 short ton)

TEMPERATURE

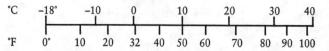

To convert degrees Celsius to degrees Fahrenheit, multlply °C by 9, divide by 5, and add 32 (example: 20°C × 9/5 + 32 = 68°F).

To convert degrees Fahrenheit to degrees Celsius, subtract 32 from °F, multiply by 5, then divide by 9 (example: 85°F−32 × 5/9 = 29.4°C).

Accommodations. *See also list of individual establishments at end of Index*
  in Ayutthaya, 192
  in Bangkok, 61–93
    around the railroad station, 91–92
    in the Business District, 75–81
    along Chao Phraya River, 62–71
    for children, 67
    money-saving tips, 64
    near the airport, 92–93
    near the Grand Palace, 71–75
    in the Shopping/Embassy area, 82–91
  in Cha-Am, 220–22
  in Hua Hin, 216–20
  on Jomtien Beach, 203–5
  in Kanchanaburi, 211–12
  in Lopburi, 227–28
  near Kwai River, 211–12
  in Pattaya, 198–205
Addresses, locating, 42
Adult entertainment
  massage parlors, 177
    in Pattaya, 208
  prostitution and, 27–28
  sex clubs, 175–77
AIDS, 28, 176, 177, 178, 194
Airport, 37–40
  accommodations near, 92–93
Air travel
  airlines, 32–34, 58
  arriving in Bangkok, 37–40
  money-saving tips, 35
  from North America, 32–34
  from the United Kingdom, 34
American Express, 47
Amporn Phimok Prasad (Disrobing Pavilion), 124
Amulet market, 132–33, 144
Ancient City, 182–83
Angkor Wat, model of, 124
Annual events, festivals and fairs. *See* Festivals
Antiques, shopping for, 152–56
Architecture, 7–10, 188. *See also specific styles*
  Western influences on, 10, 124, 133, 142, 181, 225–27
Art, 7–11, 19. *See also* Painting *and specific styles*
Arts and crafts. *See* Handcrafts
Author's Wing in Oriental Hotel, 2, 63–64
Ayutthaya, 3, 4, 7, 11, 122, 187–92
  accommodations in, 192
  restaurants in, 192–93
  river tours to, 180–81, 187–88
  sightseeing in, 189–92
  transportation in, 189
  traveling to, 187–88
Ayutthaya Historical Study Center, 189
Ayutthaya style, 9, 125, 188, 224–225

Babysitters, 31, 48
Baht, 22–23
Bamboo Island, 197
Bang Pa-In Summer Palace, 181–82
Ban Kao Neolithic Museum (Kanchanaburi), 211

Bars, 177–78
Beaches
  in Hua Hin/Cha-Am, 215
  in Pattaya, 196
  safety tips, 27
Beetle fights, 138
Bencharong, shopping for, 158
Beverages, 18
Bhumibol Adulyadej, King. *See* Rama IX
Birdwatching, in Khao Sam Roi Yod National Park, 224
Boat travel and cruises. *See also* Chao Phraya River
  to Ayutthaya, 180–81, 187–88
  to Nonthaburi, 181
  to Thailand, 35
Books about Bangkok, 18–20
Bookstores, 48, 156–58
  in Pattaya, 196
Boromaraja IV. *See* Taksin, King
Bots, 9, 128
Boxing, Thai, 138, 179
Bridge Over the River Kwai (Kanchanaburi), 210–11
Bronzeware, shopping for, 158
Buddha, 11–12
  sculptures of, 8–9, 12–13
    Emerald Buddha, 2, 12–13, 123, 125
    Reclining Buddha, 128, 143
    in Viharn Phra Mongkol Bopit (Ayutthaya), 190
    in Wat Bovornivet, 133
    in Wat Chakrawat, 146
    in Wat Kalaya Namit, 148
    in Wat Khao Prayai (Khao Tappraya Hill), 197
    in Wat Na Phra Mane (Ayutthaya), 190
    in Wat Phanan Choeng (Ayutthaya), 190
    in Wat Phra Sri Sanphet (Ayutthaya), 190
    at Wat Suthat, 134
    at Wat Traimit, 134
Buddhism, 11–14, 184
  architectural styles, 8–9
  art, 8, 10
  books about, 19
Business District, 43
  accommodations in, 75–81
  restaurants in, 100–106
Business hours, 48, 215
Bus travel, 35, 40, 44, 54, 59

Calendar of events. *See* Festivals
Cameras and film, 53
Cars and driving
  cars for hire, 46–47, 60
  driving rules, 60
  rentals, 60, 194–95, 209, 215
  traffic jams, 36–37, 43–44, 128, 214
Caverns, 213, 224
Ceramics, shopping for, 158
Cha-Am. *See* Hua Hin/Cha-Am
Chakri Maha Prasad, 124
Chandra Kasem Palace (Ayutthaya), 189
Chao Phraya Express Company, 44–46, 122–23, 129, 181, 188

Chao Phraya River, 1–3, 36, 42–43
  accommodations along, 62–71
  restaurants along, 95–97
  Royal Barge Museum, 132
  transport on, 44–46, 122–23, 129
    to Ayutthaya, 180–81, 187–88
    dinner cruises, 117–18
    night cruises, 179
    river tours, 180–81
Chao Phrya Chakri. See Rama I
Chao Sam Phraya National Museum (Ayutthaya), 189
Chatuchak Weekend Market, 129
Children
  accommodations for, 67
  restaurants for, 105
  sightseeing for, 136–37
  tips for, 31
Chinatown, 43, 129
  restaurants in, 115–16
  walking tour of, 144–47
Chinese community in Bangkok, 4, 7, 17, 144
Chon-Kai War Cemetery, 210
Christianity, 13–14, 148
Chulalongkorn, King. See Rama V
Chumbhot, Princess, of Nagara Svarga, 2, 131–32
Church of Santa Cruz, 148
Cinemas, 179
City Pillar Shrine (Lak Muang), 133
Climate, 24
Clothing
  packing, 29
  shopping for, 158–61
Cock fights, 138
Concert halls, 173–174
Cooking classes, 64, 137
Cost of everyday items, 23
Cotton, shopping for, 170–72
Credit cards, 24, 48–49, 55
Crocodile Farm, Samutprakarn, 137, 184
Cuisine. See Food
Cultural programs, 179
Currency/exchange, 22–23, 49
  in Hua Hin/Cha-Am, 215
  in Kanchanaburi, 209
  in Pattaya, 196

Damnoen Saduak, Floating Market at, 123, 182
Dance, 15
  dinner featuring Thai dance, 116–17, 174
  discos, 174–75, 208
Dawadung Cave, 213
Department stores, 161
Disabled travelers, tips for, 30
Discos, 174–75
  in Pattaya, 208
Doctors, 49
Documents for entry, 22
Dolls, shopping for, 161
Don Muang International Airport, 37–40
  accommodations near, 92–93
Drink, 18
Drug laws, 177, 208
Drugstores, 49
Dry cleaning. See Laundry and dry cleaning
Dusit Zoo, 135–136
Dvaravati (Mon), 8, 190

Elephants
  Elephant Roundup and Handcraft Fair (Ayutthaya), 25
  Samphran Elephant Ground and Zoo, 184
Embassies, 49–50
Embassy area. See Shopping/Embassy area
Emerald Buddha, 2, 12–13, 123, 125
Emergencies, 50
Entertainment and nightlife, 173–79. See also Adult entertainment
  in Pattaya, 207–8
Entry requirements, 22
Erawan Waterfall and National Park, 213
Etiquette, 50
Eyeglasses, 29, 51

Families, tips for, 31
Fast Facts, 47–57
  for Pattaya, 196
Ferries on Chao Phraya River, 44–46, 122–23, 129
Festivals, 14, 25–26, 188
  in Pattaya, 193
Films about Bangkok, 20
Fish fights, 138
Fishing, in Pattaya, 197
Flatware, shopping for, 158
Floating Market at Damnoen Saduak, 123, 182
Folklore, 14–15
  books about, 19
Food, 16–18, 94
  cooking classes, 64, 137
  festivals, 25
Funeral Hall, 124
Furniture, shopping for, 162

Gardens
  Jim Thompson's House, 131
  Kamthieng House, 134
  Rose Garden Country Resort, 183–84
  Sofitel Central (Hua Hin), 217–18
  Wang Suan Pakkard, 2, 129, 131–32
Gay bars, 178, 208
Gemstones, shopping for, 165–68
Geography, 2–3
Giant Swing, 134, 142
Golden Mount, 135, 141
Golf, 138–39, 216
Grand Palace, 2, 122–24, 144
Grand Palace area, 42
  accommodations in, 71–75
  restaurants in, 97–100

Handcrafts
  festivals for, 25–26, 188
  shopping for, 153, 162–64
Hang yao (long-tail water taxi), 44, 122–23
Health concerns and precautions, 26–28
Hinduism, 8–9
Historic Bangkok. See Grand Palace area
History, 3–6
  books about, 18–19
Holidays, 24
Horse racing, 138
Hospitals, 51
  in Hua Hin/Cha-Am, 215
  in Pattaya, 196
Hua Hin/Cha-Am, 213–24
  accommodations in, 216–22
  Fast Facts for, 215

restaurants in, 222–24
shopping in, 224
sightseeing in, 215–16
Sofitel Central, 217–18
tourist information about, 214–15
transportation in, 215
traveling to, 213–14
Hua Lampong Railroad Station, 40, 59
accommodations around, 91–92

Ice skating, 139
Information sources, 21–22, 40–41, 173
in Hua Hin/Cha-Am, 214–15
in Kanchanaburi, 209
in Pattaya, 194
for transportation, 56–57
Insurance, 28–29
Itineraries, suggested, 121

Japanese in Thailand, 5, 188, 209–11
Jazz, 174
JEATH Museum (Kanchanaburi), 210
Jewelry
collections of, 130, 132, 190
fairs, 25
shopping for, 165–68
Jim Thompson's House, 2, 129, 131
Jomtien Beach, 196, 203–5. See also Pattaya

Kamthieng House, 134
Kanchanaburi, 209–13
accommodations in, 211–12
Bridge Over the River Kwai, 210–11
cemeteries in, 210
Fast facts for, 209
restaurants in, 212
sightseeing in, 210–11
tourist information about, 209
traveling to, 209
Kanchanaburi War Cemetery, 210
Karaoke sing-along/hostess clubs, in Pattaya, 208
Karma, 13
Khao Sam Roi Yod National Park, 224
Khao Wang (Phetchaburi), 224
Khmer, 3, 7–8, 126, 128, 184, 188, 211,
225–227
King and I, The (film), 20
King's Birthday and Trooping of the Colors, 26
Kites, 25, 138
Klong Bangkok Noi, 123, 132
Klong Bangkok Yai, 123, 149
Klong Ong Ang, 42, 122
Klongs, 2, 4
exploring, 122–23
Ko Krok, 197
Ko Larn, 197
Ko Man Wichai, 197
Ko Sak, 197
Kwai River, 209–10
accommodations near, 211–12
Bridge Over the, 210–11
JEATH Museum (Kanchanaburi), 210
restaurants near, 212
River Kwai Bridge Festival (Kanchanaburi),
26, 209

Lak Muang (City Pillar Shrine), 133
Landon, Margaret, 5
Language, 51
schools, 179

Laundry and dry cleaning, 51
in Hua Hin/Cha-Am, 215
in Kanchanaburi, 209
La Wa Cave, 213
Layout of Bangkok, 41–43
Leather goods, shopping for, 168–69
Leonowens, Anna, 4–5
Libraries, 52
Literature, 11, 19. See also Ramakien
Lopburi, 226–28
Lumpini Park, 135–36, 138

Magic Land, 137
Mahachat, 11
Mail, 52–54
"Making merit," 13
Maps, street, 43
Marble Wat, 10
Markets, 144, 169–70
Maruekkhathayawan Palace (Hua Hin/Cha-Am),
216
Massage, 128–129, 143, 177
parlors, 177, 208
Minibuses, 44
in Pattaya, 194
Mini-Playland, 136
Mini Siam (Pattaya), 198
Missionaries, 10, 13–14
Mondop, 9
Money, 22–24, 48. See also
Currency/exchange
Mongkut, King, 4–5, 11, 14, 124, 126, 133,
181, 184, 189, 216, 224
Motorcycles, in Pattaya, 196
Movies, 179
Muang Boran (Ancient City), 182–83
Museums. See also National Museum
in Ancient City, 182–83
Ban Kao Neolithic Museum (Kanchanaburi),
211
Chandra Kasem Palace
(Ayutthaya), 189
Chao Sam Phraya National Museum
(Ayutthaya), 189
JEATH Museum (Kanchanaburi), 210
Jim Thompson's House, 2, 129, 131
Kamthieng House, 134
Narai Ratchanivet Palace
(Lopburi), 226–27
Phra Nakhon Khiri National Museum
(Phetchaburi), 224
Queen Sirikit National Convention Center,
136
Royal Barge Museum, 132
Somdet Phra Narai National Museum,
226–27
Vimanmek Mansion Museum, 132
Wang Suan Pakkard, 2, 129, 131–32
Music, 15–16
discos, 174–75
jazz, 174
Mythology. See Folklore

Nakhon Pathom, 184
Nanchao Period, 7–8
Narai, King, 226–227
Narai Ratchanivet Palace
(Lopburi), 226–27
Naresuan, King, 192
National Museum, 130–31
branches in Ayutthaya, 189
branch in Lopburi, 227

240 • INDEX

National Theater, 173–174
Neighborhoods, 42–43
Neng Noi Yee, 146
Nightclubs, in Pattaya, 207–8
Nonthaburi, 181

Ocean World, 186
Orient-Express Group, 34

Package tours, 35
Packing for your trip, 29
Paintings, 10–11. See also Art; Museums; Temples
  in Wat Bovornivet, 133–34
  in Wat Phra Kaeo, 125
  in Wat Suthat, 134
  in Wat Yai Suwannaram (Phetchaburi), 225
Pak Klong Talaat, 169
Palace of the Cabbage Garden, 2, 129, 131–32
Pali canon, 12
Panyarachun, Anand, 6, 37
Parks
  Erawan Waterfall and National Park, 213
  Khao Sam Roi Yod National Park, 224
  Lumpini Park, 135–36, 138
  Pattaya Park, 198
  Sai Yok National Park, 213
  Than Lot National Park, 213
  water, 185–86
Passports, 22
Patpong, 175–77, 178. See also Adult entertainment
  Night Market, 129, 169–70
Pattaya, 139, 193–208
  accommodations in, 198–205
  beaches in, 196
  entertainment and nightlife in, 207–8
  Fast Facts for, 196
  island excursions from, 197
  layout of, 194
  Mini Siam, 198
  Pattaya Park, 198
  restaurants in, 205–7
  shopping in, 207
  sightseeing, 196–98
  tourist information about, 194
  transportation in, 194–96
  traveling to, 193
  water sport in, 196–97
  Wat Khao Prayai (Khao Tappraya Hill), 197–98
Pattaya Festival (Pattaya), 25
Pavilion for Holy Water, 124
Peoples, 6–7
Performing arts, 15–16, 173–74
Pets, 53
Phetchaburi, 215, 224–26
Photographic needs, 53
Phra chedi (stupas), 9, 12, 125, 128–129, 135, 143, 146, 150, 184, 190–191
Phra Nakhon Khiri National Museum (Phetchaburi), 224
Phra Pathom (Nakhon Pathom), 184
Phra Prang Sam Yot (Lopburi), 227
Phra prangs (towers), 2, 9, 129, 188, 190, 225, 227
Phraram Ratchaniwet (Phetchaburi), 225–26

Phuket, 139
Phutthaisawan Chapel, 130
Phya Tak. See Taksin, King
Pickpockets, 54
Planning and preparing for your trip, 21–35
Police, 53, 215
Pollution, 27, 36, 194, 216
Portuguese community in Thailand, 148, 188
Post offices, 53–54
  in Hua Hin/Cha-Am, 215
  in Kanchanaburi, 209
  in Pattaya, 196
Pra sat, 9
Prasat Thong, 181
Pratunam Market, 170
Prostitution, 27–28. See also Adult entertainment
Pubs, 177–78

Queen Sirikit National Convention Center, 136

Rama I, 42–43, 121–25, 128, 130, 133, 134–135, 141, 144, 190
Rama II, 124, 188
Rama III, 128–129, 134, 142, 147
Rama IV, 4–5, 11, 14, 124, 126, 133, 181, 184, 189, 216, 224
Rama V, 2, 5, 124, 132, 133, 181, 225
Rama VI, 225
Rama IX, 5–6
Ramakien, 10–11, 14, 15, 19, 125, 190
Ratchadamnoen Klang Road, 141
Reclining Buddha, 128, 143
Recreational activities, 138–39. See also specific activities
Red Cross Snake Farm, 135
Religion, 11–14. See also Buddhism
  books about, 19
Religious services, 54
Restaurants
  in Ayutthaya, 192–93
  in Bangkok, 94–120
    in the Business District, 100–106
    along the Chao Phraya River, 95–97
    for children, 105
    in Chinatown, 115–16
    dinner cruises on the Chao Phraya, 117–18
    dinner with Thai dance, 116–17, 174
    fast food, 119–20
    high tea, 118–19
    money-saving tips, 96
    near the Grand Palace, 97–100
    in the Shopping/Embassy area, 106–15
  in Cha-Am, 223–24
  dining customs, 17–18
  in Hua Hin, 222–23
  in Kanchanaburi, 212
  in Lopburi, 228
  in Pattaya, 205–7
Rice
  barges, 148
  Royal Ploughing Festival, 25
  Wat Suthat, 134
River Kwai Bridge Festival (Kanchanaburi), 26, 209
Rivers. See Chao Phraya River; Kwai River
Rose Garden Country Resort, 137, 183–84
Royal Barge Museum, 132

Saensaep, 45–46
Safety, 54–55, 59
Sai Yok National Park, 213
Sampeng Lane (Woi Wanit I), 146
Samphran Elephant Ground and Zoo, 137, 184
Samutprakarn Crocodile Farm, 137, 183
San Phra Kan or the Kala Shrine (Lopburi), 227
Sapphire mining, in Bo Phloi area, 213
Scuba diving, 139, 197
Sculpture, 7–10. *See also* Buddha, sculptures of
   books about, 19
Senior citizens, tips for, 30
Sex, 27–28. *See also* Adult entertainment
   clubs for, 175–77
Shopping, 151–72
   in Hua Hin/Cha-Am, 224
   in Pattaya, 207
Shopping/Embassy area, 43
   accommodations in the, 82–91
   restaurants in the, 106–15
Siam Park (Suan Siam), 185–86
Siddhartha Gautama. *See* Buddha
Sightseeing, 121–37
   in Ayutthaya, 189–92
   for children, 136–37
   in Hua Hin/Cha-Am, 215–16
   in Kanchanaburi, 210–11
Silk, shopping for, 131, 170–72
Silver, shopping for, 172
Single travelers, tips for, 30–31
Sirikit, Queen, 6, 132
Slam Park, 137
Snake Farm, Red Cross, 135
Snorkeling, 197
Sofitel Central (Hua Hin), 217–18
Soi Cowboy, 177
Somdet Phra Narai National Museum of
   Lopburi, 226–27
Special events. *See* Festivals
Sports, spectator, 138
Sri Sudarak, Princess, 130
State Railway of Thailand, 34
Street vendors, 162
Student travelers, tips for, 31–32
Stupas. *See* Phra chedi
Sukhothai style, 8–9, 134, 190, 227
Sunstroke, 27
Suriyothai, Queen, 191
Swimming, safety tips for, 27. *See also* Beaches

Tai chi, 138
Taksin, King, 3–4, 128, 148
Taxes, 55
Taxis, 40, 46
   to Pattaya, 193
Tea, high, 118–19
Telephone numbers, useful
   for airlines, 58
   for emergencies, 50
   hotlines, 51
   for transportation, 56–57
Telephone/telegrams/telex, 55–56
Television, 54
Temples, 55
   Chinese Monk's Quarters,
      Temple of, 148
   Dawn, Temple of, 2, 128–30, 150
   Emerald Buddha, Temple of the, 9, 124–28
   etiquette at, 50
   Golden Buddha, Temple of the,
      134–35

Lak Muang (City Pillar Shrine), 133
model of Angkor Wat, 124
Neng Noi Yee, 146
Phra Pathom (Nakhon Pathom), 184
Phra Prang Sam Yot (Lopburi), 227
Phutthaisawan Chapel, 130
San Phra Kan or the Kala Shrine (Lopburi),
   227
Viharn Phra Mongkol Bopit (Ayutthaya), 190
walking tour of Bangkok's, 140–44
Wat Arun, 2, 128–30, 150
Wat Benchamabophit, 133
Wat Bovornivet, 11, 133–34
Wat Chai Wattanaram
   (Ayutthaya), 192
Wat Chakrawat, 146
Wat Kalaya Namit, 148
Wat Kamphaeng Laeng
   (Phetchaburi), 225
Wat Khao Prayai (Khao Tappraya Hill),
   197–98
Wat Ko Keo Suttharam
   (Phetchaburi), 225
Wat Mahathat, 132–33, 144
Wat Mahathat (Ayutthaya), 190
Wat Mahathat (Phetchaburi), 225
Wat Na Phra Mane (Ayutthaya), 190
Wat Nivet Thamaprawat, 181
Wat Phanan Choeng (Ayutthaya), 190
Wat Phra Kaeo, 9, 124–28
Wat Phra Ram (Ayutthaya), 190
Wat Phra Sri Maha That
   (Lopburi), 227
Wat Phra Sri Sanphet (Ayutthaya), 190
Wat Po, 2, 128, 129, 143
Wat Prayunrawonsawat
   (Wat Prayun), 147–48
Wat Ratachaburana (Ayutthaya), 190
Wat Ratchabophit, 142
Wat Ratchadana, 141
Wat Ratpradit, 142
Wat Saket, 135, 141
Wat Suthat, 134, 142
Wat Suwan Dararam (Ayutthaya), 190
Wat Traimit, 134–35
Wat Yai Chai Mongkol
   (Ayutthaya), 191–92
Wat Yai Suwannaram
   (Phetchaburi), 225
Tennis, 139
Thai boxing, 138, 179
Thailand Cultural Center, 173, 174
Than Lot National Park, 213
Theater, 173, 174
The Tha Chang, 144
Thompson, Jim, 129, 131, 172
Thonburi, 3–4, 9, 43, 122, 125
   walking tour of, 147–50
Tipping, 56
Tourist information, 21–22, 40–41, 173
   in Hua Hin/Cha-Am, 214–15
   in Kanchanaburi, 209
   in Pattaya, 194
Tours, organized. *See also* Boat travel and cruises
   of Bangkok, 137
   for disabled travelers, 30
   to Floating Market at Damnoen Saduak, 182
   of Hua Hin/Cha-Am, 215
   to natural sites, 137
   package, 35
   for senior citizens, 30

Traffic problems, 36–37, 43–44, 128, 214
Train travel
  to Ayutthaya, 187
  to Bangkok, 34, 40
  to Hua Hin/Cha-Am, 213–14
  to Kanchanaburi, 209
  to Lopburi, 226
  to Pattaya, 193
  within Thailand, 59
Transportation, 43–47
  in Ayutthaya, 189
  in Hua Hin/Cha-Am, 215
  information, 56–57
  in Pattaya, 194–96
Tra Sam Duang (Law of the Three Seals), 4
Traveler's checks, 24
Traveling
  to Ayutthaya, 187–88
  to Bangkok, 32–35
  to Hua Hin/Cha-Am, 213–14
  information sources, 56–57
  to Kanchanaburi, 209
  to Pattaya, 193
Tuk-tuk, 47

U-Thong, King, 188, 190–191

Vegetarian Festival, 26
Vichayen House (Lopburi), 227
Vihara (viharn), 9, 133–134, 190, 225
Viharn Phra Mongkol Bopit
  (Ayutthaya), 190
Vimanmek Mansion Museum, 2, 132
Viravaid, Meechai, 28, 37

Wai greeting, 50
Walailuke, Chulaporn, 28
Walking tours, 140–50
  of Buddhist shrines, 140–44
  of Chinatown, 144–47
  of Thonburi, 147–50
Wang Luang (Ayutthaya), 190
Wang Suan Pakkard, 2, 129, 131–32
Wat Arun, 2, 128–30, 150
Wat Benchamabophit, 133
Wat Bovornivet, 11, 133–34
Wat Chai Wattanaram (Ayutthaya), 192
Wat Chakrawat, 146
Water, drinking, 26–27, 57

Water parks, 185–86
Waterways of Bangkok, 2, 121–23, 136. See
  also Chao Phraya River
Wat Kalaya Namit, 148
Wat Kamphaeng Laeng
  (Phetchaburi), 225
Wat Khao Prayai (Khao Tappraya
  Hill), 197–98
Wat Ko Keo Suttharam
  (Phetchaburi), 225
Wat Mahathat, 132–33, 144
Wat Mahathat (Ayutthaya), 190
Wat Mahathat (Phetchaburi), 225
Wat Na Phra Mane (Ayutthaya), 190
Wat Nivet Thamaprawat, 181
Wat Phanan Choeng (Ayutthaya), 190
Wat Phra Kaeo, 9, 124–28
Wat Phra Ram (Ayutthaya), 190
Wat Phra Sri Maha That (Lopburi), 227
Wat Phra Sri Sanphet (Ayutthaya), 190
Wat Po (Temple of the Reclining Buddha), 2,
  128–129, 143
  massages at, 128–129, 143, 177
Wat Prayunrawonsawat
  (Wat Prayun), 147–48
Wat Ratachaburana (Ayutthaya), 190
Wat Ratchabophit, 142
Wat Ratchadana, 141
Wat Ratpradit, 142
Wat Saket, 135, 141
Wat Suthat, 134, 142
Wat Suwan Dararam (Ayutthaya), 190
Wat Traimit, 134–35
Wat Yai Chai Mongkol
  (Ayutthaya), 191–92
Wat Yai Suwannaram
  (Phetchaburi), 225
Weather, 24
Weekend Market, 170
Western influences, 4–5, 7
  in art and architecture, 10, 124, 133, 142,
  181, 225–227
Windsurfing, 196
Women travelers, networks and resources for, 57
Woodworking shops, 141
World War II, 5, 131, 209–10

Zoos
  Dusit Zoo, 135
  Samphran Elephant Ground and
  Zoo, 184

ACCOMMODATIONS

BANGKOK

Amari Airport Hotel (near the
  airport, E), 92–93
Amari Boulevard, The (near the Shopping/
  Embassy area, E),
  86–87
Amari Watergate Hotel (near the Shopping/
  Embassy area, E), 87
Atlanta Hotel, The (near the Shopping/
  Embassy area, B), 90
Bangkok Center Hotel (near the Railroad
  Station, M), 91–92

Bangkok Christian Guesthouse (Business District,
  I), 81
Bangkok YWCA (Business District, I), 81
Bel-Aire Princess (near the Shopping/Embassy
  area, E), 87
Bossotel Inn (on the River, M), 70
Buddy Guesthouse (near the Grand Palace, B),
  74
City Lodge (near the Shopping/Embassy area, I),
  89

KEY TO ABBREVIATIONS: B = Budget; E = Expensive; I = Inexpensive;
M = Moderately priced; VE = Very expensive.

Comfort Inn (near the Shopping/Embassy area, *I*), 89–90

Dusit Thani (Business District, *VE*), 75–76

Dynasty Inn (near the Shopping/Embassy area, *I*), 90

Golden Dragon Hotel (near the airport, *I*), 93

Golden Horse Hotel (near the Grand Palace, *M*), 72–73

Golden Palace Hotel (near the Shopping/Embassy area, *B*), 91

Grand China Princess Hotel (near the Grand Palace, *E*), 71–72

Grand Hyatt Erawan Bangkok (near the Shopping/Embassy area, *VE*), 82–83

Happy Inn (near the Shopping/Embassy area, *B*), 90–91

Hilton International at Nai Lert Park (near the Shopping/Embassy area, *VE*), 83–84

Holiday Inn Crowne Plaza (Business District, *E*), 77–78

Hotel Majestic Palace (near the Grand Palace, *M*), 73

Krung Kasem Sri Krung Hotel (near the Railroad Station, *B*), 92

Landmark Hotel (near the Shopping/Embassy area, *VE*), 84

Lek Guesthouse (near the Grand Palace, *B*), 74

Malaysia Hotel (Business District, *I*), 81

Mandarin Bangkok, The (Business District, *E*), 78

Manhattan Hotel (near the Shopping/Embassy area, *M*), 89

Manohra Hotel (Business District, *E*), 78

Menam Hotel Riverside, The (on the River, *VE*), 63

Méridien President, Le (near the Shopping/Embassy area, *E*), 87–88

Montien, The (Business District, *E*), 78–79

New Peninsula Hotel (Business District, *E*), 79

Nith Chareon Hotel (near the the Grand Palace, *B*), 74

Novotel Bangkok (near the Shopping/Embassy area, *VE*), 84–85

Oriental, The (on the River, *VE*), 63–65

Peachy Guesthouse (near the Grand Palace, *B*), 74–75

Promenade Hotel (near the airport, *I*), 93

P.S. Guesthouse (near the Grand Palace, *B*), 75

Regent, Bangkok, The (near the Shopping/Embassy area, *VE*), 85–86

River View Guest House (on the River, *I*), 71

Royal Garden Riverside (on the River, *E*), 67–68

Royal Hotel (near the Grand Palace, *M*), 73–74

Royal Orchid Sheraton Hotel & Towers (on the River, *VE*), 65–66

Royal Princess Hotel (near the Grand Palace, *E*), 72

Royal River Hotel (on the River, *E*), 68–70

Ruamchitt Travelodge (near the Shopping/Embassy area, *I*), 90

Shangri-La Hotel (on the River, *VE*), 66–67

Siam Inter-Continental (near the Shopping/Embassy area, *VE*), 86

Siam Orchid Inn (near the Shopping/Embassy area, *M*), 89

Somerset, The (near the Shopping/Embassy area, *E*), 88

Sukhothai, The (Business District, *VE*), 76–77

Suriwongse Tower Inn (Business District, *M*), 80

Swan Hotel (on the River, *I*), 71

Tai-Pan Hotel (near the Shopping/Embassy area, *E*), 88–89

Trinity City Hotel (Business District, *E*), 79–80

Uncle Rey's Guesthouse (near the Shopping/Embassy area, *B*), 90–91

Wall Street Inn (Business District, *M*), 80–81

YMCA Collins International House (Business District, *M*), 80

EXCURSION AREAS

Ayutthaya

Ayutthaya Guest House (*B*), 192

Krungsri River Hotel (*M*), 192

U-Thong Inn (*I*), 192

Pattaya City

Asia Pattaya Beach Hotel (*E*), 200

Dusit Resort (*E*), 200–201

Flipper Lodge Motel (*I*), 203

Montien Hotel (*E*), 201

Nautical Inn (*I*), 203

Royal Cliff Beach Resort (*E*), 201–2

Royal Cliff Grand (*VE*), 199

Royal Cruise Line (*M*), 202

Royal Wing (*VE*), 199–200

Siam Bayview (*M*), 202–3

Jomtien Beach

Mermaid's Rest Beach Resort (*M*), 205

Pattaya Park Beach Resort (*M*), 204

Royal Jomtien Resort (*E*), 203–4

Sugar Hut (*M*), 204–5

Sugar Palm Beach Hotel (*M*), 204

Surf House Hotel (*M*), 204

Kanchanaburi

Felix River Kwai Resort (*E*), 211–12

Jolly Frog Backpacker's (*B*), 211

River Kwai Jungle House (*M*), 212

V.L. Guesthouse (*B*), 211

Hua Hin

Fresh Inn Hotel (*I*), 218–19
Hotel Sofitel Central (*E*), 217–18
Jed Pee Nong Hotel (*I*), 219–20
Parichart Guest House (*I*), 220
Royal Garden Resort (*E*), 216–17
Royal Garden Village (*E*), 217

Cha-Am

Beach Garden Resort (*E*), 221
Cha-Am Methavalai Hotel (*E*), 221–22
Dusit Resort and Polo Club (*E*), 220–21
Kaen-Chan Hotel (*M*), 222

Lopburi

Lopburi Inn (*I*), 227–28

Please Send Me the Books Checked Below:

FROMMER'S COMPREHENSIVE GUIDES
(Guides listing facilities from budget to deluxe,
with emphasis on the medium-priced)

	Retail Price	Code		Retail Price	Code
☐ Acapulco/Ixtapa/Taxco 1993–94	$15.00	C120	☐ Morocco 1992–93	$18.00	C021
☐ Alaska 1994–95	$17.00	C131	☐ Nepal 1994–95	$18.00	C126
☐ Arizona 1993–94	$18.00	C101	☐ New England 1994 (Avail. 1/94)	$16.00	C137
☐ Australia 1992–93	$18.00	C002	☐ New Mexico 1993–94	$15.00	C117
☐ Austria 1993–94	$19.00	C119	☐ New York State 1994–95	$19.00	C133
☐ Bahamas 1994–95	$17.00	C121	☐ Northwest 1994–95 (Avail. 2/94)	$17.00	C140
☐ Belgium/Holland/Luxembourg 1993–94	$18.00	C106	☐ Portugal 1994–95 (Avail. 2/94)	$17.00	C141
☐ Bermuda 1994–95	$15.00	C122	☐ Puerto Rico 1993–94	$15.00	C103
☐ Brazil 1993–94	$20.00	C111	☐ Puerto Vallarta/Manzanillo/Guadalajara 1994–95 (Avail. 1/94)	$14.00	C028
☐ California 1994	$15.00	C134	☐ Scandinavia 1993–94	$19.00	C135
☐ Canada 1994–95 (Avail. 4/94)	$19.00	C145	☐ Scotland 1994–95 (Avail. 4/94)	$17.00	C146
☐ Caribbean 1994	$18.00	C123	☐ South Pacific 1994–95	$20.00	C138
☐ Carolinas/Georgia 1994–95	$17.00	C128	☐ Spain 1993–94	$19.00	C115
☐ Colorado 1994–95 (Avail. 3/94)	$16.00	C143	☐ Switzerland/Liechtenstein 1994–95 (Avail. 1/94)	$19.00	C139
☐ Cruises 1993–94	$19.00	C107	☐ Thailand 1992–93	$20.00	C033
☐ Delaware/Maryland 1994–95 (Avail. 1/94)	$15.00	C136	☐ U.S.A. 1993–94	$19.00	C116
☐ England 1994	$18.00	C129	☐ Virgin Islands 1994–95	$13.00	C127
☐ Florida 1994	$18.00	C124	☐ Virginia 1994–95 (Avail. 2/94)	$14.00	C142
☐ France 1994–95	$20.00	C132	☐ Yucatán 1993–94	$18.00	C110
☐ Germany 1994	$19.00	C125			
☐ Italy 1994	$19.00	C130			
☐ Jamaica/Barbados 1993–94	$15.00	C105			
☐ Japan 1994–95 (Avail. 3/94)	$19.00	C144			

FROMMER'S $-A-DAY GUIDES
(Guides to low-cost tourist accommodations and facilities)

	Retail Price	Code		Retail Price	Code
☐ Australia on $45 1993–94	$18.00	D102	☐ Israel on $45 1993–94	$18.00	D101
☐ Costa Rica/Guatemala/Belize on $35 1993–94	$17.00	D108	☐ Mexico on $45 1994	$19.00	D116
☐ Eastern Europe on $30 1993–94	$18.00	D110	☐ New York on $70 1994–95	$16.00	D120
☐ England on $60 1994	$18.00	D112	☐ New Zealand on $45 1993–94	$18.00	D103
☐ Europe on $50 1994	$19.00	D115	☐ Scotland/Wales on $50 1992–93	$18.00	D019
☐ Greece on $45 1993–94	$19.00	D100	☐ South America on $40 1993–94	$19.00	D109
☐ Hawaii on $75 1994	$19.00	D113	☐ Turkey on $40 1992–93	$22.00	D023
☐ India on $40 1992–93	$20.00	D010	☐ Washington, D.C. on $40 1994–95 (Avail. 2/94)	$17.00	D119
☐ Ireland on $45 1994–95 (Avail. 1/94)	$17.00	D117			

FROMMER'S CITY $-A-DAY GUIDES
(Pocket-size guides to low-cost tourist accommodations and facilities)

	Retail Price	Code		Retail Price	Code
☐ Berlin on $40 1994–95	$12.00	D111	☐ Madrid on $50 1994–95 (Avail. 1/94)	$13.00	D118
☐ Copenhagen on $50 1992–93	$12.00	D003	☐ Paris on $50 1994–95	$12.00	D117
☐ London on $45 1994–95	$12.00	D114	☐ Stockholm on $50 1992–93	$13.00	D022

FROMMER'S WALKING TOURS
(With routes and detailed maps, these companion guides point out the places and pleasures that make a city unique)

	Retail Price	Code		Retail Price	Code
☐ Berlin	$12.00	W100	☐ Paris	$12.00	W103
☐ London	$12.00	W101	☐ San Francisco	$12.00	W104
☐ New York	$12.00	W102	☐ Washington, D.C.	$12.00	W105

FROMMER'S TOURING GUIDES
(Color-illustrated guides that include walking tours, cultural and historic sights, and practical information)

	Retail Price	Code		Retail Price	Code
☐ Amsterdam	$11.00	T001	☐ New York	$11.00	T008
☐ Barcelona	$14.00	T015	☐ Rome	$11.00	T010
☐ Brazil	$11.00	T003	☐ Scotland	$10.00	T011
☐ Florence	$ 9.00	T005	☐ Sicily	$15.00	T017
☐ Hong Kong/Singapore/ Macau	$11.00	T006	☐ Tokyo	$15.00	T016
☐ Kenya	$14.00	T018	☐ Turkey	$11.00	T013
☐ London	$13.00	T007	☐ Venice	$ 9.00	T014

FROMMER'S FAMILY GUIDES

	Retail Price	Code		Retail Price	Code
☐ California with Kids	$18.00	F100	☐ San Francisco with Kids (Avail. 4/94)	$17.00	F104
☐ Los Angeles with Kids (Avail. 4/94)	$17.00	F103	☐ Washington, D.C. with Kids (Avail. 2/94)	$17.00	F102
☐ New York City with Kids (Avail. 2/94)	$18.00	F101			

FROMMER'S CITY GUIDES
(Pocket-size guides to sightseeing and tourist accommodations and facilities in all price ranges)

	Retail Price	Code		Retail Price	Code
☐ Amsterdam 1993–94	$13.00	S110	☐ Montréal/Québec City 1993–94	$13.00	S125
☐ Athens 1993–94	$13.00	S114	☐ Nashville/Memphis 1994–95 (Avail. 4/94)	$13.00	S141
☐ Atlanta 1993–94	$13.00	S112	☐ New Orleans 1993–94	$13.00	S103
☐ Atlantic City/Cape May 1993–94	$13.00	S130	☐ New York 1994 (Avail. 1/94)	$13.00	S138
☐ Bangkok 1992–93	$13.00	S005	☐ Orlando 1994	$13.00	S135
☐ Barcelona/Majorca/ Minorca/Ibiza 1993–94	$13.00	S115	☐ Paris 1993–94	$13.00	S109
☐ Berlin 1993–94	$13.00	S116	☐ Philadelphia 1993–94	$13.00	S113
☐ Boston 1993–94	$13.00	S117	☐ San Diego 1993–94	$13.00	S107
☐ Budapest 1994–95 (Avail. 2/94)	$13.00	S139	☐ San Francisco 1994	$13.00	S133
☐ Chicago 1993–94	$13.00	S122	☐ Santa Fe/Taos/ Albuquerque 1993–94	$13.00	S108
☐ Denver/Boulder/ Colorado Springs 1993–94	$13.00	S131	☐ Seattle/Portland 1994–95	$13.00	S137
☐ Dublin 1993–94	$13.00	S128	☐ St. Louis/Kansas City 1993–94	$13.00	S127
☐ Hong Kong 1994–95 (Avail. 4/94)	$13.00	S140	☐ Sydney 1993–94	$13.00	S129
☐ Honolulu/Oahu 1994	$13.00	S134	☐ Tampa/St. Petersburg 1993–94	$13.00	S105
☐ Las Vegas 1993–94	$13.00	S121	☐ Tokyo 1992–93	$13.00	S039
☐ London 1994	$13.00	S132	☐ Toronto 1993–94	$13.00	S126
☐ Los Angeles 1993–94	$13.00	S123	☐ Vancouver/Victoria 1994–95 (Avail. 1/94)	$13.00	S142
☐ Madrid/Costa del Sol 1993–94	$13.00	S124	☐ Washington, D.C. 1994 (Avail. 1/94)	$13.00	S136
☐ Miami 1993–94	$13.00	S118			
☐ Minneapolis/St. Paul 1993–94	$13.00	S119			

SPECIAL EDITIONS

	Retail Price	Code		Retail Price	Code
☐ Bed & Breakfast Southwest	$16.00	P100	☐ Caribbean Hideaways	$16.00	P103
☐ Bed & Breakfast Great American Cities (Avail. 1/94)	$16.00	P104	☐ National Park Guide 1994 (Avail. 3/94)	$16.00	P105
			☐ Where to Stay U.S.A.	$15.00	P102

Please note: if the availability of a book is several months away, we may have back issues of guides to that particular destination. Call customer service at (815) 734-1104.